COWBOYS
and
INDIANS

COWBOYS *and* INDIANS

The Shooting of J.J. Harper

GORDON SINCLAIR JR.

M&S

Cloth edition published 1999
First trade paperback edition published 2000

Library and Archives Canada Cataloguing in Publication

Sinclair, Gordon, 1948-
   Cowboys and Indians : the shooting of J.J. Harper

ISBN 0-7710-8082-4 (bound). – ISBN 0-7710-8083-2 (pbk.)

1. Harper, John Joseph, 1951-1988.   2. Trials (Murder) – Manitoba –Winnipeg.
3. Native peoples – Manitoba – Winnipeg.   4. Discrimination in criminal justice administration – Manitoba – Winnipeg.   5. Governmental investigations – Manitoba – Winnipeg.   6. Police corruption – Manitoba – Winnipeg.
7. Winnipeg (Man.) – Race relations.   I. Title.

HV6535.C33W55 1999   364.15'23'08997071272   C99-931857-8 rev

We acknowledge the financial support of the Government of Canada through the Book Publishing Development Program and that of the Government of Ontario through the Ontario Media Development Corporation's Ontario Book Initiative. We further acknowledge the support of the Canada Council for the Arts and the Ontario Arts Council for our publishing program.

Typeset in Minion by M&S, Toronto
Printed and bound in Canada

McClelland & Stewart Ltd.
The Canadian Publishers
481 University Avenue
Toronto, Ontario
M5G 2E9
www.mcclelland.com

3 4 5 6 7   09 08 07 06 05

For my family, Athina and Erin and Ian,
and all the families

Most people . . . especially the males, can probably remember that the first arguments they had as a kid were who is going to be the Cowboy and who is going to be the Indian. Then they set about killing each other and arguing over who was killed and who wasn't . . . One of the things that those Indians do is they kill children and they kill women around the wagon trains . . . These notions of the Indian people are reinforced as people grow older.

— Dr. Neil McDonald, testifying at the
Aboriginal Justice Inquiry, November 6, 1989

At night, when the streets of your cities and villages are silent, they will throng with the returning hosts that once filled them, and still love this beautiful land. The whiteman will never be alone. Let him be just and deal kindly with my people. For the dead are not powerless.

— Chief Seattle of the Squamish, 1853,
as translated by Dr. Henry Smith

Contents

North-Central Winnipeg

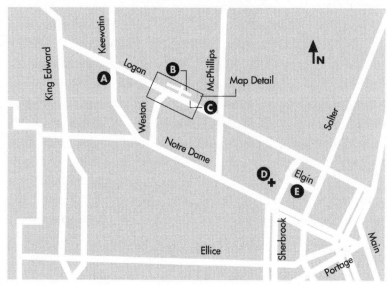

A - Harper leaves DJ's B - Pruden arrested C - Harper shot
D - Harper taken to Health Sciences Centre E - Harper's house

Map Detail

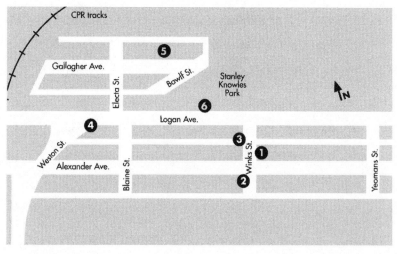

1 - Pruden drives into snowbank 2 - Allan arrested by Cross 3 - Cross and Hodgins park
their patrol car 4 - Witness Michael Tymchuk stops and sees officer with gun drawn
5 - Pruden arrested by Constable Isaac 6 - Harper shot

Maps courtesy of the Aboriginal Justice Inquiry

PROLOGUE

Thirty thousand feet over Manitoba it's easy to believe that Columbus was wrong. The Prairies slide away under the wing to a luminous blue horizon as flat and as straight as the edge of a prism. Far below, the ground glitters with glare ice dulled in sections by a thin sifting of fine snow . . . When the plane banks to starboard a tiny cluster of buildings rolls into view. Surrounded and ringed with a delicate tracery of streets and secondary roads, shimmering in the fading light from the west, Winnipeg looks like a bullet hole in a windshield.
—Carsten Stroud, *The Blue Wall: Street Cops in Canada*

It always begins the same for her, just when it's supposed to be ending. Later, like the cops and the reporters and the private investigators, the police officer's wife would try to trace his movements, starting in their bedroom. Burying her face in his pillow, inhaling the smell of him before that was gone, too. Then moving towards the living room, as if following his scent. Passing the piano in the corner. Turning towards the dining room and stopping in front of the family photo. She sensed that this was the path he had taken that awful day, before he went downstairs.

Wednesday, September 20, 1989, 9:20 a.m. He was alone at home, down in the basement in front of the big cabinet television, where he could watch the two judges and their public inquiry, but they couldn't see him. The subpoena said he was supposed to be there already, wearing the new taupe suit his wife bought him especially for his national television debut and carrying his Samsonite briefcase full of police

1

documents. But he had no intention of going to the inquiry, which to him seemed more like an inquisition. Instead, he was still in his jeans, phoning his best friend.

To the north, down Henderson Highway, a tall, greying detective groped for the bedside receiver. His buddy wanted him to come over to his house, wanted to show him something.

"Please," the voice pleaded. "Will you come *now*?"

It was 10:10 a.m. by the time the big detective wheeled his station wagon off Henderson Highway and onto his friend's street. The house was guarded in front by two evergreens and a weeping willow. He walked up the driveway, past the garage with the basketball hoop, to the high white wooden fence enclosing the backyard. There were two signs on the gate. "Beware of dog," cautioned one. "Never mind the dog," corrected the other, "beware of the owner." The gate opened onto a patio and a kidney-shaped pool. He rapped on the back door. No answer. It was unlocked so he stepped in, expecting to smell coffee perking. Nothing. He called his buddy's name. No answer. He tried the basement.

It was dark down there, except for the cold glow of the television. The Manitoba Aboriginal Justice Inquiry was on live. Constable Rick Poneira was being cross-examined about his role at the shooting scene. The detective stood there, watching Poneira, wondering where his buddy was, and waiting. A few minutes went by. He turned and moved towards the far end of the basement. The door to the Nothing Room, as his friend's wife called it, was partially open. He stopped at the doorway. He could see a weight-lifting apparatus, its black bench jutting towards him like a tongue. Open on the bench was the Samsonite briefcase that was supposed to be at the inquiry, a legal pad propped up inside, like a speech on a lectern, but the big detective was staring beyond that. At the floor. He'd found his friend. Sprawled on his right side, jack-knifed on the beige rug. A plastic tumbler was lying on its side next to the body. It looked as if the tumbler had spilled tomato juice near his friend's head. The rest was in slow motion.

He bent down by the tumbler. A purple hand-held phone was on the rug beside his friend's awkwardly bent left arm. He felt for a pulse. Nothing. There was a trickle of blood from the left ear, but little visible on his buddy's sweatshirt or powder-blue jeans. What he didn't see until the body was turned over was the jagged hole in the right temple, the kind of irregular circle you get when a sharp pencil punctures thin paper or a .38 calibre bullet shatters a skull at close range. There was something else he didn't see until the body was moved. The weapon. His eyes searched the room, looking for the gun, a clue, anything. Finally he focused on the pad of paper propped in the briefcase and the first line of the suicide note:

"I guess the first question everyone is going to ask is why . . ."

PART I

THE STRUGGLE

The struggle of today is not for today.
                                    – Abraham Lincoln

"Tomorrow might be a nice day."

It's hard to know where this story really begins. If it's to make any sense, though, it should begin eighteen months before the suicide, on the night all their lives converged, like a multi-car pile-up at rush hour, in a city without freeways.

The name Winnipeg is derived from two Cree words, *win* and *nippee*. It means muddy or murky water. But, for the more than 660,000 inhabitants of the city that lies near the geographic centre of North America, most winter days are as clear as the Prairie air that envelopes it. Snow and sky. White and blue. Sometimes, when the heavens drop low, the clouds curdle like milk. March 7, 1988, was like that. There were snow flurries during the night, but by mid-morning the next day, March 8, the snow had melted, transforming the sidewalks into a landscape of miniature islands and lakes and flooding rivers; a microcosm of the city. Winnipeg is a landlocked island, built on a flood plain at the confluence of two rivers.

By rush hour dusk had fallen, and so had the temperature, headed for an overnight low of minus five Celsius. At five-thirty, as downtown workers drove home past the Manitoba Legislative Building, few noticed the light that meant the legislature was in session. On this late winter evening it also signalled that the "assassin," as the premier later called him, was in position.

In the Legislative Assembly, slumped in the front row of the horse-shoe-shaped walnut benches, Attorney General Vic Schroeder wasn't anticipating a problem with the latest Opposition non-confidence motion. After all, the New Democrats had a majority government, even if by a tenuous single vote.

The Clerk of the Assembly, Binx Remnant, was more apprehensive. Remnant had read newspaper reports about the disgruntled former Speaker, now government backbencher, Jim Walding. Remnant instructed a page to check the government benches after he had counted the Opposition's votes. "Just in case," Remnant whispered.

During the voting Schroeder glanced over his shoulder and noticed that Walding was standing with the Opposition.

A few moments later Remnant announced, "Yeas twenty-eight, nays twenty-seven."

The Opposition Tories erupted, like looters on a spree.

Three chairs away from Schroeder, Premier Howard Pawley blinked as the blood drained from his face and his lips locked in a grim line. By the time Pawley reached the sanctity of his office, Walding was on his way to a pre-arranged hiding place. Slowly, the shaken premier phoned his wife.

"My government has been defeated," Pawley told her.

In a house two kilometres north of the premier's office, another wife was picking up the phone. Lois Harper's husband, John Joseph Harper, was a political leader, too, with the Island Lake Tribal Council. Before he left for work that morning, Lois had suggested the family go for a drive in the country. Now Harper was phoning to say he was going to be late. Someone was flying in from the reserve and he had to go to the airport.

"If you want to take the kids for a ride," Harper said, "go ahead."

"I've already got supper on," she said. "We'll wait. Tomorrow might be a nice day."

"Okay," he said. "I'll see you later."

Lois went back to feeding her three children, sliding the leftover meat loaf into the oven for later, when her husband got back. She always worried that he would go drinking and wouldn't come home. Or, worse, that he'd go drinking and he would come home. But she didn't worry about his safety on the streets of Winnipeg, despite what a young Aboriginal lawyer had said about cops and Indians on the front page of the *Winnipeg Free Press*. "Police prey on Natives, lawyer says," the headline read. The article stated that in 1988, Manitoba's Native population was less than 12 per cent of the province's one million people, yet at least half the inmates in the provincial jails were Aboriginal. The rate was even higher at the federal Stony Mountain Prison, north of Winnipeg. The Aboriginal lawyer accused police of picking on Natives, suggesting that as many as 80 per cent of the people charged in Winnipeg courts were Natives because they were "easy targets" for the police force. They were easy targets because they drank excessively, he said, and they drank excessively because they had been alienated from their culture and its values.

J.J. Harper's cultural values were rooted in Wasagamack, his reserve, a glistening, pine-forested, freshwater archipelago 400 kilometres northeast of Winnipeg. Most of the year, it was accessible only by air, but in the depths of winter a crude ice road was ploughed through the frozen land and water. Wasagamack was where he had been chief, and where his parents, and some of his fifteen brothers and sisters, still lived. It was one of a constellation of four reserves that included Red Sucker, the home of MLA Elijah Harper. Collectively the reserves were known as Island Lake.

On the southeast edge of Winnipeg there was a very different place with a very similar name. Island Lakes was a new subdivision dug out of the fertile farmland that surrounds the city. As nine-to-five Winnipeggers made their way home that day, another husband, who lived in Island Lakes, was still several hours away from going to work. Robert Cross was a police constable on night shift. Routinely before dinner Cross would bath his sixteen-month-old twins while his wife, Diane Eastwood, prepared dinner. Like Lois Harper, Diane was thirty-three. She was a surgical nurse, eight months pregnant with their third child, and still working. That's why her twin toddlers would be in bed by six, so she and Robert could eat in peace. Within three hours, he would be off to work, driving west to a suburban station on the other side of the city. Unlike many police wives, Diane never worried when her husband was on night duty. A cop hadn't been killed in Winnipeg for nearly two decades. Then there was the other kind of police shooting. In Winnipeg during the preceding five years, police had shot six people. By comparison, twenty-eight citizens had been shot by police in Toronto, six fatally, nineteen had been shot in Montreal, six in Edmonton, four in Vancouver, and only two in Calgary.

As Cross bathed his children, a pair of Native teenagers were trudging through the puddles of the city centre. Melvin Pruden, the nineteen year old, had a BORN TO BE WILD tattoo on his left bicep – and a police record. He had been waiting after school for Allan, his fourteen-year-old cousin, who looked more like he was ten. Allan had his own name for Pruden. He called him "Man." By 5:30 p.m., Allan and Man were wandering aimlessly through slushy city streets that would soon turn to ice.

—
2

"MALE, NATIVE, AH, BLACK JACKET."

At midnight on March 9 the sky was clear and the wind was blowing gently through the centre of the city. There are two centres to Winnipeg. Just over a kilometre east of the Legislature lies The Forks, where the Red and Assiniboine rivers converge. The Forks is the historic centre of the city. It was the meeting and trading place of Aboriginal peoples, and the site of the first fort built when the first white explorer arrived 250 years earlier. A railway station followed, and tracks were laid across the lacerated Indian land, like steel stitches. The Forks is now the city's most popular tourist attraction.

The other centre of the city lies a kilometre north of The Forks, where two streets intersect to form the coldest and windiest corner on the continent. Portage and Main is the symbolic heart of the business community whose office towers, viewed from certain angles, give Winnipeg a big-city look.

A few blocks north of Portage and Main, one of the country's saddest, most sordid streets starts in front of City Hall and then crawls for ten blocks past the railway lines that separate the north end from the city centre. In 1988 North Main Street was a grungy gauntlet of skid-row hotels, pawnshops, soup kitchens, and detox centres. Winnipeggers, the kind who locked their car doors as they drove past, and cursed at the drunks wandering obliviously across their paths, saw only Aboriginal faces on North Main Street. To them it was the biggest urban "reserve" in Canada. In 1986 the census reported there were nearly 28,000 Aboriginal people in Winnipeg. The migration from the reserves had begun slowly after the Second World War. Most came to the city looking for jobs and most were women who found them cleaning homes or working in restaurants. The men who followed them worked in unskilled jobs. In those years, Indians were prohibited from drinking alcohol in public places. Tommy Prince, the country's most decorated Aboriginal war hero, couldn't get a drink in a Legion Hall. In the early 1960s, the prohibition was lifted. A decade later, having pawned his war medals, Tommy Prince died a destitute drunk.

At about 1 a.m. on March 9, the wind suddenly changed direction, shifting to the south, and the sky that had looked so clear at midnight was shrouded. In a blue-collar, industrial neighbourhood just west of downtown, Ken Hayhurst, a slight, balding man walked out of the Westbrook Inn into the parking lot to discover his car had been stolen. Hayhurst, who drove trucks for a living, had left the keys in his car and the motor running, the way truckers do in winter when they stop at a wayside diner. By the looks of the shattered glass in the parking lot, someone had smashed a window and driven off.

He phoned the police immediately. In the Winnipeg Police Department's communications centre, the operator took the description: a white, two-door 1983 Dodge Aries, license two-four-four EKT – Echo, Kilo, Tango. The communications centre, or com centre as it is called, was located on the top floor of the city's central police station on Princess Street, a rather swishy address for such a macho place. Winnipeg's symbol of law and order is six storeys of off-white, fossil-filled stone. At night, from the street, it looks like an urban fortress. Narrow, perpendicular concrete slabs jut from the windows, like jail bars, which is appropriate given that two of the floors house holding cells. Court is held on another. The stark building's proper name, the Public Safety Building, is supposed to be reassuring. Half a dozen blocks southwest of the police station, inside the *Winnipeg Free Press* building, graveyard-shift copy editors were slouched in front of their computer terminals. Behind them was a scanner, set to the police channel on which the chatter between the communications centre and the cruiser cops was playing like background music.

At 2 a.m., another rush hour began. Last call. The Westbrook Inn had emptied by the time another Dodge Aries, this one a police cruiser, approached it. Constable Robert Cross was driving. His female partner, Kathryn Hodgins, was beside him in the jumpseat, so-called because normally the cop who sat there was the first one out in the event of a foot chase. Cross looked like the prototype of a Canadian cop: white, six feet tall, medium build, with a black moustache. All that kept him from looking like a model officer were the eyeglasses he was wearing, and maybe the custom rubber grips on his .38 Smith & Wesson Police Special. When he first applied to the force six years earlier, in answer to the question, "Why police work?" he wrote, "Thinking about my life & going no-where." Under "Disadvantages," he wrote, "shift work" and "being shot." That wasn't likely to happen where Cross and Hodgins worked. District Two, in suburban St. James, had the highest concentration of senior citizens in the city. The cops called it Sleepy Hollow. But the Westbrook Inn, where the car had been stolen, was on the eastern edge of District Two; beyond lay District One, the vastly more dangerous and unpredictable inner city. The two officers had just ticketed a speeder and were on their way back to the Sleepy Hollow police station for a meal, approaching the Westbrook on Keewatin Street, when they saw a white Dodge pull off a side street next to the hotel and onto Keewatin, a white Dodge just like the one that had been reported stolen.

"Kath," Cross said, "I think that's the car." He sped up to get a better look, turning on the cruiser's "wigwags," its flashing high and low headlights. The white car ahead of them sped up, too.

"Mobile N202," Hodgins identified their car, her voice crackling through to the communications centre. "We're following that stolen vehicle, two-four-four Echo Kilo Tango. We're on Worth at Pacific." The digital clock on the police reel-to-reel tape recorder read 2:24 a.m. "Received," said Carole Clark, the civilian dispatcher.

Hodgins kept broadcasting their position as the two cops chased after the stolen car. "Through a red light at Weston . . . Through a stop sign. Now northbound on Winks." Suddenly the radio transmissions stopped.

As he turned onto Winks, the driver lost control of the stolen car and it slid into a snowbank on the east side boulevard. Cross and Hodgins were right behind and saw two figures fleeing across Winks and into a lane. The cruiser followed them.

In the communications centre, the duty inspector, Eric Hrycyk, turned up the volume on the monitor. He heard a garbled voice, then "Two males out of the vehicle."

"Received," Clark said. "Two-zero-two, do you have a description for us?"

"Two males," Hodgins replied. "Dark clothing." The time was 2:26. The police pursuit, which had lasted less than a minute and a half on wheels, was now a foot chase. Cross followed the pair through a backyard just inside the lane where he had scrambled out of the cruiser. Hodgins slid over to the driver's seat and quickly backed the cruiser up to Winks, where the stolen car was stuck. She positioned the car to block the lane's entrance and turned off the headlights. She didn't have to wait long.

"My partner's got one male,"Hodgins said a minute later. "One small juvenile." The lags between transmissions grew longer.

By this time three more police cruisers had arrived in the area. Six minutes after the pursuit of the stolen car had begun, a male officer's voice cut in.

"Do we have an updated location of where Cross is?"

"I'm with the suspect at Alexander and Winks," Cross answered.

One of the officers wanted a description of the second suspect. "Any further description of the second one," Clark asked, "other than dark clothing?"

"Male, Native, ah, black jacket, blue jeans," Hodgins answered. There was a pause. "This male is approximately twenty-two years old," she added.

Nearly eight minutes had passed since the pursuit began. The police scanner in the *Free Press* newsroom fell silent for one minute . . . two . . . three . . .

It wasn't as quiet in the neighbourhood of Logan Avenue, west of McPhillips where dogs were barking and eight police officers, three of them on foot, were hunting for the second suspect. Logan Avenue is a truck route, a straight street, four lanes wide. On the south side of its 1200 block, where police and the second suspect were playing hide and seek, is a row of small, tidy bungalows that had been built for returning Second World War veterans. On Logan's north side is a pie-shaped park that runs the length of the block. The park was named in honour of Stanley Knowles, the long-serving member for Winnipeg North Centre, one of the poorest constituencies in the country. Its long side is bordered on Logan by a row of mature, evenly spaced American elms, a sidewalk and a curb-side boulevard, and a phalanx of goose-necked street standards, with mercury vapour lamps that cast a deathly yellow glow. That night, the sidewalk was mainly clear, but there was a thin, patchy blanket of snow in the park that stretches beyond Gallagher Avenue to an earthen dike and the CPR yards.

Four minutes after the last transmission a man's yell pierced the silence.

"I've got him right here, guys. He's coming out to you. Coming out to you right now. Got him, going down, down."

"What's your location?" Clark asked.

Katherine Tyler, who lived at 1262 Logan, didn't hear the cop shouting, but she was aroused by a banging, as if someone had bumped
into the back of her house. When the elderly woman looked out of
her rear window, she saw a police officer standing in the lane by her
garage looking north between her house and her neighbour's. She
hurried to the front window to see what the cop was looking at and
saw someone running across Logan and into the park. What she didn't
see was a second police officer chasing him.

"Three . . ." the pursuing cop said breathlessly.

"N203, go ahead." But the officer's transmission was garbled.

Moments later the driver of a 1982 Ford Granada moving west on
Logan saw something that startled him: a police black-and-white at
the end of the block, just past Stanley Knowles Park. The cruiser
moved north diagonally across Logan, from Blaine to Electa.
Reflexively, Randy Houston, the twenty-one-year-old driver of the
Ford, hit the brake to slow the car. His sixteen-year-old girlfriend,
Linda Morisette, sitting beside him, noticed the cruiser's taillights as
they disappeared onto Electa. Sitting in the back seat, Larry Yaworek,
the driver's buddy, didn't notice the cruiser, but seconds later he saw
something else crossing their path. So did Morisette. "Look," she said.
A figure in dark clothing had abruptly appeared from between the
houses on the south side of Logan and jogged across the street about
three car lengths in front of them. The girl instantly recognized it was
a cop, but she thought it was a woman. So did Yaworek, who hadn't
noticed the uniform when he rolled down the window, leaned out, and
let out a wolf whistle.

Houston screamed in disbelief. "Get his fucking head in the
window," he ordered Morisette. Yaworek didn't have to be told. "Holy
Christ," he yelled, "we got a cop." Morisette could be forgiven her confusion over the officer's sex. In the few seconds that she had seen the
cop, her attention had been fixed on what he was holding. Later, when
she got home, she told her mother that the officer had been grasping
his own wrist with one hand and holding a revolver at head height
with the other.

In the communications centre, Clark listened to another male police officer describe what was happening. "He's chasing him. Ah, we're on Electa or something. Yeah, Electa."

"He's going up on the dike," someone else said, trying to catch his breath. "Grey jacket. Native."

Hodgins had described it as a black jacket. The suspect's jacket had changed shades, from black to grey, a crucial difference as it would turn out. Communications relayed the description, adding another descriptive detail that hadn't been previously mentioned.

"He's on the dike. Grey jacket and pants."

Robert Cross was sitting in the cruiser beside Hodgins when he heard that the second suspect had been spotted. He decided to join the search, tracking the foot pursuit on his portable radio as he headed into the lane behind Logan. The time was 2:38, nearly fifteen minutes after the car chase had begun.

"I got him," a male officer's voice announced. It took another minute and twenty seconds for communications to confirm that "I got him" meant the second suspect was in custody.

About the time that Man, the second suspect, was being cuffed, Bob Barnes, who lived on Gallagher, was heading outside through his own backyard. A twenty-eight-year-old steel worker, Barnes moonlighted as a deejay at a bar in the Canadiana Motor Hotel. He had worked that night, and on the way home he'd heard over his car radio that Howard Pawley's government had been defeated. Barnes was so happy that when he got home he made a brown paper banner for his back fence, so drivers on Logan could see it in the morning. "Bye, Bye Howie," the sign mocked in big red letters. He had almost finished fastening the banner to his fence when he heard a loud *crack*. It startled him, and he turned towards the source of the sound, beyond the black cavity of the park, to where the street lamps cast their deathly glow on Logan Avenue.

The police recording of the broadcast didn't pick up the loud *crack* or the barking of the dogs it disturbed. But more than a block away, on Winks, Allan, the boy in the back of cruiser 202, saw the rear window shudder. "Oh, my God!" he heard Hodgins blurt. It sounded like a shot to her, and she scrambled out of the cruiser.

"I ran down the back lane," she testified later, "looking for my partner, Constable Cross, and calling his name." Allan was sure she had drawn her gun as she entered the lane, but whenever she was questioned she would deny pulling her revolver, as would every other officer who searched for the second suspect.

At 2:39, one minute and thirty-three seconds after the arrest of the second suspect was confirmed, the *Free Press* scanner picked up the sound of a click. In the communications centre the click sounded as if an officer had hit the call button on his portable radio by mistake then muted it again. Ten seconds . . . twenty . . . thirty . . . thirty-nine seconds passed. Then Cross, clearly distressed, could be heard saying, "I'm just west of Winks. I need my partner here and I also need an ambulance." There were more transmissions. Clarifications.

"Is the person conscious?" Clark asked.

"That's a negative."

More confusion. "Confirm," Hodgins asked. "Is he in the lane?"

"He's over here," a male voice answered. "We've got him over here . . ."

"N102, N102," another officer said, identifying his cruiser. "Rush that ambulance."

"Can you give us an exact location?"

"It's right in front of 1246 Logan."

The six other officers in the vicinity had already reached Cross when Hodgins arrived. She drove the cruiser onto Logan and parked it in front of a row of cop cars, their red roof lights flashing. In the back seat of the cruiser, Allan was crying. He could see a man's body writhing on the sidewalk and two cops crouched over it, giving first aid. Blood was fountaining from the man's chest. One of the cops was on his knees, leaning over and applying pressure to the wound with a bandage while a second pinned the man's arms. Allan assumed that the dark figure on the ground was Man, his cousin from the reserve. Who else could it be? What the boy didn't know, what Hodgins didn't tell him, was that Man was in the back seat of another cruiser.

What she did say, according to her later testimony, was, "You little thief." The boy had quite a different memory. He was certain she called him, "You fucking blue-eyed Indian." What both would agree on, though, was what she said next. "If you hadn't stolen the car, none of this would have happened."

Back at the communications centre Clark and her supervisor, Caroline Kwiatek, were still confused a minute and a half after the seven other cops had located Cross's position. An ambulance had been dispatched by computer to Keewatin, where the chase had started, and Kwiatek had to call to correct the location.

Then Clark relayed a question to police at the scene. "Ambulance is just asking if you know the cause of this problem?"

"Yes, we do," Constable Grant "Butch" Eakin answered. "We'll speak to you on Channel 3." Abruptly, the scanner in the *Free Press* newsroom fell silent.

Far to the north of Winnipeg, in the middle of that night, Victor Harper, a teacher on the remote Wasagamack Reserve, woke suddenly and jumped out of bed. He had seen something. A flash. An image of a man standing in the bedroom. The schoolteacher woke his wife.

"I just saw John," he told her.

—
3

"You don't want to know."

The sky had cleared by sunrise at 6:57 a.m., four hours after the ambulance had left for the hospital, followed minutes later by the fire department crew that had reached the wounded man first. But the firefighters had returned. Police wanted the scene cleaned up before day broke. There were three pools of blood, two large ones on the north sidewalk of Logan, and a splash on the narrow, curb-side boulevard. A detective, who had been assigned to make sure the clean-up was done properly, watched as the firefighters sloshed water on the three pools of blood and then covered them with sand.

Winnipeg's police chief was getting ready for work about that time. Herb Stephen and his wife of thirty-two years, Faye, lived just north of the city on Henderson Highway, in a modest brown-stained cedar bungalow set on a well-treed two acres of grass he mowed himself. At 5 a.m. the chief had been woken by the telephone ringing. "It was Inspector Hrycyk on the phone," Stephen testified later, "and he advised me that there had been a shooting, that there had been a struggle on Logan Avenue over a police officer's gun, and that a man had been shot and had died at hospital." The Detective Division wasn't staffed overnight, so Eric Hrycyk, the duty inspector who had monitored the stolen car chase, had called in four members of the Robbery Homicide Division, as well as two members from the Identification unit. Hrycyk also told Stephen that the duty executive officer, Superintendent MacDougal "Mac" Allen, had also been alerted. "Everything was under control," was the chief's understanding.

Herb Stephen was not quite six feet tall, thinning on top and thickening in the middle, as is common with men of fifty-four who spend long hours behind desks. Stephen's face was wide and fleshy, with a mouth as thin as a zipper, topped by a stubbly moustache. It was his eyes you noticed most, though. They were ice blue. Still, there was a certain warmth about the man, at least that's what the *Free Press* had suggested four years earlier when he was appointed the city's twelfth police chief. "His trademark is a smile," said the paper. Stephen had been a popular choice for the job. He had supervised two of the most sensational cases in the city's recent history. One was the 1979 arrest of the publisher of the *Winnipeg Free Press*, who was later convicted of having sex with juvenile prostitutes, and of obstruction of justice. The other was the arrest of two Winnipeg police officers who had murdered a man they suspected was going to blow the whistle on a series of break-and-enters they had been doing while on duty. As crime superintendent, his report card had been almost straight As: accessible, accommodating, affable, and admired. His only D was for decent and the lone F was for fair-minded. There was just one area in which people thought he might be weak: disciplining the department.

"In the final analysis," predicted Des DePourcq, his detective partner of eight years, "he will survive. But he may not smile as often." His survival didn't seem to be an issue in early 1988.

Stephen and his department were embroiled in a sensational case of fixed traffic tickets that had led the police to wire-tap some judges' chambers. Ticketgate, the press called it. In mid-January, the police had consulted Attorney-General Vic Schroeder and his deputies on it before charging a dozen lawyers and court officials, including the chief provincial judge, Harold Gyles, with obstruction of justice. Without Schroeder's knowledge, some of his deputies had tried to get the charges against most of the suspects dropped. But the police went ahead with the round-up. A subsequent judicial inquiry into the matter had congratulated the police on their handling of the case and chastised certain Crown attorneys, among them Assistant Deputy Minister Stuart Whitley. The inquiry's report said that Whitley had a potential conflict because of his long association with Gyles. The chief judge was acquitted, but later reprimanded by Manitoba's judicial council and demoted. Ticketgate's legacy was a bitter and lingering distrust between certain senior police officers and senior justice officials.

But for Stephen and the police department, the case was a triumph, and it couldn't have happened at a better time. Within two years of taking office, Stephen had been under fire from all sides. A *Free Press* editorial questioned why Stephen hadn't recruited more women and visible minorities, particularly Natives. A *Winnipeg Sun* editorial claimed he had been unavailable for comment on budget matters and the city's rising crime rate. And a Winnipeg radio station suggested that the chief was out of the city too much, and was neglecting his watch. Herb "Suitcase" Stephen, as he was derisively nicknamed, hotly denied that he was spending too little time on the job. But a week after Stephen fended off that criticism, another was launched, this time from inside the Public Safety Building. A letter that circulated at the police station suggested the chief was to blame for low morale, and privately there was talk among his deputies that he was uncommunicative. Meanwhile, a city psychologist was quoted as saying Stephen seemed to be suffering from a siege mentality. "It's called a defensive retreat," Toby Rutner told the *Winnipeg Sun*, "and it happens to any leader who comes into a position and can't take criticism." And there seemed to be a bottomless well of that. A city councillor had pointed out that the chief had a chauffeur while the mayor and even the premier drove themselves to work. Stephen remained unrepentant even after it was disclosed that the chauffeur had driven the chief and his wife Faye to their daughter's wedding. Defiantly, Stephen justified the use of the chauffeur by pointing out that he'd worn his uniform to the wedding. Police Commissioner Robert Lunney, a former Mountie and police chief in Edmonton, told reporters he would look into the matter. Within days, Stephen was driving himself to work.

The sun was up, and the shooting scene washed down, by the time Herb Stephen swung out of his long gravel driveway. As he drove he listened for news of the shooting on his car radio and was surprised when he didn't hear mention of it on the morning news. A police shooting was unusual in Winnipeg. A fatal shooting even rarer. He assumed reporters would have heard what had happened from monitoring their police scanners.

About the time Stephen was parking his car in the Public Safety Building's underground garage, Constable John Campbell was on his way to his second-floor desk with Crimestoppers, the city's public snitch line. With his neatly styled dark hair and glasses, Campbell looked more like a businessman than a cop, especially when smoking one of his favourite Las Pinas cigars and driving his 1984 Buick Park Avenue. Campbell's affinity for big cars and big cigars belied a social conscience, and an infinitely broader view of law and justice than most police officers'. When Herb Stephen applied for the chief's job, Campbell had been one of his hardest-working supporters. He had hoped Stephen would be an agent of change within the police department where the outgoing chief was reputed to be isolated and autocratic. But Stephen had proven a disappointment, which shouldn't have surprised anyone. He was the prime example of how the old boys' club worked.

Stephen had joined the force as soon as he turned twenty-one. His first day was January 30, 1956, and he and Faye were married later the same year. It was a more respectful era, and cops were closer to the community. In those days Winnipeg beat cops patrolled the winter streets in full-length buffalo-hide coats, the way they had since the 1920s. There was still no police academy, so young cops learned the job the way kids learned about sex, on the street. It was Stephen, only a year into the job himself, who first tutored a young, British-born constable named Ken Johnston. Twenty-eight years later, Chief Ken Johnston was succeeded by Chief Herb Stephen. In the late winter of 1988, more than a hundred years after the bison had vanished from the Manitoba plains, the buffalo coats were gone, but The Old Buffalo Coats were still in charge of the Winnipeg Police Department.

As he strode through the second-floor plain-clothes section, Campbell noticed something unusual. Several uniformed patrol officers were sitting at the detectives' desks, typing up reports. Campbell was curious. He walked over to a young constable who was hunched over a typewriter.

Constable Danny Smyth, who had been on the force for only two years, was short, dark, and soap-opera handsome. He and his veteran partner, Douglas Hooper, had been the first to reach Cross after he had radioed for assistance. Fifteen minutes later, Smyth had ridden to the hospital in the ambulance, applying pressure to the dying man's chest wound. Earlier, even before the fire department arrived, the driver of a medical van used to transfer patients between hospitals had stopped to offer assistance. Hodgins had told him he wasn't needed, the ambulance was on its way. It should have taken them only two and a half minutes to reach the hospital at that time of the morning. But by the time the ambulance arrived at the Health Science Centre at 3 a.m., the man had been bleeding for twenty minutes. He was clinically dead, but he was still rushed to the operating theatre. At 3:23 a.m., the surgeon gave up massaging the man's heart.

Inspector Hrycyk, who had gone to the scene of the shooting, joined Smyth and Hooper at the hospital, where he instructed them on what to do. Smyth accompanied the body to the morgue, and watched a nurse slide it into vault eight. He initialled the tape that sealed the door and retained the key. The nurse handed Smyth the dead man's blood-soaked clothing and personal effects in a plastic bag. Smyth then drove to the detective office to type up his report.

John Campbell was standing over Smyth's desk now.

"What's up?" Campbell asked.

Smyth glanced up from his typewriter. "You don't want to know," he said.

When he reached his fifth-floor office, Police Chief Herb Stephen contacted press liaison officer Don Peters and told him to prepare a release on the shooting and to let him see it. The statement was handed to the waiting media at 9 a.m. Darryl Sterdan, a twenty-four-year-old reporter with the *Winnipeg Sun*, was one of the police-beat regulars who quickly scanned the one-page release.

At about 2:25 this morning a patrolling police unit observed an auto in the vicinity of 60 Keewatin Street that had been reported stolen at about 1:00 a.m.

The officers attempted to stop the vehicle which was occupied by two males who ran the vehicle into a snowbank at Winks Street and Alexander Avenue and fled on foot.

A 14-year-old male youth was arrested after a short foot chase. A description of the second suspect was broadcast and about 2:30 a police officer confronted another male in the 1200 block of Logan Avenue who fit the general description of the second suspect. The police officer was knocked to the ground and a struggle ensued over the policeman's revolver and the revolver discharged striking the deceased in the chest.

A 36-year-old man was taken by ambulance to the H.S.C. [Health Sciences Centre] where he was pronounced dead on arrival.

A second suspect, a male adult, has been arrested in regards to the stolen vehicle.

When Don Peters finished answering questions, Sterdan called a taxi and headed out to the scene. He wanted to see if there had been any witnesses.

—
4

"WHO WAS HE?"

Late the same morning a phone rang at the opposite end of the *Free Press* newsroom from the police scanner. It was answered by Gordon Sinclair Jr., the *Free Press* city columnist, a tall man, six foot three, with dark hair and a close-cropped red beard that was sprouting a patch of frost. He had turned forty two weeks earlier. Sinclair had grown up at the *Free Press*. The police scanner had worn a London bobby's helmet in the late 1950s, when Gordon Sinclair Sr. was city editor and the newsroom was a second home to Gordy and his younger brother, David. Their real home was at 122 Douglas Park Road, a yellow stucco storey-and-a-half that Gordon and his wife, Dorothy, had bought from a Mountie in 1954. The *Free Press*, which was owned by the Sifton family in those days, had financed the $10,000 purchase price.

The future first female mayor of Winnipeg, whose father owned a western supply store across from city hall, lived at the bottom of the street. Susie Thompson was a year older than Gordy, skinny and freckle-faced like him. She and Gordy and the rest of the kids on the street played softball in Bourkevale Park. But it was only the boys who hid behind the giant elms of Bruce Park with their toy guns, playing Cowboys and Indians.

Gordy and David played a different game when their dad took them down to the newsroom on Saturday afternoons. While he checked the weekend assignment book and grabbed a final edition, the boys rolled copy paper into the Remington typewriters and pecked away, pretending to be reporters.

Twenty years later, in January 1976, David was a reporter with the rival *Winnipeg Tribune* and Gordy was a legislative reporter at the *Edmonton Journal* when their dad suffered a massive stroke in the *Free Press* newsroom. Their mother, Dorothy, dealt with the news in her own way.

"The rest will do him good," she said.

Twenty-four hours later doctors unhooked his life-support. He was fifty-four when he died, the victim of too much smoking, too much drinking, and his stubborn refusal to heed his doctor's order to quit.

Two years later, Gordon Sinclair Jr. moved back to Winnipeg with his wife, Shelley, and year-old daughter, Erin. The loss of Gordon Sr. sent Dorothy, who had always had emotional problems, into a psychotic spin. Over and over again, when she stopped eating and locked herself in her apartment, her sons had to obtain committal warrants and a couple of compassionate police officers would escort her to a psychiatric ward. Ten years after her husband died, Dorothy Sinclair was found dead in her hospital bed. She had suffered a heart attack.

By that time, Sinclair Jr. was living alone. Four years after returning to Winnipeg, and two years after the birth of his son, Ian, Shelley had asked him to move out. Now he had the children overnight every Tuesday and Wednesday, and every other weekend. Gordon, his children, and his girlfriend, Athina Panopoulos, had spent the evening of March 8 together. They'd been sound asleep when J.J. Harper was shot.

In the *Free Press* newsroom, Sinclair picked up the phone before the second ring. The friendly baritone on the other end of the line belonged to Marv Terhoch, the regional director of the CBC in Manitoba. Terhoch had called to talk about the fall of the government. It was a short discussion. Near the end, Terhoch asked if Sinclair had heard about the thirty-six-year-old man the police had shot the night before.

"No," Sinclair said. "Who was he?"

On the fourth floor of the Health Sciences Centre, two doctors were already at work trying to find that out in ways only autopsies can reveal. Dr. Peter Markesteyn and Dr. Charles Littman were in the post-mortem theatre standing over a corpse with stitches up the middle of the chest. There was a scrum of five police officers with them, including two Mounties from the RCMP crime lab and firearms section. They had been asked to attend by Sergeant Bob Parker of the city police Identification unit, who was also there. Normally there would be only one pathologist, but as a cop had been involved in shooting an unarmed citizen, Markesteyn had asked Littman to join him, as backup.

The two doctors found an elliptical gunshot wound just below the collar bone on the left side of Harper's body. The hollow-point bullet had shattered. The largest fragment was found in the soft tissue to the left of the vertebral column.

"This fragment was removed by Dr. Markesteyn," Littman wrote in the autopsy report, "and, after careful washing, it appeared to be the bullet jacket."

There were no powder burns at the point of entrance, and as the man's clothes were missing, the doctors couldn't check them for powder burns, an essential detail for determining how far away the gun was when the shot was fired.

"Where is the clothing?" asked Lanyse Guay, a medical examiner's investigator, who had been present in the autopsy suite before the autopsy began. Parker didn't answer. She asked again. Parker said they were back at the Identification office, but he assured Guay the man had been shot at close range and his shirt had been open. The next day, Guay learned the man had been wearing a black cloth jacket and that there were large powder burns on it. What disturbed Guay as much as the absence of Harper's clothing was something she heard before Markesteyn asked her to leave. It was a racist joke that referred to the shooting.

The police knew who the dead man was soon after he reached the hospital at 3 a.m. A search of his blue jeans had turned up a meeting schedule for the Island Lake Tribal Council in his left back pocket and in the right a black wallet containing a driver's licence and medical insurance card in the name of John Joseph Harper. The addresses on the two pieces of identification were different, though, and detective sergeants Al Cameron and Bill Rautavuori, who had been assigned to contact the next of kin, tried the one on the medical card first. But there was no one living at 290 Forrest Avenue. The second was a two-storey house a block from the Health Sciences Centre. It was around 9:30 a.m. by the time Cameron and Rautavuori pulled up in front of 594 Elgin looking for J.J. Harper's wife.

Lois Harper had been on the phone with one of her sisters-in-law, who told Lois that her twenty-six-year-old cousin, John Knott, had been airlifted to Winnipeg after being seriously burned in a house fire on the reserve and was in critical condition at the Health Sciences Centre. In the course of the conversation Lois mentioned that J.J. had stayed out all night again. Then Lois told her sister-in-law she had to go, she wanted to get to the bank when it opened at 10 a.m. She was just leaving the house when the two detectives arrived. Years later she still remembered the first words of the cops who had come to tell her that J.J. was dead:

"Where are you going?"

About the time Harper's body was being autopsied, *Sun* reporter Darryl Sterdan finished looking for witnesses and joined *Free Press* reporter Greg Pindera and photographer Gerry Cairns in a search for the shooting site. They found it on the north sidewalk of Logan, beside the park. The curb-side boulevard was marked by what appeared to be a pool of diluted blood covered with fresh sand. Then Sterdan noticed something sticking out of a patch of snow at the edge of the park. A pair of black-rimmed eyeglasses that looked as if they had been stepped on. Both arms had snapped off and the left lens had popped out. As Sterdan was gathering up the pieces, he noticed something else about the left lens. It was sprinkled with pinhead-sized spots of what looked like blood.

By late that afternoon, Harper's 1986 Ramcharger was found where he'd parked it, on the lower level of the Royal Winnipeg Ballet Parkade, a block away from the downtown offices of the Island Lake Tribal Council. Ten minutes later, at 3 p.m., Lois Harper, surrounded by a dozen family members, went to the Health Sciences Centre to identify her husband's body.

In the report they wrote later, Cameron and Rautavuori mentioned that Lois Harper had asked about something that had been found in Harper's wallet, near his children's photos. It was a letter she had written to him just before J.J. moved out a year earlier, a separation that accounted for the different address on the medical card. Harper had kept the letter with him ever since, even after he moved back home the following Christmas. The letter was highly personal and poignant, but the police saw it differently. To them it was evidence that tended to back up the constable's version of what had happened on Logan Avenue. "Due to emotional state of all persons present," the detectives' brief report concluded, "no further interviews were conducted at that time." But the police already had the answer to the question they were most interested in: Was Lois's husband ever abusive or violent with her?

Not long after Lois Harper identified her husband's body at the Health Sciences Centre morgue, Constable Robert Cross was standing in the corridor of a different hospital in the south end of the city. His shift was supposed to have ended at 8 a.m., but after turning his blood-soiled uniform over to the Identification unit, he had been sitting in the detective office, drinking coffee and trying to explain what had happened. The first senior officer he met with at the Public Safety Building was Inspector Hrycyk, who had arrived at the scene five minutes after the ambulance left.

Eric Hrycyk was the son of a cop. His father, Bill Hrycyk, was a big, gravel-voiced sergeant of detectives in the morality division. His son, who had just been made an inspector, chose to climb the police ladder on the uniformed side. But there was one piece of fatherly advice that Eric Hrycyk liked to quote to his fellow students in the Winnipeg Police Department class of '71: "There are two kinds of people: police-men and assholes."

At the scene of the shooting, Hrycyk had met with Cross and the other police officers. He'd told Cross and Hodgins to go to his office at the Public Safety Building. Then Hrycyk had headed for the hospital.

An hour later, Hrycyk met with Cross and Hodgins in his office and told them that Harper was dead. Hodgins phoned her husband, Ron, who was also a police officer, and he hurried to work. Cross decided against phoning his wife. She was less than a month away from delivering, and she had to work in the morning. He didn't ask to phone a lawyer, either. Instead he requested that Winnipeg Police Association president Norm Wickdahl be with him when he met with detectives Harry Williams and Cal Osborne to give a witness state-ment. Cross was pale and seemed agitated and "very concerned at what was going on about him," Williams testified later. The interview began at 5:20 a.m. and lasted until about 9 a.m. But even before he spoke with the detectives, Cross tried to demonstrate to Hrycyk how the shooting had happened. He pulled up his left pant leg to show the inspector how the spots of dried blood on his shin ran up his leg, not down. That fit with his story that he had been knocked to the ground and had put his foot in the man's chest. Then, Cross said, he felt a tugging at his holster. The gun came out. They fought over it. And *bang*.

Hrycyk had already noticed that there was blood on Cross's right hand. Now, as he looked down at the constable's leg, he noticed something else about the blood spots: they looked like inverted tear drops.

Cross's eyes were welling as he stood in the hallway of Victoria Hospital's main-floor surgical ward. He had come to see his wife, an OR nurse.

"Diane, can you come to the desk?" a colleague asked, poking her head into surgical theatre 10. "Bob's here."

As soon as Diane Eastwood saw her husband, she knew something was wrong. His eyes were brimming with tears, his face was twitching and his hands were trembling. "What are you doing here?" she asked. He took her off to the side, away from the desk, to tell her.

The day after the shooting, Cross was standing in his driveway when he saw his next-door neighbour return from an evening walk. Sheila Elliot was a buxom, large-framed woman. She and her short, stocky husband, Mike, had become chummy with Cross after he and Diane moved into the new subdivision the year before. Sheila worked for the federal government. Mike was a welder at CN's Transcona Shops.

Before a fence went up between their homes, Diane would put the twins in the backyard on leashes that stretched to Sheila and Mike's deck. The children would wander over to the Elliots, and Cross followed. That's how they got to know each other.

On March 10, the day after Harper died, Cross was standing in his driveway when he saw Sheila coming home from work. "I want to talk to you," he said. Then he told Sheila that he was the police officer involved in the shooting on Logan, and warned her that Natives could come to the house to harass or picket him or even retaliate in kind. They should be careful. In the days that followed, when he was drinking, Cross told Mike that there was a $75,000 contract out on his life and that police had a surveillance van watching the house. None of it was true.

—
5

"I slept like a baby."

Earlier that morning, Gordon Sinclair sat at his desk in the newsroom with the March 10 edition of the *Free Press* and scanned the front page. Under an article reporting that Howard Pawley wouldn't be around for the next provincial election, another headline caught his eye: "NATIVES DEMAND ANSWERS AFTER LEADER SHOT BY POLICE."

It was police reporter Greg Pindera's account from the news conference he and Darryl Sterdan had been at the day before.

The story said that Manitoba Native leaders were demanding answers into the police shooting of a prominent member of their community. Northern Affairs Minister Elijah Harper (no relation to John Joseph Harper) had asked the Attorney General's Department for a written report on the case, and Island Lake Tribal council spokesperson Joe Guy Wood was talking about member tribes doing their own investigation if the police didn't answer all their questions.

Wood said he didn't want to prejudge the investigation, but that it was common knowledge that the police treated whites and Natives differently.

"We just can't believe he would provoke anybody or attack a police officer," Wood had told reporters. "How was it there was such a drastic action taken on him? Why would a gun be involved? J.J. is not armed and he's not dangerous or violent. He's one of the leaders of the community. We're going to know one way or the other what happened."

From what Sinclair was reading, it seemed as if an independent investigation would be needed.

Police spokesperson Don Peters said that Harper was stopped at about the same time a man and a juvenile were arrested for car theft. The constable had asked Harper for identification, and Harper attacked the lone officer, knocking him to the ground. A struggle ensued over the constable's service revolver, and Harper was shot in the chest. The constable had been given a few days off with pay, standard practice in shooting cases. Peters acknowledged that the public might rightly question how – even in the dark of the night – an officer could mistake a thirty-six-year-old man for a nineteen year old. But he said it could easily happen.

Peters also said that the police hoped to conclude their investigation that day, although they still hadn't determined how the officer's gun was removed from its holster or how it went off. Peters had also told the *Free Press* that neither the criminal investigation nor the departmental review would be considering whether Harper was approached properly and with reasonable suspicion.

Sinclair had to turn from the front page to read the last paragraph. "Harper's broken and blood-spattered glasses were found by reporters about 2.5 meters from a pool of blood at the scene of the shooting."

Several parts of the story troubled Sinclair: the gaping age difference between the suspect and Harper; a vague reference to the officer stopping Harper "about the same time" as the two suspects were arrested; and the police blaming Harper for starting the altercation even before the investigation was over. Then there was the investigation itself. Why wouldn't it be looking into the constable's conduct in approaching Harper? And how could an investigation into the death of a citizen from a police bullet be over just a day after the shooting? But it was the last sentence that bothered him most. He re-read it: "Harper's broken and blood-splattered glasses were found by reporters . . ."

The image of the eyeglasses that Darryl Sterdan had found and turned over to police reminded Sinclair of the last time a cop was killed in Winnipeg, in the summer of 1970. The killer had escaped by swimming across the river, but he had been easy to trace. Police identified "Peeping" Tom Shand from a serial number on the prison-issue glasses found at the scene. Obviously Winnipeg cops could do a thorough job of searching the homicide scene when a fellow officer was the victim.

What else had the police missed at the Harper shooting scene besides the dead man's glasses, Sinclair wondered.

Over the lunch hour Chief Herb Stephen began paging through the reports he'd received on the shooting from the officers involved in the case. The first was from the Firearms Review Board of Enquiry. Three of the four board members were away, including Deputy Chief of Crime Paul Johnston, so their roles had been filled by officers from lower ranks.

The board met briefly for the first time at 9:30 on the morning of the shooting and again the following morning. Less than three hours later, Herb Stephen had the board's conclusion. Stephen also read the special reports that had been typed up in the detective office by the eight uniformed officers directly involved at the scene, the four who had support duties plus one by armaments officer William Kehler. Among the specials was one from Constable Glen Spryszak, the acting supervisor who had taken charge until Hrycyk got there. Spryszak, a former partner of Cross, had seized the revolver when he arrived, and on Hrycyk's instructions he had later done a canvass of the houses on Logan that faced the park. There were seventeen homes on the block and on Gallagher eight more that backed onto the park. Spryszak had knocked on just six doors before he left at 6 a.m. Three people answered, but the only one with any information was Katherine Tyler, the woman who had heard a banging behind her house and who had seen a police officer in the alley and someone running north through the park.

The chief had also read a report from the only eye witness to the shooting the police had found: Constable Robert Cross. Herb Stephen knew the officer's father, "Hap" Cross, who had been a civilian photographer with the department. The chief's own son, Tim, was on the force.

When Stephen got to the bottom of the pile of specials he found a report from Eric Hrycyk. It began: "On speaking to everyone at the scene it was apparent that no one had witnessed the event and a subsequent canvass of the houses in the area did not turn up any witnesses . . ."

It ended: "In conclusion, I would like to add that all the officers in this incident and in the subsequent investigation, including Crime, Ident and the Trauma Unit, acted in a professional competent manner . . ".

Stephen flipped back to the front and signed the Firearms Review Board's covering report. "I concur with the findings of your copy of the report." Then the chief began to write the news release.

Herb Stephen knew what it was like to be the subject of a Firearms Review Board investigation of a fatal shooting. On January 22, 1971, Stephen and his detective partner, Ivan Klepatz, were staked out in the basement of a downtown Toronto Dominion Bank when two masked men entered the bank. According to the police, one of the robbers began shooting. Klepatz returned fire with a twelve-gauge shotgun, wounding the gunman in the leg. The second robber was standing by a cash drawer. He turned when Stephen yelled, "Police. Hold it." Stephen fired at him twice, killing him. At the inquest, Stephen described seeing a flash of metal in the bandit's hand. It was a screwdriver. The bank robber had been using it to pry open the cash drawers.

The Firearms Review Board cleared Stephen of wrongdoing, as did the inquest. The Canadian Bankers' Association went further. It awarded Stephen and his partner gold medals. Years later, when a magazine writer asked Stephen how he felt about killing a man, he answered, "Police officers are expected to assess the situation in seconds . . . and then act accordingly. If a fellow is punching you, you would not expect to take your gun out and shoot him . . ." On another occasion, Judge Harold Gyles heard a more candid Stephen remark on how he felt after killing the young bank robber: "I slept like a baby."

Shortly before 3:30 p.m. on March 10, exactly thirty-six hours after John Joseph Harper had been pronounced dead, Herb Stephen strolled across King Street to City Hall to meet the media.

"As you are already aware," he began, reading from the release he had prepared himself, "a patrolling police unit observed a stolen motor vehicle in the vicinity of 60 Keewatin Street at approximately 2:25 a.m., March 9, 1988. The vehicle was abandoned at Winks and Alexander by two males who fled on foot. A 14-year-old male youth was arrested after a brief foot-chase and this resulted in a description of a second suspect being broadcast.

"At approximately 2:40 a.m. a lone police officer who was searching the area for a second suspect observed John Joseph Harper walking east on the north sidewalk of Logan Avenue approaching Winks Street. In the opinion of this officer, Harper matched the general description of the second male. The officer approached and advised him he matched the description of the second male. The officer took hold of Harper by his right arm. At this time Harper turned to face him and pushed the officer with both hands on the shoulders. The officer lost his balance and fell backward onto the ground. As he fell he grabbed Harper by both arms and he fell on top of the officer. As the officer attempted to push Harper back, Harper reached down and grabbed at the butt of the officer's service revolver. In the ensuing struggle, the revolver came free from the holster and the officer managed to hold the butt while Harper pulled on the barrel of the weapon. The officer felt the weapon sliding out of his hand and at that time it discharged, with the bullet striking Harper in the chest. Harper let go of the revolver and slumped to the ground. Assistance was requested and Harper conveyed to the Health Sciences Centre, but was pronounced dead shortly thereafter.

"The police department's Firearms Review Board of Enquiry convened and reviewed the details of the incident. They reached the conclusion that the death was precipitated by the assault of the officer by Harper and the subsequent struggle for his service revolver, which accidentally discharged. They found no negligence on the part of the officer and," Stephen said, looking up from his statement, "I have concurred with their findings. The report on this incident has been reviewed by the senior Crown attorney, Bruce Miller. He found no evidence of a criminal offense and no charges will be laid."

In the questioning that followed, Stephen hinted at something that wasn't in the release: that Harper had been intoxicated.

Later that day, at a news conference in the Island Lake Tribal Council's downtown office, with Elijah Harper at his side, a spokesperson for the group read a prepared statement: "We feel the police are trying to sweep this under the rug and we will do everything in our power to see that this does not happen."

Dave Courchene, Honorary Grand Chief, rebutted Herb Stephen's contention that Harper had attacked Cross. "He wasn't that kind of person," Courchene said. "But people can be provoked into any situation. If you kick a doggie long enough, he's going to bite back."

Years later, Paul Johnston told Gordon Sinclair that, on his return to work, he had read the Review Board's findings. His assessment of it echoed Courchene's metaphor: "I've seen better reports on shot dogs."

$$\overline{6}$$

"Just a reporter came and asked me."

The Winnipeg police's exoneration of their officer was the lead story on CBC Radio national morning news on March 11, the day after a candlelight vigil was held at the shooting scene. Aboriginal leaders were demanding a public inquiry. "The mentality of the police force is the same as what is happening in South Africa," one of them told a reporter. "I don't see any difference."

That morning Herb Stephen was on the local CBC morning radio show. "Our investigation goes forward now to the chief medical examiner," Stephen said. Inquests are mandatory where police officers are involved in a shooting death, the chief explained. "And," he added confidently, "there will be evidence brought forward there which will certainly, I'm positive, substantiate our findings."

Two days after the shooting, Gordon Sinclair was still troubled by the police's having missed Harper's eye glasses, and what that suggested. If his friend Deputy Chief Paul Johnston had been in town, Sinclair would have contacted him for some background on the case. Instead, after lunch, Sinclair dialled the chief's office for an appointment to talk about the Harper shooting. The chief suggested 2:30 that afternoon. That gave Sinclair only an hour. He called a taxi. There was something he had to do before he saw the chief.

The taxi turned onto Electa Street at the west end of Stanley Knowles Park.

"Wait here," Sinclair said.

He got out and walked towards the houses on Gallagher Avenue and the lane that backed onto the park. There was an elderly Chinese man wearing a wide-brimmed hat standing in his backyard. Sinclair decided to try him first.

It was almost 2:30 p.m. when the *Free Press* columnist returned to the taxi. As the cabbie drove, Sinclair scribbled a list of questions for the chief, starting with the first one that came to his mind. Was this case being investigated the way a homicide would be?

Herb Stephen greeted Sinclair at the threshold of his fifth-floor corner office. He looked relaxed and friendly. Sinclair was struck by that, and by how white Stephen's shirt was. "Whiter than white," was the way he described it when he began writing later that afternoon. Sinclair sat down and opened his notebook to the first question: Was the investigation being handled as a homicide?

"The scene is protected and Ident attends," Stephen answered. He hadn't said yes, but at the time it sounded as if he had.

What about missing the eyeglasses?

"That was an unfortunate thing," Stephen said. "They're not really necessary for the investigation. But it's unfortunate they were missed." Stephen speculated the glasses could have been buried in the park snow when the police examined the area initially. The Identification unit had taken a video of the scene on the afternoon of the shooting, after Darryl Sterdan had found the glasses, and there had been a lot of melting.

Sinclair asked if the chief was upset about Ident having missed the glasses. "Not really," Stephen said. "I think they did a thorough job."

Sinclair flipped back to the questions at the front of his notebook. Were there powder burns on Harper's hands? Stephen said he didn't know that, either.

Next, Sinclair asked how the revolver had been removed from the holster and how it came to be fired.

"That's something that will be explained fully at the inquest, both by officers and experts who have examined that," Stephen said. He went on to emphasize his belief that the inquest would vindicate the officer and his department's investigation. "As I say, a lot of questions will be explained there and will back up what we said. I'm confident of that." Sinclair had a query in his notebook about Harper. "Was he intoxicated?"

Stephen had suggested he was during his news conference the day before, but now he deflected the question, repeating that those kinds of questions would be answered at the inquest. As diplomatically as he could, Sinclair asked Stephen if he felt there was a problem with racism on the force. The chief got the message.

"There's no truth to that whatsoever," he said indignantly. "I'm on the mayor's race relations committee, and we don't get that many complaints."

"How many Native policemen are there?" Sinclair asked.

"Half a dozen anyway and maybe some with mixed blood," Stephen said. "We would be glad to get them. We have a difficult time recruiting them."

Sinclair returned to the investigation. "Are you satisfied with how the officer conducted himself?" he asked.

"I am, based on the information I have," Stephen said. "Plus it was reviewed by our shooting review board." He said the Identification unit had collected enough physical evidence to back up the constable's story.

Twice Sinclair asked the chief if he was satisfied that the investigation had been complete. Twice Stephen said his officers had done a thorough job.

Now Sinclair had something to tell Stephen, something that would show that the glasses weren't the only thing the police had missed. Sinclair told Stephen that he had just been in the neighbourhood where Harper was shot. He had gone to six homes and spoken to three potential witnesses. None of them had been canvassed by police. "Just a reporter came and asked me," the first man, eighty-four-year-old Sam Lim, had told Sinclair.

Stephen looked momentarily startled. He had reason to be. He had personally cleared Cross of any negligence in the shooting of an unarmed citizen, yet there were still potential witnesses that the police hadn't interviewed.

Sam Lim hadn't seen anything; the others said they hadn't either. Sinclair offered Stephen their names and addresses.

"I know many people were interviewed," Stephen said, "and some people may not have been home when we were there."

"So the investigation continues?" Sinclair asked.

"Oh," Stephen responded, "there's always little pieces to clean up, certainly."

Little pieces? Sinclair drew a box around the quote, then flipped back to the front of his notebook. There was one question left. It was circled, too.

"Why has there been no public expression of sympathy and regrets from the department to the family?"

Stephen said police had been to the home to talk to Harper's wife and he had arranged for his victim's services department to visit her.

"It was very unfortunate," Herb Stephen said.

When the interview ended, Stephen left for the detective office. He was angry. He wanted the canvass completed. Half an hour later, two detectives had been assigned to look for witnesses. A few days later, Lois Harper received a letter expressing Stephen's personal condolences. It was dated March 11, the day Sinclair interviewed the chief.

Back at the newsroom, Sinclair started his next-day's column the way he always did, by writing his own headline. "CIRCLING THE PADDYWAGONS," he titled it.

At the same time Sinclair was meeting with Stephen, Attorney General Vic Schroeder and three senior bureaucrats from his department were secretly conferring with Manitoba's head Mountie, Assistant Commissioner Dale Henry. Schroeder was concerned and suspicious about the speed with which the police department had cleared the constable, whose name still hadn't been made public. He wanted the RCMP to take over the Harper investigation. "We were looking for some way to make sure the facts would come out and the public would be satisfied," Schroeder explained years later.

Dale Henry was reluctant to take on the case. Petty jealousies plagued the Winnipeg department's attitude toward the "Horsemen," as the city cops called the RCMP. Henry thought that the Mounties riding in and assuming control of a city police investigation could do irreparable damage to an already strained relationship between the two law enforcement organizations. "But, if that's what you want," Henry told Schroeder, "I'll do it."

When the meeting ended, Schroeder was still undecided.

—
7

"You better take your rifle to school."

The Island Lake community of Wasagamack was still buried deep in snow three days after its former chief was mortally wounded on a bare Winnipeg sidewalk. Buses, trucks, cars, and power-toboggans lined the parking area outside George Knott School where 600 mourners had come to J.J. Harper's funeral, among them his wife and her three children, MLA Elijah Harper, and J.J.'s friend and mentor, Dave Tomasson, a consultant who had been hired four years earlier to create the Island Lake Tribal Council.

Two caskets were positioned side by side in the gymnasium, where the service was held. One contained the body of John Joseph Harper, the other the remains of his young cousin, John Knott, who had died from his burns in the same hospital and on the same day. The death of men in the prime of their lives was common among First Nations peoples. The mortality rate of Aboriginal Canadians between the ages of twenty-five and forty-four was five times the national rate. Then there was suicide. Indians killed themselves at double the rate of other Canadians. Still, the nature of J.J. Harper's death had shocked the community and the coincidental tragedy of his cousin's death had compounded the grief.

Lois Harper sat on a front-row folding chair, her three children beside her, Vince, age twelve, Elliot, age eight, and Lori, age seven.

Lois had first met J.J. while he was partying his way through a two-year attempt at a Bachelor of Education degree at the University of Brandon, in southwestern Manitoba. He was twenty-one, she nineteen when they married on August 11, 1973. They had spent most of their married life in Wasagamack, where, in 1982, J.J. became the band chief. After he died, when he was described in the media as a Native leader, critics sneered that the only place J.J. Harper had ever led anyone was to the nearest bar. But Dave Tomasson, an Icelandic Canadian who, three months after the funeral, would become deputy minister of northern and native affairs, dismissed that slur.

"That's bullshit," Tomasson said. "J.J. had a lot of ability. He was a good leader for his age and where he was at. But the question, could he have been a great leader? Well, we'll never know. He had the makings of being a very, very good leader. He was articulate, the man was smart." Tomasson gave an example: when Harper had become chief, the band was hundreds of thousands of dollars in the red. "J.J. told me his priority was to get the band out of debt. And he did."

Lois, who was a Métis from southern Manitoba and didn't speak the Island Lake dialect, a blend of Ojibway and Cree also known as Oji-Cree, had always felt his role as chief took him away from her and the children too much. So, in 1984, he resigned and moved to Winnipeg, where he went to work under Tomasson for the newly created Island Lake Tribal Council, the political and socio-economic arm of the four bands that made up Island Lake. Within five months he had taken over from Tomasson as executive director of the tribal council and co-manager of the reserves' Nor-win Construction Co. Ltd, which built and maintained the winter road. Harper's combined annual salary of nearly $68,000 easily allowed him to buy the two-storey house on Elgin, a block away from the hospital where he died.

The wailing of babies tucked inside traditional teekinakins mingled with the sobbing of the mourners in the overheated gymnasium. One woman wasn't crying. No one really knew how much J.J. Harper's mother understood. Clara Harper seemed like an infant in an old woman's body. She had suffered a stroke some months earlier and was unable to communicate.

Her husband, James Harper, approached their son's casket alone.

Since Clara's stroke, James had looked after her as best he could, and J.J. had looked after both of them. He brought them food, repaired their house, took them to the hospital. He even bought them a truck so they could get around more easily and sent his father seeds for his garden. Now James stood for the last time by his son and in a loud and moving voice, told J.J. that he would see him again one day.

J.J.'s sister Bernadette was the last of his fifteen siblings to approach the coffin. When she saw his body she knew it was true; J.J. was dead. Bernadette thought she would never stop crying, remembering vividly the way as children he used to send her in search of stones for his slingshot. He always wanted them perfectly round. He always wanted everything perfect and in order.

As Victor Harper watched the line filing past the casket, he remembered the last time he'd seen J.J. It had been in a vision that had jolted him awake on the night of the shooting. Victor wasn't related to J.J., but they had grown up together. They had spent their early years in camps in the bush, where their families fished and hunted and trapped. The two boys grew up speaking Oji-Cree, immersed in the culture and customs of the Island Lake people. Then, late in the summer of 1956, their world changed. Victor was seven and his father was out hunting at their camp at Kalliechollie Lake when a float-plane swooped across the water, like a bird of prey. A man in a red coat Victor assumes was a Mountie got out and began rounding up the school-aged children.

"I can still hear the mothers crying and hanging on to their kids," Victor said. "They didn't want to let them go. I went and hid. I was hiding under a bed and this guy in the red cloth came and got me. My mum was hanging on to me. And I remember looking back and my sister was crying. I think J.J. was out at Willow Lake or Stevenson Lake, and the same thing happened to him that summer."

The plane took them to a school at Norway House, 170 kilometres due west across the wilderness. The Oblate Order of priests and Grey Nuns operated the Jack River Residential School there. Victor and J.J. were two of the 1,237 Aboriginal children who went to the eleven residential schools in Manitoba in 1956. The Jack River school, a big stone building, became their prison. "When we got there, they didn't even know who we were. We had Indian names."

Victor and J.J. were placed in kindergarten. "Even in kindergarten J.J. was one of the top students in school," Victor said. "He would finish his work way ahead of anyone else."

The school's mission was to teach the children the basics, but to reading, writing, and arithmetic they added another lesson: assimilation. "We were taught that every white man was your master," Victor said. "They wanted to de-Indianize us. They wanted us to forget our culture."

The children were forced to speak English only, and if they were caught speaking their native tongue, they were punished. J.J. resisted and was strapped.

One teacher at residential school taught them something that wasn't on the curriculum. "He was a Brother, I guess," Victor said. "He was next to being a priest. He used to take us up to his room with a banana or apples or a little toy. He'd play with us. Sometimes he would show us his dick and make us play with him. That went on right through till we realized what was going on. I thought it was part of education because there's this holy man doing this.

"And then you'd have the Brother taking you to the altar for communion. And sometimes he would give you some of that holy wine in the chapel. Now that I think about it, to be raised like that, we kind of lost track of how to respect people. That's why I have this problem after being abused like that, especially by a holy man.

"You kind of get lost. Then you get angry. " Victor said. "You get frustrated and then sometimes you abuse your family. But that's because of what happened to you."

J.J. and Victor went to Winnipeg for high school at the Assiniboine Residential School. Then, in grade 11, they were enrolled at a regular high school, Vincent Massey Collegiate, in suburban Fort Garry, where they endured a different kind of abuse. "People thought we still lived in teepees. Even the teachers told the kids, 'You better take your rifle to school, 'cause there are Indians coming.'

"It was rough the first two months. A lot of name calling. But after they started to get to know us, they started to back us up. We played sports with them as a class team, and as soon as they started to know us, they liked us. They started to accept us through sports."

The funeral service lasted for more than two hours. Then J.J.'s casket was placed in a pick-up truck for the short trip across the lake to the island where he would be buried. Elijah Harper was among the mourners who followed the truck. The day after the shooting, as minister of northern affairs, he had demanded a written report from the Attorney General's Department. At the funeral, in front of his people, Elijah Harper made a personal pledge that there would be a public inquiry into why J.J. Harper died. But that's not what Attorney General Vic Schroeder had been saying in the days immediately following the shooting. Although he had issued a statement saying he was concerned and that many questions needed answering, Schroeder had rejected the idea of a public inquiry. He had also heeded Dale Henry's words and decided against calling the RCMP to investigate.

An inquiry wasn't what mattered most to J.J.'s eighty-year-old father. "He always told us not to have angry thoughts," Bernadette said years later. "He wasn't angry for what happened. But he always said he believed the truth will come out somehow." James Harper said something else Victor Harper would remember, too. Standing by the casket, speaking loudly in Oji-Cree, J.J.'s father prayed that the police officer would come and talk with him, so he could be forgiven.

At the time no one in the Harper family knew anything about the constable James Harper wanted to absolve of blame. They didn't know that while J.J. was attending Vincent Massey Collegiate in Winnipeg, Robert Cross was walking through the same hallways on his way to shop classes. The two men whose paths would intersect again so tragically nearly twenty years later had more in common than either of them ever understood.

$$\overline{8}$$

"A SINCERE AND CONSCIENTIOUS YOUNG MAN."

As a child, Tim Hanford had lived on the same street as Rob Cross, as he was known at Viscount Alexander Junior High. Later, he would go by the name of Bob, but those who knew him from his school days would always call him Rob. Hanford liked Cross.

"He was a big kid, and he was kind of crazy," Hanford said. "He used to go to parties and get the biggest container he could find, fill it with beer, and chug it."

Rob had a reputation for being a bit of a bully, but to Hanford he seemed more like a bodyguard when they walked to the neighbourhood high school, Vincent Massey Collegiate, for classes in shop. "If he liked you, he would stick up for you."

Robert Andrew Cross was born in Ottawa on April 26, 1954, the third child and only son of William and Marjorie Cross. "Hap," as his father was known, was employed by the RCMP lab in Ottawa. Marjorie Cross was the dominant force in the family. She loved to talk, a trait her son would inherit. When Cross was in his mid-teens, Hap took a job as photographer with the Winnipeg Police Department. Cross was an easygoing, fun-loving child who was very close to his parents and his older sister, Judy. He grew more quickly than most of the boys in junior high and developed an aggressive attitude and a reputation as a tough guy. In 1970, wearing a wispy moustache and hair over his ears, Bob entered grade 10 at St. Paul's High, a Catholic boys' school.

Cross got through high school with marks in the fifties, mostly. A few years later, in 1975, he married Charlene Glenesk. Like J.J. and Lois Harper, he was twenty-one and she was nineteen when they exchanged vows. They had met when she was in grade 12. Charlene thought Cross was handsome and fun to be with, "a real crowd pleaser." Except when he was drinking. Then he tended to get down on everything and everybody.

Charlene had found a job out of high school as a payroll clerk at St. Boniface Hospital and later moved to the Great West Life Assurance Co. across the street from the Legislative Building. Cross, meanwhile, bounced around. He went to work for National School Studios taking student photos and briefly attempted some courses in university. For a while he leased cars for Century Motors, then switched to Chrysler credit and leasing, doing phone collections. He and Charlene joined the Downtown Y and started playing racquetball with another couple. Drinking didn't seem to be as much of a problem then. The way Charlene saw it, Cross traded the bottle for the natural high of athletics.

Then he tried selling condos, and for a time he was regional manager for Suzuki Canada. But none of the jobs lasted. Between pay cheques he would start drinking and get down on life. What Cross really wanted to do was join the police department, but he had been turned down once. He decided to try again, though. "The reason I wish to become a member of the Police Department," he wrote in his application, "is simply that I believe I have a lot to offer, an example would be I enjoy working with people, solving problems, and seem to work best when under pressure. I have been told I always have an excellent way of dealing with people."

On March 26, 1984, exactly one month short of his thirtieth birthday, Cross entered recruit class 103. The Winnipeg Police Department brought out the best in him, at least when it came to fitting in and showing enthusiasm. The younger recruits liked him and so did the older training staff. That was Cross. People liked him, as was evidenced in his letters of reference from former employers and friends. One of them read, "I have known Robert Cross for 15 years and have had the pleasure of seeing him mature into a sincere and conscientious young man."

By the second week of recruit classes, his fellow officers in training had selected Cross to be class president. An early performance evaluation praised his appearance, deportment, and effort. When it came to classroom work, though, he struggled, almost to the point of flunking out: "One week prior to the final examination Cst. Cross was interviewed and told that he would have to receive a high mark in order to meet the recruit standard. He took this challenge and received a much higher mark. He came through when the 'heat' was on. Good job."

Cross graduated eighteenth in a class of twenty-one, making standard in eight of thirteen areas on his evaluation report, and above on the rest. Measured against what would happen four years later, the four areas in which he did best were significant: public contacts, employee contacts, effectiveness under stress, and acceptance of responsibility. The evaluation also praised him for his knowledge of the law and the way he handled suspects. Finally, there was this: "Constable Cross is . . . married. He accepts the discipline of Police Work and the effects it will have on his personal and family life."

Cross told Charlene he envied the single guys in the class. They could go out drinking without having to phone home. At about the time Cross was entering recruit class, Charlene became pregnant. She was walking their dog one day when Cross drove up beside her, and she told him the news. He said nothing and just drove off towards their small, two-storey brick house.

Just before Christmas 1984, Charlene gave birth to a baby girl. She wanted to name her Jennifer, but Bob insisted on Sasha. Eighteen months later, not long after their tenth wedding anniversary, Cross came home from his night shift. "We have to talk," he said.

Cross was involved with another woman. Charlene was hurt. But she wasn't surprised. He didn't have to tell her who he was seeing. Charlene sensed it was Diane Eastwood, his girlfriend in junior high. Three months earlier, she and Cross had chatted with Diane at the Vincent Massey Collegiate high school reunion.

"Too bad she hasn't got a boyfriend," Cross remarked to Charlene later.

"Yeah," Charlene said. "She's a nice girl."

A week or two after the reunion, Cross phoned Diane and asked her out for a drink. Diane said no. But a couple of weeks later, when he called again, she agreed to meet him. It was a Saturday and Charlene was in Denver on business. Cross and Diane ended up on the patio at La Taverna, on Corydon Avenue, near Winnipeg's Little Italy. It was there that he told Diane that he and Charlene were having marital problems. By that time there was only one thing that mattered to Diane. Cross was back.

"We just seemed to click," Diane said later. "It felt like we had picked up where we left off all those years ago. It was just bang, bang, bang. It was just like a wild, hot, and heavy romance. And then he left his wife."

Charlene was devastated by Cross's departure. She knew the marriage hadn't been going well, but she never would have ended it. Citing "unhappy differences," Cross and Charlene were divorced a year later. By that time, he and Diane were already living on Charbonneau Crescent in the new housing development of Island Lakes, and Diane was pregnant. When he found out she was expecting, Cross asked Diane if she really wanted to go through with it. "Of course I do," she said. In November 1986 Diane gave birth to twins.

By the time Cross and Diane married the following year, she was pregnant again with their third child. He wanted to drive her straight to an abortion clinic. Diane refused. During the pregnancy, she was plagued by mood swings, which led to frequent arguments with Cross. It didn't help that, while she was pregnant, Cross gave her crabs. It was in the midst of this domestic turmoil that J.J. Harper was shot.

8

"A MODEL CITIZEN."

The racist letters arrived anonymously in Gordon Sinclair's newsroom mail slot. "Next time you get mugged," advised one, "call an Indian." "Since Winnipeg has become Canada's largest reserve our crime rate has jumped sky high," wrote another. "You're making such a fuss over that Indian that was shot accidentally," said another name-less critic. "Did you make a fuss over the other murders committed by these people – taxi drivers, old ladies and the rest."

The boil of bigotry had been lanced by a series of columns Sinclair had written about trying to find out what had happened in the hours before and after the shooting. By that time Sinclair had found Bob Barnes, who had been putting the Bye Bye Howie sign up behind his house when he heard the shot. Barnes hadn't seen the shooting, but he and his wife, Carole, had watched first the fire truck and then the ambulance arrive, and they both wondered what was going on and why it took so long for the ambulance to leave.

Sinclair knew that the shooting had happened between 2:38 and 2:40 a.m. The ambulance received the call at 2:41, the service's director, Jake Enns, told the columnist. It arrived eight minutes later and was at the scene for another eight minutes before leaving for the hospital. The attendants had treated Harper at the scene, using pressurized, inflatable anti-shock trousers in an attempt to pump blood from his lower extremities to his vital organs. Great in theory but, in the case of a chest wound, a dubious practice.

Chief medical examiner Dr. Peter Markesteyn told Sinclair that Harper would have had to have been shot in the operating theatre to have had a chance. He practically was. The Health Sciences Centre was less than 2.5 kilometres east of the sidewalk where Harper lay bleeding to death. But, by the time the ambulance arrived, twenty minutes had passed sinced Harper was shot, and he was dead. He had bled to death.

There were other matters to consider. The police still hadn't explained adequately how the gun was drawn from Cross's holster. One day, not long after the shooting, Sinclair got a chance to test the holster when he saw a uniformed police officer standing in the news-room lobby. Sinclair hurried over and explained that he wanted to try removing his revolver from his holster. The cop understood why and obliged. Facing the officer, Sinclair reached out with his left hand, grabbed the butt of the gun and pulled it forward in one buttery-smooth motion. Sinclair was surprised by how effortlessly the revolver slid out. So surprised that he neglected to consider the safety feature designed to foil just such an attempt. The holster had a leather strap that held the gun in place. The constable in the lobby had unsnapped it. If he had left the strap in place, as police always do unless they're pulling their weapon, Sinclair would have had to yank at the revolver, and even then it was unlikely he could have drawn it out.

The revolver didn't have a safety, a locking mechanism that prevented the gun from being discharged accidentally, but the .38 Smith & Wesson Police Special was a double-action revolver, which meant that cocking it allowed the trigger to be pulled more easily. The gun could be fired without cocking the hammer, but that required more pressure and a more deliberate squeeze of the trigger. Sinclair didn't learn that until the inquest.

There was a vital detail shown by the demonstration that Sinclair missed as he stood there in the lobby with the answer in his hand. If Harper had pulled Cross's gun, it would have been upside down and backwards. And the barrel would have been pointing toward the cop. But it was Harper who had been shot in the chest.

In the newsroom lobby, Sinclair carefully handed the city police officer's weapon back, and thanked him. Sinclair briefly reported his findings in his next column. In every column since the shooting, Sinclair had been unrelentingly critical of the police. In his own mind, he knew he had performed the little experiment with the holster and gun more to show he was willing to examine both sides of the story than because he expected the demonstration to prove anything. It was a perfunctory effort. In one of his earliest columns on the case, Sinclair had shown his bias, and that he hadn't done a thorough investigation, either. He had read the glowing character references that Native leaders had offered after the shooting, and accepted them as true. He had also called Lois Harper's sister, Bonnie Ross, who told him that the weekend before the shooting, J.J. had helped the police when he pulled an OPP cruiser out of a ditch near Kenora. Then, in a phrase that must have made Herb Stephen laugh, Sinclair wrote that J.J. Harper was a "a model citizen." That was long before Sinclair sat down with J.J. Harper's girlfriend and learned what he had been doing on the night he died.

—
10

"WHY DO YOU WANT TO GO THERE? DO YOU WANT TO GET SHOT?"

Around 9 p.m. on March 8, the phone rang in a west-end duplex that Kathy Bushie shared with her sister. Kathy was a pretty, plump twenty-two-year-old Ojibway with shy eyes that were masked by large, thin-framed glasses. She had been sitting home alone waiting for a couple of girlfriends to pick her up. Like Kathy, Joyce Williams and Tanya Sinclair were from the Hollow Water Reserve, seventy miles north of the city.

Joyce had called earlier to ask Kathy to go bar hopping with her and Tanya, but Kathy hadn't wanted to go. She had a feeling that if she joined them she would run into J.J. and they would end up together, the way they used to when he was separated from Lois. She didn't want to start that again. But she missed him. He was easy to talk to, always out to have a good time, to meet people. Laughing and dancing. Buying drinks for friends. Above all, though, he made Kathy feel special.

They had met when she was the secretary for Nor-win Construction. At first they talked on the phone when he called up and sometimes she would see him in the office. Then they bumped into each other in bars. When J.J. and Lois separated in 1987, Kathy started seeing him. They would drift together for the night. Then drift apart. They never spoke of love, but the relationship was warm and caring. It lasted about six months, and three months later J.J. moved back home with Lois and the kids.

"I think I was more of a close friend," Kathy said, "because at the time of his separation he told me there was something missing, there was a space in his heart. He said I filled that space. I guess he was lonely at times without the children. He would just say, 'My wife and I cannot get along.' His children meant a lot to him. I knew by then I didn't want to get involved, or close to him, because I knew that somewhere in his mind he wanted to reconcile with his wife. But I always told him I'd be there anytime he needed someone to talk to."

Despite her mixed emotions about J.J. and her premonition about running into him, Kathy eventually decided to join Joyce and Tanya. The first stop was at The Front Page Lounge, so named because it used to be up the street from the *Winnipeg Tribune* building. The bar was still in the same spot, but The Trib was now a parking lot. The Front Page was on the ground floor of the St. Regis Hotel, a medium-priced inn which actually welcomed Native families visiting the big city. The place was packed at 9:45 when Kathy walked in. She spotted J.J. right away, sitting with friends. He looked the same. He was wearing his black jacket and blue jeans, his black-rimmed glasses and that smile.

"There's your old girlfriend," someone remarked to him, loud enough for Kathy to hear.

"No," he said quickly, emphatically. "She's a good friend of mine."

He made room for Kathy beside him. She was happy to see him again, even though she was now seeing another man, a former counsellor at Stony Mountain Penitentiary. Frank didn't have an ex-wife and children, and Kathy really wanted her relationship with him to work. But being with Frank wasn't the same as being with J.J. The question came up as they sat together in The Front Page, catching up on each other's lives.

"Are you seeing anyone?" he asked.

"Yeah," she said.

It was the first he knew of her new relationship. Kathy didn't tell him Frank's name, and J.J. didn't mention that he had gone back to Lois.

"I'm happy for you. You deserve the best," he told her. "As long as you're happy." But she wasn't, even though she didn't know that until

Frank left her a year later. Maybe that's why, that night, she was drawn to J.J., and she sensed that, despite what he said about being happy for her – he still wanted to be with her.

He gave her a hug. His arms made her feel safe again. Safe and comforted.

By 10:30, Tanya wanted to try another bar. Kathy would have to go, too. "Can I come along with you?" J.J. asked.

They were going to the Sherbrook Inn, a bar where management had put up a sign for the benefit of the bikers who used the place as their clubhouse away from the clubhouse. The sign advised patrons, among other things, to check their knives at the door.

"Why do you want to go there?" J.J. Harper said. "Do you want to get shot?"

J.J. got into the back seat with Kathy, and they cruised west on Portage Avenue, looking for somewhere other than Winnipeg's answer to the Longbranch Saloon. Then someone had an idea. "How about the Westbrook?"

The Westbrook was distinguished by a twelve-foot wooden replica of the famous cartoonlike cowboy from the Las Vegas strip. Next door the squat, square windowless DJ's Saloon featured live country bands. Typically, as soon as J.J. and the others arrived, he grabbed an OV spotted some friends across the bar, and drifted away, leaving Kathy with her girlfriends. Later, they all went next door to DJ's Saloon, where J.J. began playing pool.

It was after midnight, while J.J. and Kathy and the others were at DJ's, when the two native teenagers stole the white Dodge Aries from the Westbrook parking lot. Around 1:30 a.m. J.J. asked Kathy to dance. Kathy wasn't in a party mood. But she agreed to a slow dance, and then another. The band was playing "Momma, he's crazy," and J.J. was singing along. He actually made her laugh. J.J. always made her laugh. But when the song was over, he drifted off again. Kathy and her friends decided to leave.

"Why don't you go and see if he wants a ride home," Joyce suggested to Kathy. "I'll get the car and wait in front."

But Harper wasn't quite ready to leave. "I'm going to finish my beer first," he said. He wrapped his arms around Kathy. "Hang on," he said, as if she had any choice.

"The girls are waiting in the front," Kathy said.

He began to kiss her on her lips. Kathy pulled away. She was embarrassed.

"Let's go now," she said.

"Okay," he said. "Let's go."

But J.J. wasn't interested in a lift from Tanya. Once he and Kathy were outside, he suggested they take a cab instead. Kathy knew why. He didn't want the girls to drive him home, because then she would know he was back with his wife. "No," Kathy answered. "If you don't want me to know where you live, why don't you just come home to my place? You can sleep there."

But he was insistent, they had to get a cab.

"No, get in the car," Kathy ordered. "We'll get a ride. Why would we want a cab when we have a ride?"

But he kept talking about getting a cab. Kathy was starting to waver, glancing at the car, then back at him, wondering what she should do.

But, she thought to herself, where's he going to go? I've got to work tomorrow. Then there was Frank . . .

"If you want to come, come," she said finally. "But I'm getting a ride."

"Okay, fine," he said.

"Good night," she said. "I'll see you later."

Then he walked off.

As Kathy got in the car, she looked over her shoulder and watched J.J. walking, his hands in his pockets, towards the big Las Vegas cowboy.

The phone was ringing at the Harper home. It was loud enough to wake Lois, who was sleeping in Lori's room. She hurried to answer it. Just as she picked it up, it stopped ringing. Lois looked at the time on the bedside digital clock radio.

It was 2:07 a.m.

"I thought it was probably him," Lois said. "And he'd probably be drunk and . . . and he'd probably be with whatever guys he'd be with."

11

"ALL OF A SUDDEN, BOOM, THIS COMES UP."

Three days after the funeral, and a week after the shooting, Native community leaders spoke in front of city hall at a noon-hour vigil. The mood of the crowd was angry, defiant, and, at times, extreme.

"I think we should take this as the sixth murder this year," said Yvon Dumont, the president of the Manitoba Métis Federation. "I urge you all to keep off the street at night and to keep out of dark corners."

Damon Johnston, speaking for thirty-five Winnipeg Native organizations, called for Herb Stephen's resignation. "If he thinks he can walk away and answer to no one," said Johnston, "he's mistaken."

Marilyn Fontaine, a cousin of Phil Fontaine, the soon-to-be Grand Chief of the Manitoba Assembly of Chiefs, spoke as a Native woman and mother. She told the crowd that Harper had died a victim of one police officer's racism, but the police department's handling of the investigation made him the victim of a more insidious form of bigotry.

"It's too easy for [Mayor] Bill Norrie and Herb Stephen – known for protecting his boys in blue – to be satisfied that the death of J.J. Harper was not racially motivated."

The mayor was the chairperson of the city's race relations committee, on which Herb Stephen also sat. And Bill Norrie had already told reporters, "This is not a racial incident. It was just timing, circumstances, and events. The Native community's demand for a public inquiry will be satisfied by the inquest." There were those who agreed with Norrie that the shooting related to time, circumstances, and events, but in a historic sense, not the narrow way the mayor meant.

The demonstrators wanted an inquiry that would look beyond the shooting and into the justice system's treatment of Aboriginals as a group. This wasn't the first time the Aboriginal community had called for just such a public inquiry. Two years earlier, in 1986, three white men were charged in the slaying of Cree teenager Helen Betty Osborne, who had been abducted off the streets of The Pas. Her naked body was discovered in snow-covered bush near the town. She had been stabbed more than fifty times, and her head ferociously bludgeoned. It had taken the RCMP fifteen years to make the arrests, even though the identity of the suspects was common knowledge in the town shortly after the killing. That had prompted Oscar Lavalin, the chief of The Pas reserve, to call for a public inquiry.

The pressure that was building on the still-governing New Democrats wasn't just coming from the Native community. As Schroeder went door-to-door in his predominantly Mennonite riding in North Kildonan, Schroeder was hearing concern from his constituents, who had questions about the shooting that he couldn't answer.

The next day, Elijah Harper stood on the broad stone steps of the Legislative Building, in front of 500 demonstrators, and kept the promise he had made at the funeral in Wasagamack. There would be a public inquiry into the shooting of J.J. Harper. It would follow the inquest. Schroeder explained why he had changed his mind.

"I am moved by the concerns of the community at large," he told the crowd, "and have felt pressure from constituents who've said this thing smells."

Following the wishes of the Native community, the inquiry would be much broader than just the Harper shooting. It would look into the murder of Helen Betty Osborne and the justice system's treatment of Aboriginal people generally in Manitoba. "There is a belief they are treated differently on our streets and in our courts and prisons,"

Schroeder said. "What needs to be done is to ensure that justice is the same for all of us."

Later, a reporter asked Herb Stephen for a comment. "I have no problem with him having an inquiry, but I don't think it's necessary." The police chief said he had never seen an incident of racial harassment in his thirty-two years on the force. "All of a sudden, boom, this comes up and there's a racial problem."

12

"Why don't you shoot me like you shot the Indian?"

Many years later, it occurred to Gordon Sinclair how little the rest of the Winnipeg media, including his own paper, initially seemed to care about the Harper shooting. They reported the vigils and demonstrations and the war of words between Native leaders and the allied mayor and police chief, but left the investigating to him, a columnist. He concluded he wouldn't have been the only Winnipeg journalist still investigating weeks after the shooting if the victim had been a white businessman shot walking his dog in River Heights, instead of an Indian on Logan. Any more than the police would have wrapped up the case in thirty-six hours.

On the day after Elijah Harper announced the creation of the Aboriginal Justice Inquiry, Sinclair found a witness the police hadn't interviewed about the shooting. It wasn't difficult. Melvin Pruden was in the third-floor courtroom, appearing on remand for theft over $1,000 and dangerous driving. Pruden was in the same clothes he had been wearing the night he stole the car: a grey tweed jacket, red shirt, and powder-blue jeans. He was about five foot eleven and slim, with a wispy moustache and a mane of black hair that fell nearly to his shoulders. Sinclair followed Pruden out the front door and tapped him on the shoulder. He introduced himself, and asked Pruden if they could talk. There was a restaurant across the street.

While Pruden wolfed down a hamburger, Sinclair went to a pay-phone and called his boss, Murray Burt, the managing editor. Sinclair told Burt whom he had found, and that Pruden had agreed to return to the scene of the shooting and tell them what happened. In Sinclair's estimation that was a news story, so he asked Burt if the city desk wanted to take over. Burt said he would check with the city editor, David Lee. Lee, whose brother was a Mountie, had a reputation for having an astute sense of news, of knowing what was and what wasn't a good story. But when Burt returned to the phone, he told Sinclair the city desk wasn't interested. Still, Sinclair wanted a photographer to go with him. A few minutes later Gerry Cairns joined Sinclair and Pruden, and the three of them drove to the intersection of Logan Avenue and Winks Street. On the way Pruden told the journalists that he had stolen the car from the parking lot at the Westbrook Inn about 12:30 a.m. He had driven it a block over, parked it, and walked back to the Westbrook, where he stayed until closing. Then he went to pick up his young cousin, Allan, and they drove around the area for fifteen minutes. It was almost 2:30 a.m. when Cross and Hodgins spotted Pruden and the boy passing the Westbrook. The police chased the stolen car for over a mile until Pruden swerved off Alexander onto Winks, a block-long street connecting Alexander and Logan, and ended up in a snowbank.

Sinclair, Pruden, and Cairns were standing on Winks where Pruden and Allan had ditched the car more than a week earlier. As the boy had scrambled from the back seat and out of the driver's side door, Pruden told him to run. They both did, dashing diagonally across Winks towards the lane south of Logan. As he ran, Pruden had seen the police cruiser rounding the corner of Alexander and Winks. Sinclair looked up. There was a street light on the boulevard across from the lane. The cops should have got a fleeting but reasonably good look at both of them.

Pruden said the cruiser had followed them to a backyard just inside the lane, at which point the teenagers split up. The male cop chased the younger boy between two houses and back onto Alexander, while Pruden ran west. For a while, maybe five minutes, Pruden had crouched behind a bush in the backyard of a house on Alexander and watched police cars driving right by him in the lane. Pruden showed where he'd scooted across the lane north towards Logan, hiding between a tall wooden fence and a car in another backyard. It was when he'd looked around the fence that he'd seen a cop standing in the lane. The officer had raised his revolver and pointed it at him, Pruden said. He demonstrated, his arms outstretched, his two hands together, the grip police are taught on the shooting range.

"He said, 'Stop, or I'll shoot.'"

Pruden had turned and run towards Logan. "There were a whole bunch of cops chasing me."

The young man retraced his path across Logan, through the park to the base of the dike, back to a yard behind a house on Gallagher Avenue. Here he had crouched between a fence and a bush roughly 200 metres from where Harper was struggling with Cross. Pruden said that's when he heard the shot. Just before the police caught up to him.

Pruden claimed that after he was cuffed, he was slammed against the hood of the cruiser and called a "fuckin' Indian."

Sinclair then asked him the same question he had asked the neighbours in the area. "Have police asked you about what you saw that night?" Pruden said no.

A few hours later, Sinclair got Allan's phone number from Heather Pullan, his legal aid lawyer. When he came to the phone, Allan sounded nervous, but he agreed to meet. Sinclair took a cab to the boy's home, a rundown north-end house just off Main Street.

"He's gone roller skating," said the man who let Sinclair in. The boy's mother said the police had been around early that morning to question him. Two big detectives had knocked on their windows, waking them up at 7:20 a.m. They turned out to be Dave Shipman and Ron Morin, the police department's ace homicide team.

According to Allan's mother, he had told the cops that he hadn't seen the shooting, but he'd overheard officers talking about it. Sinclair asked her if what he had heard matched what the police said happened.

"No," she said. "It was different. A lot different."

Late that afternoon, Robert Cross and Kathryn Hodgins went back to work for the first time since the shooting.

Their first call was a break and enter in progress. Half a dozen other officers raced to the scene, but it was the two partners and a couple of other cops who caught the male suspect. The identity of the officer involved in the Harper shooting hadn't yet been made public, and wouldn't be until Cross and Hodgins testified at the inquest, so the suspect couldn't have known who had just arrested him. But, as he was being led away, he said something that Hodgins remembered word for word nearly two years later.

"Why don't you shoot me like you shot the Indian?"

13

"You'll do good."

There are certain events that forever alter one's life. The death of a child is one. Winnipeg lawyer Harvey Pollock had experienced that tragedy just five years earlier. Now the death of J.J. Harper, a man he had never known, was about to alter his life again, in a way Pollock could not have anticipated.

Pollock had been retained by the Harper family to sue the city, Police Chief Herb Stephen, and the constable involved. One of Harper's stepbrothers, Harry Wood, also used Pollock to launch a complaint with the Law Enforcement Review Agency (LERA), the provincial watchdog agency. LERA had rarely ever barked at a police officer accused of a misdeed, and certainly had never bitten one.

Pollock, a slightly built, outgoing, and energetic man of fifty-five, was well known in the Aboriginal community. Early in his career, he had frequently represented Native clients and Aboriginal political organizations, and in 1971 he had been made an honorary chief and given the Cree name Si-naki-to-nam, which Pollock was told means He Who Interprets Difficult Meanings. A faded framed photo of Pollock, wearing a feather headdress as he accepted the honour, hung on a wall outside his corner office on the sixteenth floor of a downtown commercial tower.

Like his Aboriginal clients, Harvey Pollock knew what it was like to be a member of a minority. He was the youngest son of Jewish immigrants, Shloima Pollock and his wife, Sluva, who had fled Russia, one step ahead of the state police. They had gone first to the Netherlands, and then to a farming community on the Canadian prairie, where they opened a general store.

The family moved to Winnipeg in 1944, when Harvey was ten. Growing up during the late 1940s in Winnipeg's north end, Harvey was sarcastically nicknamed "Toughie," by the other kids. Harvey Pollock was a featherweight, but he was tenacious, an admirable quality for a lawyer specializing in personal injury suits, as Pollock would.

Pollock had another talent. In 1977 he had been the first winner of the International Whistling Championship at Carson City, Nevada. Winning had earned him an appearance on "To Tell the Truth." He had even appeared with the Winnipeg Symphony Orchestra. But Pollock didn't whistle professionally any more. Nowadays, he didn't do much criminal work either, and no impaired driving cases. No one in Pollock & Company had been allowed to defend anyone charged with failing or refusing a breathalyzer test, not since the November night in 1982 when his younger son Nathan had been driving home late from playing hockey with some pals. He was at a blind corner, turning from Sherbrook onto Broadway, when a drunk in a pick-up truck with its lights off ran a red light and broadsided Nathan's car.

Incredibly, two police officers had been at the downtown intersection and witnessed the collision.

Nathan died a few hours later. Pollock was devastated.

When the case went to trial, the Crown appeared to have a solid case. One of the officers who had witnessed the accident testified that he had never seen anyone drunker behind the wheel of a motor vehicle than the truck driver who killed Nathan.

The case was assigned to Stuart Whitley, a Crown lawyer who was later criticized for his conduct during Ticketgate. On the face of it, the charge of criminal negligence causing death appeared solid, especially with two cops as eyewitnesses. But to Whitley's astonishment, the jury found the driver guilty only of dangerous driving. Harvey Pollock was furious and he never forgave Stu Whitley for not getting a conviction on the more serious charge.

Pollock's older son, Martin, had been at Dalhousie Law School in Halifax when his brother died. Three years later, Martin returned to Winnipeg and joined his father's law firm.

On Friday March 25, just over two weeks after the Harper shooting, Harvey Pollock was sitting at the conference table in the office library when Martin got off the elevator and pushed through the heavy glass doors to Pollock & Company. Martin Pollock, a handsome, fresh-faced young man, was slightly built like his father. Through a second glass door, Martin could see his father hunched over, reading through a stack of documents.

The pile of papers were from William White Morton, the director of special prosecutions for the Attorney General's Department, who had been assigned to lead the evidence at the Harper inquest scheduled to start on April 5. There was a typewritten covering letter, itemizing the documents, at the bottom of which Bill Morton had penned: "Item 3 (f) is for your info only, not for Inquiry purposes." The item was a transcript of the letter from his wife found in Harper's wallet. Pollock and Morton had agreed the letter was personal and wouldn't be introduced as evidence.

Pollock didn't know it then, but there were police reports missing from the bundle sent over by Bill Morton.

Three days later, the Pollocks received a police report that had just been completed. A pair of Winnipeg police detectives had consulted a Winnipeg Hydro engineer to determine whether the mercury vapour lighting used on Logan would distort the shades grey and black. The report concluded that it wouldn't. The detective's signature at the bottom of the report was illegible. But on the day the inquest was to begin, the author of that police report was in the police headquarter's fifth-floor boardroom, directly across from Herb Stephen's office. Staff Sergeant Ken Dowson was in his early forties, tall, with the face of an earnest schoolboy, and a floppy choirboy haircut. He was waiting for the constables who had been at the shooting scene that night. One at a time, the officers entered the boardroom and Dowson, pretending to be Harvey Pollock, listened to their testimony, tested it, and instructed them to be calm, clear, and concise when they gave their answers at the inquest. One of them was Kathryn Hodgins. "You'll do good," Dowson assured her.

In late March, as Diane Eastwood's due date approached, she asked her doctor to induce labour. She wanted the baby delivered before the inquest began. Her obstetrician wanted to wait. Then, one afternoon in early April, a month after he had gone there to tell his wife about Harper's death, Cross returned to Victoria General Hospital to watch his son being born, while his police buddies guarded the hallway. One of them was Butch Eakin, the constable at the shooting scene who had directed the communications centre to switch to Channel 3, so the media wouldn't hear that a man had been shot. They named the baby Stephen, a name Cross would tell people he chose in tribute to Herb Stephen. Nature's timing was perfect. The inquest started the next day, Diane's thirty-fourth birthday.

PART II

---⊗⊗⊗---

THE INQUEST

Canadian policemen and policewomen feel they can only safely love their fellow cops. Only the buddies understand. Only the buddies can be trusted. This kind of schism is self-sustaining.

– Carsten Stroud, *The Blue Wall: Street Cops in Canada*

14

"IT WOULD TAKE SECONDS, RIGHT?"

Courtroom 230 lies at the end of a long marble hall in the Old Law Courts Building, across Broadway from the Manitoba Legislative Building. The room is the size of a university lecture hall, with a cross-beamed ceiling and green-veined marble walls, dominated by the judge's oak bench and an ornately carved thronelike black leather chair. From this majestic position, the judge looks down on the simple wood tables where the lawyers sit. Behind them is a polished brass rail, and beyond that is the public gallery, eight tiered rows of fold-up seats upholstered in green leather. At a right angle to the public gallery are two rows of six seats for the jurors. In the middle of the room is a big oak box, where the accused sits, his or her back to the gallery. But on the opening day of the inquest into the death of John Joseph Harper, there were no jurors and there was no accused in the grand courtroom, just one white-haired, black-robed judge and a line of lawyers.

The judge was John Enns, a former Crown attorney and *Free Press* reporter. As fate would have it, the judge's son, Martin Enns, a firefighter, was one of the first responders who arrived the night of the shooting to help the wounded man. The coincidence was not all that surprising in a city that boasted only one degree of separation. The city's legal community was similarly close-knit. In front of Enns at the inquest were six lawyers, including one he had graduated with thirty years earlier, Harvey Pollock.

Gordon Sinclair was sitting in the public gallery, with *Free Press* reporter Heidi Graham, who was doing the daily stories. Sinclair didn't know Pollock or Enns, but he did know Martin Minuk, the co-counsel for the Winnipeg Police Association. They had met through a mutual friend who owned Picasso's, a Portuguese seafood restaurant. Minuk was wiry and well tailored. He was also single, which qualified him for a column Sinclair had written listing Winnipeg's ten most eligible bachelors.

Minuk and Alvin R. McGregor, QC, were co-counsel for the Winnipeg Police Association. McGregor was a dark-haired, pointy-nosed barrister with a gruff, intimidating courtroom style and an impish smile. He was the only lawyer to remain seated when Judge Enns entered. He had a good reason. In 1971, McGregor had been at a wedding reception when he picked up a glass, and dropped it. That seemingly innocent episode was the first indication that McGregor had been stricken with multiple sclerosis. He was thirty then. Now, at forty-seven, his MS had progressed to the point at which he used a motorized scooter to navigate the courthouse halls.

There was one more lawyer of note: Crown Attorney Bill Morton, whose thinning, slicked-back grey hair, rimless spectacles, and heavy mid-section made him look like Mr. Wilson, Dennis the Menace's comic-strip foil. "Whitey," as Morton was known, had graduated from law school at the University of Manitoba two years before Harvey Pollock and in illustrious company. Three of his fellow graduates from the class of '60 went on to become judges, and three others went on to do time in a penitentiary.

Like Judge Enns, Morton had started work in an era when the provincial courts were in the Public Safety Building. Crown attorneys not only robed on the same floor that the detectives worked, they would drink with them at the police association's Call Box Lounge. Their common purpose of putting bad guys behind bars made for a symbiotic relationship, but the chumminess was viewed with suspicion by some. The Crown attorneys had since relocated from the police station, but for veterans like Morton the coziness with the cops continued. Within months, Chief Justice Archibald Dewar would write his inquiry report into the Ticketgate affair, urging that independent counsel be hired when the Crown is perceived to be too close to a case. But the advice arrived too late for the Harper inquest.

The Crown's role at an inquest wasn't to prosecute, because no one faced a charge. It was simply to lead evidence. While the other lawyers represented their clients, McGregor and Minuk for the police, and the Pollocks for the Harper family, Morton was supposed to occupy the middle ground and be impartial. He was the attorney general's representative, the public's counsel. RCMP Sergeant Wes Border had been assigned to assist the inquest with any further investigations that might be needed. Since Vic Schroeder had decided, at Dale Henry's urging, not to have the Mounties take over the Harper investigation, having Border at the inquest was a way of injecting some outside scrutiny. "We are ready to call witnesses," Morton said.

The first witness was the chief medical examiner, Dr. Peter Markesteyn. He testified that when Harper was shot, the police revolver's muzzle was either touching or nearly touching his chest.

That hadn't been his initial finding, Markesteyn explained. The police hadn't brought Harper's clothing to the autopsy, so when he found no gunshot residue around the wound, and in the absence of Harper's shirt and coat, Markesteyn assumed that he had been shot at a distance.

The bullet had entered between the first and second rib on the left side, fracturing the fourth rib. The copper-cased hollow-point bullet had shattered in the chest and severed the subclavian artery, a major blood vessel. In terms of bleeding, it was almost like being shot in the heart itself.

Markesteyn backed up what Herb Stephen had alluded to at the day-after news conference, that Harper was legally drunk when he was shot. His reading was 2.2. "Almost three times the legal limit for him to have driven a motor car," the doctor said in a voice tinged by his Dutch background.

"That usually means somebody who is belligerent," Morton said, standing parade-ground straight, as usual. Belligerent was the word Robert Cross had used in his witness report.

"Yes," Markesteyn agreed.

"May verbally and even physically attack people?" Morton added.

"Yes, sir," Markesteyn said.

The medical examiner wasn't of much help in determining whether Harper had been wrestling for the gun when it discharged. Other than the gunshot wound, and abrasions on the right knee and right elbow that were consistent with Harper collapsing after being shot, there were no obvious signs that he had been involved in any struggle, let alone a life-and-death fight.

If he had been in a fight over the revolver, there might have been skin under Harper's fingernails, but no one had taken scrapings. There was no visible gunpowder residue on Harper's hands, and an RCMP firearms officer who had been present at the autopsy had told Markesteyn there was no test available in Canada that could detect invisible chemical residue. The RCMP had been invited to the autopsy because they had the only crime lab in the province and the exhibits would be taken there for analysis.

This point brought Markesteyn to the most surprising and disturbing portion of his testimony. City police hadn't dusted the revolver or the holster for prints at the time of the shooting. The gun wasn't fingerprinted until a week later, when it was delivered to the RCMP forensic lab. A single thumb print had been found. It belonged to the RCMP technician.

The next witness was Sergeant Bob Parker, the Identification officer who was called out on the morning of March 9 and took charge of gathering physical evidence at the shooting scene. The next day he'd delivered some of the exhibits to the RCMP. He had also videotaped the autopsy.

On the morning of the shooting, the Winnipeg police department's three most senior Identification officers were with Deputy Chief Paul Johnston in Orange County, California, checking out a fingerprint computer. That left Parker to deal with the physical evidence. Now, a month later, it was left to Parker to explain the three questions that would forever haunt the Harper case, and the lives of every officer who was part of it: Why wasn't the gun examined for fingerprints on the day of the shooting? Why did the police order the bloody scene washed down so quickly? And why didn't the police find Harper's glasses?

Parker told Harvey Pollock that he decided not to print the weapon shortly after he arrived at the shooting scene at 4:30 a.m.

"At any time did you believe that the gun ought to be fingerprinted, even up to today's date?" Pollock asked, speaking quickly and rocking on the balls of his feet.

"No, I do not."

"Why?" Pollock snapped in an accusatory tone, a trait of his cross-examination style.

"The presence of his fingerprints on the weapon or the holster would not be conclusive proof of anything."

That, Parker contended, was because there were three scenarios fingerprints would have suggested: that Harper touched the gun inadvertently; that he was trying to take the gun away; or that he was trying to defend himself against Cross.

"All those theories and postulations are very interesting, witness," Pollock said, "but it is your duty to collect and maintain evidence in any investigation, is that not true?"

"I believe that the responsibility of a person collecting evidence is to ensure that the evidence will lead to some form of conclusion or that it will offer something in the way of an explanation as to the occurrences," Parker replied.

"Isn't that something for a judge or a higher authority to determine and not you, sir?"

"That will be for the court to decide," Parker said.

Eventually, Pollock got around to asking about Harper's glasses. Parker said he and Ident photographer Craig Boan had searched the area where the glasses were found, and he could think of only one explanation: the snow had melted during the day, exposing the glasses to view. He claimed he'd intended to search the scene again after the morning rush hour, but had been prevented by the autopsy.

When Pollock asked why the police had washed down the scene before daylight, Parker maintained that that was standard procedure "to deter any morbid curiosity seekers."

Parker's answer didn't satisfy the judge. "You have said earlier, officer, that you had intended to return after the rush hour," Enns said. "What did you think ordering the fire department to wash everything down did? Destroy possible scenes? Possible important —"

Parker interrupted Enns, assuring him that the scene had been "photographed, measured, and examined quite thoroughly."

If Enns seemed troubled about how quickly the police had washed down the scene, he was even more perplexed about why the gun hadn't been fingerprinted immediately after the shooting. He asked a series of questions in an attempt to make sense of police thinking on that, but Parker's answers seemed to leave him even more puzzled.

Pollock had a single follow-up question for Parker. How long did it take to dust for prints?

"The amount of time that it takes to run a powdered brush over an object," Parker said.

"Seconds, right?"

"It would take seconds, right."

There was supposed to be one other witness on the first day. But Melvin Pruden didn't show up. Enns issued a warrant for his arrest.

15

"OR WAS THE WORD 'SAY'?"

When Gordon Sinclair's girlfriend, Athina, dropped by the inquest on its second day, she noticed something about the fourteen-year-old boy on the stand besides his small stature. "It was his eyes," she told Sinclair over dinner that night. "They were piercing blue."

After the startling revelations of the first day, Sinclair was anxious to hear what Allan's mother had meant when she said the boy had a different story to tell from the one the police had released.

Morton began by taking the boy through the sequence of events, to the point at which he was being chased by Cross. "The policeman said to me 'Stop,' and I seen him fall, and then he said 'Freeze.'" The boy said the officer then grabbed him and put him in the car. Later, the male cop left. After he'd been arrested, Allan heard the sound of the shot, and the female constable pulled her cruiser up to where a body was lying on the sidewalk. She had parked the cruiser the wrong way on Logan behind two other police cars. Allan was in the back seat, on the driver's side closest to the curb, looking out the window.

"You thought it was Melvin," Morton said.

"Yeah."

The boy said that soon the male cop who had caught him got into the car, beside the female cop. He looked shaken and his eyeglasses were askew. The boy listened to the conversation. "When he took his glasses off, he says, 'Oh, my God.' He goes, well, I don't remember what happened, exactly his words, eh. I remember he says – all I remember these part words, like, 'I happen to reach for my gun,' and then he said, 'I pulled the trigger,' and then they went off."

That's not exactly how Detective Sergeant Dave Shipman, who had taken Allan's statement, had written down the boy's recollection in his March 17 report, which Morton had in front of him. In his police statement, the boy said the male cop told his partner "he had pushed the guy, and the guy had grabbed his gun, and he had shot him. He stated the officer was upset and was questioning aloud why the male had to wrestle with him."

There was more. "And then," Allan told Morton, "there's this 'nother male cop that pulled up beside us, an older one." The uniformed officer got out of the car and he heard the older officer say, "I want to talk to you first." The passenger side window was rolled down about three inches, but Allan hadn't heard anything else until the younger cop opened the car door again to get back in. "You just say that," Allan heard the older officer say, and the younger one had replied, "I will say that."

In a statement he had given to Harvey Pollock after the shooting, Allan had mentioned other details. He said the "old man cop" had grey hair and had stripes around his uniform sleeves.

Morton questioned how much Allan could have heard, pointing out that there was a plexiglas barrier between the front and back seats of the police car. The police had a name for this, the Silent Partner. Morton suggested that the Silent Partner would have made it difficult for Allan to hear conversations in the front seat, although the cop who'd caught him had no trouble asking him questions through the Silent Partner's small sliding door.

"And you . . . you can't remember exactly what people were saying?" Morton said.

That brought Pollock to his feet, objecting to the way Morton had put the question, the way he had suggested that the boy "can't" remember.

"You are leading him constantly through this," Pollock said.

"This is just an inquiry, Mr. Pollock," Morton replied condescendingly. "Do not worry about it."

"Let's do it right," Pollock shot back.

"It is being done right, Mr. Pollock."

Pollock began his cross-examination of Allan with some background questions, until Enns cut him short. He didn't want Pollock going over the same testimony. In his view the Fatalities Inquiries Act did not give lawyers acting for a witness at an inquest the same right of cross-examination that a defence lawyer had at a trial. Enns added that he didn't want to curtail lawful inquiry, but he also didn't want the hearing to become adversarial.

It already had.

Pollock's next move was to dispute the police contention that Harper matched the description of the suspect. Why had Allan initially thought that Pruden was the body he saw on the ground?

"It looked something like his jacket."

In fact, they had both been wearing dark, hip-length jackets, although Harper's was black and Pruden's grey. But that wasn't the answer Pollock wanted. He tried again. There was another reason, the boy agreed. He'd just assumed that because the police had been chasing his cousin, that it was Pruden who had been shot.

Pollock moved into an aspect of the statement Allan had given detectives Shipman and Morin that Morton had ignored. He wanted to know exactly what the female officer had said to Allan after the shooting.

"Like it was all my fault and all that. Like that if I wasn't screwing around that this wouldn't have happened."

"What else did she say? Anything else?"

"And after, she called me a blue-eyed fucking Indian."

"And do you have blue eyes?"

"Yeah."

"And is your skin light?"

"Yeah."

Minuk started his cross-examination after lunch. As he was out to attack Allan's credibility, he began with differences between what the boy had said on the witness stand and what was in his statement taken eight days after the shooting. Why was there no reference in his statement to seeing the cop who was chasing him fall?

"I didn't tell them that he fell down," Allan said.

Minuk next suggested that his mother had prompted him to tell police that the female officer had called him a fucking Indian.

"She told me to tell," the boy agreed, "but I didn't want to tell it, eh."

"But you did not tell them everything," Minuk said. The words "blue-eyed" were not in Allan's statement.

"No, I told them. I said how she called me a blue-eyed fucking Indian."

Minuk now turned to a more vital discrepancy between Allan's statement and his testimony: his overhearing Cross say he had reached for his gun and pulled the trigger.

"You did not tell the police officers you heard that conversation?"

"No, I didn't. I didn't want to."

"You did not want to? Why did you not want to talk to the police officers?"

Allan said that he was afraid of getting in more trouble with the police, which perhaps explained why his mother had had to prod him to report what Hodgins had called him.

Minuk turned to the description of Pruden the police said the boy had given the two officers after he was captured. He wanted to know if Cross had questioned the boy.

"You did not tell that police officer that the person you were with had a black jacket, blue jeans, and was in his twenties?"

"No. . . . He just asked me, 'How old is he?' I said, 'He's about in his twenties.'"

Before Enns could dismiss the witness, Pollock pleaded for a chance to re-examine the boy. Enns refused. Pollock persisted, arguing that Minuk's examination of the boy's police statement hadn't been complete. Morton misunderstood. He thought Pollock was suggesting the statement hadn't been complete. "I take grave issue from my learned friend to suggest that a police officer took a statement from a witness and made it deliberately incomplete," Morton huffed.

"No, I'm not saying that," Pollock said.

Enns asked to see the statement. Quickly, he read it. It was the end of the statement that Enns found most interesting:

I can't remember exactly what the policeman looked like, but he had a moustache and black hair and glasses. He was standing about five feet from the body. He said he pushed the guy back and the guy grabbed his gun and he shot him. He said, "Why did the guy have to wrestle with me?" He was shaking pretty bad, nervous I guess, scared. Some old man said, "See, the gun went off accidentally." Then the girl was yelling at me, blaming me for the guy getting shot, calling me a "fuckin' Indian." That's all I remember, and I didn't see any of the shooting. Is what I said going to help the guy that got shot?

"Mr. Morton," Enns said when he finished reading, "I do find there are some aspects of the statement that give me concern."

Pollock was allowed to continue. He asked Allan about the sentence, "Some old man said, 'See, the gun went off accidentally.'"

"Do you remember hearing the word 'see'?" Pollock asked, "or was the word 'say'?"

"Say," the boy said.

Pollock wanted to make absolutely clear the difference between what Shipman wrote and what the boy said.

"So you understand then that sentence to mean 'Some old man said, "*Say* the gun went off accidentally."' Yes?"

"Yes," Allan said.

Morton called the next witness. "Constable Robert Cross, please."

16

"I DON'T RECALL ANY BLOOD ON MY HANDS."

On the day the inquest opened, Gordon Sinclair was walking down the Law Court's marbled hallway when he saw Robert Cross for the first time. At that point, Cross's identity was still a secret. But there was something about him that caused the columnist to suspect he was the constable at the centre of the case. He was in uniform, standing in the hall outside the witness room, chewing gum, his hands on his hips. The at-ease body language mimed indifference. What gave his identity away was the way he reacted when Sinclair stared at him. Cross looked away, as if he didn't want to make eye contact.

In the witness box now, Cross stood with one hand on the Bible. To his left, on an easel, was a diagram drawn by Identification Sergeant Bob Parker to the scale of one inch to forty feet. It showed the area bounded by Gallagher Avenue on the north, Alexander on the south, Winks on the east, and Blaine and Electa on the west. In the centre were Logan Avenue and Stanley Knowles Park. It also numbered the seventeen houses on the south side of Logan and another twenty-two across the park on Gallagher. Parker had marked three locations with circled letters. "A" marked where the stolen car had ploughed into the snowbank on Winks, "B" the backyard behind 2037 where Pruden had been arrested, and "C" the place in front of the park and across from 1254 Logan where Harper's body was found.

Morton started with basic questions about the events of March 9, 1988. Cross ran through how they were on their way into the station for a meal, approaching the Westbrook Inn, when he saw what looked like the stolen car turning from Ross onto Keewatin. Cross was driving and sped up to get a better look, and the other car sped up, too.

"I remarked to my partner, 'Kath, that's the car.'"

They had chased the car until Pruden ploughed it into the snowbank.

"As I rounded the corner," Cross said, "I observed that the vehicle was up on a snowbank. The driver's door was open, and I observed two suspects fleeing into the lane." Cross steered the cruiser up the alley and into the backyard where the pair had run. He quickly caught the shorter one and escorted him back to the cruiser, which Hodgins had backed up to block the entrance to the lane.

"Once he was in the rear of the vehicle I opened up the small passageway – our Silent Partner. I opened up that to speak to him."

"Yes, go on," Morton said.

"At this point my main concern was getting a description of the other suspect that I had lost. I asked him, 'What did the other guy look like?' He answered me, 'He's a tall guy in his twenties, wearing a black leather jacket and jeans.' I then proceeded to ask him, 'Do you know him?' He answered, 'No.' Then I asked him, 'Is he a Native?' He said,

'Yes.' This information was relayed to Constable Hodgins to broadcast the same. The information was also broadcast due to the fact that other cruiser cars were attending the area to help us in the search."

Three other patrol cars had responded to the dispatcher's call for assistance. While officers from the other black-and-whites searched the area on foot and by car, Cross remained in the cruiser with Hodgins and their prisoner. Ten minutes ticked by. The next time recorded in Cross's notebook was 2:38 a.m. "I received a radio message that November 203 was in pursuit of a male."

Pruden had been flushed out of his backyard hiding place by the police officer who, according to the Native teenager, had pointed a revolver at him. The cop's name was Randy Hampton.

"Shortly after that I got out of the vehicle and headed west in the lane of Alexander and Logan in case the male started doubling back towards me." Cross checked his notebook again. "Okay, then I received a radio message that the police had a male in custody on the dike, the water reservoir north of Logan. This is 2:39."

Gordon Sinclair stopped scribbling and glanced up, stunned by what he had just heard. Pruden had told him that he heard the shot just before he was caught. But he couldn't have. Cross was saying he had approached Harper after he knew a second suspect was already in custody. Why hadn't Herb Stephen included that in his news release?

Morton suggested Cross leave the witness box to show the court on the police map of the area where he had encountered Harper.

"He was just walking along the sidewalk," Cross said, pointing to the north side of Logan in front of the park.

"At this point, constable," Morton asked, "you have heard that police have in fact apprehended an individual?"

"That's correct."

Did the officers who'd arrested the second suspect say something that made Cross doubt they had the right guy?

"Their description that they broadcast was different than what I was looking for," Cross said. "They described it as a sweater jacket."

"Yes," Morton said.

No is what he should have said. There was never any mention of a sweater jacket, as the audiotapes of the incident proved when they were played later.

"I thought to myself, he matches the description, the other one doesn't," Cross said. "I'll just angle across the street, talk to him, find out some identification and just basically talk to him at that point."

Cross recalled what he said to Harper when they came face to face on the sidewalk. "I asked him, 'Sir, can you show me some identification?' At this point he looks at me, says, 'No, I don't have to show you nothin'." He noticed the smell of liquor and a belligerent tone in Harper's voice.

"I feel [it] necessary then to explain to him why I wanted to see some identification, why I was questioning it."

"What did you tell him?"

"I said, 'Sir, you match the description of a suspect that I am looking for, for a theft of auto. Could I please see some identification?' At that point I received the same answer, 'No, I don't have to show you nothin'. Mr. Harper starts to walk on."

"In the easterly direction?"

"Yes, correct. Just continued on his path. I reach out my hand, take hold of his arm. I turn him around to talk to him again."

In all his answers this far, Cross had seemed composed, as if he was giving evidence in some routine speeding case, instead of the final moments of another man's life, and the pivotal moment of his own. Then, just as he was beginning to describe the struggle, Cross asked to sit down. Then he said, "At the point where I touched him on the arm just to turn him, he spins. I feel two hands on my shoulders. I am getting pushed. I am losing balance. I'm just waving my arms trying to clutch onto him. I'm going down. I remember striking him in the face with an open hand and I caught onto his glasses and they went flying away."

That accounted for Harper's glasses being found just off the sidewalk, in the park. But that detail had been added only after

Sterdan had found the glasses. In his witness statement made two hours after the shooting, Cross had made no mention of striking Harper in the face.

"I'm still going down," Cross continued. "I remember trying to grab onto his jacket. Whatever. I wind up on the ground. I pulled Mr. Harper along with me. I'm laying on my back. My knees are drawn up and Mr. Harper is standing one foot between my legs and one on the other side of my legs. He's reaching down. I . . ." Cross paused momentarily.

"Just reaching down at my waist area. I plant my left foot on his chest trying to push him off me. At that point I feel a tugging at my right side. He's got hold of my holstered gun. I don't know at that point. I panic. I'm trying to move his hands away from my firearm. The gun comes out. We are both fumbling for it. He's pulling. I'm yanking. The gun goes off. I hear a loud bang. There's a very large flash that emanates from the muzzle of the gun. He stands up. My first thought is did he get hit? He backs up a little bit and I see that he has been hit. He looks at me and crumples to the ground.

"At that point I stood up and I got out my radio to broadcast that I need some help. I turn on the mike and all of a sudden I realized I didn't know where I was. I turned off the mike. I thought. Looked around from where I am. Gathered my thoughts." One of those thoughts concerned the possibility the media was monitoring the police channel.

The police tape of the incident later revealed that Cross spent thirty-nine seconds gathering his thoughts before he turned on his portable again and asked for his partner and an ambulance, in that order.

"Tell us what happened after that."

"Various cars started arriving."

"Where was the gun at this point?"

"I was holding it in my right hand."

Morton asked where Cross was standing.

"We'd be in the park."

"And where was Mr. Harper at this point?"

"I believe he was on the sidewalk."

"Did you approach him?"

"No."

"Was he moving, could you tell us?"

"Yes, he was moving quite a bit. He was – I don't know quite how to describe it. Twitching. Clutching at his throat area." Cross said he just stood there and watched. "All I'm concerned with at that point is retaining the handgun to turn over to the first officer in charge."

"What, if any, contact did you have with acting Inspector Hrycyk?" Morton asked next.

"He just informed me to go downtown, wait in his office. There would be detectives coming in to interview me."

"And where were you when he told you this?"

"I was outside of one of the police cars."

"You were outside?" Morton asked.

"I wasn't standing beside my own car."

Morton returned to the struggle with Harper.

"I just felt the tugging on my right side. . . . If you tug at the butt, the holster gets tugged, the tugging of the holster tugs on my belt. And I don't know exactly what he had hold of."

"Then what happened?" Morton asked.

"The gun came out."

"Do you know how it came out?"

"No."

"Where were your hands when it came out? Or do you know?"

"No, I don't. When it came out I might have had a small portion of it. I don't really remember."

"Immediately after that what happened?"

"The gun came out. We were both fighting for it . . . I remember the gun being up. I got one finger in the trigger."

I got one finger in the trigger, Sinclair scribbled in his notebook, trying to keep up.

Morton asked where Harper's hands were on the gun.

"One on the butt and one on the barrel."

"Was it a constant pull, pull?"

"Tug-of-war, I guess. Both trying to get hold of the gun."

"And you held onto that gun for what reason?"

"I feared for my life . . . The whole time I felt, like, I mean, I was losing it. The gun was going from my grip."

Morton moved to Allan's testimony.

"Did you at any time, Constable Cross, in speaking to any of the officers at the scene or subsequent to that ever use the phrase, 'I happen to reach for my gun'?"

"No."

Had Cross said, "I happen to pull the trigger"?

"I might have," Cross said. "I don't remember saying that."

Morton asked what made Cross think he might have admitted to pulling the trigger.

"My hand was on the gun. My finger was on the trigger."

"Did you pull the trigger or was it yanked?"

"I don't really know. There was a pulling and yanking on both parts. I don't remember a conscious effort to pull the trigger."

Sinclair waited for Morton's next question, waited for him to go after the logical inconsistency of Cross being conscious of so many details – using his left hand to swipe at Harper's glasses, having his finger on the trigger – but not remembering if he had consciously pulled the trigger and shot J.J. Harper.

"Just taking you back now before the incident," Morton said. The Crown attorney's probing of the most important issue of the inquest – how Harper was shot – was finished.

Harvey Pollock started his cross-examination by trying to show that Cross would have had a good look at Pruden as he fled the stolen car, good enough to know he was much slimmer and younger than Harper. Pollock also wanted it on the record that Harper was within his legal rights not to produce identification when Cross asked for it.

Morton and Minuk promptly objected, and Enns agreed with them. "It is a question of law, Mr. Pollock," the judge said, "not for the witness to answer."

"Now, let us get on with other pertinent issues," Enns added.

"I think it is very pertinent," Pollock said. "We are right at the pertinent issue, Your Honour, and I am trying to deal with it as best I can. I may be lacking in some capacity, but I am doing my best."

Pollock asked Cross if, after he reached out and grabbed Harper to turn him, he then grabbed the Native man's right wrist.

"He was making a motion to strike me."

That was news to Pollock.

"Why did you take him by the right wrist?"

"I believe he was pushing me."

"That is not what you said in your statement."

Again Pollock asked why Cross grabbed Harper's right wrist.

"My memory leads me to believe like, he was pushing me and I was just warding off his hands."

"That is not what the statement says. I am asking you, why did you take him by the right wrist?"

A flurry of objections followed, but Pollock persisted.

Cross looked down at his statement.

"I guess he was pushing at me because my next line [is] 'The suspect leaned forward, pushing me with both hands on the front of my shoulders.' I imagine he was making a gesture towards me and I was trying to remove his hands."

"What was the next thing that happened after you took him by his right wrist is what I want to know."

"Suspect leaned forward, pushing me with both hands on the front of my shoulders."

"So he pushed you away, is that what happened?"

"Correct."

At that point, Cross said, he lost his balance, swiped at Harper's glasses and fell backwards, grabbing at the Native man's jacket sleeves and pulling him down. He was still clutching the sleeves when he landed on his back, with his legs drawn up and his left foot in Harper's chest.

"So you did not pull him all the way down onto the ground?"

"No, I didn't."

Pollock was trying to visualize the struggle.

"You are on the ground flat at that point, are you?"

"Yes."

"And you tell us that he is extended over you?"

"Yes, that's correct."

"And you've still got hold of him by both arms?"

"I believe so."

"And that foot remained in the position until your gun went off and Mr. Harper crumpled to the ground, is that not so?"

Cross agreed. Pollock wanted to know why Cross had put his left foot in Harper's chest.

"To push him off me."

"And you have the leverage of the ground against Mr. Harper, who has 220 milligrams of alcohol in him and he is leaning over you, maintaining his perfect balance?"

Once again Morton and Minuk both objected. "It's not a question. It is a speech," Minuk said.

"Nevertheless, it is cross-examination," Enns said. "The witness, I'm sure, can respond."

"He was standing between – one foot between my legs, one foot on the outside. I had my foot planted on his chest and at that point you're focusing on one split second. His arms – I had hold of them as I was going down. As soon as I was down, his arms moved and I felt a tugging on my holster. I was trying to push him off. I was trying to get his hands off. That's what I remember."

"He was falling on top of you is really what was happening, wasn't that so?" Pollock said. "You were pulling him towards you, he was off balance, he was coming towards you. Is that not so?"

"At one point, yes."

Now Pollock was going to try his Perry Mason question, the one that had worked for him twenty-five years earlier in Portage la Prairie when he got a witness to confess to murder.

"And you reached for your gun, is that not so?"

"No, that's not true."

"He was trying to hold on because he was coming down, and you were going for your gun. Is that not true?"

"No, that's not true."

"And you removed your gun from your holster because you were going to frighten him off with the use of your gun. Is that not so?"

"No, that's not true."

"You did have the gun in your hand first, didn't you? Not Mr. Harper. Harper did not get the gun out of your holster. The gun was in your hand first, is that not true?"

"No, that's not true."

Pollock glanced down at Cross's statement. "And did you say in your statement, 'He grabbed ahold of the butt and the holster of my revolver pulling it forward.' Did you say that?"

Cross searched for the paragraph. "He grabbed ahold of the butt and holster of my revolver, pulling it backward."

"Is that correct?" Pollock asked.

"Correct."

"The gun was still in the holster, wasn't it?"

"At that point, I guess, yeah. The gun was still in the holster."

Silently, Pollock read the next sentence in Cross's statement: "He took hold of my right hand, which the gun was in, and started to yank at the gun . . ."

"'And then he took hold of your right hand which the gun was in,' is that correct?"

Cross appeared confused. "No," he answered. Then he seemed to contradict himself, adding, "To the best that I can remember this is correct."

"How did the gun get into your right hand?"

"I don't know."

"With the gun in your right hand Harper is still over you, is that correct? He is in the position over you, suspended sort of, while you are still on the ground."

"I don't understand," Cross said. "You're stating that I'm holding the gun?"

Cross was reacting as if Pollock had delivered one too many head blows; he seemed to be waiting for his corner to rescue him.

"I am just going on the basis of the statement, sir." Pollock said.

"No, you are not," Morton interjected, "because that is not the way it is in the statement."

"The gun is in your right hand," Pollock began again. "You have already told us that in your statement, right?"

"I wound up with the gun in my right hand," Cross said. This remark seemed to startle Enns.

"I wound up with the gun in my right hand?" Enns repeated. Supposedly Cross was using both hands in the life-and-death tug-of-war with Harper, and now he was agreeing the gun was in his right hand.

Pollock sensed a knockout coming. "But you did not say that in your statement, did you?"

Before Cross could answer, Morton stood up. "Well, Your Honour," his tone now more anxious than angry, "I would be pleased to allow you to look at this. I have the statement that this witness has given, and that is not what my learned friend is putting to the witness."

"Sure, I am," Pollock said.

Enns had had enough. He lamented how difficult conducting the inquest had become. Then, abruptly, he adjourned the hearing until the next day.

Gordon Sinclair was angry with Bill Morton. Just when Pollock had Cross with the gun in his right hand and his finger on the trigger, the Crown attorney had stepped in and Enns had stopped everything.

Sinclair waited until the courtroom cleared, then he walked over to Morton, who was collecting his files. Wes Border, the RCMP officer

Attorney General Vic Schroeder had assigned to assist Morton, was standing beside him. Bluntly and angrily Sinclair accused Morton of being biased.

"I'm watching you," Sinclair said as he turned to leave. Morton began to bluster.

"Don't even say it," Sinclair said over his shoulder, and kept walking.

When Pollock resumed cross-examination the next day, Morton was subdued. But the Harper family lawyer still had Enns to contend with. Pollock began by asking Cross to step out of the witness box and demonstrate the struggle, but Enns said no. The judge also refused to allow Pollock to explore the origins of the three pools of blood as they related to where Harper's body was found. Nor would he permit questions about the blow-by, the soot that escapes from the gap between the barrel and the cylinder when a revolver is fired, that police had found on the webbing of Cross's right hand.

Ironically, when it was his turn, Cross's counsel, Marty Minuk, did Pollock's work for him. Minuk referred to Allan's statement, in which he claimed to have heard Cross telling Hodgins: "He shouldn't have fought. I had to pull my gun, I had to pull the trigger."

"Did you make those comments to your partner?" Minuk asked his client.

"Part of the comments I might have said. I never said I pulled the trigger. I don't believe I said that."

When Minuk had finished, Enns permitted Pollock one last question on behalf of the Harper family.

"Was Harper under arrest by you?"

"At that point, no."

"At any point?"

"At no point was he under arrest," Cross said.

Enns had a question, too. He wanted to know if there was blood on his hands when Cross turned his revolver over to Spryszak.

"No," Cross said. "I don't recall any blood on my hands."

(above) John Joseph Harper, 1952–88.
(*Winnipeg Free Press*)
(inset) J.J. at sixteen.
(Courtesy Maurice Hogue)

Robert Cross (left) and partner Kathryn Hodgins (centre) leaving the inquest. (Stu Phillips, *Winnipeg Free Press*)

Melvin Pruden, wearing his grey jacket, one week after the shooting. (Gerry Cairns, *Winnipeg Free Press*)

Inquest Exhibit 39, Cross's service revolver. (Wayne Glowacki, *Winnipeg Free Press*)

The sidewalk between Logan Avenue and Stanley Knowles Park, where Harper was shot. (Winnipeg Police Service)

Three pools of blood mark the sidewalk where Harper was fatally wounded. (Winnipeg Police Service)

The cowboy sign outside the Westbrook Inn, today joined by a Mohawk gas station sign. (Gordon Sinclair photo)

Diane Eastwood and Robert Cross on their
wedding day. (Courtesy Diane Eastwood)

Kathie Bushie.
(Gordon Sinclair photo)

Kathryn and Ron Hodgins.
(*Winnipeg Free Press*)

Native drummers at a demonstration at city hall demanding a public inquiry into J.J. Harper's death. (Wayne Glowacki, *Winnipeg Free Press*)

Mayor Bill Norrie.
(Dave Johnson, *Winnipeg Free Press*)

A demonstrator protesting the four-day leave with pay Cross was given following Harper's death. (Wayne Glowacki, *Winnipeg Free Press*)

Police Chief Herb Stephen.
(Winnipeg Police Service)

Deputy Chief Paul Johnston.
(Gerry Cairns, *Winnipeg Free Press*)

Inspector Eric Hrycyk.
(Winnipeg Police Service)

Gordon Sinclair in the *Winnipeg Free Press* newsroom during happier times. (*Winnipeg Free Press*)

Jeff Funnell's drawing of Allan testifying at the inquest. (Courtesy Jeff Funnell)

Martin (left) and Harvey Pollock. (Courtesy Dr. Morley Lertzman)

Judge John Enns.
(Glenn Olsen, *Winnipeg Free Press*)

Crown Attorney Bill Morton.
(Manitoba Archives)

Winnipeg Police Association
junior counsel Marty Minuk.
(Gordon Sinclair photo)

Al McGregor, Police Association
senior counsel.
(Gordon Sinclair photo)

That's not the way Inspector Eric Hrycyk remembered it, though. He had seen blood on Cross's right hand. The one Cross said the gun ended up in.

By the third day of the inquest, there were already some regulars in the public gallery. One was a big plain-clothes detective named Rex Keatinge, who was taking notes for Herb Stephen. Another cop, Inspector Joe Gallagher, was also an articling student and was there to assist the city's lawyer. There was a farmer who should have been preparing to seed, but he'd made time for the first day and become hooked. There was also a group of Natives in the gallery and one other regular of note: Jeff Funnell, a long-haired, middle-aged local artist. He had decided to attend because he had been disturbed by Harper's death and Stephen's attitude. Funnell sat at the back of the gallery sketching the witnesses with pencil and ink, and jotting down fragments of testimony. He had sketched Allan as a tiny head peeking over the witness box with the judge looking down on him. Under the drawing Funnell had written: *Some old man said see say the gun went off accidentally.*

Funnell sketched Cross, shading his eyes so darkly it looked as if he was wearing a mask. Around Cross, Funnell had scribbled a swirl of dialogue: '*No point was he under arrest... Laying on my back Harper standing ... Large flash ... There was blood all over me ... Gathered my thoughts request an ambulance ... Part of comments I made. I never said I pulled the trigger.*'

———

17

"Some personal papers."

"Exhibit number one," said Constable Kerry Armit. The Winnipeg police Identification unit officer held up a pair of brown cowboy boots.

J.J. Harper's cowboy boots had been piled on the same rectangular wooden exhibit table as Robert Cross's service revolver, with its custom black rubber grips and bulbous trigger guard. Cross's rubber overboots were there, too, and his bloodied uniform pants and jacket. But most of the exhibits on public display belonged to the deceased: The black jacket and blue jeans that Cross said caused him to stop Harper. A bloodstained white shirt, with a bullet hole above the pocket. A pair of blue and red socks. A gold watch. Two keys on a hand-shaped key fob. An Island Lake Tribal Council schedule found in the left rear pocket of the jeans. There were other, clinical exhibits: A vial of Harper's blood and the single hair pulled from his scalp to compare it with any hairs that might have been on Cross's clothing. The RCMP lab had found none. Harper's eyeglasses were there, too.

"They're black framed," Armit said. "One of the eye pieces is out of the frame and both arms are broken off the glasses."

There was also a loose-leaf album on the exhibit table containing the colour photographs Ident officer Craig Boan had taken at the autopsy, including a close-up of the elliptical chest wound and a photo of Harper stretched out naked on a stainless steel table. There were no photos of Cross in the album, but there were pictures of his patrol jacket, muddied on the upper back in the shoulder area, with a large bloodstain on the front lower right side, a smaller stain on the lower back right corner, and a third stain, the smallest, on the bottom of the right sleeve.

The uniform pants had also been photographed. "Specifically the right leg of the pants showed soiling below the knee and along the right side of the knee area," Armit reported. "A large bloodstain was noted on the right knee . . . There was a white, almost white, coloured soiling, staining. Possibly salt, I noted."

Morton clarified that Armit was talking about road salt, used to melt ice.

Armit said the salt stains were found above the right knee and on the outside right thigh. He also noted that there was a large amount of blood on Cross's left boot, the one Cross said was in Harper's chest when the gun discharged, but none on his right boot. There were no photos of the boot.

Armit picked up a clear plastic pouch and announced the next exhibit. "Number seven is a black leather wallet." Inside the pouch that contained the wallet was Harper's driver's licence and other identification that Cross had wanted to see; the ID that might have saved J.J. Harper's life if he had produced it on demand. Then Armit mentioned something else that the police had found in the wallet and which was also in the clear plastic pouch. "Some personal papers."

Melvin Pruden followed Armit on the witness stand. The teenager was describing how a police officer had pointed his revolver at him in the back lane when Enns called for a ten-minute afternoon recess. During the break Harvey Pollock noticed a glaring light by the exhibit table. A television cameraman and a pack of reporters, including Marc Gage from CTV, were pressing against the exhibit table like wolves at a kill. Pollock scurried over and began shouting at Gage and the cameraman, telling them they had no right to film the exhibits. But it was too late. Gage and his cameraman already had what they wanted: the "personal papers" from Harper's wallet, the letter Morton had referred to in a handwritten post script to Pollock: "Item 3 (f) is for your info only, not for Inquiry purposes."

When the hearing resumed, Morton seemed flustered and angry. He told Enns that he and Pollock had an agreement that the letter wasn't relevant and would be excluded from the exhibits, but "inadvertently" it had ended up on the exhibit table. Enns appealed to the media not to publicize the contents until argument could be heard on the letter's relevance and admissibility. But that night, on the CTV news, Mark Gage revealed to the nation the letter Lois Harper had written to her husband, which he had always kept with him.

> J.J.
> We can't go on like this. I need a home where I can feel safe. I can't seem to find it with you. The couple of days we spent up north were nice, it almost made me hope we could work it out.
>
> You said, (the other night) 'I wish I could make it easier for you.' I don't know what you were referring to, but each time you drink it drives us farther apart and makes it seem easier to leave.
>
> For a long time I've wondered if I really love you. A lot of [the] time I feel I don't, but for some reason the leaving is very hard to do. But I've got to leave. I can't spend the rest of my life like this.
>
> Maybe I'll never in this life find peace and happiness. But I've got to do something. You have given me some precious memories for which I thank you. The happiest time of my life was when we made Ell & Lori.
>
> Maybe it was too much. Me and Vince had some very nice peaceful days with you in our first house.
>
> Maybe that's all I'll get and if so, surely my life will be over soon.
>
> I've always had trouble saying things so that's why I'm writing this. I just hope you can understand me a little better.

After the hammering they had been taking in the *Free Press* during the inquest's first two days, the police were delighted with the letter. Before the TV cameras, Al McGregor, representing the Winnipeg Police Association, made sure that no one missed the connection he saw between what Harper's wife had said in the letter and Harper's behaviour on Logan Avenue on March 9, 1988. "Specifically," McGregor said, as if he were thinking about every word, "his attitudes and actions while under the influence of alcohol."

Two years after the shooting, Gordon Sinclair finally spoke with

J.J. Harper's wife. Lois Harper was waiting in the Island Lake Tribal Council boardroom, where her husband's Chicago Blackhawk–style hockey sweater hung on the wall in tribute.

Nervously she lit a hand-rolled Export "A" and haltingly, at times tearfully, she talked about the last time she had spoken to her husband on the phone, when he told her he had to meet someone at the airport. Two hours later, frustrated and angry because he still hadn't come home, Lois drove downtown.

She knew he would be drinking. She just didn't know where. She found his Ramcharger in the Royal Winnipeg Ballet's new parking lot near his office. Obviously he was back from the airport. He was probably sitting around at the Beachcomber or the St. Regis or one of his other favourite downtown watering holes. She tried the Aberdeen, the seventy-five-year-old log-walled basement pub that still masqueraded as a hotel. There was no one down there but old men nursing glasses of draught, and pickled eggs floating in an oversized jar. Frustrated and angry, she gave up the hunt for her husband. "This is ridiculous," she thought to herself, "chasing around after him." She drove back to her children, put the meat loaf in the oven, and spent another night without him.

Lois mentioned that when the police found the letter in the wallet, they wanted to know if J.J. had been abusive or violent with her. "I said, 'With me sometimes. But I never heard of him being in a fight with anybody.'"

Years later, Dave Tomasson, J.J. Harper's friend and mentor – and now deputy minister in Gary Filmon's government – concurred with Lois. Over a coffee at a Second Cup outlet next door to the building where he had worked to create the Island Lake Tribal Council, Tomasson recalled a surprise phone call he had received from Harper one day. He was calling from the drunk tank.

"Dave, can you come and get me?" Harper asked.

Tomasson was shocked. In all the years he had sat in bars drinking with Jay, as he called him, Harper had never been the belligerent drunk that police wanted the public to believe he was. On the contrary,

Tomasson said, Harper was easygoing, never argumentative or out to pick a fight. There had been the time he was slashed on the arm at Club Morocco, but that had happened when he intervened to stop a woman from being assaulted.

"What the hell's going on?" Tomasson demanded over the phone.

"I got into a little problem at home," Harper said. "I need a place to stay."

Tomasson said he was on his way, but before he left he called Lois, who told him they had had an argument, during which he'd hit her, and she'd called the police.

"Dave," Lois implored, "you've got to talk to him." She said she'd drop some things off for J.J. at Tomasson's house. "But I'm not going to talk to him."

When Lois arrived with her husband's clothes, and Tomasson saw her black eye, he was furious. After Lois left, Tomasson lit into Harper, warning him that if he didn't shape up, he was risking both his family life and his job.

Harper stayed with his friend for a week, then Tomasson called Lois and made sure she was comfortable about her husband returning home. Before Harper left, Tomasson cautioned him. "If things get tough, you get the hell out. I never want to hear of you hurting her again."

Harper promised he never would. Lois never called the police again.

Shortly after he spoke with Lois, Sinclair finally located Marc Gage, the CTV reporter who had publicized her anguished letter. He was now working in Vancouver for CBC Radio. Sinclair didn't expect Gage to tell him anything significant, but on the phone he asked anyway. How had he managed to find the letter on the exhibit table that day?

"I knew it was there," Gage said.

Who had told him?

"It was a cop," he said without hesitation.

The pen in Sinclair's hand froze.

"A friend of mine on the force," Gage continued. "I'd met him through a friend of a friend."

Gage said he used to drink beer with the cop and one day, during a recess at the inquest, he took Gage aside and told him things were looking bad for the police, the full story wasn't coming out. That's when the cop told Gage about the letter and what was in it.

"He knew exactly where it was. He said, 'You gotta find that thing, Marc. You gotta get that out.'"

Sinclair knew Gage wouldn't reveal his source, so he tried an indirect approach. He asked if the guy was a uniformed officer.

Gage said he was, but he hadn't been in uniform at the inquest.

"He said his ass would be grass if anyone found out."

18

"A KANGAROO COURT."

In the early 1980s, writer Carsten Stroud spent a year researching Canadian street cops for a book called *The Blue Wall*. The title had a dual meaning. It referred to the protective line police form between society and crime, and to the barrier that cops erect between us and them. Stroud concluded that of the three basic rules that street cops live by, "Stand by your partner was the first, possibly the premier rule. A man could fail his wife, his children, his parents and himself, but the loyalty to the police partner was perhaps the strongest social bond I've ever seen."

Four police officers had gathered round Robert Cross as he stood fidgeting and trembling on the sidewalk after Harper went down on the dark, early morning of March 9. All four – Grant "Butch" Eakin, Rick Poneira, Glen Spryszak, and Kathryn Hodgins – had partnered with him at one time or another. At the inquest their recollections of what Cross said to them about the shooting were cryptic and, at times, confused.

Spryszak later testified that Cross told him: "Smacked me, went for my gun, went off," although in Spryszak's written report he had switched the order of events: "Went off, smacked me, went for my gun."

Poneira hadn't recorded anything in his notebook and gave his testimony from memory: "He indicated that he went to check a male, this male attacked him, knocked him to the ground, went for his gun, the gun came out and the gun went off."

Eakin had recorded what he claimed was a verbatim account of what Cross said: "I approached him. I asked him for ID. He hit me, knocked me down and went for my gun. It came out and he got shot."

The fourth officer who comforted Cross at the scene was his longest-serving partner, Kathryn Hodgins. She was the first of the four to take the witness stand at the inquest on Friday, April 8.

Her full name was Kathryn Marie Dzogan Hodgins. She grew up in a middle-class Winnipeg suburb, just off the Trans-Canada Highway. Her father, Walter, had been a pilot for Transair, a regional carrier, and Kathy was just entering her teens when he died. It was her first experience of tragedy. The shot in the night on Logan Avenue had signalled the second.

Hodgins told Morton what she did on hearing it: "I ran down the back lane, looking for my partner, Constable Cross, and calling his name." Then she heard him asking for his partner on her radio, and she dashed back to her car. Cross was just around the corner from where she was parked at the mouth of the lane on Winks, but in her frantic state, she ended up being the last of the four cruisers to find him. After she parked cruiser N202 the wrong way on the north side of Logan, Hodgins saw Cross standing next to Eakin, about ten feet east of Harper.

"As I walked up to Constable Cross I saw there was snow and blood on the back of his reefer jacket collar, arms, on his legs. He seemed pretty dirty. I didn't know what to do. I walked up to him and started brushing him off to see if he was okay."

She recalled Cross had a blank, shocked look on his face. "He stated to me: 'He jumped me, Kath. I was on my back, on the ground, and he went for my gun.'"

Hodgins suggested he should come back to the car, but Cross just wanted to stand there.

"I went back to the cruiser car. I asked for assistance. I realized I was basically the senior officer there at the scene. Decisions had to be made. I was asking for a duty inspector to come out. I was asking for someone to come and attend."

In the meantime, Eakin took charge of the situation. He told Bill Isaac and Randy Hampton, who had Pruden in the back of their cruiser, that they weren't needed at the scene. It had been Hampton who flushed Pruden out of the back lane and Isaac who caught and cuffed him. Eakin instructed the two downtown patrol officers to go back to Winks, where they were to guard the stolen car until the tow truck arrived.

Eight or nine minutes after the shooting Spryszak, who had to drive all the way from the suburban District Two station, arrived in time to see the ambulance pull away at 2:57. At 3:02, Inspector Eric Hrycyk arrived and took charge of the scene.

The "old man" Allan had heard give Cross instructions could have been Hrycyk. He looked to be in his late thirties, with light brown hair that could be mistaken for grey in the night light. Within minutes of his arrival, Hrycyk testified later, he told Cross and Hodgins to leave for the Public Safety Building and wait for him in his office.

"Where were you when you received these instructions from Acting Inspector Hrycyk?" Morton asked Hodgins.

"Myself and my partner were outside [our] vehicle. The accused had already been taken away. We were in front of the vehicle."

If Allan had already been transferred to another cruiser and taken away from the scene, he couldn't have overheard any instructions Hrycyk gave Cross, assuming it was the duty inspector the boy saw. But Hodgins was wrong. Allan was still in the back seat. Hrycyk later testified that he hadn't ordered the boy transferred until after he'd spoken with all of the officers at the scene, around 3:10 a.m., eight minutes after arriving.

Hodgins went on to make the point that it would have been impossible for the boy to hear anything outside the car anyway, because of the noise from the engine, which she said had been left on to keep him warm. She also mentioned the sound-inhibiting factor of the Silent Partner.

Morton asked Hodgins for the exact words she spoke to Allan as he was being turned over to the other constables.

" 'If you hadn't been a little thief to begin with, none of this would have happened,' " she said. Hodgins denied that she'd called him a blue-eyed fucking Indian.

Morton next took Hodgins back to the end of the car chase. "Constable, how far were these males [Pruden and Allan] from the stolen vehicle when you first observed them?"

Pollock paid particular attention here. If they had had any kind of look at Pruden there was no way Cross could have mistaken the much older Harper for him. Pruden was thirty pounds lighter than Harper and nearly twenty years younger.

"I didn't really take a good notice of the persons as they were running," Hodgins said.

"As we had seen the persons fleeing from the vehicle, we observed..." Hodgins paused. Cross had testified that he had seen them only as dark shapes. She corrected herself. "Excuse me. I observed that the first person that was running appeared to be much taller than the second person. The only description that I could find at that point, the first male appeared to be male, Native, black hair, and dark clothing. The second also appeared to be male, Native, and dark clothing."

"Just one last question," Morton said. "At any time during or after this incident did you have occasion to remove your revolver from your holster?"

"No, I did not," Hodgins said.

Now it was Pollock's turn.

Pollock started at the point at which Hodgins saw Pruden and Allan fleeing the car.

"Constable, how far were these males from the stolen vehicle when you first observed them?"

Hodgins said that Allan was in the centre of the street, and Pruden had almost reached the lane on the other side of the street. She agreed with Pollock that the distance between them might have been a hundred feet, and that it shrank to about twenty-five feet when the cruiser followed them into the alley and the pair ran between some houses.

"Now," Pollock continued, "you broadcast that the taller of the two youths was twenty-two years of age. Is that right?"

Hodgins didn't respond.

"That is in the tape," Pollock reminded Hodgins.

"That is correct," she finally said.

"Where do you get that information from?"

"I don't know."

Cross had testified that he had relayed the description Allan had given him as "in his twenties."

"Did you estimate the taller of the two youths to be twenty-two years of age when you observed him?"

"No, I did not."

"Did Constable Cross tell you that he thought that the taller of the two youths was twenty-two years of age?"

"No, he did not."

Then why had Hodgins picked the specific number twenty-two, instead of "in his twenties," as Allan was supposed to have told Cross?

"I can't answer that," she said.

Pollock wanted to hear about the conversation between Hodgins and Cross when she first approached him at the shooting scene.

"What did you say to him?"

Again Hodgins didn't respond.

"Anything?" Pollock prodded.

"Nothing," she finally said.

Pollock was having trouble believing that Hodgins hadn't asked her shaken partner anything when Cross had radioed for her before he had even called for an ambulance.

"How long were you in his presence before you first uttered a word?"

"A minute."

"And during that minute, did you speak to any of the other officers?"

"No, I did not."

What did Cross say to her then during that minute?

"He said, 'He jumped me, Kath. I was on my back, on the ground. He went for my gun.' He said nothing further to me."

"And you didn't ask him anything further about it?"

"I did not."

"Why didn't you?"

Again, she didn't respond. Kathryn Hodgins was redefining the term Silent Partner.

"So you were at the scene involving the death of a man, and for three minutes you did nothing except brush off the constable. Is that correct?"

"I walked over to Mr. Harper and watched as the persons attended to see if they required any assistance."

Then she'd suggested to Cross that he sit in their cruiser, which he did, just prior to Spryszak arriving at 2:58. Hodgins estimated they were in the cruiser about forty-five seconds before Cross got out, saying, "I've got to stand." Allan had said it was while Hodgins and Cross were in the front seat together that he overheard Cross talking about the struggle. Pollock asked Hodgins if Cross had said anything to her when they were sitting in the car.

"Not that I recall."

Pollock asked if, as Allan said, Cross had left the cruiser when the "old man cop" arrived.

"I don't recall anybody approaching the cruiser car," Hodgins said. She acknowledged only that Cross spoke to Spryszak at some point after leaving the car. Pollock wanted to follow that up, but Enns interrupted.

"The act clearly directs the Fatality Inquiry judge to limit cross-examination. And if you are going to go over with a fine-tooth comb every step of the way – he went to the Public Safety Building, and so on – that I can't allow. So you will either finish now, or discontinue."

A few minutes later, Harvey Pollock gave up.

That wasn't the end of the day, though. The next witness was a reel-to-reel tape of the police radio transmissions, starting with the stolen car chase and ending with Cross calling first for his partner and second for an ambulance. During the hunt for Pruden, the descriptions of his jacket changed colour, from black in the first broadcast, to grey when he was being chased and finally caught. But, contrary to what Cross said he heard, there was no mention of the second suspect wearing a sweater jacket, the discrepancy in the description that supposedly caused him to stop Harper.

Before the end of the fourth day, the group of Natives who had been gallery regulars had left. Jeff Funnell glanced up from his sketch pad and watched them go. "This is a fucking kangaroo court," he heard one of them say.

They never returned.

—

19

"THE SUN'S COVERAGE WAS DIFFERENT."

On day five of the inquest, Marty Minuk asked Judge Enns to instruct the witnesses to speak more loudly and clearly, "So that we don't have what I believe to be a continuing problem of inaccurate representations of verbatim quotes from witnesses."

Free Press reporter Heidi Graham took this to be another jab aimed at intimidating her, this time publicly. Privately, Al McGregor of the police association had been hounding Heidi, accusing her of mis-quoting witnesses.

"I think he saw it as part of his job to try to keep the media in line," Heidi later told Gordon Sinclair. "He said I got a quote wrong. So I went and looked at what the *Sun* had and what I had, and it was the same."

That reminded Heidi.

"The *Sun*'s coverage was different. You remember that?" Sinclair remembered. Quotes aside, the *Free Press* and the *Sun* rarely read the same on the Harper inquest. The *Sun* managed to put the police slant on everything. All any reader had to do was compare a couple of the lead paragraphs of the same day's testimony.

The *Free Press:* "Constable Robert Cross knew police had two suspects in custody when he stopped John Joseph Harper as a possible suspect in an auto theft early on the morning of March 9."
The *Sun*: "Flat on his back, Const. Robert Cross stared in terror as an intoxicated J.J. Harper hovered over him and tugged at his gun, an inquest heard yesterday.

"'I feared for my life,' Cross calmly said . . .'"

The *Free Press:* "Minutes after a bullet from his gun killed John Joseph Harper Const. Robert Cross told his partner he had taken the revolver out of his holster and pulled the trigger, a witness testified yesterday."
The *Sun*: "A 14-year-old boy's hazy description of a driver of a stolen car led a Winnipeg Police officer on a chase which ended in the death of J.J. Harper, an inquest heard yesterday."

The *Sun* didn't report the discrepancy between Cross saying he had heard the suspect was wearing a sweater jacket and the fact that the words weren't on the police tape. Instead, it made this surprising interpretation: "The radio tapes appear to support Cross's testimony that he approached Harper because he thought he matched the description of the car theft suspect."

Heidi Graham was the *Free Press* reporter on all of those stories. The *Sun* stories were written by Bruce Owen, a handsome young rookie reporter, who looked as if he belonged in front of a television camera. His name didn't mean much then. But it would. As would the name of the next witness.

20

"I SHOT HIM."

"Can I refer to my notes, Your Honour?" Bill Isaac asked.

Enns asked if they were the notes that he had made shortly after the incident.

"Yes."

"Yes, you may refer to such notes."

Isaac, the six-foot-eight cop from Lethbridge, Alberta, who had arrested Pruden, had been parked on Gallagher, north of the park, when he first saw Pruden running across Logan towards him. Isaac estimated he was 200 metres away. "I attempted to back the cruiser car up in order to intercept them, but the roads were icy. So I abandoned the vehicle."

Just as he was leaving the car, he spotted Pruden running across Gallagher and into the backyard at number 2039. Isaac caught him there. Pruden cheekily remarked, "It took you awhile to get me, didn't it?" Isaac turned him over to Rick Poneira and Butch Eakin.

"Did you hear anybody in your presence make any comment to Mr. Pruden about being a Native?" Morton asked.

"No, I didn't."

Isaac said they heard only two complaints from Pruden. He wanted the twelve-pack of OV beer that was in the front seat of the stolen car, and he said his handcuffs were too tight. Police often tighten handcuffs as a way of punishing disrespectful suspects, but Isaac wasn't asked about that. Isaac said that when Eakin and Poneira turned Pruden over to them and complained, his partner, Randy Hampton, loosened the cuffs.

"What was Mr. Pruden wearing?" Morton asked.

"Mr. Pruden was wearing a grey jacket, cloth jacket, blue jeans, and a red shirt."

"All right, sir. You, this morning, are wearing a sports jacket that appears to be somewhat greyish in colour. How would you compare Mr. Pruden's jacket, as you saw it that night, in terms of the colour of grey to the jacket you're wearing this morning, constable?"

"My jacket is basically two-tone grey. Mr. Pruden's was grey with a black effect to it."

"In terms of degree of lightness, how would it compare to the grey you have got?"

"His jacket was darker."

"Did you call him a fucking Indian?" Pollock began.

"Certainly didn't," Isaac said indignantly.

"Did anybody else in your presence call him a fucking Indian?"

"No, no one did."

Minuk stood up to object, saying, "I believe that this question is not within the proper realm of cross-examination set out in Section 17 of the act."

"I appreciate your comments," Enns said. "And of course, it's been the problem of the conduct of the inquest all along. Where should the court draw the line?"

Pollock moved on to other areas. At one point he looked down at his notes and inadvertently stumbled into an area that later would suggest that Isaac was hiding something. He asked Isaac if he had returned to the shooting scene that day. Pollock thought he had heard Isaac tell Morton that he had.

"Not – not that day," Isaac stammered. "In the course of general patrol I have had occasion to go by there."

"Did you ever return to the scene where Harper was found for any reason connected with this investigation?"

"No, I didn't," Isaac said.

Not knowing how close he had come to uncovering the truth, Pollock moved to another area that would ultimately prove important.

"Who did you report to when you got back to the station?"

Isaac said he reported to his sergeant and later, upstairs in the detective office, to an inspector.

"Which inspector?" Pollock demanded.

"I'm not sure of his name."

"Does he have a number?"

"I'm not sure what his number is."

"Who else was there besides you and this inspector?"

"Really, we had no involvement with anybody else."

Pollock continued to prod Isaac about whom he had talked to before he testified.

"Did you discuss with anyone the matter of this evidence that you are giving here this morning?"

"I don't understand what your question is."

"Well, did you have a meeting with any of the inspectors or with any of the sergeants or any of the other constables in this matter in relationship to the evidence that you're giving here today?"

"Well, I met with Inspector Keatinge when we went to listen to the transcript of the event."

"Who else?"

"I was at Mr. Minuk's office."

Pollock tried to find out who else was at Minuk's office, but Enns said no, and told him to go into another area. Pollock protested. He wanted to know whom else Isaac had discussed the shooting with, or who might have been present when he talked.

"Far too broad a question," Enns said. Did Pollock want to know if Isaac had discussed the case over breakfast with his ten-year-old son or his wife? the judge added sarcastically.

"I will narrow it," Pollock said.

"No," Enns barked. He suggested Pollock could elicit this kind of detail during the course of a civil suit. Pollock continued to plead until Enns relented.

"Did you have any discussions with Chief Stephen?"

"No, I didn't."

"Did you have discussions with any of the lesser officers in his office, inspectors, sub-inspectors, about this matter?"

"No, I didn't."

Harvey Pollock had been going in the right direction, but he didn't go quite far enough.

Up in the gallery, Funnell sketched Isaac standing in the witness box in his grey blazer, hands behind his back. Beside Isaac's likeness, Funnell wrote: *Who else did you discuss case with?*

Partners Butch Eakin and Rick Poneira were the next to testify. Poneira, the son of a local piano player, had been a cop for seven years. It had been Poneira who chased Pruden across Stanley Knowles Park after Randy Hampton flushed him out of the back lane and onto Logan. Like the other constables who had been part of the search for Pruden, Poneira denied drawing his revolver on the early morning of March 9. He also denied calling Pruden a "fucking Indian."

Minutes later, after he heard Cross radio for help and reached the shooting scene, Poneira had used his bare hands to apply pressure to the blood that was pumping from Harper's chest. Harper had tried to fight him off, so Poneira pinned the fatally wounded man's arms, and Constable Danny Smyth took over applying pressure to the wound.

Later, after he was relieved by the fire department first responders, Poneira tried to console Cross. But he'd made no notes of what Cross told him because, he said, he couldn't remember the comments verbatim. Pollock was incredulous about both what Poneira had excluded and included in his notes.

"Did you write in your book that you thought Harper was in his twenties?"

"Yes, I did."

"Is that after observing him?"

"Yeah."

"When did you make those notes?"

"During the time I was there."

"Right at the scene?"

"At the scene."

"There's a big difference in age between nineteen and thirty-six when it comes to appearance. Wouldn't you agree with me on that?" Pollock asked.

"Could be."

"Well, there is, isn't there?"

Poneira didn't say anything.

Butch Eakin was a former minor league pro hockey player. He was blond and looked like a bodybuilder. Gordon Sinclair knew of Eakin by reputation. A few years earlier Sinclair had been phoned by a guy who played goal in a local recreational hockey league. The goalie claimed that he and Eakin had had an argument on the ice at The Highlander sportsplex. After the game, Eakin had allegedly jumped the goalie. The goalie told Sinclair he had reported the incident to police, but got nowhere. He took it to the Crown but they wouldn't do anything either.

Eakin hadn't been involved in the foot chase on the night Harper was shot. Instead, he'd roamed the area in the cruiser after dropping Poneira off to search on foot. Eakin left the car twice, once to help place Pruden in the back of his cruiser and once to speak with Cross and take charge after the shooting.

Two areas in Eakin's testimony were of particular interest. One concerned Randy Hampton, the officer Pruden claimed had pointed a gun at him in the lane. About the time Pruden was first spotted, Eakin had seen Hampton standing in the lane. Eakin testified that he was in his cruiser at that point, parked on Blaine, at the west end of the lane, and could see Hampton waving his right hand in a throwing motion. Eakin had gone further in his report. He'd said Hampton was motioning with a flashlight, and he made it sound as if Hampton was speaking into his two-way radio as he was gesturing.

"And how far were you from him?" Pollock asked.

"Exactly, I don't know," Eakin said. "It was several yards down."

"He was using his flashlight – was he?"

"His flashlight or a portable radio. He was doing it with his right hand, gesturing. I believe it was his flashlight."

What Pollock didn't know then, and what Judge Enns didn't know until long after he delivered his findings, was that Eakin couldn't have seen Hampton motioning with his flashlight. Hampton had left it in the cruiser.

Eakin's most important contribution to the inquest came from his testimony on what happened moments after he'd seen Hampton motioning. Eakin had driven to the corner of Blaine and Logan, the direction in which the second suspect had run. There, about seventy yards to his left, walking east towards him on the north sidewalk of Logan, was Harper. But unlike Cross, Eakin hadn't stopped him.

During his examination-in-chief, Morton had asked why he hadn't.

"At the time I was assisting my partner and Constable Hampton in pursuit of a male."

Pollock asked how long he'd watched the man walking towards him on the other side of the street.

"Just seconds."

Pollock asked what he observed about the man.

"That he fit the general description of the suspect we were chasing, black leather jacket and blue jeans."

Pollock held up Harper's jacket to show Eakin that it was cloth, not leather. Then he suggested that Eakin wouldn't have expected a suspect to be walking back towards the scene of a crime where police were looking for him. "You would assume he would be running away from the scene rather than towards the scene, wouldn't you?"

"I guess you could say that," Eakin replied. "Yes."

Pollock turned to what, at the time, seemed like a subtle, inconsequential difference in detail. Pruden's jacket was grey – the colour Poneira had broadcast as he chased him from Logan across the park, not black, as Hodgins had originally broadcast. And it was cloth. Now Pollock had a surprise for Eakin and the inquest. He showed Eakin a photograph.

"The man that was subsequently caught was Pruden, and he was wearing this jacket, is that not so?"

Eakin was looking at the photograph that *Free Press* photographer Gerry Cairns had taken of Pruden eight days after the shooting, when he and Sinclair took the young Indian back to the scene.

"Mark that," Pollock said quickly, handing the photograph to the court reporter.

"Just a minute," Enns said, angrily.

"What?" Morton snapped, starting to object.

"Mr. Pollock," Enns said, "I know it's nice to be dramatic and show a photograph out of nowhere, but this is not a movie. We are not trying to be dramatic and impress somebody outside."

Pollock tried to explain that he was simply putting the photograph to the witness for identification. But Enns was angry with him, so upset his words and thoughts started to snarl and tangle. "Why don't we have TV cameras here and show what a beautiful – I'm upset. I'll call a recess."

When Enns returned he had cooled off. Morton and McGregor wanted to know where the photo had come from, but Enns wasn't interested. He allowed that Pollock had been within his rights to show the photo to Eakin, it was just the way it was done that had infuriated the judge.

Pollock wasn't finished with Eakin. Earlier he had established that Eakin had known Cross for about three and a half years. But now, Eakin only reluctantly admitted that they had been partners on occasion. He had already told Morton the first thing Cross said to him at the scene.

" 'I approached him, asked for some ID and he hit me. Knocked me down and went for my gun. It came out and he got shot.' "

"What question precipitated that response?" Pollock asked.

"I would have just asked him, 'What happened?' "

"Did you say anything else to him?"

"No, I never."

Pollock didn't believe that Eakin hadn't wanted more detail about how one of his former partners had become involved in a struggle that ended with a citizen being shot.

"Did you ask him how the gun came out?"

"No, sir. He stated . . ." Eakin paused, and began again. "No. Just that the gun came out."

"Did you ask him how he got shot?"

"No, I never."

"Were you not interested at that time?"

"At that time I was – there was a body on the ground. I wasn't going through a whole – wasn't talking long to Constable Cross."

"You were interested in protecting Constable Cross to that point, weren't you?" Pollock said bluntly.

"No, I wasn't."

"Didn't care about how well he was going to do in this matter?" Pollock asked.

"Just told him to go sit in the car, that would be the best."

"That's all you told him?"

"Ah-hum."

At the back of the gallery, Jeff Funnell was sketching Eakin coolly leaning on his elbow as he testified. As he had done with earlier witnesses he surrounded the drawing with fragments of testimony that seemed to swarm like flies around Eakin's head: *Hampton gestured to you w [with] flashlight. What happened? Did you ask him how he was knocked down how gun came out? 3 half years I've known Cross. Partner from time to time. Pruden cuffed and brought back to cruiser car. It would appear to be grey jacket.*

Pollock wondered if Eakin had checked the ground around the shooting by flashlight. Eakin hadn't.

Then Pollock asked if Eakin would have searched the area if it had been the other way around, if it had been Harper who killed Cross?

Before Eakin could answer, Enns cut in.

"I'm afraid that is a whole hypothetical question."

Pollock had another question for Eakin.

"Do you know who found the keys?"

"No, I don't."

Danny Gerald Smyth was the one who found Harper's keys. He was the first cop to talk to Cross after the shooting, and the last officer to testify on day five of the inquest.

Smyth was the most junior officer at the shooting scene, the son of the police armament officer, and a university graduate.

When he took the stand that spring afternoon, a month after the shooting, it became rapidly apparent that the tone of his testimony was different from the rest. In contrast to Isaac, Poneira, and Eakin, Smyth's answers were direct and detailed and there was nothing defensive about his demeanour. Maybe it was because he was a relative rookie who hadn't been conditioned or socialized to be one of the boys. Maybe it was because he had worked only in the downtown district and he had never met Cross before. Maybe it was education and upbringing. Whatever it was, there were no "I don't knows" from Smyth, the way there had been from the other three constables that day.

Smyth had located Harper's keys on the sidewalk, six feet east of body, before he joined Poneira in an effort to save Harper's life. Harper was still thrashing around when Smyth climbed into the ambulance and tried to comfort him, telling him to hang on until they got to the hospital.

As his testimony began, Smyth explained that he and his partner, Hooper, had been the last of the three cars to leave the area where

Pruden had been caught after Cross called for help. As soon as they turned onto Logan, Smyth and Hooper saw what the other officers had driven past in their haste to get to the stolen car on Winks, where they assumed Cross still was. Smyth saw Cross standing halfway down the block on the north side of Logan.

"He was standing facing to the south and his revolver was drawn. It was in his right hand. It was pointing to the ground. He was standing over Harper, [who was] perhaps five feet away from his feet. He didn't have a hat on. His jacket was on, but done up halfway. There was snow visible on his back, on his top right shoulder, and also snow visible on his right pant leg. His hair looked mussed up."

Smyth could see Harper lying across the sidewalk. "He was lying on his right shoulder with his arms tucked into his chest. I would describe it as a recovery position." Morton asked Smyth to put his notebook down and demonstrate where Harper's hands were. Smyth bent his elbows, pulled his arms in tight to his body, his fists clenched against his chest.

Morton seemed impressed with the exactness of Smyth's notes. "Yes, please constable. Please tell us what else you observed."

"There was a pool of blood visible, quite a large pool of blood, around his chest area onto the sidewalk. Blood was visible on his clothing, on his jacket, on his shirt, on his hands, on his neck and face area.

"We were the first unit to actually get there and the first thing I did was jump from the car and ask Constable Cross if he was all right. He said to me: 'Yeah, I'm okay.' He looked shaken up. My partner pointed at Harper lying on the sidewalk and asked Cross if this guy had been shot."

According to Smyth, Cross's answer, his first words describing what happened, were simple and direct: " 'He went for my gun. I shot him.' "

Eight hours after the day had started with Minuk's attack on her credibility, Heidi Graham was in the *Free Press* newsroom, typing the lead on her summary of the day's testimony.

"Minutes after John Joseph Harper was fatally wounded, Const. Robert Cross told fellow officers he shot the Native leader . . .

"'My partner asked him (Cross) if this guy had been shot,' Const. Danny Smyth, one of the first officers on the scene, told the hearing.

"He said, 'He went for my gun and I shot him.'"

At the *Sun*, Bruce Owen chose a different angle to start his story. He wrote that even though J.J. Harper had lost a lot of blood, he still fought off two cops who were trying to stop the bleeding from his gunshot wound.

Cross's first words to Smyth and Hooper – "He went for my gun and I shot him" – didn't appear in Owen's story.

21

"THE BEST I COULD DO."

Glen Joseph Spryszak was the acting sergeant, the officer in charge, who arrived just as the ambulance was leaving and who seized Cross's service revolver. Spryszak had a broad, friendly face and was built like a football lineman, which he had been at Sisler High School in north-end Winnipeg. He was yet another cop's son, and yet another former partner of Cross.

Spryszak had just finished studying for a sergeant's exam, but on Logan that night he was a constable, one who had more experience than Cross and Hodgins combined. Normally a confirmed sergeant would have been sent out, but the District Two station was short-staffed that night. This was the first time in his fourteen-year career that Spryszak had been involved in a shooting.

When he arrived, he carefully pulled his vehicle into the tire tracks vacated by the ambulance. It was 2:54 by Spryszak's watch, which was running four minutes slow. Spryszak saw Hodgins sitting in the front seat of cruiser N202. Allan was in the back. As the 270-pound cop got out of his truck he could see Cross standing about thirty feet away with Poneira and Eakin.

Spryszak asked them what had happened. Eakin told him that someone had been shot.

"And," Spryszak now testified, "I asked who was involved with this, and Constable Cross said that he was." Apologetically, Spryszak asked him for the revolver, which Cross had put back in its holster. Cross drew his gun and handed it to Spryszak with two fingers. Spryszak pulled his own gun, accepted Cross's with two fingers, and slid it in his own holster. "It was the best I could do," he testified.

Spryszak suggested to Cross that he go back to his cruiser and sit there, which he eventually did, climbing into the passenger seat beside Hodgins.

Five minutes after Spryszak arrived, Duty Inspector Eric Hrycyk pulled up.

Spryszak said later that he broke open Cross's revolver and together he and Hrycyk checked that only one round had been fired. Spryszak then closed it and reholstered it. He later noticed a whitish salt stain running the length of the barrel and a spot of blood on the left side of the grip.

Eakin and Poneira were still there when Hrycyk left Spryszak in charge of the scene, with instructions to seal it off and do a witness canvass of the neighbourhood. The site was sealed off by tape at 3:30 a.m. Two Ident officers arrived an hour later, and Spryszak left for the Public Safety Building around 6 a.m.

While he was at the scene, Spryszak said, he searched the street on his hands and knees and held a flashlight while an Ident officer collected blood samples. Afterwards, he did the witness canvass, knocking on six doors. Three residents answered.

When Pollock learned that Spryszak knew of Ident's plans to wash down the scene before dawn, he asked, "Did you say, 'Don't do it because we're not finished with the scene yet. It's too early. The sun hasn't come up. We should leave the scene intact for a while.'?"

"No, I did not."

Pollock turned to Spryszak's handling of the revolver.

"Why did you hold it so gingerly with two fingers?"

"I didn't want to get my finger in the trigger for any reason."

"You didn't want to get your fingerprints on it. Isn't that right?"

"I didn't want to contaminate it."

Pollock wondered why he hadn't wrapped the gun in something to preserve it. Spryszak said that if he had had something, he would have used it. "At the time that was the best I could do."

Earlier, during Morton's examination-in-chief, there was one exchange that passed so quickly, so innocuously, that no one gave it a second thought. Morton asked on whose instructions Spryszak was acting when he turned over the revolver to the armaments officer.

"On the instructions of Inspector Hrycyk, and I talked to Staff Sergeant Dawson, who reminded me to turn the firearm over to Constable Kehler."

It wasn't Staff Sergeant Dawson whom Spryszak spoke with, but he got the name almost right. The name was Dowson. Ken Dowson

When Morton examined Spryszak, he asked for a description of Hrycyk, the most likely person to be the "old man" Allan had heard telling Cross to say the shooting was an accident.

"Your Honour," Spryszak said, "Inspector Hrycyk is approximately thirty-eight years old, perhaps forty. He is about five foot ten or eleven, about 190 pounds. He is not of an unusually heavy build or a slim build. Fairly average in build. When he arrived he was wearing an inspector's uniform, which consists of a crest similar to mine except it's gold in colour and he wears a white shirt."

"And what colour is his hair?"

"It's a light-coloured brown."

Eric James Hrycyk had been with the Winnipeg Police Department for seventeen years, but he had been an inspector for only one month when Harper was shot. He had been monitoring the chase in the communications centre. On the stand, he acknowledged that he had had a conversation with Cross once he got to the scene. Cross had told him about his struggle with Harper. "Constable Cross said he had both hands on the butt of the revolver and the male was holding the revolver in the space left over. He wasn't sure exactly where he was holding it. Cross said the revolver was beginning to slip from his hands, and as it slipped free, the gun went off. The male fell back and Cross called for help."

Hrycyk said there was no discussion of fingerprinting the revolver. To his knowledge that had never been done in an officer-related shooting. Hrycyk said it was up to detectives to decide how to do the investigation.

"My rule in an incident like this is not to be the investigator," he told Harvey Pollock. "It's to allocate resources of the appropriate people at the scene. Let the investigators investigate the incident." His duty was to notify the duty executive officer of the incident and to make sure that the proper people were sent to the scene.

The duty executive officer was Superintendent MacDougal "Mac" Allen. Hrycyk had phoned him, as well as Identification unit officer Sergeant Bob Parker, and the three detectives of the Division 23, the Robbery Homicide unit, who were on call that morning: Sergeants Angus Anderson, Harry Williams, and Cal Osborne. "And," said Hrycyk, "they also requested that Acting Inspector Dowson be called." Shortly after 4 a.m. he also called Herb Stephen at home.

Throughout the inquest, Pollock's line of questioning suggested that he suspected the police had conspired about the evidence they were giving. "Did you talk about the evidence that had been tendered?" he asked Hrycyk.

Enns exploded at the question and what it implied. "Don't put the insinuation that if the police officer speaks to his neighbour or his wife about what happened in an inquest, or even a fellow police officer, that immediately raises a sinister obstructing justice allegation, unless you have in your possession evidence that statements provided weeks ago differ."

Harvey Pollock waited for the judge to finish his tirade. When it was over, Pollock said calmly, "I never did receive a report from my learned friend, because I assumed he didn't have one from Inspector Hrycyk."

"I see," said Enns.

It wasn't the only report Morton failed to give Pollock.

Jeff Bedosky, who worked for a private medical van company, had driven past the scene just before the shooting and again just after it on his way to pick up his partner, Doug Ennis, who lived at 2262 Gallagher Avenue. He'd noticed an abandoned car on Winks, stuck in the snow, its driver's door wide open, and as he neared the end of Stanley Knowles Park, he saw a police cruiser turn onto Logan, heading in his direction. And then, as he got to Electa, he saw a cop running along the sidewalk on the north side of Logan.

"The only thing that I could note," Bedosky told Morton, "outside of him running, is what I assumed to be a two-way radio in his right hand, close to his ear."

On the way back from picking up his partner, Bedosky passed Stanley Knowles Park again. This time there were several police cruisers parked midway down the block. Bedosky drove on to the abandoned car on Winks and stopped to make sure no one needed assistance. Then he turned the medical van around and drove back to where all the police cars were. There Bedosky parked close to where a man lay on the sidewalk. He could see a police officer applying pressure to the man's chest. Ennis jumped out of the van to ask the police if they needed a blanket or bandages for the injured man. Kathryn Hodgins told him everything was under control and an ambulance was on the way.

Bedosky and Ennis stayed to see the fire department first responders arrive a few minutes later and left after the ambulance took Harper away.

In his cross-examination Pollock asked Bedosky about the officer he'd seen running along Logan.

"You say he had something in his hand?"

"That's correct."

"You are not able to say what it was?" Pollock asked, trying to shake Bedosky's assumption.

"I would say it was a two-way radio because it was close to his ear and it had a long, wide body towards the base of his hand."

"And you're not able to say here today, now, under oath positively that it was a radio. It could have been something else."

Morton stood up. "Well, your Honour, I really don't know . . ."

Pollock tried to fend off Morton's objection.

"I just want to ask him questions," Pollock said.

"You want something more than that," Enns said. "You want him to say it looked like a gun."

Enns was angry again.

"So say it," Enns ordered.

"Did it look like a gun?" Pollock finally asked.

"No, it did not."

"You couldn't say it wasn't a gun," Pollock persisted.

Morton began to object again, but Judge Enns was ahead of him.

"I'm sorry, Mr. Pollock, you have asked the question and he has given you an answer."

At the time, Pollock thought he had lost a crucial point. If Bedosky was certain the officer was carrying a radio, it would undermine Pruden's evidence that it was a gun and Pollock's theory that Cross already had his revolver out when he approached Harper. It would also weaken his suspicion that other cops had their revolvers drawn that night, too, and were conspiring to say they hadn't to protect Cross.

Long after the inquest was over, something surfaced that gave weight to Pollock's attempts to shake Bedosky's testimony and Morton's effort to hinder him. Bedosky had talked to the police twice, but Morton gave Pollock only one of the two statements, the second, dated March 15, which read: "He was carrying what looked like a two-way radio in his right hand . . ." Pollock was missing Bedosky's first statement, given on the day of the shooting, in which Bedosky said that the "Constable at the west end of the park ... was carrying a radio or gun in his right hand."

The constable at the west end of the park was Randy Hampton, the same policeman Pruden said had pointed a revolver at him.

The next day, April 13, with the provincial election less than two weeks away, the NDP government passed an order-in-council formally creating the Manitoba Aboriginal Justice Inquiry and, within the week, the names of the co-commissioners were announced. The appointments of judges Alvin Hamilton and Murray Sinclair were welcomed by Native leaders. Al Hamilton, an associate chief justice of the Manitoba Court of Queen's Bench, was sixty-three and had the distinction of presiding over the creation of family court in Manitoba. Murray Sinclair, an associate chief justice of the provincial court, had been sworn in the week before Pawley's government fell and J.J. Harper was shot. At age thirty-seven he was the first Aboriginal judge in Manitoba since Confederation, and only the second in the country. Sinclair's appointment to the bench had drawn predictable charges of patronage because he had once worked as an executive assistant to Howard Pawley, during the years the premier had served as attorney general. He was also the young Aboriginal lawyer who had been quoted on the *Free Press* front page less than four years earlier accusing police of preying on Natives.

The Aboriginal Justice Inquiry would hear that charge repeated during its hearings, which would take the inquiry into forty communities, and several jails and prisons, beginning in September. The Harper portion of the inquiry would begin in August of the following year. Pollock wouldn't have to wait that long to learn there were others who'd seen a gun out on Logan on March 9.

—
22

"A CHILDISH DISPLAY OF POWER."

One night around the time the inquest was starting, Harvey Pollock returned home to find a message on his answering machine. It was from a woman who said her teenage daughter and two friends had driven along Logan on the night Harper was shot, and they had seen something. Her daughter had been reluctant to come forward with the information, that's why the mother was calling Pollock.

Pollock was excited. He sent private investigator Milt Brown to interview the surprise witnesses: Linda Morisette, sixteen, her boyfriend, Randy Houston, twenty-one, and his boyhood buddy Larry Yaworek, also twenty-one. Later, Morton dispatched RCMP Sergeant Wes Border to interview the three friends. On the afternoon of April 12, Border went to Morisette's home. Morisette and her boyfriend, Houston, had been expecting Border, but he wasn't alone. He had a Winnipeg police detective with him, Staff Sergeant Ken Dowson, a big guy, tall, about forty, with a moustache and sandy-coloured hair whom Border introduced by his last name. Border taped the interviews with Morisette and Houston, and the next day the two cops drove north through the flat farmland that circles Winnipeg and into the Interlake area, to Powerview, near the pulp and paper town of Pine Falls. At the Powerview RCMP detachment, they interviewed the other witness, Larry Yaworek. The accounts given by the friends varied in places, but their stories were fundamentally the same. They had been at Yaworek's home in Pine Falls on the evening of March 8. It was late by the time the three climbed into Morisette's 1982 Granada to drive to Winnipeg. They were on the way to stay overnight at Morisette's mother's place. Houston was behind the wheel, his girl-friend was beside him, and Yaworek was drunk in the back seat, although, as Houston said, sometimes it was hard to tell with Larry. He acted the same when he was sober. Goofy.

Once in the city, they drove south down McPhillips Street to Logan. By that time it was after 2:30 a.m., although they all thought it was earlier. On Logan near Winks, Houston saw something and slowed down. At the end of the block, just past the park, a police cruiser drove across Logan from Blaine, heading towards the dike and city reservoir. Seconds later a pedestrian ran right out in front of their car, headed north or northwest. Morisette thought it was a woman. So did Yaworek. He rolled down the back window, leaned out, and whistled. Inside the car, Houston screamed in disbelief.

The pedestrian Yaworek had been whistling at was not only not a woman, but a policeman. Morisette recognized the uniform right away, but she didn't get a good look at the cop himself. Her eyes were drawn to what the officer was holding head high, in his right hand. It looked like a gun.

All three witnesses told the investigators that they saw the gun. Border wrote down one more fact, which none of them had mentioned, but the Mountie believed was relevant. All three of Pollock's surprise witnesses were Native. No, they all answered when Border asked. They had not known J.J. Harper.

Ken Dowson noted something else in his report. There was a warrant for Houston's arrest. He owed $99 for an unpaid parking ticket.

By the penultimate day of the inquiry, Jeff Funnell had added three more drawings to his growing collection. In the courtroom below Funnell, Enns was wondering out loud why the three youths had taken so long to come forward. The judge then asked Morisette if it could have been a two-way radio she had seen the officer holding.

"No, that's one thing I'm sure of, is the gun," she replied. "And I told my mom that, too. As soon as I talked to her about it, I told her I was sure."

Yaworek's testimony wasn't as detailed or coherent as his friends'. But that was understandable, he had been drunk at the time. He had told Border he'd had eight beers.

"I was drunk, but I wasn't drunk drunk."

"At what stage would you get drunk then?" Enns asked Yaworek. "After you drank fifteen or twenty beer?"

"About twenty-four."

"Pardon?" the startled judge asked.

"About twenty-four. At least."

Enns was incredulous. "On these many trips that you say you take to Winnipeg, do you sometimes drive yourself?"

"No, I have no licence."

That's why Yaworek and his pals had driven to Winnipeg that night. Yaworek was hoping to get his suspended licence back the next day. Enns wasn't aware of this, but Ken Dowson had run a check on Yaworek's background and his pal Randy Houston's as the friends would find out when they finished testifying. Jeff Funnell was standing outside the courtroom during a break and saw what happened. Later, after Enns delivered his findings at the end of May, Funnell wrote a letter to the editor of the *Free Press* describing the scene.

During the hearings I had the unfortunate opportunity to witness first hand police harassment of the Natives testifying. Larry Yaworek, Linda Morisette and Randy Houston had just finished stating under oath that they had clearly seen a police officer run across the path of their car brandishing a revolver. They were precise about the fact it was a gun and not a radio. After their testimony, court was recessed for a break and I went out in the lobby for a cigarette. Mr. Yaworek, Miss Morisette and Mr. Houston were quietly sitting on a bench while representatives of the police force were badgering and laughing at them.

"You couldn't see anything, you were so drunk. You could see a gun but not whether the officer was male or female." The three remained composed. I was already uncomfortable about this when suddenly two uniformed police officers walked up and arrested one witness. My mind reeled. I felt I must be in a different country to witness police coming into a courthouse and brazenly arresting a witness. Miss Morisette and Mr. Yaworek appeared visibly upset that their friend had been taken away. I found out that he had been arrested for [ninety-nine dollars in parking tickets]. The police had chosen to enforce the law, right at that time, in the courthouse. This can only be perceived as an intimidation tactic. It was a childish display of power . . .

After lunch, the last of the scheduled fifty witnesses took the stand. Harry Williams, a twenty-five-year member of the Winnipeg department, had taken Cross's seven-page statement on March 9, beginning two hours after Harper was pronounced dead. Later that morning Williams had seized the bloody uniform pants from the shaken constable. Williams was still at the station at 1 p.m. when Darryl Sterdan brought in Harper's broken glasses. Williams described what he saw when he first met Cross that night at the police station.

"When I first approached him – I didn't know Constable Cross prior to this – he seemed to be agitated, like very pale, as if he was in shock. Very concerned at what was going on about him, and excited or accelerated."

Cross had asked police association president Norm Wickdahl to be with him in the room rather than a lawyer. "At one point during the statement," Williams continued, "I noticed he was rubbing the palm of his right hand and I asked to see his hand and I noticed from the web of the right hand, between the thumb and the hand across the outside, a black mark which I identified in my mind as blow-by from a revolver cylinder."

To Williams, the position of the blow-by on Cross's palm appeared to corroborate Cross's recollection of where his hands were when the .38 discharged. He explained: "Well, I would take it from the mark on his hand and from his demonstration that his right hand was around the front of the gun."

Williams used his own hands to demonstrate. As the detective understood it, Cross had his right hand across the six-chamber cylinder, while his left hand held the pistol grip. His left index finger was in the trigger.

Morton asked if Williams made any other observation about Cross that morning. He had, and to Williams it was further evidence that verified Cross's account. "I noticed the right inside leg, at the knee, had a large amount of blood staining, and both legs, to the knee."

The left leg – which Cross said was on Harper's chest when the gun discharged – was splattered with dried blood, Williams testified. "Just small droplets of blood, from the top of the socks, which had rolled down or slid down his leg, to about two inches above the top of his boot. And the right leg was stained, like a wiping stain, as if the blood had gone through the cloth."

When Williams started to describe how Cross had got down on his back to demonstrate his position during the shooting, Enns had a surprise. He wanted to recall Cross for a re-enactment. The judge made one more ruling. Cross would demonstrate alone, no one would play the role of J.J. Harper.

At this point, Morton could have said, but didn't, that a week after the shooting, Williams had watched his partner, Cal Osborne, and Cross re-enact the struggle over the revolver in front of a video camera. It had taken four rehearsals to get it right. One minute and thirty-three seconds had elapsed between the radio report that Pruden was in custody and the time Cross clicked on his portable radio to report the shooting and immediately clicked it off again. But from the re-enactment of the struggle on the videotape, the police esti-mated only twenty-eight seconds passed between Cross first con-fronting Harper and the moment the gun discharged.

On the video, Cross is sitting up on the floor, in a tug-of-war over his service revolver, and Osborne is standing over him. At one point Cross appears to cock the double-action Smith & Wesson. But the inquest never saw that. During the pretrial disclosure Morton did not mention the existence of the videotape to Pollock or Enns. What's more, he had instructed Williams not to mention it during his testimony at the inquest.

Pollock made one last request of Enns. "I think we should hear from Chief Stephen," Pollock said. "He's the senior officer in charge of the investigation."

"No he's not," said Morton.

Enns refused to call Stephen, adding that he could still be called by the Aboriginal Justice Inquiry.

"Subject to the availability of Constable Cross," Enns said, "we will adjourn until tomorrow at 10 a.m."

23

"I TRIED TO TELL THE TRUTH."

On the final day of testimony, Cross arrived at the court with Al McGregor. The lead counsel for the Winnipeg Police Association hadn't been in court the day before, but he knew that today Cross would be asked to demonstrate what had happened in his struggle with Harper, and he was concerned. He didn't want Cross to be required to get down on the floor to re-enact the incident.

"I'm just concerned it might be somewhat demeaning to the witness to take that kind of position," McGregor told Enns.

The judge assured McGregor that wasn't his intent. McGregor also wanted it understood that there would be no cross-examination by Harvey Pollock, although he didn't identify him by name. Enns told him, "The total questioning will be from me. There will be no questioning by counsel at all."

This made Pollock angry, and he wanted it on the record.

"I had not completed my cross-examination of Mr. Cross when I asked him to demonstrate what happened."

Enns noted Pollock's concern, then he called a brief recess so Cross could put on a holster, a police issue .38, and the jacket he'd worn the night of the shooting.

Then Enns directed Cross's attention to the street map, set up on an easel, that showed the area of the foot chase. A circled "C" marked the place on the sidewalk where Harper's body was found. Gordon

Sinclair and Heidi Graham took seats in the jury box to get a better look. Enns asked Cross to indicate on the map where he was walking when he encountered Harper.

Cross pointed to between 1238 and 1250 Logan, where he'd cut through from the alley to the front of the houses, and then across Logan to the opposite sidewalk.

"I angled across northwest," Cross said.

"And while you were doing that, where, in connection with the letter 'C,' did you first approximately see Mr. Harper?" asked Enns.

"Oh, twenty-five, thirty feet west of that."

"Walking in an easterly direction on the north sidewalk?"

"That's correct."

"So if you both continued in a straight path, without changing paths, you were actually meeting. You facing his right side and front. Is that correct?"

"That's correct."

Then Cross went through his story again, to the point at which he fell backwards.

"All right," Enns said. "Assume, as best you can, the position you ended up in as you fell backwards."

Cross positioned himself on the floor, half sitting up. He flexed his left knee and raised his foot, as if it were on Harper's chest as the big Indian stood, bent over from the waist, leaning on the prone police officer.

"And then what happened?"

"The gun came out."

Then Cross showed Enns how he was holding the gun, and the judge described it for the record.

"Indicating with your right hand over the cylinder and –" Enns stopped. Cross had his left hand on the cylinder, but Williams had seen the blow-by on Cross's right hand. The judge quickly corrected himself. "And your left hand on the cylinder?"

"My left hand," Cross confirmed.

"Your left hand on the cylinder?" Enns asked again.

"Right." Cross said he had grabbed what he could of the gun to keep Harper from taking it.

"Where were Mr. Harper's hands?"

"As best I can remember, right at that specific time, one hand on the butt and one on the barrel. You're talking about something that happened in a split second ... I imagine during the course of the struggle for the revolver, hands were all over. I can't pinpoint exactly. All I remember, he had a hand there," Cross said pointing to the butt, "and one up here . . ."

"Your hands and his hands were more or less touching each other's all the while," Enns surmised.

"Yes," Cross agreed.

That revelation made the failure to take fingernail scrapings from Harper and Cross all the more glaring, Sinclair realized.

"Can you explain why, if I understand rightly, you fell so suddenly, so quickly?" Enns asked. "You say he turned, put his hands on your shoulders. You were already in the act of falling, is that correct?"

"He shoved me. I wasn't expecting to be shoved to the ground."

"He was about your height, I presume?"

"I think he was about my height, yes. I had no reason to expect that he – a physical confrontation. I wasn't braced for anything like that."

Enns turned to the mystery of how the gun discharged.

"Can you describe once again how you best recollect the trigger actually being activated?"

Cross began to demonstrate the way he was pulling and Harper was yanking. Then he said, "I don't remember. Like it takes a certain amount [of force] to pull it. I don't remember making a conscious effort pulling the trigger, or anything like that. It's just the both of us are like that and then a bang and a flash. I keep saying it. It was a second. It was the briefest amount of time."

Enns asked how easily the revolver could be pulled out by someone standing in front of a police officer, then paused briefly to check his notes.

"Do you recall any movement or anything to do in the course of his pushing you, or thereafter, about Mr. Harper's glasses?"

"Yes. As I was falling down, I swung out. I remember hitting his glasses and knocking them to the side."

Instead of asking Cross how he could fall, hold onto the sleeves of Mr. Harper's jacket, and swipe at his face with enough force to knock his glasses off, all at the same time, Enns wanted clarification of Harper's position once Cross was on the ground.

"Are you saying, then, that Mr. Harper was in a position somewhat over your body when the loud flash occurred, not upright at the time?"

"He was bent over at the waist over top of me."

"What were his actions, as best you can recall, immediately after the flash, or the gunshot?"

"He stood up and then backed up about two or three feet."

"And you told us earlier, that after the shooting, the gun was only in your hand?"

"Yes," Cross said.

Enns seemed to be zeroing in.

"And your hand was approximate to the trigger and butt, so that it ended up in a natural position to hold the revolver?"

"No."

"How did you end up holding the revolver immediately after if it was in an unnatural position? Can you demonstrate that to me?"

"I can't," Cross said. "I remember struggling for the gun and having my hands in this position." Cross was holding the gun with both hands around the cylinder.

"Yes?" Enns said.

"Immediately afterwards, I don't know. My next recollection is having the gun in this hand "– the gun was in his right hand – "just holding it down at my side."

Enns never did ask Cross the obvious question: How, if Harper had drawn the gun from Cross's holster, did the barrel end up pointing at his chest, or, conversely, how did Cross get his hands on the butt end?

Enns was finished with Cross. But McGregor wasn't finished with

Enns. At the time Sinclair didn't see the significance of McGregor's remarks. The police counsel was arguing over something he had spoken about in chambers with Enns, something to do with "other evidence" that might help corroborate Cross's story because it would "show a temperament." But Enns had ruled the subject matter too prejudicial.

"I would humbly suggest to this court," said McGregor, "that the only prejudice that flows from the non-entry of those reports and those events, the last of which was as late as August of 1987, goes toward Constable Cross and no one else. He is the one that is being prejudiced by those, if the reports and the supporting evidence are not going in."

Pollock stood up. "My learned friend is now putting in evidence before you, Your Honour, the thing that we talked about in chambers that we were not to be referring to, and I think that's unfair."

"I will go no further on that point," McGregor said.

"You've done it already," Pollock snapped.

"I've been learning from my learned friend over the last three weeks," McGregor retorted.

Enns tried to wrap up the inquest on a civil note.

"I thank all counsel for their assistance in this difficult inquiry."

Pollock had one last question. Did the judge want closing arguments? But evidently Enns had heard enough arguing.

"I've decided against submissions and arguments. Thank you. That concludes the inquest."

On the same day Enns concluded hearing evidence at the inquest, another case was being heard down the hall. Two Indians, Garry Bunn and Gordon Ross, had been charged with the murder of a taxi driver. Minutes before their trial was to start, Richard Beamish, a young lawyer who was assisting the renowned Winnipeg defence counsel Hersh Wolch, was standing in the hall outside the courtroom. Beamish was talking to one of the detectives who had arrested Bunn and Ross. It was Ken Dowson, the cop who had accompanied RCMP Sergeant

Wes Border when he interviewed Morisette, Houston, and Yaworek.

"You've got the wrong guy," Beamish told Dowson, who just laughed. But minutes later, something happened to suggest Beamish was right. The star witness, Virginia Cook, was supposed to describe how, two years earlier, she had seen Bunn and her then-boyfriend, Ross, murder taxi driver Gurnam Singh Dhaliwal. In the witness box, Cook haltingly began to tell the story in her own words. It was a night in early April 1986. They all got into the cab together. Bunn and Ross were saying something to each other in Ojibway or Sioux. She wasn't sure which. Cook paused. Crown Attorney Jack Montgomery urged her to continue and she began again. Her boyfriend, Ross, plunged a knife into . . .

Cook stopped again and she bowed her head.

"Are you lying to the jury?" Montgomery asked, his voice rising.

"Yes," Cook said.

"Why?"

"I don't know. I wasn't there. I don't care if I have to go to jail, I will," she cried, weeping.

"Why are you lying?"

"I tried to tell the truth. But they wouldn't let me."

"Who?"

"The detectives."

"Why did you lie to the detectives?"

"I told them I didn't know anything about it, but they kept on bugging me. The cop kicked the door open."

"Which cop?"

"The one in Pine Falls."

Beamish had been right. The charges against Bunn and Ross were stayed, and a young white man on crutches was led out of the courtroom by the police. Midway through Cook's testimony she had been asked if she'd ever seen the man on crutches before. She hadn't. Outside the courtroom reporters wanted answers from Wolch. He explained to the microphones and wagging pens that the police had fingerprint and other evidence against someone else, the young white man on crutches. But they had disregarded that evidence and had pursued Bunn and Ross, charging the pair and keeping them in custody. As the scrum of reporters listened, Dowson walked out of the courtroom. Beamish watched him coming. Neither man spoke. But as the big cop passed, he shoved his shoulder into Beamish, like a tight end brush-blocking a corner linebacker.

"Did you see that?" Beamish asked Wolch as Dowson walked away. "What an asshole."

Less than two weeks later, on May 2, Dowson addressed an internal report to Herb Stephen. He was writing in anticipation of Enns making recommendations about the police investigation. The two-and-a-half page report was captioned "Investigative Procedures Officer-Related Shooting Incidents." It began:

> I respectfully submit for your information and attention, the following report, relative to the captioned subject. On 88 04 05, the writer and Staff Sergeant R. Keatinge, #564/23 were seconded to the Special Prosecutions Branch of the Attorney General's Department at the request of Senior Crown Attorney W.W. Morton, Q.C., to assist in the J.J. Harper Fatality Inquiry.
>
> As you are well aware, during the course of this much publicized inquiry, the Police Department was taken to task, albeit sometimes unjustly, for the manner in which the initial investigation was conducted, as well as the manner in which certain decisions were arrived at in terms of the processing of certain exhibits.
>
> With respect to certain of the evidence, I myself, as well as Staff Sergeant Keatinge, agreed that perhaps some criticism was warranted. The most glaring example, you will recall, dealt with the decision made at the time not to fingerprint the weapon issued to Constable R. Cross. During those initial days of the inquiry, which dealt chiefly with police evidence, other areas of concern arose in

terms of procedures followed at the onset of, and during, the early stages of the investigation. For the sake of brevity, I will list some of the more obvious in point form:
– Officer's handgun and holster not printed.
– Handgun not photographed prior to any forensic examination.
– No test available (in Canada) to test hands and/or clothing for gunpowder residue.
– Clothing from victim not present for autopsy.
– Incomplete residential canvass during the first day of investigation.
– Incomplete scene examination.

Dowson went on to say a homicide team should have been called out to assist at the scene, but police terms of reference on officer-related shootings were too restrictive. He said a new section should be added to the procedural manual. "Such a section would remove any ambiguity as to the duties of those attending such a scene," he said, "and hopefully prevent our Department from being subjected to the type of negative media criticism which arose during the J.J. Harper Fatality Inquiry."

Dowson ended his report: "I will be attending the conclusion of the inquiry on 88 05 26. I would assume that we are not in a position to submit any proposals until after that date."

—

24

"Why don't you shoot me?"

On May 26, a month after Gary Filmon and his Progressive Conservatives had won a minority government and Attorney General Vic Schroeder had lost his seat, Judge John Enns reconvened the inquest to present his findings. Gordon Sinclair looked around Courtroom

230 and saw that all the familiar faces and principal players were there, all but one. Robert Cross hadn't shown up. Sinclair took a seat beside Heidi Graham and glanced around the gallery. Behind him, a few rows up, there was one person he hadn't seen in court before. It was Lois Harper.

Enns entered the courtroom and, after declaring his frustration at attempting to conduct a fair and open inquest within what he saw as the limits of the act, he got to his conclusions.

When Enns was halfway through the twenty-three page report, Heidi Graham leaned over and whispered to Sinclair, "He's coming down on the police side on everything."

"The following factors," Enns said, "have led me to the conclusion that both the allegations of racial slurs and the allegations of drawn revolvers are not credible."

He went on to give nine reasons for his conclusion, which boiled down to two. All the police had told the truth and none of the Native witnesses was credible.

Enns mocked Pruden's account of a police officer holding his revolver with both hands as he pointed it at him in the back lane. Unaware that police are trained to hold their revolvers exactly the way Pruden demonstrated, Enns dismissed the claim as being "more reminiscent of a TV police show than reality." He also dismissed the testimony of Morisette, Houston, and Yaworek, suggesting that they had come forward with their stories about seeing an officer with his gun out because of what they had learned from the media.

He went on to cite the evidence that supported Cross's story, from the blood on his uniform and left boot that the constable said was on Harper's chest, to the quotes his fellow officers had recorded in their notebooks that supported Cross's account.

As for the discrepancy about the colour of Pruden's jacket, Enns found it immaterial to Cross's search for a second suspect.

"Whatever description he may have heard on his hand-held radio," Enns said, "would not change his own recollection of the fleeing suspect seen only minutes earlier."

As the judge spoke, police association lawyer Marty Minuk glanced back over his shoulder at Sinclair and gave him a smug smile.

Enns had only two quibbles with the police conduct that night. The service revolver should have been fingerprinted, and the washing down of the scene before daylight had been a bit hasty.

"In conclusion," he said, "despite certain shortcomings in the area of police investigation, it is my view that the shooting occurred as a result of the deceased pushing down the officer and then attempting to take his revolver. The officer's attempt to keep control of his gun is justified and the ensuing shooting I find to be accidental. I therefore exonerate Constable Cross."

His conclusion was summarized in a different way by the Aboriginal community: the white-haired judge had believed all of the white cops, but none of the Native witnesses.

Sinclair turned to look at Lois Harper. Her arms were folded tight across her chest, and she was staring straight at Judge Enns with a look as fixed and cold as the courtroom's marble walls.

There were three recommendations, only one of which involved the police department and the Aboriginal community: "In view of the obvious distrust displayed by many members of Winnipeg's Native community towards the Winnipeg Police Department, that the City of Winnipeg vigorously pursue a program of recruiting minorities to the police department."

Lois Harper was already pushing through an exit door to a side stairway when Gordon Sinclair caught up to her. He asked how she felt about the decision.

"Very disappointed," she said. Then she began to weep, and the heavy stairway door closed behind her.

J.J. Harper's stepbrother, Harry Wood, was bitter: "You kill a dog and the Humane Society is up in arms. You kill an Indian, what happens?"

The sound of a party and the smell of Chinese food coming from the boardroom lured Ellen Gordon. The young criminal lawyer was on her way to her office at the firm of Simkin Gallagher when she chanced by the inquest victory party in the room across from Al McGregor's office, with the neon "Al's Bar" sign that a grateful client had given him. Gordon was twenty-nine, petite, with a husky voice and a little girl's smile. Ellen had chanced into law the way she happened on the inquest celebration. She followed the sound of a party when a bunch of her arts faculty friends were accepted into law school. Ellen ended up practising criminal law in part because she had a soft spot for petty crooks and handsome cops. There were lots of good-looking cops at McGregor's party. Sergeants Dave Shipman and Ron Morin were there, the storied homicide team that had taken Allan's statement. Randy Hampton, the cop Pruden claimed had pointed his gun at him in the back alley, was seated at the boardroom table. Hampton's partner, Bill Isaac, was missing, though, because Hampton was doing a stint in plain clothes. His new partner, a veteran cop, was getting drunker, louder, and more obnoxious as the party progressed. Ellen's guard went up when she noticed a stocky young blond cop seated at the boardroom table. As a Jew she was wary of men who looked very Aryan. At the time she didn't know she had just had her first glimpse of Butch Eakin.

Curiously, Cross, who should have been the guest of honour, wasn't there. Ellen noticed Kathy Hodgins and she recognized Rex Keatinge, the sergeant who sat through the inquest taking notes for his daily reports to Herb Stephen. Ellen sat down between Keatinge and the detective from the Bunn and Ross murder trial, Ken Dowson. Ellen loved the guy like a brother as she later told Sinclair. She liked everything about Ken Dowson: his intelligence, his sense of humour, and his looks. She even had snapshots of him in her desk drawer.

There were more than a dozen cops and lawyers at the party when Dowson and Shipman decided to borrow McGregor's scooter and run time trials up and down the halls. Not long after, the mood of the party abruptly changed. Hampton's new partner was getting even louder, and at one point he made an anti-Semitic remark that prompted a Jewish lawyer named Kerry Pearlman to leave. Others

around the table told the drunk detective to shut up. The next thing
Ellen knew, his service revolver was on the table and he was offering
an open invitation.

"Why don't you shoot me?" he asked.

Ellen was tempted. "I will shoot you," she said. "And no one will
charge me." She turned to Dowson. "You won't, will you Ken?"

"No," he said.

Hampton snatched the revolver off the table and unloaded it.
Randy Hampton with a gun in his hand at the inquest victory party.
The irony was lost on those present. As for Cross, he had his own little
party the next day.

<hr/>

25

"WHO IS EVER GOING TO FIND OUT?"

The morning after Judge Enns delivered his report, a good-looking
scholarly man in his early thirties flicked on the TV in his Winnipeg
hotel room. "Canada AM" was on, and Herb Stephen and the
spokesperson for the Island Lake Tribal Council, Joe Guy Wood, were
being interviewed. Stephen dismissed any notion of problems
between the Winnipeg police department and the city's Native population. Wood disagreed. "The judge says there is no racism. He's living
in a dream world. The report is a whitewash."

Don Gillmor, a freelance writer and contributing editor to
Saturday Night magazine who was in town to interview Robert Cross,
was dismayed by Stephen's attitude and made note of the conversation.

As teenagers, Cross and Gillmor had gone to the same school.
Gillmor now lived in Montreal, and the last time he had seen Cross
was in 1985. He had been in Winnipeg for his sister's graduation when
he ran into Cross at a dinner party. Cross still had the moustache he

had grown as a teenager. He was married and had been with the police department for a year. Cross was happy being a cop, he told Gillmor. He enjoyed the towel-snapping camaraderie. Over dinner, when Gillmor pushed him for details about what it was like to be a cop – was it dangerous, boring? – Cross finally said, "Stop, or I'll shoot."

When Gillmor heard about the shooting of J.J. Harper, he thought it would make a good magazine piece. He could draw on his boyhood memories in his portrait of Cross.

As teens one summer, they had gone looking for a place to buy beer in Cross's Vauxhall Viva and had come across blood on a side-walk and two unconscious Natives near the Occidental Hotel. Cross had got out of the car to buy the beer. When he returned, they had headed home along the Pembina Highway, turning up the Rolling Stones on the tape deck, opening the cold beer, driving with one arm out the window, and imitating Indian accents.

Now Gillmor wanted to explore in writing how someone who grew up in an innocent middle-class neighbourhood could wind up in a life-and-death struggle with an Indian man roughly his own age.

In early May, Gillmor had phoned Cross. They talked briefly about the shooting and what Cross had been doing since and then Gillmor tried to persuade his boyhood pal to do an interview. Cross reluctantly agreed, on the condition that Gillmor wouldn't identify him as a source.

After Gillmor's call, Cross had confided to his neighbour Sheila Elliot that he was going to do a magazine interview with an old friend from junior high days. Since the shooting Cross had been talking a lot more to Sheila.

"Do you think this is a smart move at this time?" Sheila asked.

"Who is ever going to find out it was me?" Cross replied.

It was afternoon by the time Gillmor arrived at Cross's house in a typical 1980s subdivision. Over Coors Light in the backyard, the two old school friends reminisced for a while about what had happened to people they had gone to junior high with in Fort Garry. As the twins romped around the yard, Cross talked about his second marriage, and the break-up of his first. When they had finished with the old days, Gillmor eased into the questions for his story. Cross said he thought he had always wanted to be a policeman, that he had found a job and a place where he belonged, but he didn't want to be a detective. He liked being in uniform.

The talk turned to the shooting and police work and the Native "situation" in general. Cross felt Judge Enns's report had resolved the Harper case, and that eventually the relationship between the police and the Natives would mend on its own. He had one complaint, though: the media weren't treating him fairly. There seemed to be some biases, he told Gillmor.

By the time Gillmor left that afternoon he thought Cross seemed almost euphoric. The inquest was behind him, he would be able to get on with his life again. It was as if he'd forgotten that the Aboriginal Justice Inquiry had yet to happen. Or that he still faced a complaint with the Law Enforcement Review Agency that had been filed by Harper's half-brother, Harry Wood. That very day, the new Tory government had appointed a new LERA commissioner, Herb Stephen's old partner, Des DePourcq.

——
26

"THE USUAL EXCELLENT PROCEDURES."

On June 9, two weeks after Enns delivered his report, Diane Eastwood went to see Dr. Danny Globerman, who practised psychiatry at the hospital where she worked. Diane was feeling overwhelmed by first the birth of Stephen two months earlier, then the three-week inquest, and now the prospect of more public scrutiny during the Aboriginal Justice Inquiry. And through all of this she had to look after the children and be supportive of a husband who was stressed out, drinking excessively, and who had given her crabs when she was pregnant. It was all too much. Later, Globerman wrote a report on his first session with Diane:

> She presented as a well groomed woman appearing her stated age, who had no past psychiatric history. She informed me that she was depressed and was "crying all the time," as well as having a feeling like she wanted to "crawl in a hole and die." She had some similar feelings in September of 1987, and this occurred largely in the context of adjusting to the change in her and her husband's lives which came as a result of the birth of their twins, which were approximately 6 months old at that point in time. These mood swings in September 1987 manifested themselves by frequent arguments with her husband, Rob, but they settled down over time until the birth of their third child . . .

After the initial visit Diane was prescribed trimipramine and placed on disability.

"Her mood did not improve in spite of gradual increments in the dosage," Globerman wrote, "and she developed suicidal ideation." Diane was having a hard time coping with three children under the age of two and was frequently enraged by her husband's behaviour in the wake of the inquest. He wasn't helping much with the kids and she found it difficult to find the energy to support him emotionally. This aggravated Cross's own anger and frustration and he sought refuge in drink.

Five years later, Diane recalled those dark days. "I was trying to survive on my own with post-partum depression and three little babies. The most important person at the time was me."

She remembered how she had introduced herself to Globerman on that first visit: "My husband's the one who shot J.J. Harper."

"You've got a lot on your plate," the doctor replied. But Diane didn't remember his telling her his connection to the case, that his father-in-law was Harvey Pollock. In early August, Globerman diagnosed her with a major post-partum depression and admitted her to hospital.

Two weeks after Enns released his report, Bill Morton met with Herb Stephen and his executive at the Public Safety Building. Late that afternoon, Morton walked back to his office, and wrote a note to file.

> Met this afternoon at 2:00 p.m. with Chief Constable Stephen, Deputy Chiefs [John] Urchenko, [Paul] Johnston, [Stan] Scarr. We discussed the general conduct of the fatality inquiry vis a vis the City of Winnipeg Police Department and his officers. We also discussed the findings of His Honour Provincial Judge J.J. Enns as they directly affected the City of Winnipeg Police Department. I was satisfied from discussions that the Chief Constable was fully cognizant of the criticism that had been leveled at the Police Department both during the inquiry and as a result of the findings by Chief Provincial Judge Enns.

Morton was unaware of Ken Dowson's May 2 report to the chief that had acknowledged the failings of the Harper investigation. This was apparent when Morton went on to deal with the criticism.

First was the failure to fingerprint the gun. The meeting felt that proper procedures had been followed.

The second criticism had centred on the fact that Harper's glasses had been found by a newspaper reporter. Even though Stephen admitted his department was responsible for not finding the glasses, Morton still thought it necessary to add that he thought the police had done a thorough job.

Next was the criticism that the scene had been washed down "somewhat hastily." Again, Morton wrote that he felt proper procedures had been followed before the area was cleaned.

There was also the criticism that the police had not conducted the canvass for witnesses as promptly as they should have. Once again, Morton wrote that he'd been satisfied "that the usual excellent procedures were used to speak to all persons in the neighbourhood who may have been in a position to see or hear anything." He went on to note that the people Harper had been with earlier that evening had not come forward to talk to police.

Another area of concern was the poor relationship between the police and Natives. Morton wrote, "I am satisfied from my discussion with the Chief Constable that his Police Department is fully aware of the animosity that exists between the Native population and the City of Winnipeg Police Department. All expressed a mutual concern that high standards not be set aside in the recruitment of any new personnel."

The last area of concern was the testimony that some officers that night had made "derogatory remarks" to the two Native suspects and that they had been seen with guns drawn. Morton wrote, "It was unfortunate that these witnesses had made the comments that they had as it seemed to support the view of the animosity between the Native population and the City of Winnipeg Police Department."

Morton's memo went on for another page, including this entry: "It was generally agreed that in future any death caused by the actions of a City of Winnipeg Police Department Officer should be investigated at the level of a homicide investigation."

There was one more area of note: a reference to Harper being arrested twice under the Intoxicated Persons Detention Act, the information McGregor had been trying to bring out at the end of the inquest. "It appeared that the two incidents which involved Mr. Harper prior to his fatal shooting clearly indicated in my mind a predisposed attitude of Mr. Harper towards Police Officers, particularly when he was intoxicated."

Years later, Martin Pollock would characterize the Crown's relationship with the police during the Harper inquest. "Morton," he said, "was a cop without a badge."

27

"I ALMOST SHOT ANOTHER ONE."

Typically, police officers involved in the shooting of a citizen are back to a normal working, social, and family life within five months, at least according to a survey of fifty-six RCMP officers that had been completed just two years earlier. But Robert Cross wasn't typical. Almost six months after the Harper shooting, on August 23, 1988, Cross, carrying a gun in a grocery bag, walked into the psychiatric department where Diane had been a patient for the past three weeks. He wasn't there to see her. He had an appointment with his own psychiatrist.

Cross had been under enormous stress even though the inquest had cleared him. It hadn't helped that Diane's hospitalization left him alone to look after their three children. He was a mess, emotionally and physically. He had lost twenty pounds, he was suffering from chronic diarrhea and constant headaches, and his eyes twitched intermittently, the way spent fluorescent bulbs flicker just before they burn out. At work he was having trouble with his memory and concentration. Then there were the almost daily panic attacks during which he felt dizzy, his heart raced, and his breathing quickened. Sometimes he fainted. His right hand shook so badly he couldn't write.

Cross had come to the hospital for something to make it all go away. He had already found a home remedy for his insomnia: booze. He had prescribed himself four or five drinks, taken before bed, a total of three bottles of liquor a week. But sleep wasn't always an escape. Sometimes the panic attacks tracked him to a blurred and frightening netherworld of nightmares, where he was being chased and killed. That's why, when he was off duty, he carried his revolver in a plastic bag, the way department store security guards conceal their two-way radios.

Cross's appointment was with Dr. Linda Loewen, to whom he had been referred by Diane's psychiatrist, Danny Globerman. At this first session, Cross denied feeling depressed, but said his moods constantly swung from anger to sad to tearful. Loewen prescribed Clonazepam to relieve his anxiety and block the panic attacks. He was to return the following week for the second of what would be many sessions with Loewen over the next two years. After that first session she wrote:

> He denied any homicidal or suicidal ideation. There were no delusions. He did express exceedingly high expectations. He feels his inability to cope at this time is a failure. He has a "macho" self image and sees any emotional problems as evidence of weakness ...
>
> Mr. Cross described three areas of particular stress, including his job, his wife's absence from the home because of a depression, and the care of his children. Mr. Cross is the policeman who shot and killed Mr. J.J. Harper in the line of duty. There was, however, an inquiry into his behaviour and Mr. Harper's death. Mr. Cross was cleared of any negligence, but the Native community was not satisfied with this judgment. Mr. Cross states that they have, in fact, a contract on his life. His house is under surveillance, he carries a weapon at all times, and he is escorted to and from work. This constant threat of harm to himself or to his family has been a tremendous stress on Mr. Cross. He stated that his wife has been unable to appreciate this stress or to support him through these difficulties in his work ...
>
> Mr. Cross has great difficulty understanding mental illness and is somewhat unsympathetic toward her. He sees her as uncaring, unsupportive and selfish. He complains that she is uninterested in sex and has no concern for the welfare of him or their children.

Loewen then made the first diagnosis of Robert Cross's emotional problems.

> I feel that Mr. Cross is suffering from severe anxiety, which includes some symptoms of panic disorder, as well as some symptoms of post traumatic stress disorder. In addition he is extremely angry at the Native population, at his wife, and at himself. He is developing maladaptive coping strategies, in particular his increased

alcohol intake. I discussed possible interventions with Mr. Cross, including his taking a leave of absence from work, or his sending the children to stay with relatives for at least two weeks. He refused to consider either alternative and was quite hostile to my suggestions. He stated that what he really needed was a pill that could glue him together until his wife was discharged from hospital . . .

In passing, Loewen mentioned something else:

For the most part his judgment seems good, although he does admit to excessive use of force if he is provoked by a suspect . . .

Nearly three weeks later, on the day Diane was released from Victoria General, Robert Cross saw his neighbour Sheila Elliot in her driveway and called her over, the way he had the day after the Harper shooting. While Diane was in the hospital, Cross had spent a lot of time talking to Sheila, confiding in her. Now he had more to tell her. Something had happened on his shift the night before. He and Kathryn Hodgins had been involved in a car chase that had ended with three people being arrested. The people they apprehended had been drinking, but they were neither armed nor dangerous. Later, a fellow officer who witnessed what happened testified that Cross pulled his service revolver and pointed it at the head of one of the passengers. Bob Cross's version of the incident, as Sheila Elliot remembered it, was more revealing:

"I almost shot another one."

28

"ELEVEN YEARS OLD."

Gordon Sinclair knew nothing of Cross's emotional and marital problems in the fall of 1988, although Al McGregor of the Winnipeg Police Association unintentionally offered a picture of them to the press. The police association and the city were locked in an acrimonious arbitration hearing over a new contract, and McGregor was portraying the association's membership as underpaid, overworked, and stressed out. A psychologist who counselled police officers went further. He said the force was being affected by growing drug and alcohol abuse problems, family breakdown, divorce, and extramarital affairs.

At about the time the cops were trashing their public image, a letter arrived in Sinclair's mail that made the police problems seem trivial by comparison. The letter was about the reality of Native despair, but it took the issue out of the realm of social work files, prison ratios, and Statistics Canada bulletins and put it in a context that meant something to a white, middle-aged, middle-class parent like him. It prompted Sinclair to start writing a column. First, he composed the headline. It was just three words: "ELEVEN YEARS OLD."

Sinclair, using a fictitious name and address for the boy, quoted the letter:

Sir:
Tuesday night young Matthew Redcloud of Apt 2, 361 Cumberland hanged himself. Matt was a little Native boy who was 11 years old.

I think this is an ideal case to illustrate the sad state of the Indian people in our community.

The letter writer, a family friend, said the boy read a lot about Indian traditions and customs.

Sinclair called the boy's mother. At first, as she relived the day it happened, the mother's voice was calm. Matt was home from school that day. He had been home, in fact, since the second day of school when he had a problem with a male teacher. Matt refused to say what.

In the afternoon Matt persuaded his mother to take him and his brother Craig, three, and sister Tanis, two, to the park, but they hadn't stayed long as it was cold. Matt didn't want to leave. That evening the mother went to an Alcoholics Anonymous meeting, leaving the boy to babysit his siblings. Before she left, he had hugged her and told her he loved her.

She got home around midnight and found Matt hanging in the closet with her best dress scarf wrapped around his neck. His face was blue. She touched him.

"He was cold. He was cold."

Sinclair's column concluded:

Apparently there was a string of circumstances that led to 11-year-old Matthew Redcloud taking his own life. But I wanted to know if being Native was the overriding reason. His mom thought so. "He hated being poor. He used to say, 'When I get a job I'm going to buy you the biggest car.'" I wonder, in his reading about North American Indians, if Matt ever came across the Manitoba Métis leader Louis Riel. In the 100 years since Riel was executed while fighting for Native self-determination and Native self-respect Canada has come a long way.

We don't hang Native men anymore. Now 11-year-old Native boys hang themselves.

29

"How do you wink at an Indian?"

Herb Stephen had kept a low profile since his appearance on "Canada AM" the day after Enns's verdict. But in early December he attended the St. Andrew's Society 118th annual dinner at the Westin Hotel. Stephen wanted the police department to be well represented. Earlier, he'd issued a memo confirming who would be sitting at which police tables. Among those on the list were John Campbell and Rex Keatinge. Conspicuously absent was Deputy Chief Paul Johnston. Unlike Stephen, Johnston wasn't a joiner of clubs and he wasn't a fan of pomp and circumstance. He would rather be up to his elbows in grease, rebuilding a car engine.

About that time the December issue of *Saturday Night* arrived on Gordon Sinclair's desk. Don Gillmor's article was inside. "The Shooting of J.J. Harper" gave new details about the case, some of them different from what Cross had told the inquest.

Gillmor reported that, after Harper refused to show his ID the first time, Cross had said " 'Well excuuuuuuuuuuse me,' . . . Steve-Martin-style, thinking it might break the ice."

That was relatively minor. But the more Sinclair read, the more disturbed he was by the new information. According to Gillmor, when the ambulance crew put Harper into the inflatable anti-shock trousers, which had the unintentional effect of forcing more blood out of the chest wound, one of the police officers at the scene had said, "That's right, bleed him dry."

The quote was unattributed. So was a racist joke that had made the rounds at the Public Safety Building after Harper's death: " 'How do you wink at an Indian?' The answer was the pantomimed pull of a trigger." It was the same joke that Guay, investigator for the medical examiner's office, said she heard at the autopsy on the morning Harper was shot.

Other parts of the article also stood out.

"When news that Rob Cross had shot a man reached those of us who had known him as a boy, there wasn't too much surprise. He had always had a knack for being in the middle of things.

"He is remembered as having a temper, as being a bit unpredictable..."

A few months before the shooting a mutual friend of Cross and Gillmor put a sharper point on the same sentiment. "There's one guy who shouldn't have a gun," he told Gillmor. Cross's boyhood friend remembered the time, in junior high, when Cross lay in wait with some pals outside school to beat up a teacher he didn't like. The episode ended with the teacher peering warily through a glass door with the principal beside him and the pack grudgingly dispersing.

There were no direct statements about the shooting in the article, but Gillmor quoted an anonymous Winnipeg police officer. "Harper was the author of his own demise," the cop said. "The Natives drink and they get in trouble. Blaming the police for their troubles is like an alcoholic blaming the liquor store for being open late."

In November 1988, just before *Saturday Night* hit the newsstands, James Harper had a stroke. The loss of his son, coupled with the strain of looking after his invalid wife, had been too much. Harper was evacuated to Winnipeg by air. On December 18, nine months after vowing that one day he would be with his son again, James Harper kept his promise. He was buried beside J.J. on the island near Wasagamack. But James Harper had died without ever having the chance he wanted to meet and forgive the police officer who had killed his son. By that time, though, it seemed that Cross had been absolved in another way. LERA commissioner Des DePourcq had dismissed Harry Wood's complaint against Cross. Martin Pollock had been given the Law Enforcement Review Agency file by his father, and now all he could do was file an appeal with the Manitoba Police Commission and wait for its decision.

30

"IT'S SUCH AN UNUSUAL REQUEST."

Some time in the late spring or early summer of the following year, a man wearing hospital greens walked into the Island 99 Food Store in suburban St. Boniface. It wasn't the first time the customer had dropped by. Victor Sorensen, the owner of the strip-mall convenience store, recognized him as a regular.

"I could see right away that he was drunk," Sorensen said later. The customer's breath smelled of liquor, and he was unsteady on his feet.

"He told me that he had had a tough day, that he had spent all day in surgery working on an accident victim. I think he said the patient had died. I just assumed he was a doctor. I remember him telling me he'd had such a tough day that he needed to stop for a drink on the way home, just to unwind."

Sorensen knew the "doctor's" name, because he used to take cheques from him. But he didn't realize who he really was until he saw his picture in the paper that fall. It was a photo of Constable Robert Cross.

Cross hadn't been able to work since the car chase in September 1988, when he'd bragged to Sheila Elliot that he'd almost shot another one. By the end of the year he was just trying to survive. He had been drinking heavily, he was feeling inadequate and useless, and his marriage was falling apart.

In February 1989, the Manitoba Police Commission overturned Des DePourcq's ruling and ordered LERA hearings into Cross's conduct on the night Harper was shot. Meanwhile, on the advice of Dr. Linda Loewen, the police had tried to ease him back to duty by having him work as a community-based policeman. He wouldn't have to respond to calls, all he had to do was patrol the neighbourhood, something that, under normal circumstances, he would be good at. But by the summer, Cross had stopped working again.

"He was not able to function in this limited protected role," a psychiatrist noted some years later, "and this approach was abandoned in July of '89."

When Gordon Sinclair arrived for work on Tuesday, July 4, a phone message was waiting for him from someone named Mike Elliot. Offhandedly Sinclair tossed the slip of paper on his desk. He was preoccupied that morning. The Winnipeg Police Association's lawyers Al McGregor and Marty Minuk were still setting up legal roadblocks in an attempt to stop the portion of the Aboriginal Justice Inquiry that would deal with how J.J. Harper had died. In June, when the Harper hearings had been scheduled to start, McGregor and Minuk had convinced the courts to declare the inquiry invalid because the authorizing legislation had been drafted in English only. Fixing that with a French translation of Bill 28 was easy enough. But then the inquiry attempted to subpoena twenty-four notebooks from the officers known to be involved in the Harper investigation. McGregor and Minuk filed another motion with the court. Anticipating the association's next move, the inquiry asked the Manitoba Court of Appeal for a ruling on whether it had the right to compel Robert Cross to testify. Until the court ruled on both issues, the Harper portion of the hearings was on hold.

The Winnipeg Senior Police Officers' Association, which represented the "white shirt," executive officers, was also busy after the long weekend. It, also, decided to fight the inquiry's demand to see the notebooks. Superintendent Lawrence Klippenstein, a tall, stiff-looking officer, acted as the association's spokesperson.

"It's such an unusual request," Klippenstein said, "it's hard to believe. It says you don't trust the policemen that were there."

But trust hadn't been the issue that had moved Aboriginal Justice Inquiry co-counsel Randy McNicol to ask for the notebooks. "I wanted to see what each of them had written independently about the event at the time and immediately after. That's all."

McNicol was a duck hunter, with the methodical, patient, personality that wading through water and hiding in tall marsh grass requires. The more the police resisted, the more determined McNicol became.

"I wasn't doing it because I was expecting any smoking gun and anything out of the usual or ordinary."

In the *Free Press* newsroom, it was nearly noon. Mike Elliot's message still lay unreturned on a corner of Gordon Sinclair's cluttered desk, and the phone was ringing. Sinclair picked it up. The woman on the other end was talking quickly, spewing words, the way people do when they're angry or agitated or just in a hurry to tell a story. She identified herself as Mike Elliot's sister. Mike Elliot, she said, lived next door to Robert Cross. Sinclair groped through the jumble on his desk to find a pen. Then he flipped over the phone message and began scribbling.

The sister said she was calling because Mike's wife, Sheila, and Cross had been drinking at the house that weekend and Mike had walked in and caught Cross on top of Sheila.

It was salacious stuff, Sinclair thought, but Cross's fooling around with a neighbour's wife wasn't something he would write about unless it had some relevance to the Harper case. And what possible link could there be?

Later that day, unbeknownst to Sinclair, Robert Cross was admitted to the Victoria General Hospital psychiatric ward. He had arrived at the hospital in tears, Dr. Linda Loewen noted in his file, his mind racing, and he was talking about committing suicide, shooting or asphyxiating himself.

Cross told Loewen what had happened with his next-door neighbour's wife. "His behavior had been inappropriate while drunk," Loewen wrote. "He was very ashamed of this incident."

Diane was at her parents' cabin in northwestern Ontario for the long weekend. When she returned, Cross was already at the hospital, and Mike immediately told her why.

"I just fell apart," Diane said years later. The same day she called Child and Family Services and asked to place the children in foster care. The twins weren't three yet, and Stephen was fifteen months. Diane stood on the front step as the van pulled away with her kids.

"I was crying and crying," she said. "I knew deep down it was best for them and me. I just couldn't cope."

It was autumn before the children returned.

Cross was still in hospital at the end of July, when the Manitoba Court of Appeal ruled that the inquiry could subpoena Cross and the notebooks. It looked as if the Harper hearings would finally begin in late August.

PART III

───✦───

THE SACRIFICE

The most common reactions to stress are anxiety and depression. The anxious person feels tense, nervous, fearful, restless and apprehensive. Anxiety usually occurs in anticipation of a stressful encounter. Depression, on the other hand, usually occurs after the occurrence of serious stressful experiences and involves feelings of loneliness, worthlessness, fatigue, blame and pessimism. Recognition and identification of emotional signals are the first steps to the coping process; otherwise, long-term personality reactions to stress, such as alcoholism, suicide, psychosis, chronic depression and similar problems, become a possibility.

– A. Daniel Yarmey, *Understanding Police and Police Work: Psychosocial Issues*

31

"WE'LL SEE."

The Harper hearings began, on August 21, 1989, nearly a full year after the start of the Manitoba Aboriginal Justice Inquiry (AJI).

The hearing room was in the basement of the Norquay Building, a provincial office tower opposite the Law Courts Building on York Avenue, It was a stark venue, with a low ceiling and the ambiance of a jailhouse cafeteria. Commissioners Murray Sinclair and Al Hamilton sat at a table covered in blue and white cloth, as if presiding over a hotel banquet, instead of a historic legal proceeding. To their right was a similarly draped table, where the witnesses would sit. The lawyers' tables and a simple lectern were lined up in front of rows of folding chairs that served as the public gallery. A local public access TV station had set up cameras so the proceedings could be televised live and taped for the public archives.

Gordon Sinclair was in the gallery. In a month, he and Athina would be getting married. He'd slipped the engagement ring on her finger as they cruised over Kenora at 30,000 feet on the way back to Winnipeg from a business trip to Toronto. It was his parents' wedding anniversary, and a flight attendant with whom Athina had gone to school broke open the champagne.

As he surveyed the crowd in the hearing room, the wedding was far from his mind. He noticed some familiar faces. John Campbell, an old friend, was there in his new role as Winnipeg Police Association president. Joe Guy Wood from the Island Lake Tribal Council was in the gallery. Most of the lawyers had familiar faces: Al McGregor and Marty Minuk for the police, Harvey and Martin Pollock for the Harpers, Doug Abra for the city, and Hersh Wolch, who was appearing for the Island Lake Tribal Council.

There were two lawyers Sinclair didn't recognize. Ruddy-faced Randy McNicol, the duck hunter with a scalpel-edged style of cross-examination, and his less flashy partner, Perry Schulman. McNicol and Schulman were co-counsel for the AJI, as they had been earlier throughout its community hearings and examination into Helen Betty Osborne's murder in The Pas.

The two commissioners, Al Hamilton and Murray Sinclair, were studies in contrast. Hamilton was thin with short, white hair, Sinclair burly with a long, black braid. Hamilton, associate chief justice of the Court of Queen's Bench, was two days shy of sixty-three, and near the end of his career on the bench. Sinclair was thirty-eight, and just beginning his as associate chief justice of the provincial court. Hamilton's father had been a judge, Frank Hamilton of the Juvenile Court. Sinclair's father, Henry, left young Murray and the rest of the family after his wife died. After working for a time as a miner, pulp cutter, and cook, Henry Sinclair ended up living the life of a drunk on Main Street. Murray Sinclair and his three siblings were brought up by their grandparents.

Hamilton looked straight and stern, just what a judge is supposed to look like. Sinclair also looked the part of a judge, but in a different way. There was an aura of authority about him that seemed to come from an inner peace. Murray Sinclair was a bright child, skipping grades 3 and 7. In high school he was named athlete of the year and was the only Aboriginal in his graduating class. But, although he was obviously a gifted student, teachers at Selkirk Collegiate suggested, because he was Aboriginal, that he take a trade at Red River Community College, as it cost less than going to university. He enrolled at the University of Manitoba, anyway, but dropped out within two years to look after his grandmother, who was in failing health. He went to work as a program director at the Selkirk Friendship Centre and by 1972 he was regional vice-president of the Manitoba Métis Federation. A year later Attorney General Howard Pawley, MLA for Selkirk, asked the twenty-two-year-old Sinclair to serve as his executive assistant. It was during this period that Sinclair became intrigued by law. Encouraged by Pawley,

Sinclair enrolled at the University of Manitoba. He graduated in 1979.

Murray Sinclair's initiation into private practice was indicative of why the Manitoba Aboriginal Justice Inquiry had been called. He had appeared in court one day with a white client who was wearing a business suit. The judge mistook Sinclair for the accused. By 1984, Sinclair was speaking out about the prejudice within the justice system, at a conference on Native alcohol and drug abuse, which is how his comments ended up on the front page under the headline: "Police prey on Natives, lawyer says."

Sinclair had told the conference that the justice system was oppressive and abusive for Indian people, whose crimes were usually impulsive and triggered by alcohol.

"You don't find a lot of Indian people convicted of drug trafficking or fraud," he said. "They are convicted because they are drunk," and they drank excessively because they had been alienated from their culture and its values. They also were more likely to be convicted, and more likely to be handed longer sentences than whites, because most were charged with summary offences for which they couldn't get legal aid. The result, Sinclair suggested, is that the police target Natives because the higher conviction rate makes the police look good.

Sinclair had been practising law for only nine years when he was appointed to the bench in early 1988. For a time he served as legal counsel for the Four Nations Confederacy. It was in that capacity that the young lawyer briefly met a young chief from northern Manitoba, John Joseph Harper.

In mid-August 1989, the Aboriginal Justice Inquiry announced that its hearings might be expanded to look at a trial that happened the same day the Harper inquest was ending. The commissioners were curious about how the police had come to charge Garry Bunn and Gordon Ross with the murder of a taxi driver. Hersh Wolch, who defended Gordon Ross, still remembered how his junior counsel, Richard Beamish, had been shoulder-shoved by Ken Dowson on the way out of the courtroom that day.

By now even the police department agreed that they had arrested the wrong men. Their new suspect, Christopher Glenn Grywinski, was the young white man on crutches whom the police had escorted into court the day Bunn and Ross walked. Since then Grywinski had written a letter to a Winnipeg TV station confessing to stabbing the taxi driver. The police report had shown all along that Grywinski's fingerprints were on the taxi and that the cabby's last call had been to the apartment block where Grywinski's sister lived. At Grywinski's trial a year later another taxi driver, Ravindar Singh Grewal, testified that he repeatedly told police they had the wrong men when Bunn and Ross were charged. Grewal had seen a white man driving the victim's stolen cab. Gordon Ross had been in jail for a year waiting trial. Wolch wasn't surprised when he heard about Grywinski's arrest, but he was disturbed. "I've got a guy here who's innocent and he's been branded a killer. I think there should be an inquiry into this." Wolch had another client who had been accused and, in that case, wrongfully convicted, of murder. It would be three more years before David Milgaard was released.

Ultimately, the commissioner decided not to look into the Bunn and Ross case because Grywinski still hadn't been tried.

As the Harper portion of the AJI opened on August 21, something was troubling Martin Pollock. Just before the first day's testimony began with questions about why the police hadn't fingerprinted Cross's revolver right away, Martin spoke to commission counsel Randy McNicol.

"Randy," Martin asked, "do you think there may be a phantom involved in this matter?"

McNicol knew what he meant. Was there a senior officer buried deep in the background who was responsible for covering up what had happened on Logan?

"We'll see," McNicol said.

32

"A RIGHTEOUS MAN."

On August 22, two days before Robert Cross was scheduled to testify, Al McGregor told the inquiry he wanted him to be excused. He said that appearing could do serious damage to Cross.

"J.J. Harper's family weren't the only ones to suffer since March 9, 1988," McGregor said, peering over the top of his glasses at Hamilton and Sinclair. "The documents I'm about to give you will show there has been a great deal of suffering on the part of Constable Cross and extensive suffering on the part of his wife."

The documents were psychiatric reports. By this time Cross had been out of hospital for three weeks, but his looming date with the inquiry had exacerbated his emotional problems. That was the opinion of Dr. Stanley Yarin, the province's chief forensic psychiatrist, who did an independent assessment for the inquiry. Yarin concluded that Cross's mental function was so impaired that he was incapable of giving coherent evidence and that appearing before the inquiry would likely trigger a "catastrophic," potentially life-threatening reaction.

"Mr. Cross demonstrates symptoms of severe anxiety," Yarin wrote. "He has prominent facial twitches, he stutters, and he is quite fidgety. His mood is labile, swinging precipitously from tears to nervous laughter. His cognitive thought processes are impaired. He is distractible, has poor concentration, and impaired memory. He frequently loses track of his thoughts in mid-sentence. He cannot touch on certain topics without trembling and breaking down in tears. There are major events for which he has no memory. For example, he was unable to give me a coherent account of the investigations related to the shooting which have already occurred. He had disturbed sleep, with frequent awakenings and nightmares in which he relives the shooting incident." Yarin also said the police officer was preoccupied with thoughts of suicide.

"Mr. Cross has not made any suicide attempts or gestures till this point, however his current state of hopelessness and helpless despair together with his impaired judgment and tendency to use alcohol excessively are all factors which create a high degree of suicidal risk."

Outside the inquiry, Harvey Pollock dismissed Yarin's report. "You can't hide behind a psychiatric report. Mr. Cross is no doubt suffering from the proceedings but it's a natural consequence of commissions and inquiries."

Joe Guy Wood said he felt for Cross and his family.

"But we want to get at the truth. It's all speculation at this point – maybe he's racked by guilt or maybe he's afraid – we don't know what it is."

"McGregor has been throwing a lot of blocks in the way," Wood reminded reporters, "this could be one of them."

During the following week, while Al Hamilton and Murray Sinclair were deciding whether Cross should testify, the inquiry heard from a number of witnesses who had appeared at the inquest. Allan was now a pudgy fifteen-year-old, but he still looked young for his age. Again he recounted hearing the "old man" cop instructing Cross to say the shooting was an accident. He described Cross sitting in the car telling Hodgins, "It happened so fast. I just pulled the trigger," and Hodgins blaming him for what happened and calling him a "blue-eyed fucking Indian." Allan also repeated that, just before Cross caught him, the cop slipped and fell, but he added a detail about what the cop did just as he was yelling for him to stop and falling.

"He was reaching for the back where his gun was, and that's when I stopped at the fence."

Allan mentioned another development. He had been seeing a therapist because he was having nightmares about the shooting, in which he would cry out in his sleep, "Don't shoot me."

There was something familiar about Melvin Pruden's reappearance a week later. Once again he didn't arrive on schedule, and again police arrested him, this time on a failure-to-appear court warrant still outstanding from the stolen car incident nearly a year and a half earlier. On August 28, 1989, he was finally sentenced for stealing the car. He received twenty-one days. The next day, when he took the stand, Pruden repeated his testimony about seeing a cop pointing a gun at him when he was in the lane and then being roughed up and called a "fucking Indian" as he was being arrested.

Next up after Allan was Detective Sergeant Harry Williams, who was raised with Natives from the Long Plain reserve, where his father taught school. Williams brought the police videotaped re-enactment of the shooting, which Crown Attorney Bill Morton had suppressed at the inquest. It was shot at the police academy a week after Harper died. Cross and Williams's partner, Cal Osborne, rehearsed four times before finally taping the fifth version. The elapsed time, from encountering Harper to shooting him, was twenty-eight seconds. The alleged tug-of-war over the gun took five seconds.

Throughout the fight for the gun Cross's right hand appeared to be holding the gun's butt. When Murray Sinclair saw the video he was curious about the way Cross's right thumb moved towards the hammer.

"Did you notice if Constable Cross drew back the hammer before it was fired? . . . it looked like he drew it back," Murray Sinclair said.

Williams didn't see it that way.

"It's a double-action revolver . . . and it's as easy either way to cock it or pull it back. There's no more energy required."

But commission counsel McNicol got Williams to admit that it's easier to pull the trigger once the hammer is cocked in the single-action position.

Williams had also taken Cross's witness statement, having been briefed beforehand by Sergeant Angus Anderson that Harper had attacked Cross.

"I asked him, 'Do you wish to offer a statement, and describe your part in the shooting?' He says, 'Sure, I've got nothing to hide.'"

Williams said he cautioned Cross that whatever he said could be used in evidence but he didn't interrogate Cross, he simply helped him clarify his "witness" statement.

"He wasn't a suspect, sir." Williams told Randy McNicol.

Hersh Wolch was incredulous. "In interviewing Cross, do I take it you asked him no questions in two hours?"

"Yes, sir."

There was more surprising testimony from Harry Williams about other evidence Bill Morton didn't call. On the morning of the shooting, Williams said, he noticed a revolver blow-by mark across the outside of the fleshy webbing of Cross's right hand. The fidgety, ashen-faced constable had been rubbing the area.

On March 17, two days after doing the video re-enactment, Williams conducted an experiment at the police firing range. Williams said in the normal firing position the sooty debris escaping from the gap between the cylinder and barrel lands on the top of the exposed hand, not where he saw on it Cross. So Williams put on a pair of grey work gloves, placed his right hand under the cylinder, where Cross said it had been, and fired. The blow-by mark was left in the same location as it appeared on Cross's hand, Williams said. But when Morton didn't ask for the gloves during the inquest, the detective said he took them home.

"I felt that I should get the use out of them," he told McNicol, "and I used them for gardening."

Then he discarded the gloves, Williams said.

The inquiry heard other police officers give variations on their inquest testimony. Ident Sergeant Bob Parker, looking tense and flushed, vowed, "I wasn't trying to cover anything up." And if he had it to do over again he would have fingerprinted the gun and holster.

"Quite frankly, I was surprised at the extent of the handling of the gun," Parker said.

It was Constable – then Acting Sergeant – Glen Spryszak who seized Cross's revolver and slid it into his own holster because, he testified, it was the only place he could put it. Spryszak, now a sixteen-

Cross."

another quote on the same page. "‹"If Harper had
cer said, "he would have had a different version, no
ally happened."›"

you that?"

Cross," Gillmor said, adding that Cross had been
ething another officer had said.

eferred to one more quote.

f Rob's felt it was largely a question of shooting the
If it hadn't been someone politically prominent, it
ecome an issue. "Maybe they should give him a medal
Indian. I don't really mean that, but you know, I mean
out what the police actually have to put up with every
ody basically hates their guts."›"

t said that.

Cross had phoned him after the interview. He'd been
ecker from *Saturday Night* had called Cross to cor-
ns of the story, including an anecdote about him and
to a hotel to buy beer when they were underage teens.
about that.

lained the point of the article: "What were the series
ot Rob to this point, and conversely what were the
that perhaps got Harper to this point? And as such, I
nt of memoir, which included myself in it, to offset –
t cultural differences that had existed at the time for
d in our area, where we had no contact whatsoever
cept for these isolated instances of occasionally going
beer."

ondered how Cross had reacted to that rationale.

t his personal life was his own and that he had denied
lieve that he felt by denying it to the fact checker that
be removed from the story."

er Hamilton had some questions for the writer. "You
The thing that made the incident possible, the thing

year veteran, admitted he removed and reholstered the gun at least
two or three more times, including once when he broke it open in
front of Inspector Eric Hrycyk.

Hrycyk denied that, although he acknowledged knowing at the
time the gun hadn't been handled properly by Spryszak. Yet in his
report to Stephen, Hrycyk assured the chief that all of the officers had
acted in a professional and competent manner. As for the canvass of
the area that he instructed Spryszak to do, Hrycyk said he had just
learned a week ago that only six doors were knocked on that morning.

On cross-examination Hersh Wolch wanted to know why Hrycyk
didn't question Cross about why he grabbed Harper.

"My presumption at the time," said Hrycyk, "was that he was
arresting him. I thought if he wasn't arresting him he was assaulting
him."

Randy McNicol's decision to ask for the officer's notebooks paid
off early, when Butch Eakin testified. It was from Eakin's notes that
the inquiry learned that when he saw Randy Hampton waving his
flashlight he also heard him on the car radio screaming "I've got him
right here guys. He's coming out to you . . .," referring to Pruden being
flushed out onto Logan Avenue. But Hampton wasn't carrying a
flashlight. So what was Hampton motioning with at the same time he
was broadcasting? Eakin couldn't explain it.

The day before Hampton took the stand, Linda Morisette testified
again about driving past the scene with her friends and seeing a cop
running across Logan with his gun out. Since then, Morisette said, an
AJI investigator had taken her back to the scene where a man dressed
in police clothing re-enacted what she saw. Sometimes he ran holding
a police radio, sometimes a revolver. Morisette testified she had no
problem telling the difference.

When Randy Hampton took the stand, he acknowledged that he
must have been the officer Morisette saw, but he insisted he had only
his portable radio in his hand. Again he denied having his revolver
drawn in the back lane. But when he was asked to demonstrate how
he was taught to shoot, Hampton clasped both hands together, arms

outstretched, the way Pruden had described it, but Judge John Enns had said only happened on TV.

During his examination of Hampton, Police Association lawyer Marty Minuk asked him whether his partner, Bill Isaac, the officer who'd caught Pruden, would ever call anyone a "fucking Indian."

"I have never heard Constable Isaac in the five years that I have known him swear one single word," Hampton said. "I have never heard him to utter a racial comment of any type ever."

"Is this something which stands out in your mind about your partner?" Minuk asked.

Hampton said it was. "I think, he's basically, Biblically speaking, what would be called a righteous man, because he is that."

"You are embarrassing him, you realize that?" Murray Sinclair said.

It wasn't until the following week that the judge understood just how embarrassing Isaac found the public flattery.

—

33

"A CERTAIN KIND OF RACISM."

Cross's boyhood buddy, Don Gillmor, the magazine writer, was the next witness. Gillmor had been accompanied to Winnipeg by *Saturday Night's* legal counsel, Julian Porter. When Gillmor had promised Cross confidentiality before their backyard chat the day after the inquest verdict, he hadn't thought the Aboriginal Justice Inquiry could compel him to reveal his sources for his December 1988 article, "The Shooting of J.J. Harper." Now he knew he could be jailed for refusing. That's why *Saturday Night* had asked Porter to accompany him. What remained to be seen was whether Gillmor would co-operate and, if not, whether the commissioners would actually send him to jail. It was Monday, August 28, the sixth day of the Harper hearings.

Commission counsel P
through his magazine story

"At page 44 of the article
to walk across the street. H
was aware of his rights; he
have to show you any."

" " "Well, excuuuuuuuu
thinking it might break th

"Who gave you that inf
Gillmor asked if he was
was. Then he said: "That ca
Schulman turned to th

" " "That's right," one of
that information?"

"Constable Cross," Gill
Schulman referred to
" 'Before Harper was load
turned to Cross and said, "
you that information?"

"Constable Cross," he
Schulman flipped to a
" " "Harper was the au
the Winnipeg force. "Th
Blaming the police for th
liquor store for being ope

"Who gave you that ir
"Constable Cross."

"On page 52 of the arti
gallows humour of a dan
Indian?" is a joke that ma
in Winnipeg after Harper
of a trigger.'

"Who told you that?"

"Constable
There was
lived," one off
matter what re
"Who told
"Constable
expressing som
Schulman r
" 'A friend
wrong Indian.
wouldn't have l
for shooting an
when you find
day. And everyl
Cross hadn'
Gillmor said
angry. A fact cl
roborate portic
Gillmor driving
Cross was upse
Gillmor exp
of things that
series of things
used this eleme
to show the vas
people that live
with Natives, ex
out and buying
Schulman w
"He said tha
everything. I be
it, in fact, would
Commission
say on page 47,

that framed Harper's death, was racism . . . not overt racism, but a subtler systemic brand.' Are you saying that it was inbred racism, that it was inbred in Constable Cross that caused the problem?"

"No, not at all." Gillmor tried to explain, that when two cultures have been segregated, a mutual suspicion can develop that allows something like the Harper shooting to happen. He called that "casual racism," which he defined as a dismissal of the other group rather than a hatred towards it.

"But you saw that as part of the character of Constable Cross?" Commissioner Hamilton asked.

"I saw the separateness as part of his character having grown up in an area where he had no social dealing . . . no discourse with Native people. And then he's thrust into what is being described by me as an adversarial position on the police force."

Gillmor also believed there was institutional racism at work. He explained institutional racism by referring to Herb Stephen's appearance on "Canada AM" the morning after Judge Enns released his verdict, when the police chief said police relations with Natives were good.

"There was a blindness there that constituted a degree of institutional racism."

Commissioner Sinclair asked Gillmor to elaborate.

"I didn't perceive him as being an individual. I saw him as being a spokesman for the police force in that capacity. And that he was putting forth the idea that there wasn't in fact any problem, when in fact there was this hue and cry across the city that, at this point – when a conciliatory gesture would have gone far to placate matters and at least examine them in some more rational light – that he in fact had taken the opposite route and exacerbated things. And I felt that this could be – that this element of blindness in fact could be symptomatic of a certain kind of racism."

Murray Sinclair turned to other quotes from the article that Gillmor had attributed to people who had known Cross growing up.

"There is a reference here in particular that causes me a bit of concern," Sinclair said. " 'When news that Rob Cross had shot a man reached those of us who had known him as a boy, there wasn't too much surprise.'"

The commissioner was concerned that Gillmor hadn't offered any factual basis for a comment that seemed to suggest Cross was known to be violent. Gillmor said he didn't believe that was the implication, suggesting that the perceived accidental nature of the shooting, coupled with Cross's being at the centre of so much when he was a kid, was the true context of the quote.

Murray Sinclair moved to another quote that bothered him. It had been said to Gillmor at a bar a few months prior to the Harper shooting, when the writer had been in town for Christmas and out playing hockey with some guys who knew Cross. Sinclair read the passage aloud: "'We wondered at the fact that he had become a policeman. "There's one guy who shouldn't have a gun," one of the hockey players said.' And again, that particular statement portrays Constable Cross as a man with a bent for violence. Do you agree with that?"

"I don't think I'd use the phrase 'bent for violence.' I think . . . a certain lack of responsibility, would perhaps be more accurate."

Sinclair had detected an overall message in Gillmor's article. "That a situation like this, whether it was J.J. Harper and Robert Cross, that you felt it was almost inevitable that this would happen."

"I did," Gillmor said.

The following day, Hamilton and Sinclair released a ten-page written decision on Cross's status as a witness. Halfway through, they got to the heart of the matter:

"We have to balance our concern for the mental health of Constable Cross against our responsibilities to examine the circumstances surrounding the death of J.J. Harper . . .

"We are very mindful of the fragile emotional condition of Constable Cross and the fact that he has at times given doctors concern about the possibility of suicide. We certainly do not wish to cause him harm. On the other hand we are not persuaded, considering all the evidence and submissions of counsel, that Constable Cross is not competent to testify."

There was one other matter the judges addressed at the end of their decision. They questioned whether McGregor, as lawyer for all members of the Winnipeg Police Association, had acted in Cross's best interests in trying to block the inquiry. Cross had said he wanted to testify, and the stonewalling had only delayed his appearance and prolonged his anxiety. Sinclair and Hamilton said Cross should get new counsel, independent of the police association.

After the inquiry had wrapped up on its seventh day, Al McGregor called Perry Schulman and asked to meet him at the Simkin Gallagher offices that evening. McGregor had something he was duty bound to tell the commission. It had to do with the police notebooks. Constable Bill Isaac would be there, too.

34

"WHY DID YOU CHANGE THE COLOUR?"

On the morning of August 30, the "righteous" Constable Bill Isaac stood at the witness table, holding a Bible in his right hand. To administer the oath the clerk had to look up at the six-foot-eight-inch officer.

Isaac, who was now a plainclothes constable, was wearing a blazer, the way he had at the inquest sixteen months earlier. Except this one was blue, instead of grey.

Before the questioning began, Isaac asked, just as he had at the inquest, if he could refer to his notes.

"You made them at the time?" Murray Sinclair asked, echoing Judge Enns's query.

But this time Isaac's reply was different.

"I have two sets of notes here," Isaac answered. "One was made at the time and one was made some time after." That's why Perry Schulman had been summoned to McGregor's office two days earlier. Isaac had confessed to McGregor that he'd rewritten his notes on the shooting. In fact, he had rewritten a whole notebook, a month's worth of notes, ostensibly just to make some minor corrections and add detail. In July, when the appeal court ruled that photocopies of all notes pertaining to the Harper shooting had to be produced, Isaac had turned over only portions of his rewritten second version. Now, on the stand, Isaac told Schulman that he had discovered the first set of original notes while searching through a box of notebooks he kept at home, just four days before he was scheduled to testify at the inquiry.

The notebook he had been looking for was from March 1987, a full year before the Harper shooting.

"I see," said Schulman. "You're looking for March of 1987 and you come across the original notebook from March of 1988?" Schulman's question was sceptical.

"Do you remember preparing the second notebook?"

"No, I don't."

Isaac had recopied and revised thirty-five pages of notes from between February 19 and March 17, but he didn't remember doing it.

Schulman asked Isaac which set of notes he'd referred to during the inquest.

"The notes that are marked 'revised.'"

Curiously, while Isaac said he couldn't remember rewriting his notebook, he could recall why he did it.

On March 17, 1988, more than a week after the shooting, he had prepared a supplemental report on the case. Someone – again his memory failed him – had noticed an error in the report. Isaac had recorded the address where he arrested and cuffed Pruden as 2047 Gallagher instead of 2037.

"After the error was pointed out to me I returned to the area of 2037 Gallagher and I found out that indeed the correct address was

2037. And at that time I realized my notes were in error and that it was something that should be corrected and that any details that I failed to put in the first time, I should add."

Of particular interest was an alteration Isaac had made, changing the colour of Pruden's jacket from grey to black.

In his original notebook Isaac had written, "Suspect: male, 22 yrs, grey jacket, jeans." Pruden had been wearing a grey jacket when Isaac caught him, but Isaac had altered his notes to conform with Hodgins's broadcast description of Pruden's jacket as black. In fact, Pruden's jacket was grey and Harper's was black.

Isaac remained composed throughout his embarrassing testimony. But when Schulman asked him what he did after discovering the original notebook, the big cop started to choke back tears.

"I first of all explained the situation to my family." Isaac reached for a glass of water, took a sip, and cleared his throat. "And early the next morning I explained it to my boss." Isaac's pointed chin was quivering.

"Did you offer to do anything?" Schulman asked.

"Yes. I . . ." Isaac bowed his head. "Excuse me," he continued, struggling to keep his composure. "I offered to resign."

Schulman looked at Isaac sympathetically. "It's obvious that what you've done has caused you concern. Is there anything that you would like to say to the commissioners about that?"

Isaac glanced at the two commissioners, then looked away. "I'd like to apologize for this mistake, for any problem that it causes the court." Isaac tried to go on, but couldn't. Fifteen seconds went by before he added, "I would like to apologize to the department. And to my family and to the people I serve."

Schulman then asked him whether he had called Pruden a fucking Indian. Isaac, still clearly upset, denied that he had. Marty Minuk suggested the inquiry take a five-minute break so Isaac could compose himself.

There were still tears in Isaac's eyes when he returned to face Hersh Wolch, counsel for the Island Lake Tribal Council. Wolch adjusted his glasses and zeroed in on why Isaac had rewritten his notes about the colour of the jacket.

"Would you agree with me that if your evidence was that the description you received was of a man in a grey jacket, that that could be detrimental to Officer Cross's position?"

"I suppose you could interpret it that way, yes."

"It might have been then that the revised notes were done so that you wouldn't cause Officer Cross any added burden or problem."

Isaac denied that this had ever been his intention, insisting he had only wanted to correct any mistakes and add more detail.

"Yes," Wolch said, "but if you had crossed out 'grey jacket' and written in 'black jacket,' I'm certain that some nosy lawyer would have said to you, 'Why did you change the colour?' But with a new set of notes, nobody could see that."

"That's true," Isaac said, smiling for the first time. "But that wasn't my intention."

Commissioner Hamilton had a question.

"Do you remember anyone speaking to you or suggesting to you that you make a change or clarify any of your notes?"

"No, no," Isaac said, more emphatically than when he'd denied abusing Pruden. "I know for a fact that no one would do that."

Hamilton thanked Isaac and McGregor for their honesty in bringing the original notebook forward.

"I think," added Murray Sinclair, "we both recognize as well that you could have easily withheld your discovery of your first notebook and not told anyone. And that, although you would have had to live with that, it would have saved you from the difficulties that you are facing now and I am sure you are going to face in the near future. And again, we sincerely appreciate the candour that you have brought to these proceedings."

"Thank you," Isaac said.

"We are adjourning these proceedings until 9:30 on Friday morning," Murray Sinclair said. "We trust that counsel will be able to arrange for the attendance of Constable Cross appropriately at that time."

Late the following day the police department issued a press release saying it would do an internal investigation into Isaac's confessions.

"Suggestions have been made previously to have such incidents investigated by an external agency," the release said. "Chief Stephen has given consideration to this, but is confident that the department is competent to carry out this investigation and provide a complete report to the Department of the Attorney General for its decision on possible criminal charges."

The next day the police held a news conference. Joe Gallagher, the cop-cum-lawyer who had monitored the Harper inquest for the department, took questions. CBC television sent two reporters to question Gallagher: George Jacob, an old newspaper reporter turned TV researcher, and a new reporter at "24 Hours," as the supper-hour news was called. Jacob had some questions. The investigation aside, what were the police going to do about Isaac's admission that he rewrote his notebook? What form of discipline was the force considering? Gallagher answered by not answering. He said Isaac should be commended for stepping forward.

Years later, Jacob remembered that answer and laughed. Criminal charges were never laid against Isaac. Jacob remembered something else about the news conference. The new reporter, the guy who was supposed to help Jacob, seemed to freeze.

"He just didn't ask anything," Jacob said. "He just started backing away."

It wasn't as if Jacob's sidekick was a rookie or was unfamiliar with the case. Before moving to television he had covered the Harper inquest for the *Winnipeg Sun*. His name was Bruce Owen.

Two weeks later, Isaac received his punishment. He was transferred back to uniform, put on general patrol, and slapped with a $4,000 pay cut.

174 GORDON SINCLAIR JR.

35

"OH GOD, WHAT'S HAPPENING?"

For more than eighty years there has been an underground pedestrian passage connecting Manitoba's Legislative Building to its Law Courts and the network of government buildings beyond. Cross was escorted through this tunnel on the way to the inquiry. He walked in the centre of a convoy of sheriffs and cops that entered the tunnel from the Law Courts' furnace room. The door was marked "caution." Cross ducked to avoid a large blue utility pipe on the other side.

The officers had met him at McGregor's office at 363 Broadway, just two blocks away. Ellen Gordon, the young criminal lawyer with a fondness for handsome cops, watched curiously as Cross left, led by Winnipeg Police Association president John Campbell.

The inquiry had arranged for Cross's secret entry in an effort to shield him from the prying eyes of the media waiting on York Avenue. It was only a temporary reprieve. As soon as Cross emerged from the tunnel he passed by a storage room that had been converted to a media centre. And just around the corner in the inquiry room was a TV camera Cross couldn't avoid.

By 9:30 a.m. on September 1, 1989, the 150 folding chairs in the public gallery were taken and thousands more people had tuned in to watch the proceedings on local cable or on CBC Newsworld.

Gordon Sinclair was standing, looking around when he noticed a familiar face. Burly Butch Eakin stood out in his turquoise sweater. Eakin was poised like a bodyguard, near the side door where Cross was expected to enter, the way he had stood guard outside the hospital delivery room the day before the inquest started, when Stephen, Cross's and Diane's third child, was born. There were twelve lawyers with standing at the inquiry, all sitting at the front of the room. At 9:40 one of them stood up. It was Bill Olson's first appearance at the inquiry. Olson, who was tall, fit, and had the bearing of a CEO, had recently been appointed to represent Cross personally, taking over from McGregor. Olson began by reading from the psychiatric report. He stressed that his client was on a high dose of Valium, and cautioned that Cross could suffer a catastrophic breakdown if pushed too hard.

When Olson finished, Cross was summoned. He entered through the door where Eakin was standing. Cross was wearing a striped tie and white shirt, a light grey sports coat, and blue-grey slacks. Gordon Sinclair noticed Cross walked quickly, but mincingly, like an impaired driver trying to walk a straight line.

Al Hamilton must have noticed this, too. He carefully explained that if Cross needed a break at any time, all he had to do was ask.

Cross was thirty-five now. His hair was still dark, like his eyes, and his moustache full, the style of Old West cowboys. Randy McNicol had drawn the assignment of doing the examination-in-chief on Cross. Months earlier, Cross had asked McNicol to represent him, but McNicol had already been retained by the inquiry.

McNicol took Cross through the events leading up to and following the shooting of J.J. Harper. Cross acknowledged, as he had at the inquest, that he had heard a second suspect was in custody when he approached Harper. Cross had been in the lane behind Logan when he heard Isaac say, "I got him." But Cross said he also heard someone say the second suspect was wearing a sweater jacket.

"Has it subsequently been brought to your attention that no such description was broadcast on the radio?" McNicol asked. "That the description broadcast was, in fact, that the suspect was wearing a grey jacket?"

"Several things have been brought to my attention, but I can only go by what I heard and that was what I heard." Gordon Sinclair made a note of Cross's "loud, clear, and steady" voice.

McNicol continued in his typically stern-sounding, purposely paced manner, but his questioning didn't sound as aggressive as usual.

"Given the doubt that you must have had . . . in your mind at that point concerning the suspect that had been apprehended, can you tell me, Constable, why you wouldn't have communicated that to the other officers on the radio? For instance, saying to them, 'That doesn't sound like the right guy,' or 'The description doesn't fit,' or something to that effect?"

"I can't answer that."

Cross went on to say that he had cut through the backyard of 1242 Logan and emerged on the street to see Harper on the other side, approximately five houses west, dressed in the jacket he said Allan had described.

McNicol got Cross to agree that Harper had been walking east towards the stolen vehicle, not running west, away from the police. So why, McNicol wondered, had he approached Harper? Cross replied that when he saw the jacket Harper was wearing, he decided to ask for identification.

"How would that assist you in making any decision about this individual?"

"I've already given my answer for that. I mean, he matched the description of the suspect."

"If he had produced identification would he then have been allowed to proceed along his way?"

"Yes, he would have."

"And if he had failed to produce identification he would not?"

"I can't really answer that question."

McNicol rewound the scene a bit, and again asked why Cross hadn't radioed the other officers. This time Cross said, "I didn't feel there was a need to contact the other officers."

McNicol seemed to be suggesting that Cross was simply spot-checking Harper. That if he really thought he was a suspect, he would have alerted the others to what he was doing, just in case. McNicol continued on the same path.

"At what point, as the two of you were approaching each other, did you also notice that this individual was a Native?"

"Not until I got fairly close to him."

"As you approached towards him, did you have your service revolver out of the holster and in your hand?"

"No."

"Did you ever have your service revolver out of the holster that evening, prior to speaking to the individual who we now know was J.J. Harper?"

"No."

"You say he was being uncooperative and trying to get away. By uncooperative, I take it you're referring to his belligerence and his failure to show you identification?"

"I believe I treated him with respect. I explained the situation, and given those circumstances, the lateness of the hour, no one being around, I do not feel that he would have felt threatened by just producing some identification."

"Well, as a result of his conduct, and his demeanour, as he commenced to walk away from you, did you decide that you had reasonable and probable grounds to effect his arrest?"

Cross said he hadn't made that decision at that point. "The last thing I wanted was a struggle and what happened. I mean, I didn't want that."

"You did not arrest him?"

"No."

"And at no point in that encounter between you and he was he under arrest?"

"No."

"If you were not in the process of effecting an arrest," McNicol asked, "what right do you say you had to reach out and take hold of this individual?"

"Simply because I wanted to talk to him some more to explain to him, so he would understand as to why I wanted to see some identification."

Had Cross anticipated that grabbing a man who had been drinking and was in no mood to co-operate with a police officer might result in a struggle?

"No, I didn't anticipate that at all."

Next, McNicol asked Cross to describe what happened after he took hold of Harper's arm.

"Okay. He turned quickly, caught me off guard, pushed with both hands on my upper shoulders. I went down. I was trying to grab hold of his jacket, grab hold of him. Grab hold of anything to break my fall. I remember lashing out with my left hand and knocking off his glasses. I believe I had hold of both sleeves. . . . I'm trying to give you an approximation of what happened."

"I understand, sir."

"He came down on top of me. I planted my left foot on his chest to kick him off me, but due to my leg being compressed so much, I could not push him off. I felt a tugging in the area of my holster and revolver. I thought to myself, 'Oh, my God, what's happening?' The gun came out. We fumbled for it. I remember having my hand around the cylinder. He had his hand, I believe, on the butt and barrel of the revolver. I managed to get a finger in the trigger, around the trigger guard and on the trigger. Through the pulling and yanking, the gun discharged. There was a loud flash. It took seconds. It seemed like hours, but I wondered, like, 'Did he get shot? Am I shot?' It's not like on TV, people don't fly away. It's an awful feeling. Mr. Harper stood up, backed up a few feet, and then slowly sank to the ground. At that point I realized he'd been shot."

During his recall of the struggle, Cross had omitted something that he had mentioned in his statement. McNicol picked up there.

"When you reached out with your right hand and turned Mr. Harper towards you, did you with your left hand then take hold of his right wrist?"

"You know, you're getting into areas now that become extremely confusing for me," Cross said.

McNicol referred him to the statement he had given Sergeant Harry Williams three hours after the shooting.

"I mean, my statement is there. I signed it. Obviously that's what I said." But he didn't recall grabbing Harper's wrist.

"When that statement was given I was not in the best frame of mind. The people are asking me, they want details . . . I mean, it is of my own free will, but to describe something that took place in a matter of seconds, to know every movement that I made, I can't do that."

McNicol said he understood. "Why would you not just say that, rather than attempt to give people detailed descriptions of the event?"

"That's another toughie, you know. I guess I was in a state of shock that night. Part of me – I was wondering, Do I have a job? What's going to happen to me? Do I call a lawyer? Does a lawyer come and say, 'Don't say anything?' In my heart I know I have nothing to hide, so I gave a statement freely, and now I wind up getting picked apart because of it. It's very difficult for me."

"Do you need a few moments, Constable?" Murray Sinclair asked.

"Yes."

When Cross took the stand again, McNicol began with those parts of his statement that gave the details of the struggle for the gun.

"I have – I have difficulty with this statement," Cross said.

"Tell me about it. What difficulty do you have, Constable?"

The difficulty was that holding the butt of the gun while it was in its holster would keep it in place, Cross said. "Reading this statement," he continued, "it almost appears like I've got my hand around the whole butt of the gun, which I didn't." But that's the way it appeared on the video. "I remember trying to retain my firearm. I remember fumbling with it and having hold of different parts of it at different times. But it bears down to my earlier statement. They were asking me, 'You know, Bob, you just can't say you fumbled for the gun and the guy got shot. Like, what happened? Where were your hands?' I can't really remember it."

McNicol tried to help him remember. "Are you right-handed?"

"I'm right-handed."

"In this passage," McNicol continued, "you have commenced with, 'He took hold of my right hand which the gun was in and started to yank at the gun . . .' Are you saying in that statement that the gun was in your right hand, with your right trigger finger through the trigger guard?"

"The statement confuses me. If I would be allowed to have my firearm, I could best demonstrate the last position I remember my hands being in."

The clerk handed Cross the revolver, and he took hold of the frame and cylinder with his right hand and put his left forefinger through the trigger guard.

McNicol thanked Cross and pointed out that the statement hadn't been clear on that point. "Indeed," the commission counsel said, "there's no reference at all to your left hand or your left trigger finger."

"It was not clear at the time of giving the statement and it is not clear now. I wish I could give a clear answer."

McNicol wasn't finished with Cross's account of a tug-of-war over the .38 Smith & Wesson. He turned from his witness statement to Cross's notebook account. "You say, 'The snap came undone and the revolver came out. He had both hands on the gun and I had my right hand on the frame and my left index finger on the trigger.'"

"Right, as I demonstrated to you earlier."

"As best you recollect, is that what you told Sergeant Williams when he took your statement from you?"

"I, you know, I find it so difficult, but I don't recall giving the statement. I remember sitting there asking, 'Can I have a cup of coffee? Can I have a cigarette?' Like, it just seemed like this took forever."

McNicol rewound the sequence again, to when the revolver was secured in the holster by a leather strap. The holster tilted forward and the trigger fit under a retaining mechanism. The two design features made it difficult for someone to sneak up and take the weapon from behind.

"To remove it," McNicol pointed out, "the snap has to be undone."

Cross agreed. "There are two ways of removing the gun when it's on your side, a thumb pressure down releases the snap and then the drawing motion forward. If the gun was to be taken from you from the front, somebody grabbing the butt, putting their thumb in there releases it."

Commissioner Sinclair asked to see the holster. "The snap appears to be pretty easy to undo," he said.

McNicol continued: "And as I understand it, at some point, as you struggled with Mr. Harper, you say that he got hold of the butt of the handgun, pulled it forward and out of your holster?" Cross agreed with McNicol's summary.

"Do you agree that if the gun was pulled forward and out," McNicol said, demonstrating the motion, "the individual pulling it out would have it both upside down and pointed back towards you?"

"The hand that you demonstrated was your left hand," Cross said. "It would have had to have been the right – I'm guessing at this – simply for the thumb to hit the mechanism to release the lock."

That would have meant the intoxicated Harper would have had to reach across Cross's body, an awkward motion even for a sober individual. But McNicol didn't pick up on Cross's interpretation of the choreography.

"What you do know," McNicol said, "is at some point the handgun was right side up with the barrel or muzzle pointing towards Mr. Harper?"

"I remember a bang, a flash, and where my hands were."

McNicol moved on to the moments after the shooting, after he had radioed for help, and Douglas Hooper and the rookie Danny Smyth arrived. He asked if Cross recalled being asked if he was okay.

"It becomes very blurry to me. Several constables came up to me and asked, 'Are you okay?' Some suggested that I sit inside the car. I went and sat in the car. I couldn't sit in a confined space. I felt like vomiting. I kept stepping out of the car to get some fresh air."

"Do you recall Constable Hooper, with Smyth at his side, pointing at Mr. Harper, asking you if he had been shot and your responding to him, 'He went for my gun. I shot him'?"

"No."

Did he remember Eakin arriving and asking him what happened?

"I'm sorry, my memory's not that great. I don't remember. I

remember people saying to me, you know, 'Take it easy, Bob, sit in the car.' "

"Do you recall your partner, Kathryn Hodgins, at some point asking you what happened?"

"No, the only thing I recollect about Constable Hodgins is she was brushing the dirt off my back."

Cross did remember Spryszak asking for his revolver. He also remembered Inspector Hrycyk's arrival.

"Did you have any conversation at the scene with either Spryszak or Hrycyk or indeed any of the other constables, where they suggested to you what you ought to say about the incident and the manner in which it happened?"

"No," Cross said, "not that I remember. No one suggested anything to me."

McNicol next moved to Gillmor's *Saturday Night* article, and its quoted comments attributed to unnamed police constables at the shooting scene. He directed Cross to the words allegedly spoken as Harper lay on the ground bleeding to death: "That's right, bleed him dry."

"Mr. Gillmor has told this inquiry that you told him that. Is that so?"

"No."

"In the same article, Mr. Gillmor goes on and relates: 'Before Harper was loaded into the ambulance, one of the officers turned to Cross and said, "If you're lucky, that fucker dies."' Mr. Gillmor has told the inquiry that you told him that that comment was made to you. Did you?"

Cross denied telling Gillmor that.

McNicol turned to a quote from an anonymous police officer.

"Harper was the author of his own demise . . . The Natives drink and they get in trouble. Blaming the police for their troubles is like an alcoholic blaming the liquor store for being open.' Mr. Gillmor has told this inquiry that you were the anonymous police officer that spoke those words. Is that so?"

"I'm not sure of that, but I might have said that."

"Is it, was it your view that Mr. Harper was the author of his own demise?"

"No."

"Why would you have used words to that effect in your conversation with Mr. Gillmor then?"

"I believe that maybe Mr. Gillmor took that out of context."

Cross explained that he'd agreed to talk to the writer about what it was like being a police officer. He brought up the joke 'How do you wink at an Indian?' as an example of the humour he had to put up with from fellow officers.

McNicol backed up to the previous quote.

"Was it your view, and did you say to Mr. Gillmor, 'Blaming the police for their troubles' – that's a reference to Natives – 'is like an alcoholic blaming the liquor store for being open late'?"

"I don't really recall that, no."

"Is that and was that your view, constable?"

"No, that's not my view."

"Also in the article, at page 52, Mr. Gillmor quotes another unnamed police officer as saying the following: 'If Mr. Harper had lived, he would have had a different version, no matter what really happened.' Mr. Gillmor told us that it was you that told him those words. Did you?"

"No."

Moments later, McNicol said, "Those are all my questions."

It was nearly 12:30 p.m., and Cross had been on the stand for almost two and a half hours.

The hearing was recessed until one o'clock. Cross left through the door he'd come in, headed for a back room where lunch awaited him. Moments later McNicol walked over to Cross's new lawyer. "Any objections if I shake hands with Constable Cross?" McNicol asked Olson.

When the hearing resumed after lunch, McGregor didn't have any questions for his client. Neither did the city's lawyer, Doug Abra. Hersh

Wolch was next. His initial questions were designed to point out the discrepancy between Harper's age and the age of the two suspected car thieves. Cross agreed with Wolch that Harper matched the description Allan had given him in three ways; he was wearing a black jacket and blue jeans and he was Native.

"I take it you might agree with me that the age didn't match?"

"The – well, yes, that's correct, the, you know, thirties versus twenties. Yes, there's a discrepancy in age."

"He didn't look like the kind of fellow that would necessarily be chumming around with a person of twelve years of age?"

"That's – I can't form an opinion on that."

Commissioner Sinclair interjected: "It's a tough question for a lot of people to answer."

"In any event," Wolch continued, "did he look like he was perspiring, as if he had been running a race with somebody?"

"You know, I keep going back to the thing, it's a matter of seconds. You know, people have asked me, 'Did he have glassy eyes? Did he have this? Did he stagger?' You know, I didn't notice if he was perspiring."

"Isn't that something you would look for if you were interested in somebody who has been leading you in a race?"

"Not necessarily. I was most interested in just obtaining some ID."

"Well, I don't wish to belabour a question that Mr. McNicol posed to you, but whether his name was J.J. Harper or John Smith, how would that help you in ascertaining if he was the car thief?"

"If I had a driver's licence . . . I had someone else to contact the next day, someone I could fingerprint, maybe match fingerprints of the stolen auto. That was my reason for approaching him and getting identification."

"And when he exercised his right not to answer your question, you grabbed him."

"I did not grab him. I took hold of his arm to turn him around to try and explain to him . . ."

"You say the word 'grab' doesn't describe what you just described?"

"I guess, you know, people's interpretations of grabbing or holding or turning . . . I did not use an open hand, I cupped my hand."

"Did it not enter your mind that if this was a man who had been drinking and appeared to be a little belligerent, that putting your hands on him might cause some sort of confrontation?"

"Not at that point," Cross said. "Once I explained to him that he matched the suspect, he still informed me that, 'I don't have to show you nothing,' and walked away. That's when I wanted to turn and talk to him some more. I just felt that if I could explain the situation in a little bit more detail and say, like, 'Look, just around the corner there, there's a stolen car, like, you know, you're one of the few people in this area. I'd just like to see some identification.' But I never got a chance to go on with that."

Wolch looked down at Cross's statement. "I'm reading from your statement to Officer Williams: 'I reached out with my hand and he turned to face me, so I reached out with my left hand to take hold of the right wrist.' Is that an accurate description of what occurred?"

"You know, as I said earlier, I have great difficulty with this statement. It was taken at a time that . . . I was under great duress. People were asking me, 'Where were your hands?' You know, I do not know exactly. I know I turned to him, and he shoved me, and that's all I can remember."

"Okay, but your statement says you took hold of his right wrist. Is it your evidence now that you have no recall of that happening, or it didn't happen?"

"I have no recall of that happening."

"So it may have happened and you may have described it accurately to Officer Williams?"

"I may have, yes."

"And it is my understanding as well, that as a police officer you are trained as to how to confront people to protect yourself."

"There are various techniques that you are taught – to maintain a safety zone, you know, to stay away from striking distance. That sort of thing. I did not feel particularly threatened by Mr. Harper."

"A man who was drinking and belligerent?"

"I deal with people who are drinking and belligerent most days that I work."

"Are you trained to expect the unexpected?"

"Yes, and sometimes we get caught off guard."

Wolch was closing in on his own view of what had happened during the struggle. He directed Cross to his testimony that after grabbing Harper, the Native man turned quickly and pushed him.

Wolch said he was puzzled by how an impaired man could have knocked Cross down so easily. "I'm going to suggest to you that the reason he was able to knock you down was because your gun was drawn when you confronted him."

"My gun was not drawn."

"I'm suggesting to you that because you were guarding your gun, that is the reason why you went down that easily."

"My gun was not drawn."

Wolch reminded Cross that Allan had testified he had seen Cross reaching for his holster area when he slipped and shouted at him to "stop" or he would shoot.

"I never made any reference to a gun whatsoever. I said, 'Stop, you're caught.'" Cross pointed out that Allan was under five feet tall. "That's not a threatening person."

"But it's a nice way of making a person stop."

"Using a gun?"

"No, but saying that. 'Stop or I'll shoot,' might stop a person."

Wolch had a reason for asking these questions. "At any time that night, was your gun on the ground at all?"

"Not that I'm aware of, no."

"I'm just wondering. One of the officers testified at the inquest at least, that he found some white, perhaps salt type, stains on the barrel of your gun. Do you recall anything about that?"

"No."

Wolch read from Spryszak's testimony: "He said: 'I observed there was a stain of some sort running down the length of the barrel. It had dried and it was just the outline of something similar to a salt stain, or something to that effect.'"

Cross still didn't remember. Wolch tried again.

"When you were chasing the young fellow you did slip, didn't you?"

"Yes, I did. I went down on my, I believe it was my right knee."

"And your hand as well?"

Wolch reminded him of his earlier testimony, that his hands had touched the ground when he slipped chasing Allan.

"If that's what I testified then, then that's probably what happened."

"Did you have a gun in your hand at that time?"

"No, I didn't."

Wolch turned to Cross's notebook.

"After you finished your statement, you recorded your notes?"

Cross wasn't sure. "I did it – either I started then and finished it the next day or I finished it then, it – as time progresses it becomes blurrier and blurrier for me. I was not in a great frame of mind and, to be quite honest, when I looked at my notes it looked like I did a pretty good job on them. Like, you know, my hand is fairly steady and what not."

"I would suggest your notes are exceptionally legible and read right through very easily, would you agree with that overall assessment, then?"

Cross agreed that the notes didn't look as if they had been written by someone who was upset.

"But you acknowledge there are some differences between your notes and the statement that you gave Williams. And you attribute that to the probing and questioning, is that the idea?"

"Yes, I mean, once you start writing your notes, maybe little things come back into your mind that you remember and stuff. I remember that these notes were made as soon after the event as possible."

Later, Kathryn Hodgins would testify that she was dictating her reports to her husband Ron, who was typing, when Cross dropped by the detectives' lunchroom where they were working. It was afternoon, and Cross told them he was going to the hospital to tell Diane about the shooting.

"I'm leaving now," Hodgins recalled Cross saying. "You're stuck with the reports."

A month and a half later, the United States Secret Service reported an interesting finding about Cross's notebook. After Isaac's admission, the inquiry had asked the Secret Service to analyse and authenticate the notebooks of the other eight officers known to be involved in the Harper investigation. John W. Hargett, chief document examiner for the U.S. federal law enforcement agency, noticed Cross's four sample notebooks from before and after the incident used the same format for the date. But the March 9, 1988, notebook that dealt with the Harper shooting exclusively used a different format. "This format," Hargett wrote, "is similar to the format used by Constable Hodgins at the beginning of duty on March 8 and 9, 1988."

In the hearing room, Wolch continued his questioning. "I just want to take you back a moment to after Mr. Harper was shot."

He was asking Cross about the thirty-nine seconds that elapsed between the moment he first keyed his portable radio and when he keyed it again to call for his partner and an ambulance.

"And I take it," Wolch said, "thoughts went through your mind about how you're going to explain what happened and matters of that nature?"

"There are many things that go through your mind. I realized the news media is monitoring our channels. I'm trying to ascertain what I need. My first thoughts were for my partner because I didn't feel that I was, like, in control. I needed some help, I needed some guidance as to what needed to be done. I knew I needed the street supervisor, I needed an ambulance, I needed someone to think for me, so I had to determine where I was exactly so I could give a proper description, and I guess the thirty-nine seconds as you say was spent determining these things."

Wolch was struck by the first thought Cross mentioned: the media listening in.

"I hadn't appreciated the news media monitored your channels, but is that something that crossed your mind right then?"

"Yes."

"And obviously what preyed on your mind is that it was a very difficult situation to describe, given the fact that an innocent person, unarmed, had been shot with a police gun?"

"Yes."

Wolch turned to the quotes from the *Saturday Night* article, starting with the comment, "If you're lucky that fucker dies," which Cross had denied either saying or hearing.

"Now you're saying that Gillmor is either mistaken or lying?"

"Mistaken, lying, or he heard it from someone else, but not me."

But what would Gillmor's motive have been for identifying Cross as the source of the material? Gillmor, Cross agreed, held no animosity towards him.

"You see," Wolch said, "I can see you denying it because you don't want to place your fellow officers in a very awkward position."

"I never said it."

Wolch got Cross to acknowledge it would be highly embarrassing if a fellow officer had said it. "And," Wolch added, "even if it were said, you would be reluctant to name names, wouldn't you?"

"If it was said I would not be reluctant to name names."

"Well," said Wolch, "name one name who said, 'How do you wink at an Indian.'"

"I don't remember. Several people say that to me. I am known. The whole force knows me, I don't know the whole force. It's my picture that's in the paper all the time, they all know me."

"Are you saying that casual police officers, who barely know you, would walk up to you and make racist jokes?"

"I do not classify that as a racist joke. It's . . . a gallows humour to try and lighten the load for me, maybe a feeling of sympathy."

Had that been the sum total of racist remarks Cross had heard, Wolch wondered.

"That's the sum total."

"Just that one little comment that you passed on to Mr. Gillmor that he happened to get right?"

"Yes, that's a comment that I passed on to Gillmor that he got right."

"And as far as you saying, 'Harper was the author of his own demise,' that's a comment that you neither made nor adopt?"

"That's correct."

But that's not what Cross had told McNicol that morning, and Commissioner Sinclair caught the discrepancy.

"I believe he said he might have made it," Sinclair said.

"I might have made it," Cross quickly agreed.

Wolch appeared perplexed, although his follow-up question suggested he was feigning confusion.

"Unless I'm mistaken I thought you said you didn't say that, but you may have said the things about the liquor store. Maybe I'm wrong. If you could correct it, please."

"To be quite honest, I'm getting quite confused. I'm getting asked the same questions over and over and I'm losing track of what's going on."

Wolch pounced. "We would expect the same answer to the same question." It was the parting shot of his cross-examination.

By the time Harvey Pollock got to Cross, the constable had been answering questions for five hours. There was a row of twelve police officers seated behind Pollock, all in street clothes, and as the lawyer got to his feet, they began groaning audibly and shuffling their feet. One of them, a big, balding cop in cowboy boots, even began heckling Pollock. Pollock ignored him.

"You said earlier that you were aware of the physical evidence that was on your body. What were you talking about when you said that?"

"The back of my jacket was dirty from laying on the ground. I was covered in blood, my pants, my shoe. I had blood on my glasses which I washed off myself. Mistake again. Something that should have been seized. I had blood on my leg and I had powder burns on my hand.

I've always felt that these things – my condition, my arrival at the station – should have been photographed right there as soon as I got out of the car. . . . I did not ask for it to be photographed. I remember pointing out to Sergeant Williams my markings on my hand and the teardrop bloodstains going up my leg to my knee."

Murray Sinclair asked Cross if he had received any training about dealing with Aboriginal people during his police academy classes.

"We did some training. It was a lecture from a professor at the university. I don't remember too much about it. The training is what I would call very elementary. It's just basic background on Aboriginal people. I don't – I guess I don't like to say it, but I guess it's, considering the circumstances, it's limited."

By now Cross had been on the witness stand for almost six hours. Murray Sinclair alluded to that, and the stress the constable had been under answering so many questions about so much detail.

"I'm curious about whether, after having gone through all of that, you feel that you have said everything that you want to say. Is there anything else you would like to say before we end the day?"

"I'm sorry it ever happened," Cross said.

His eyes were tearing.

"Well," Murray Sinclair said, "I think we all are."

"Thank you, Constable."

The cop in the front row, the one in the cowboy boots, was talking out loud again.

"He's going to break down."

Cross bowed his head and put his hands to his face.

"He told the whole truth," the cop in the cowboy boots said, "and nothing but the truth."

Outside the court, Harper's step-brother, Harry Wood, was unconvinced. "I don't believe the statement we saw today is the truth, and I'll have to live with that. I don't believe his testimony about the way the gun was drawn. It's not the truth."

When John Campbell got back to his Winnipeg Police Association office, the phone was ringing off the hook with calls of support – fifty in all. "A lot of people were congratulating him," Campbell said later of Cross. "A lot of people saw him as the victim."

Harvey Pollock had phone calls after his cross-examination, too. They were all angry or abusive. In the *Free Press* newsroom, Gordon Sinclair wasn't taking calls. He had a column to write, and he started with the headline: "THE VALIUM FACTOR."

He felt that Cross had conned the doctors and the inquiry about his condition, and he was angry. It was early evening by the time he began typing the last few sentences:

As the inquiry adjourned, a newspaper reporter summed up Cross's testimony thusly:

"I'm stunned. I thought this man was supposed to have a mental disorder."

Yeah. But don't discount the Valium factor. The inquiry had repeatedly heard the psychiatric evaluation that Cross had agreed to make public. So yesterday, when Olson rehashed the constable's sad situation, it was inevitable. Everyone just opened wide. And swallowed.

Later that day, Herb Stephen drove over to Robert Cross's and had a cup of coffee with him. It was the first time Stephen had spoken to Cross. And it was the last.

It was around that time, during a recess at the hearings, that Hersh Wolch casually mentioned something to Gordon Sinclair.

"I have a feeling there's someone out there who saw something, and he's going to come forward."

Either Wolch was psychic, or he already knew about "the mystery man," as CBC national radio referred to Michael Tymchuk on the morning he testified, two weeks later.

36

"ARE WE GOING TO HEAR FROM HIM?"

Michael Tymchuk decided to park his car at the far end of Broadway, across from the Hotel Fort Garry. The morning of September 13, 1989, was warm and sunny – Indian summer weather – and Tymchuk had decided to walk to the Norquay Building.

Tymchuk was a short, soft-spoken thirty-three-year-old shift supervisor at Varta Batteries. Early on the morning of March 9, 1988, he had been driving home from work when he saw a cop with his gun out. The officer turned out to be Randy Hampton, the same cop that four Native witnesses at the inquest had said they saw with his revolver drawn, but Judge Enns wouldn't believe.

Tymchuk was white, though. So there was no reason to suspect him of having an ethnic bias. And he'd also had a longer look at Hampton while his car was stopped at the intersection of Weston Street and Logan Avenue. Hampton had also been stationary at the time. As he watched Tymchuk testify at the AJI, Gordon Sinclair decided that the blue-collar father of three was more representative of the city's attitude about the Harper shooting than the racist hate mail he had received.

After Tymchuk finished and was hurrying back to his car, Sinclair caught up with him, wanting to know why he hadn't come forward earlier. Tymchuk said that he had phoned the police within a month of the shooting, but they hadn't seemed interested in what he had to say. "The impression I got was that there was already enough information around."

Sinclair wondered if he was afraid of police payback now. Tymchuk joked about needing a bank loan to cover his next speeding ticket. Then he said, "You hear stories about repercussions. I can't see that happening in a reasonable society. Can you?" Sinclair didn't answer.

So why had he decided to testify? "I didn't want to go through the rest of my life knowing this," he said.

Meanwhile, back at the Law Courts building, Harvey Pollock had drawn a direct line between Tymchuk's testimony and the question of whether Cross had drawn his revolver.

"We believe there is a high probability he had his gun out," Pollock said, referring to Cross. "We have to assume the police lied and that they are covering up."

In the two weeks since Cross had testified, something else had happened. McGregor had produced the two police reports about J.J. Harper which he hadn't been able to get Judge Enns to enter as exhibits. Now he wanted the inquiry to consider them. Both involved drunken domestic incidents, but there was more to them than that. The first was dated Christmas 1986. Harper had been arrested and taken to a drunk tank after Lois had called police. The police had found Harper drunk and yelling obscenities, but Lois seemed fine. According to the report, the police had tussled with Harper, at one point hitting him with a baton before handcuffing him.

Harper was released later Christmas Day. Although the incident had occurred at the end of 1986, the report wasn't written until March 31, 1988, twenty-two days after Harper died and fifteen months after the arrest. Constable Phil Siatecki had prepared the report on the orders of Sergeant Rex Keatinge. That same day, March 31, 1988, Constable Marty Lucas prepared a report on a similar incident, again at Keatinge's request. This one had happened in August 1987, seven months before the shooting, during Lois and J.J.'s separation. Again, Lois had called police, this time to complain of a prowler. The retroactively written report said that Harper had broken into his former home and again fought with the police before being subdued. Lucas specifically noted that at one point he drew his gun, but Harper kept coming. When his partner, Stan Kondrat, grabbed Harper, Lucas said he'd holstered his revolver and assisted Kondrat.

It was up to Al Hamilton and Murray Sinclair to decide whether the police reports should be made public and tendered as exhibits, but that decision was made for them. On September 18, McGregor and Minuk served notice to the commission that, out of respect for Lois Harper, they would not be proceeding with calling evidence on the two previous police incidents. Later that day, Harvey Pollock wrote to Schulman and McNicol.

> Mrs. Harper is surprised to learn that a police officer drew his revolver given those circumstances referred to in the said letter. Further, had such an incident occurred as alleged by the police, then surely it would have been recorded in the police officer's notebook because of the gravity of the incident. We verily believe that there is no reference made to the alleged incident in any of the police officers' notebooks who were in attendance in respect to the I.P.D. [Intoxicated Persons Detention act] incidents.
>
> Should commission counsel believe that calling the four police officers involved in the I.P.D. incidents would assist the Inquiry in arriving at the truth of how J.J. Harper met his death, then Winnipeg Police Association counsel ought not to concern themselves with Mrs. Harper's personal feelings.

The four police who had no notes on the alleged incidents weren't called to testify and their reports were never filed as exhibits.

For the first three weeks, the commission had rolled along without the police association erecting any barricades. On their own, the commissioners had decided not to look into the Bunn and Ross murder case because Grywinski still had to stand trial. But the day before they decided that, the case came up when Hersh Wolch was cross-examining Sergeant Harry Williams.

"Were you involved in the Bunn and Ross case?"

"Yes, sir."

"Mr. Ross has indicated that when he was questioned for the murder for which we have found him to be innocent, he was taken to Portage la Prairie for two days and interviewed. Were you party to that?"

Williams not only denied going to Portage la Prairie, he denied knowing Ross was taken there. Williams said he was busy on other cases at that time. "My partner, who at the time was Inspector Dowson, he became involved, and I believe he was the chief investigating officer."

"So when he comes here we can ask him about that?"

"That's right, sir."

Murray Sinclair had another question for Williams. "Just one other thing, sergeant. You keep talking about senior executive officers throughout your testimony, and you've mentioned a couple of them. Can you tell me who, in your estimation, were the senior officers with respect to this investigation who had decision-making power?"

"In our division it was, at that time he was Staff Sergeant, and he was Acting Inspector Ken Dowson."

"How do you spell Dowson?"

"D O W S O N."

"Are we going to hear from him?"

"Yes, sir."

Gordon Sinclair wasn't at the inquiry on August 23, the day Harry Williams appeared. If he had been, he would have been surprised by his testimony. Sinclair had covered the case for a year and a half and he had never heard of Ken Dowson. And it would be another month before he would.

37

"IT'S EVEN NOW."

Gordon Sinclair's mind wasn't on the hearings when he arrived at the *Free Press* on Wednesday, September 20, 1989. His stag was that night, and the wedding was on Sunday. Then, late that morning, word reached the newsroom that the inquiry had adjourned for the day. Someone had committed suicide. Sinclair called Harvey Pollock.

"Gord, I can't tell you. We've been told not to say anything."

It was tragic, that's all he would say.

"Who do you think it was?" Pollock asked.

There was only one person Sinclair could think of: Bob Cross.

John Campbell heard the news over the phone in his office at the Winnipeg Police Association. At 11:30 a.m. Campbell and a colleague pulled up outside Robert Cross's home.

"I know why you're here," said the man who answered the door. Then Bob Cross turned, walked into the kitchen and put on some coffee. Before Campbell arrived, Cross had looked shaken when he told Diane the name of the cop who had shot himself. Now, to Campbell, Cross appeared emotionless. Stiff, and cold, like a living corpse. "We were concerned that you might feel some guilt," Campbell said.

On the other side of the city, in East Kildonan, a police officer walked into Munroe Pharmacy. He was looking for the short, middle-aged woman who did the drugstore's books. At first, when Jill Dowson saw him, she thought there had been a robbery. He asked her to come with him and she followed the policeman without question. He tried to lead her out the back door, but it was blocked by boxes. Finally, on the front sidewalk, Jill laughed in bewilderment.

"What's going on?"

The officer took her hand.

"Rex is waiting around back," he said softly.

It was then she knew; her husband was dead.

"*No! No!*" she screamed.

Three days earlier, on Sunday, Jill Dowson had been resting in their bedroom when her husband came in.

"Come on, honey," Ken Dowson said. "Let's get up and go out to Lockport for an ice cream."

The traditional Winnipeg Sunday drive north eighteen kilometres to Lockport would have taken them right past Herb Stephen's brown bungalow. Instead, Dowson veered west across the Chief Peguis Bridge, named after the Ojibway leader who befriended the first white settlers to the Red River Colony. The bridge led to Main Street, and the long way to Lockport.

"Let's go see Vic," he said when they reached the other side.

They could see Vic's place from the highway. It was at the top of a grassy hillside, in front of a long, low hedge and marked by a rectangular, bronze plaque set flush with the grass of the Glen Eden Cemetery.

Victor N. Bozyk

1936 – 1986

Vic Bozyk was someone Ken Dowson had looked up to, a beefy detective who had survived a legendary level-crossing tango with a train.

Jill bent down and brushed a leaf off the plaque. Ken was standing behind her.

"You know," he said, "I was always happy around Vic." Then he looked around. "It's a nice place here," he said. Jill sensed his sadness. He had been anxious and depressed lately about the Harper case. But she didn't make the connection. Instead, she tried to deflect his depression.

"Yeah," she agreed. "But there are other cemeteries."

"I wonder if they have any plots here?" he wondered aloud. Jill was still bending over the grave. She didn't want to look back at him. She didn't want him to see her tears.

"I'll see," she said.

Jill's father was with Rex Keatinge behind the drugstore waiting for her. Keatinge was Ken Dowson's best friend, the person he trusted to find his body in the basement that morning.

Late the previous night Dowson had called Keatinge at home and invited himself over. Half an hour later Dowson walked in, poured himself a drink, and sat down on the living room floor.

"In hindsight," Keatinge said at the inquest, "I guess that was his way of asking me to have a last drink with him."

But Keatinge didn't have a drink that night. He just listened as Dowson talked fondly about Vic Bozyk, the place he was buried, and how he had been out to visit it on Sunday.

"I didn't see anything unusual because I knew he had a lot of respect for this man," Keatinge said.

What was unusual, given how anxious he'd been lately, was how relaxed Dowson seemed, especially since he was to testify the next morning.

It was after 1 a.m., and Dowson was on his way out the door when he turned back.

"You're a lucky son of a bitch," he said.

"What do you mean?"

"You only have two more years left before you can get out of that goddamn place."

Keatinge was taken aback. Dowson never talked about retirement. Never. Keatinge followed him out the door, into the darkness.

"Are you okay?" Keatinge inquired.

"Yes," Dowson said.

Eight hours later, Keatinge's phone rang. It was 9:20 a.m. and Dowson was on the line. He wanted Keatinge to come over to the house. He wanted to show him something.

Keatinge was reluctant.

"Please," Dowson said. "Will you come now?"

Less than an hour later Keatinge wheeled his station wagon off Henderson Highway and onto Fraser's Grove. Dowson lived near the bottom of the street, in a bungalow guarded by two evergreens and a weeping willow. Keatinge rapped on the back door. When no one answered, he stepped in and called Ken. There was no answer. Keatinge took the stairs to the basement. It was dark, except for the cold glow of the cabinet TV. The Manitoba Aboriginal Justice Inquiry was on and Rick Poneira was being cross-examined. Dowson was supposed to be the next witness. Keatinge stood there, watching Poneira, until something pulled him towards the utility room. The Nothing Room, Jill Dowson called it. The door was partly open. Keatinge peered in.

There was a weightlifting apparatus, with a black bench jutting toward him, like a tongue. On it was an open Samsonite briefcase and inside was a pad of legal-sized paper propped up, like a speech on a lectern. But Keatinge wasn't looking at the briefcase.

"I see him laying on the floor over against the wall," Keatinge later told the inquest.

Dowson was sprawled on his right side, blood trickling from his left ear. Keatinge bent down by the body and felt for a pulse.

"I knew he was dead. I wondered how he died."

Dowson had fallen on his service revolver.

"I began to search the room . . .

"I walked over and looked at these two notes. One was a torn page. One was four pages with my name on it."

It began: "*I guess the first question everyone is going to ask is why? To anyone who really knows me the answer should be obvious . . .*"

Herb Stephen and Deputy Chief Paul Johnston were visiting Assistant Commissioner Dale Henry that morning when the chief received a call about the suicide. Without explaining why, Stephen and Johnston excused themselves and drove to Dowson's house.

In law the authority of the medical examiner's office supersedes police authority at a death scene. But the police weren't cooperating with Hedie Epp, the investigator sent from medical examiner Peter Markesteyn's office. When she asked if the suicide had anything to do with the Harper investigation, they told her no. And when Stephen arrived he took charge. After he, Johnston, and Crime Superintendent Joe Gallagher viewed the body in the basement, Rex Keatinge took the chief aside privately in Dowson's upstairs bedroom. At that point, as far as the homicide detectives knew, Dowson hadn't left any notes, which is what they told Hedie Epp at first. Keatinge hadn't told anyone he had the notes because he was thinking about secreting them. Years later, he told Gordon Sinclair that, by the time Stephen arrived, he'd decided to turn them over to the chief, which is what he did in the bedroom. Stephen slid them into a pocket and left the scene without even telling Crime Superintendent Joe Gallagher about the suicide notes. Gallagher drove him to see Jill Dowson at her parents' home.

It was a short drive to the same house Jill had been living in when she began dating Ken in high school. By the time John Campbell arrived, Manitoba's Chief Provincial Judge Kris Stefanson, a friend of Dowson's, was there holding Jill's hand. Herb Stephen had already been there to hold the widow's hand.

"How many lives does this thing have to take?" Jill Dowson had asked Herb Stephen.

"Yes, yes, I know," the chief had said.

It was mid-afternoon when Herb Stephen began reading the press release. Dowson, it was learned by the end of the day, was the officer in charge of the Harper investigation, but Stephen wouldn't refer to him that way in his statement.

"At 10:30 today, a member of the department attended at the home of Inspector Kenneth George Dowson, 43 years, a 19-year veteran of this department. Inspector Dowson was found dead from an apparent self-inflicted gunshot wound.

"Inspector Dowson has served in a number of areas in the department, specializing in criminal investigation through most of his service. He was appointed inspector 89 01 29. Inspector Dowson was a staff sergeant in crime division at the time of the J.J. Harper fatality. As a result, he was to appear at the Aboriginal Justice Inquiry today.

"This tragedy is under intense investigation at the present time. It would be premature to speculate whether his pending appearance before the inquiry had any influence in this terrible event."

In the course of the news conference Stephen mentioned the four-page suicide note.

"It's entirely possible there may be more victims," Stephen warned.

Then, ignoring the last line of his own news release, he assigned blame. "It was definitely caused by the inquiry that's going on."

Later, Mayor Bill Norrie took the chief's verdict and pronounced sentence. The inquiry had been going on too long. He wanted it to wind up. Manitoba's Justice Minister Jim McCrae agreed.

Meanwhile, Randy McNicol was defending the inquiry to reporters, saying they had had no plans to hear from Dowson until city lawyer Doug Abra asked them to call him as a witness.

"The City of Winnipeg Police Department suggested that he would be an important and knowledgeable witness," McNicol said.

But not everyone blamed the inquiry. "If you're looking for who's responsible," Police Commissioner Robert Lunney told a group of reporters, "look around you."

Gordon Sinclair was stunned by the news of Ken Dowson's suicide. He had never thought to ask the name of the lead investigator of the Harper case. From day one he always considered the chief to be in charge, if for no other reason than it was Herb Stephen's review of the file that had cleared Cross.

There was something else Sinclair would learn about Dowson later from a lawyer who lived across the street from the columnist. Richard Beamish told him that Dowson was the detective who had shoulder-shoved him outside the courtroom when Bunn and Ross were acquitted on the last day of the inquest.

Over the years Sinclair would learn much more about Dowson, but that late afternoon, as he sat down to write the next day's column, all Sinclair knew was that he didn't know anything about Ken Dowson. He had been all but invisible since the night Harper died.

As usual Sinclair began with the headline.

POINTING THE FINGER

Yesterday morning, mere hours before he was supposed to testify at the aboriginal justice inquiry, a police officer pointed his service revolver at his temple and pulled the trigger.

By yesterday afternoon, the police department was pointing fingers. In less time than the department took to clear Robert Cross in the J.J. Harper shooting . . . the police commissioner and police chief assessed blame. The aboriginal justice inquiry was "definitely" a factor, said Chief Herb Stephen.

The unrelenting news media pressure played a role, suggested commissioner Robert Lunney . . .

I don't know if Ken Dowson was under pressure from above because of the Harper investigation's obvious inadequacies. I don't know if his suicide had anything to do with his own directing of the Harper investigation.

Maybe Dowson's four-page suicide note will tell us more about that.

What I do know about assessing blame is this.

It wasn't the inquiry or the media that botched the investigation.

It wasn't one of the inquiry investigators who failed to knock on every door in the neighbourhood the night Harper was shot.

It wasn't a reporter who failed to fingerprint Cross's revolver.

It wasn't an inquiry investigator who broke down weeping and offered to resign because he rewrote his notebook of the Harper investigation.

What was odd about what the police chief did yesterday afternoon wasn't so much that he went on the offensive with the inquiry by suggesting it was directly linked to the suicide.

What was surprising was that his comments came minutes after he issued a four paragraph news release that ended with these words.

"This tragedy is under intense investigation at the present time. It would be premature to speculate whether his pending appearance before the inquiry had any influence in this terrible event."

What occurs to me when I read those words is not that they're inconsistent with his later comments. Inconsistency, after all, is a trademark of the Harper investigation.

What occurs to me, instead, is the sad irony of the words the chief used.

"This tragedy is under intense investigation. . . . it would be premature to speculate."

If the department had taken the same approach to the Harper investigation, it wouldn't be part of the aboriginal justice inquiry. And that's pointing the finger where it belongs.

That morning, medical examiner Dr. Peter Markesteyn had been at a conference in Edmonton when his investigator, Hedie Epp, finally learned there was a suicide note, but the police wouldn't give it to her. He immediately drove back to Winnipeg, arriving in time that evening to see Jill. Markesteyn felt a bond with Dowson's family, as cops and coroners usually work closely together. In the emotion of the moment, he promised Jill that he would protect the family's privacy.

It wasn't until the following day that the police grudgingly gave Markesteyn the long letter addressed to Keatinge, and the other note. The police claimed Ken Dowson hadn't left a letter to his family. But years later, Anglican priest Robin Mather told Gordon Sinclair that there was a third note, one left for the family. Jill Dowson had asked him to read it to her children at their grandparents' home on the evening of the suicide.

Grief and anger hung in the air like a combustible vapour in Jill's parents' home that night. Understandably, some of it was directed at Ken Dowson. But most of the rage was directed at Herb Stephen, someone who was there told Sinclair later. His source left the why to his imagination.

That night, detectives Harry Williams and Cal Osborne, the pair who had taken Cross's statement, sat outside the Dowson home, guarding Ken Dowson's family.

Gordon Sinclair didn't feel like going to his stag that night. Marty Minuk was supposed to be there, but he was late. The shock of the suicide had left him looking drained and depressed. Sinclair remembered the over-the-shoulder smirk Minuk had given him when Judge Enns was reading his inquest report that blamed Harper for his own death. Now Minuk was staring blankly at a stripper in the final throes of tossing off her sequined costume, when the junior counsel for the Winnipeg Police Association said something Sinclair hadn't considered. "It's even now."

––––
38

"THE PHANTOM OFFICER."

The morning after the suicide a banner headline in the *Free Press* announced Dowson's death: "STAR OFFICER SHOOTS SELF: *Inspector idol of every constable – 'he had it all,' one says.*" There was a grainy black-and-white photo of Ken Dowson below the headline that looked as if it had been taken from a television screen.

Gordon Sinclair stared at the front-page photo of Dowson. He was in his inspector's uniform, with the four shoulder epaulets. It still bothered Sinclair that he had never heard of him, or even seen him before. Then he remembered. He had seen him once before. Dowson had walked in and taken a front-row seat at the inquest one day. For some reason, maybe because he looked like a cop and he didn't know him, Sinclair remembered that.

The day after the suicide the *Free Press* article began by trying to paint a picture of the man.

He was described by other officers as a crackerjack, happy-go-lucky cop. Reporters who knew him talked about his cooperative, friendly attitude.

Later Gordon Sinclair talked to several people who knew Dowson.

"He was one of the best, one of the smartest," said Police Association president John Campbell. "He'd take you through two hours of conversation and he would tell you what the two inconsistencies were."

"Smooth and charming," was the way defence lawyer Hymie Weinstein described him.

His police academy instructor, Dennis Scott-Herridge, said Dowson's service in the Canadian army helped him get into recruit class, that and a promise to finish grade 12.

"He just so impressed everyone with his motivation and desire to become a police officer that they took him on and said during training he would have to complete his grade 12," Scott-Herridge said.

Dowson had gone on to graduate at the top of a recruit class that included Eric Hrycyk. Scott-Herridge presented Dowson with a gold tie tack, shaped like handcuffs, the first and last officer he honoured that way.

Al McGregor and Marty Minuk had been close to Dowson, too. But there was another lawyer at their firm who liked him even more than they did. Ken Dowson was the big cop Ellen Gordon had sat beside during the inquest victory party at Simkin Gallagher. Ellen remembered one weekend when Dowson was working as sergeant of detectives and she wanted him to recommend to a magistrate that her client should be given bail. The client was Native and Ellen told Dowson his problems with the law could be linked to especially tragic circumstances that went beyond boozing and neglect. His mother had tried to kill him when he was a small child. Dowson listened to the story, then released the kid on condition that he report once a week directly to him.

But there were other lawyers who wondered about Dowson's ethics and his tactics. Hersh Wolch was one of those. He recalled the time Dowson had extracted a signed confession from one of his clients by letting the man mistakenly assume he was a defence counsel.

Sinclair also spoke with Jeff Gindin, who lectured law students at the University of Manitoba and liked to use Dowson as a witness in the mock court. "I knew he'd be difficult to deal with and bright," Gindin explained.

At the inquiry Dowson was supposed to testify about the report he had written to Herb Stephen two months after the shooting. In it

Dowson acknowledged the investigation's flaws – failing to finger-print the gun, the missed eyeglasses, the incomplete canvass – and suggested policy changes designed to prevent the same mistakes being made. But eventually it became clear to Gordon Sinclair that Dowson's involvement in the Harper case went way beyond writing a lessons-learned report on an investigation he'd taken charge of after being called out by Eric Hrycyk.

According to Dowson, he and Keatinge had been seconded to the inquest at the request of Crown Attorney Bill Morton. Morton shouldn't have needed any help. The attorney general had already given him RCMP Sergeant Wes Border.

It was Dowson who had accompanied Border when he interviewed the three young Native witnesses, Morisette, Houston, and Yaworek, whose arrest outside the inquest so outraged artist Jeff Funnell. It was Dowson who had noted in a report that Yaworek had an outstanding warrant for a traffic offence. It was Dowson who had checked with the city to see if grey would be seen as grey under the lights of Logan and black would be black.

At his office that morning, Martin Pollock wrote a memo to file. "At the commencement of the hearings into the shooting death of J.J. Harper, I, off the cuff, asked Commission lawyer Randy McNicol, 'Randy, do you think there may be a phantom involved in this matter?' Today, one day after the tragic news [of] Ken Dowson's suicide, I believe him to be the phantom officer. I believe that Ken Dowson was at the shooting scene with acting Inspector Hrycyk, Field Supervisor Spryszak, Constable Hodgins, Cross, Eakin and Poneira . . ."

More specifically Martin suspected Dowson might be the "old man" cop Allan said he had overheard telling Cross to say the shoot-ing was an accident.

Dowson's death had unleashed pent-up rage on both sides. "To put it bluntly," Inspector Lou Spado said, "I'm pissed off at the witch hunt that so-called inquiry has become. I think Kenny was a victim of the

meat-grinder they were going to put him through. They were supposed to be looking for prejudice, but they wound up hounding us,
looking for things that don't exist."

Native leaders counterattacked. Manitoba Grand Chief Phil
Fontaine called a news conference where he demanded Mayor Norrie
and Chief Stephen apologize or resign for suggesting the inquiry
should quickly conclude. Fontaine was also dismayed by Justice
Minister McCrae's attitude. "His remarks don't give us any confidence
that this government will implement the inquiry's recommendations."

There were no apologies or resignations.

In the wake of this emotional storm, on a perfect Prairie autumn
Sunday, Gordon Sinclair and Athina Panopoulos were married at St.
Demetrios Greek Orthodox Church. Sinclair had invited police asso-
ciation lawyer Marty Minuk to the reception afterwards, but not the
Pollocks, with whom he hadn't yet become close.

The next day, the newlyweds flew off for a honeymoon in Europe.
Sinclair asked his brother, David, to wire the Canadian Embassy
in Bonn, West Germany, when the chief testified. As it turned out,
Herb Stephen wouldn't be testifying until after they got back in
November. The inquiry had decided to postpone hearings until after
the Dowson inquest.

Later, in what McNicol characterized as a decision based on the
AJI being blamed for Dowson's suicide, a private investigator was hired
to look into the detective's background. Over the next few years
Gordon Sinclair would do his own investigation of Ken Dowson, and
what he uncovered about the pressures that led to his suicide pointed
to more complex circumstances than his appearance at the AJI.

39

"THEY KNOW WHO THEY ARE."

On the Monday after Dowson's suicide, Martin Pollock decided he needed a shoeshine. The shop he usually went to was a few blocks from his office. Martin had his choice of routes to take, but on this fall morning he decided to take Graham Avenue down to Donald Street.

Ken Dowson's body was there.

Cruiser car 106, the one Danny Smyth had been in the morning Harper died, blocked the intersection long before the flag-draped casket was carried into Holy Trinity Church across from Eaton's. As Martin neared Graham and Donald he could see hundreds of mourners lining the street and filling the Gothic church's courtyard.

Inside Holy Trinity nearly a thousand people filled every corner of the hundred-year-old church. Ken Dowson was being treated as if he had died in the line of duty. The Winnipeg police choir was there, so were police officers from all over Canada. Rex Keatinge sat at the front with Jill Dowson and her children. Farther along the front-row pew, Ellen Gordon sat weeping beside Marty Minuk.

Oddly, the family had chosen to share their pew with the police association law firm, rather than the police chief. Herb Stephen, his wife, Faye, and Deputy Chief Paul Johnston were ushered to seats several rows back. So were Assistant Commissioner Dale Henry and Robert Cross. At the front, a clergyman stood behind a brass lectern, shaped in the form of an eagle.

"Remember a man who loved pomp and ceremony," said the minister. "Remember a man who laughed at his own jokes. Remember a man who hated the cat, but still gave it a sardine. Remember a man who was allergic to holidays . . ." Dowson, the minister added, "was totally honest and couldn't tell a lie."

Inspector Wayne King, the investigator on the Ticketgate case, gave the eulogy, saying that Dowson was always handed the toughest, high-profile cases, and pushed himself to the limits, and beyond.

"When I chided him about the extra stress he was enduring he'd laugh and joke. 'Hey buddy, don't worry about me. Look where it got me. Look where I am.'"

King suggested there was a lesson to be learned from Dowson's death. "Grown men do cry. Don't expect perfection every time. Don't give it all. Keep some for yourself. We're only human."

Jill Dowson listened to the eulogy awash in tears and memories. The last time she saw her husband was as she was leaving for work on the morning he was scheduled to testify. The time was 8:50.

"When are you leaving?" Jill asked.

"In about half an hour," he said.

"Good luck."

"OK," he said.

"I'll talk to you later," she said.

Their daughter, Kelly, was taking just one course at high school and she would be coming home later in the morning. Afterward Jill thought he must have panicked at the thought of Kelly finding his body.

"When you come home from school, just take my car and go to work," he told his daughter.

"But Dad," she said, "I don't have to be at work until 1 o'clock."

"Just take my car and go to work," he ordered.

It was four days before Jill could go back to the house. By that time her girlfriend Bev had shared a feeling she had about the house.

"There's something there, Jill," she said. "You've got to go and look." Bev thought it was something to do with a photograph.

On Sunday Jill, Rex Keatinge, and two of the children returned to the house. It was after dark, about 10 p.m.

"I wanted to touch things," Jill remembered. She stroked the soiled shirt he had discarded in the bathroom, and buried her face in his pillow, before the smell of him disappeared, too.

Then, as if following his scent, she wandered into the living room and over to the piano. She moved pictures and looked behind things, but she couldn't find anything. Then she turned and walked into the dining room, pausing in front of the family photo on the wall. Jill had found what Ken left behind, Bev told her later. "You walked where he walked."

Jill decided that Ken had taken a few minutes after Kelly left for school to stand by the family photo and remember.

"I don't think he could have committed suicide if he hadn't done that," Jill said.

A lone piper played "Amazing Grace" and the bells tolled as the casket was wheeled into the crowded courtyard. Bruce Owen was outside, covering the funeral for CBC TV. He watched Jill Dowson emerge from the church, sobbing and clutching her husband's police hat to her face while Rex Keatinge steadied her. Across the street, *Free Press* photographer Glenn Olsen snapped pictures from an overhead crosswalk. As the mourners filed out behind the family, the piper could still be heard inside the church, the tune reverberating alongside the poison-tipped spear remark that Wayne King had flung as he began the eulogy.

"And I'll dwell not on what and who caused his death – for they know who they are."

The hearse led the procession past City Hall and the Public Safety Building, and along Main Street. Two police officers had been stationed on every corner and as Ken Dowson's body passed, they stood at attention and saluted. The procession drove slowly out of town to the countryside, and the open hole beside Vic Bozyk's grave.

After the interment, the mourners drove to the Kildonan Canoe Club. Ellen Gordon had never before been to a wake and couldn't believe the boozing that was going on. At one point, Jill put her drink down and went to the washroom with a girlfriend. While she was there, Herb Stephen's wife walked in. As soon as Jill saw Faye Stephen, she turned to her girlfriend and said something that would echo through the halls of the Public Safety Building. "Get me the fuck out of here."

At the time Dowson was buried, Sinclair was in Europe, and *Free Press* Ombudsman Barry Mullin was receiving calls from angry readers who thought the columnist was wholly responsible for the suicide and should be fired. Mullin published some sample comments.

"Why keep that Indian-lover on staff?" observed one caller who refused to give his name. Another wrote: "I am certain he has something against the Winnipeg police force and I just hope they in turn get Gordon Sinclair really good. Why would the *Free Press* allow a man to chastise a man [Cross] so badly and repeatedly? He [Sinclair] is judge and jury all by himself and I feel this is terrible." One woman said: "You've got the blood of that police officer on your hands now." Another woman added: "I hold Gordon Sinclair and the *Free Press* responsible for his death. He crucified the force and killed a good man." A man wrote: "Are you satisfied? Sinclair's been on the side of the Natives since day one. He's done such a good job, a good cop is dead." Another said: "No cop should have to die for a Native."

The Ombudsman's column, which appeared three days after the funeral, concluded with a reference to Wayne King's eulogy.

"Earlier this week, Insp. Wayne King delivered a solemn and personal eulogy to his friend and fellow police officer Insp. Dowson. King said: 'I dwell not on who caused his death, for they know who they are.'

"I strongly doubt Insp. King was talking about the media."

40

"IT'S ALL YOUR FAULT."

When the inquest into Ken Dowson's death began on Halloween 1989, it was obvious that Chief Medical Examiner Markesteyn had kept his word to Jill Dowson about protecting the family's privacy. The exhibit list had been sanitized. Unlike the Harper inquest, there would be no photos of a corpse naked on the stainless steel autopsy table. No bloody clothes. No wallet. No private papers for the media to find. No gun. The exhibits were limited to documents, among them the autopsy report describing a military tattoo of a boy with helmet and rifle and the words, Never Again. As for the "why," Bill Davis, the City of Winnipeg's psychologist, said a combination of factors had caused Dowson to kill himself. Dr. Anthony Valentine testified that Dowson had a history of job-related stress and anxiety and could have been clinically depressed for as long as seven years. In April 1982, a year after putting Dowson on Ativan to help him cope with anxiety attacks, Valentine had made a note: "Uptight about work, especially taking responsibility."

The inquest's most compelling witness, the man he trusted enough to find his body and the suicide notes, saw Ken Dowson quite differently.

"He really seemed to handle the anxiety," Rex Keatinge said. "He really seemed to thrive on it. He had an inner drive for perfection. He wanted to accept responsibility for every investigation he undertook. He was always prepared to take the flak or heat."

Keatinge referred to Dowson drafting the new policy on officer-related shootings. "He wasn't at the scene of the shooting, he wasn't involved in it, but he knew it wasn't perfect, that mistakes had been made and he wanted to accept the responsibility for it. He took it personally and he took the humiliation personally. He refused to pass the blame onto anyone else. He knew that criticism would be levelled at the entire police department and he felt that was unfair."

Keatinge also told the inquest about Dowson coming over to his house for a farewell drink the night before he shot himself.

Dowson had visited others the day before he killed himself. He met with Herb Stephen, then walked down the hall to Deputy Chief Paul Johnston's office. Johnston told Gordon Sinclair later that whatever dealings the chief and Dowson had over the Harper investigation had always been private. The other deputies would ask Johnston what was going on, and the deputy chief of crime would tell them he didn't know. In Johnston's office on the morning of September 19 Dowson spoke briefly about his scheduled appearance at the inquiry the next morning. Then he talked wistfully about the good old days, and the New Year's Eve on which then Detective Staff Sergeant Johnston had ordered Chinese food and poured a few drinks for the boys. Dowson often reminisced about that night with fondness. At the time, Johnston didn't realize that this was Dowson's way of thanking him. The same day, he had dropped by unannounced on Al McGregor, who was surprised to see him. "What are you doing here?" the lawyer asked. Dowson told him he wanted to go over his evidence one more time. "In retrospect," McGregor said long afterwards, "I realize he wanted to say goodbye."

Dowson said goodbye to others without them knowing it. He dropped by to see LERA commissioner Des DePourcq, the grandfatherly former detective partner of Herb Stephen. And he met with flamboyant Crown Attorney Jack Montgomery, who got Virginia Cook to recant her police statement against Bunn and Ross, the two Indians wrongfully arrested for the murder of taxi driver Gurnam Singh Dhaliwal. Dowson wanted to talk about the case with Montgomery, which wasn't surprising given what Dowson wrote in the second suicide note.

At the inquest it was left to Keatinge to read the suicide note Dowson left for him. Keatinge had trouble composing himself as he began.

I guess the first question everyone is going to ask is why? To anyone who really knows me the answer should be obvious.

This investigation was screwed up from the beginning. I've never seen so many things go wrong. The glasses missed at the scene, the gun not printed, the photos that weren't taken.

And then the media took over and it's gone downhill from there. The effect on all of us has been devastating, especially [for] Cross and those young guys at the scene.

No one will ever realize how I wish my phone had never rung that morning, but I guess that's fate. The die was cast when Melvin Pruden stole the car.

The guys involved in the investigation did the best they could and it's not their fault. I failed to provide the leadership and direction. I just didn't make the right decisions.

The disservice done to Cross is immeasurable. I've been feeling this way for a while now and I guess when I learned that Cross was suicidal, well, that was it.

I find it almost unbelievable that anyone could believe that the shooting of Harper was racially motivated. I guess the commission counsel may have believed it before the hearings started, but I now think that their independent review of the forensics has established that this is not the case.

It doesn't matter, though, the hearing goes on and so does the daily condemnation of the department. The media has turned it into a circus. Nothing is private anymore, not even a grieving constable's mental condition.

Then, to watch supposedly mature individuals berate and humiliate a naive officer on the stand in front of a national audience is incredible, and to top it off our tax money is paying for it. The whole thing is a joke.

The media eats it up and the circus act continues. They have no shame. I've listened to the despair in the voices of some of the young officers – Randy Hampton begging Al to put him back on the stand because Tymchuk contradicted his evidence. Bob Parker because he feels he didn't adequately answer the questions the right way.

I don't know how Al McGregor takes the pressure. It's difficult to do the job when you don't have the tools and for Al, it's been one nine of hearts after another.

If I had only ordered the weapon printed, we may have all been spared this – but I didn't . . . a judgment call, and the worst one I could have ever made.

Anyways they will never be satisfied until they have their pound of flesh, so I'll be the sacrifice. I was the one in charge and I was responsible.

Harvey Pollock lost his son and knows the despair. I hope he understands what my family will go through.

I'll miss the special people in my life – my family and my good friends. I was proud to have served as a police officer. When I contemplated resigning after the revelation of Cross's condition, my wife told me to remember I had done a lot of good things in 19 years. She's right but that was all wiped out Mar 9/88.

I have no objections to the commission reading this, just don't make it public. My family will suffer enough. To the Chief, I'm sorry. I let you down.

Rex – sorry I dumped on you but you're the only one who really understood me. Look after Jill and the kids and keep the damn media away. I am going to join Vic. Maybe God has a place in heaven for cops. Nobody else understands us. Jill knows where I want to be buried.

Ken

Dowson added a P.S.: "*Don't forget to print the gun.*"

The last line was Dowson's macabre last laugh on the Aboriginal Justice Inquiry. Dowson knew that, despite what you see in movies, it's rare to find fingerprints on a handgun. They're blurred by the recoil and the heat when the gun is fired.

Judge Charles Rubin placed a prohibition on the contents of the second suicide note, because it related to the taxi driver murder. Confessed killer Christopher Glenn Grywinski was still facing trial. But the essence of the note had been published soon after Dowson died. Dowson had left it for Hersh Wolch, who represented Gordon Ross. The note read:

Hersh,

I refuse to be humiliated. Sorry Hersh. You never got your chance. The worst thing is you know Bunn and Ross are responsible.

Ten months after the suicide, a jury convicted Grywinski of the murder Dowson went to his grave insisting Garry Bunn and Gordon Ross had committed. Yet it came out at the trial that Grywinski's fingerprints were found on the taxi, and another cabbie had told police he saw a white guy driving the murder victim's taxi, but the police hadn't believed him.

There was more to it, though. By that time Sinclair had read the transcript of Hersh Wolch cross-examining Harry Williams about his client Ross being driven an hour west of Winnipeg to be interrogated for two days. Williams had claimed he wasn't personally involved, but had referred Wolch to someone who would know.

"My partner, who at the time was Inspector Dowson, he became involved and I believe he was the chief investigating officer."

"So when he comes here we can ask him about that?" Wolch asked.

"That's right, sir."

That was a month before the suicide. Later the inquiry commissioners had said they weren't going to allow questions about Bunn and Ross, again because of the Grywinski trial. But either Dowson didn't know that, or he was afraid to take a chance. Now Sinclair understood the meaning of the second note, and why Dowson was afraid of being humiliated by Wolch. Sinclair thought he had figured out some of the other reasons Dowson would rather die than take the stand at the AJI. When he looked back at the Harper inquest transcripts of Isaac's testimony, he saw where Harvey Pollock had come close to uncovering the invisible inspector.

Pollock: "Did you have a meeting with any of the inspectors, or with any sergeants in this matter in relationship to the evidence that you're giving here today?"

Isaac: "Well, I met with Inspector Keatinge when we listened to the transcript of the event."

Pollock: "Who did you report to when you got back to the station?"

Isaac: "To our sergeant."

Pollock: "Who is that?"

Isaac: "Sergeant Vokey at that time."

Pollock: "Yes?"

Isaac: "And later we transferred Mr. Pruden upstairs. The inspector at the time was present and I informed him of the details."

Pollock: "Which inspector?"

Isaac: "I'm not sure of his name."

Pollock: "Does he have a number?"

Isaac: "I'm not sure what his number is."

Pollock: "Who else was there besides you and this inspector?"

Isaac: "Really, we had no involvement with anybody else . . . I believe the inspector came by the desk where we were typing and that's when we advised him of our involvement."

Later, during the LERA process, Isaac remembered something he hadn't mentioned during his tearful AJI confession. Martin Pollock said Isaac told him in a casual conversation that it must have been a senior officer who ordered him to rewrite his notes because they weren't complete enough.

Sinclair also learned from the city's lawyer, Doug Abra – who had advised the inquiry to call Dowson – that it was Dowson's decision to send Detective Angus Anderson to watch firefighters wash down the shooting scene.

Long after the Dowson inquest, Sinclair attempted to get inside Dowson's head by creating the cross-examination he might have feared facing on the morning he shot himself:

Tell us, Inspector, you're an experienced homicide investigator, why didn't you make sure the neighbourhood canvass for witnesses was completed the day Mr. Harper was shot? . . . Can you tell us why you didn't overrule Bob Parker and have the gun and holster printed? How about the photographs of Cross's leg and boots, why didn't you make sure they were taken? . . . I direct your attention to Constable Isaac's testimony before this commission. He said he couldn't remember why he rewrote his whole notebook. But earlier, at the inquest, he said that some inspector came by and looked at his notes that morning. Was that you, Inspector Dowson? . . . What did you tell Constable Isaac about his notes? . . . Inspector, help me if you can. Why did you send Sergeant Angus Anderson out to the scene to watch the fire department wash away the shooting scene before daybreak? . . . Why was Cross helped with his statement, instead of interrogated? ... Inspector, we have documents here, your May 2 report to Chief Stephen, that show you and Inspector Keatinge were seconded by Mr. Morton to help him with the inquest when he already had Staff Sergeant Border from the RCMP for that purpose. ... Inspector, you'll recall at the inquest before Judge Enns, that there were three Aboriginal witnesses who testified about seeing an officer running across Logan with his revolver out on the night Mr. Harper died. And you'll remember that police appeared at the Law Courts Building and arrested one of them, Mr. Houston, on an outstanding traffic warrant? And it was you, Inspector Dowson, who ran a check on Houston and discovered the outstanding warrant for the traffic offences, was it not? ... Yes, so was it also you, sir, who ordered officers to arrest Mr. Houston on the same day and in the same place where he gave evidence? ... Would you not agree with me, sir, that you could have waited for another time and place? Or were you trying to send a message with the arrest? ... Well, inspector? We're waiting ...

Ken Dowson's fingerprints may not have been on his service revolver, but, Sinclair decided, they had been on almost everything else connected with the Harper case.

Later one night over dinner and a cigar, Police Association president John Campbell offered Sinclair a more sympathetic perspective on Dowson's involvement.

Spryszak had already mishandled the gun, Parker had already decided not to print it. The canvass that was supposed to have been done, wasn't.

"If Ken had really been in charge that night, it never would have happened. Someone had to be the scapegoat. He was the sergeant of detectives. Who else was left? By the time Kenny got on it what are you gonna do with the gun now, sergeant of detectives? The buck stops there. Superintendents, inspectors, all phone the sergeant of detectives for direction." Campbell took a slow drag on his cigar and exhaled. "He was a big detective. He wasn't afraid of anything. He'd grabbed more guys with guns. He was always the first guy in. And he was afraid. He couldn't face this?"

Then Campbell told Sinclair what he read between the lines in Dowson's suicide note. He said Dowson was being asked to do something he wasn't comfortable doing. "And there was no way out of this."

On the second day of the Dowson inquest, as Herb Stephen waited to be called to testify, a middle-aged woman in the gallery began cursing at him. Police Commissioner Robert Lunney attempted to calm her, but before she could be led away by sheriff's officers, the irate woman flung a cup of coffee on the chief. "You prejudiced bastard," she screamed. "It's all your fault."

41

"YOU'RE A PRETTY BRAVE LADY."

The October issue of *Blueprint*, the Winnipeg Police Association newsletter, featured a cover photo of Ken Dowson and the text of Wayne King's eulogy. Farther inside, there was a birth announcement. Kathy and Ron Hodgins had a baby boy. They named him Robert.

By early November, when the Aboriginal Justice Inquiry resumed with Hodgins on the stand, the commissioners heard that she also had been suffering from post-traumatic stress. Hodgins described the moment after the shooting when it started for her. It was when she looked into her partner's eyes.

"Constable Cross had a look in his eyes . . . The look is he's about to die. I don't know what to say to him. I walk up to him and I start brushing him off. I can't speak. I'm looking for the hole. My God. He's got to be injured. I can't find anything. A few seconds pass by. I don't know how much time has elapsed and he speaks to me. He states, 'He jumped me, Kath. I was on my back, on the ground. He went for my gun.' I will never, ever, forget what he said. How he said it. And the way he looked."

Hodgins might never forget that moment, but her memory wasn't as good when it came to the testimony she gave at the inquest. She said she couldn't even remember being there. As for her testimony at the inquiry, it was sometimes at odds with what other officers remembered, including Cross. Hodgins testified that she was in the front seat, the boy in the back and Cross was standing outside when he asked the boy for a description of the second suspect. Cross then shouted Allan's answers to her, because she said she hadn't heard them. The Silent Partner prevented that, she suggested. Hodgins's unspoken message was that if she couldn't hear Allan in the back seat, he couldn't have overheard her and Cross talking in the front seat.

The problem was that Hodgins's recall of the questioning didn't match Cross's.

"I got in the front seat with Kathy," Cross had told Harvey Pollock during cross-examination. "Once in the front seat with Kathy, I started asking questions of the young offender."

But commission counsel Perry Schulman didn't pick up on that. No one did. Instead, he directed Hodgins to the period just after Cross had left the cruiser and headed down the back lane to look for the second suspect.

"I heard the sound of what appeared to be a gunshot or the backfiring of a vehicle . . ." She wasn't sure what it was, but she knew what it wasn't. "It wasn't the backfiring of a car because I remember listening after it happened and I heard no traffic sounds, and that concerned me."

So she locked the car and headed into the alley, calling Cross's name.

Schulman followed up on Hodgins's remark about being concerned because she knew the shotlike sound wasn't a backfire.

"Did you have any concerns at this point?"

"At that point, no," Hodgins said, seeming to contradict herself. "It was a sound. It was strange. It was fairly close by. But no concerns. I was going to get my partner and we were going to go and investigate."

When he didn't immediately answer her call, Hodgins decided to return to the cruiser. Just as she turned to go back, she heard Cross calling for help on her radio.

Schulman asked if she had been concerned then.

"I had concerns. You hear a shot in the dark in the middle of the night and you think somebody is right beside you and they're not there. Of course you're going to have a concern. It's an unusual sound."

Hodgins described how she had backed the cruiser up to the intersection of Winks and Logan, where she met another cruiser manned by Isaac and Hampton. She got out of the cruiser and stood by the driver's door; Hampton did the same thing. They were a car length apart and Hodgins said she shouted at Hampton, asking if he knew where Cross was and telling him she would drive down the back lane looking for him.

Schulman pointed out that at the inquest she had testified that it was the six-foot-eight Isaac who got out of the car, not his partner Hampton.

Hodgins said she had been wrong at the inquest.

Schulman was puzzled.

"Help me understand this. Would your memory be more accurate in April of 1988 than in November of 1989?"

"When I went through the inquiry, to the best of my recollection, I was still in shock over the whole incident."

"So your evidence today is that you were wrong in April of 1988 and your memory is you have a clear recollection now of speaking to Constable Hampton?"

"I have a clear recollection of speaking to Constable Hampton. Yes, I do."

Schulman then explained that, according to the other officers, neither of her versions was accurate. Hampton and Isaac testified that they didn't stop at Winks and Logan to talk to Hodgins.

"I can't speak for what they said. I never watched their testimony. I recall speaking with Constable Hampton," Hodgins said.

Schulman then noted that Eakin had testified that it was his cruiser that stopped at Winks and Logan and that his partner Poneira got out of the car.

Hodgins said Eakin was wrong.

There were more important discrepancies, though.

Schulman asked Hodgins what she had said to Allan when he was being transferred from the back of her car to another cruiser.

Hodgins said she opened the rear passenger door and told Allan "somewhat in apologetic terms" – because she had never had to hand over a prisoner to another crew in mid-investigation – "that he was being transferred to another cruiser and that he was still under arrest. And I told him that if he hadn't been such a little thief to begin with, nothing would have happened. He was then turned over to –"

"Well," Schulman said, "just let's talk about that for a moment. Were your words: 'You little thief. If you hadn't stolen the car, none of this would have happened'?"

"No."

Schulman read from a police report done by detectives Dave Shipman and Ron Morin eight days after the shooting: "Respective of the alleged racial comments which Allan claims were uttered by PC Kathy Hodgins, this team had occasion to interview her on 88 03 17. Hodgins recalled specifically saying . . . 'You little thief. If you hadn't stolen the car none of this would have happened.'

"I'm asking you once again whether you said to the youth, 'You little thief, if you hadn't stolen the car none of this would have happened?'"

"I don't recall saying those exact words."

Schulman wasn't through. He wanted to know what she meant by "none of this would have happened."

"What were you referring to? Mr. Harper lying on the ground?"

"No, the fact he was still being charged and cautioned with theft of a vehicle."

"Well, let me understand it. Mr. Harper is lying on the ground not far from the car. You've seen your partner with an unusual look on his face like you saw in someone else at the moment of death?"

"H'mn, h'mn."

"Weren't you blaming him for the shooting?"

"No."

Schulman wasn't convinced.

"Is that appropriate to say to a fourteen-year-old boy, 'If you hadn't been a little thief to begin with, none of this would have happened'?"

Murray Sinclair interjected.

"Whether or not it is appropriate, it is a question for us to decide."

Schulman asked Hodgins about calling the boy a "fucking blue-eyed Indian."

"I didn't even know the youth was blue-eyed until all of this happened. It was dark."

"Was he a thief?"

"He was being charged with theft over $1,000."

Schulman had one more question.

"You know the charge was dropped, don't you?"

"No, I did not."

"Officer," Hersh Wolch began, "you mentioned that you looked in Officer Cross's eyes and you graphically described what you saw. You compared it to somebody who was facing something traumatic in the future."

"That is correct."

Wolch was into his second question when Hodgins asked him about his first.

"Did you say facing something in the future?"

Wolch suggested that, given the circumstances of the shooting – both suspects in custody, a passerby fatally wounded by a police revolver – officers knew they would have a lot of explaining to do.

"At no time was I thinking of things in the future that I'd have to explain. I would have to dare say that Constable Cross wasn't thinking of that either."

"Well, do you think Officer Cross at that stage was capable of thinking whether or not he should be transmitting on a radio band the newspapers might pick up?"

"I couldn't tell you. He came across to me on Channel 1. That was the channel that we were using."

"But from what you could assess of his state of – it might have been shock – do you feel he was even capable of addressing his mind to media coverage and things like that?"

"No."

It was Pollock's turn. Pollock wanted to know if Cross gave his partner any further account of the struggle with Harper, other than, " 'He jumped me, Kath. I was on my back on the ground and he went for my gun'?"

"At that point in time, no."

"At any time after he made that statement to you, did you inquire from him further about the circumstances of that incident?"

Hodgins said she hadn't.

"Were you not inquisitive about what happened?"

"I knew he'd tell me when he was ready to state it again."

"Did you ask him whether he had his gun out?"

"No. Three years of working with Constable Cross dealing with people time and time again in so many different instances. On all – on any but one occasion, I have never seen him approach anybody carrying a weapon. That thought would never have crossed my mind."

Harvey Pollock left that area for the moment and moved on.

"Constable, you remember you told us earlier that you heard what appeared to be a gunshot?"

"It sounded like possibly a gunshot."

"You got out of the car and you went down the back lane looking for your partner."

"Correct."

"When you thought you heard a gunshot, I take it you were apprehensive about what might be out there?"

"I didn't know it was a gunshot. I had never heard a gun outside a range with headphones on. It sounded somewhat like it, but it wasn't."

"Well, at that time, did you think it was a gunshot?"

"At that time I didn't know what it was, no."

"Did you suspect it was a gunshot?"

"I suspected it could have been almost anything. I did not single out a gunshot, no."

When Schulman had examined Hodgins earlier in the proceeding Harvey Pollock had noted her words: "I heard the sound of what appeared to be a gunshot or the backfiring of a vehicle . . ." And later: "It wasn't the backfiring of a car because I remember listening after it happened and I heard no traffic sounds. That concerned me." Pollock didn't challenge her further, though. Instead, he got to his pivotal point.

"When you left the car did you take your gun out of your holster as you proceeded into the back alley?"

"I never had my gun out."

"You're a pretty brave lady. Weren't you afraid something might happen to you there?"

"No."

Minutes later Pollock returned to the issue of how much Cross had or hadn't told his partner about the struggle.

"Constable, at no time did Constable Cross say to you that morning that Mr. Harper had tried to remove his gun from his holster, did he?"

"He said he took the gun from his holster," Hodgins answered.

"No, he said, 'He jumped me, Kath. I was on my back, on the ground, and he went for my gun,'" Pollock quoted.

"Oh, no. When we got back to Inspector Hrycyk's office he told me what happened then. He was able to talk to me then."

"I thought you told me earlier that you didn't discuss that particular matter?"

"Not while we were in the car. Not to that point."

"You're sure of that?"

"Yes."

"It's not an afterthought?"

"No."

Pollock asked if she had put what Cross told her in Hrycyk's office into an incident report.

"No."

Pollock pressed her on that answer.

"Didn't you think it was an important point to put into the incident report?"

"Obviously not," Hodgins answered.

Then Pollock went fishing, and Hodgins bit.

"Did you have occasion ever to speak to Inspector Dowson about this matter?"

"Yes, I did."

Pollock asked when.

"I remember speaking to him the day before the inquest started. Prior to that, I don't recall. I may have."

"What did you speak to Inspector Dowson about?"

"Inspector Dowson was . . ." She paused, then she said that Dowson and Keatinge had met her and the other constables from the shooting scene, and Dowson had played lawyer-witness with them.

"And all he was doing was sitting back and listening to testimony. One at a time officers were going into the boardroom of the fifth floor and basically presenting themselves, and he was just telling us to be calm and be clear and concise and to give our testimony. He just said, 'You'll do good.'"

It sounded like something Al McGregor would do, Gordon Sinclair thought when he heard that. But not a lead investigator. Unless he was concerned someone might inadvertently say something they weren't supposed to. It seemed to Sinclair that Ken Dowson would have had even more explaining to do had he not shot himself.

When he finished, Pollock told reporters how he felt about Hodgins's testimony.

"We were given Valium with Constable Cross's testimony. I don't know if we're getting 222s or 292s with Constable Hodgins."

Harvey Pollock would come to regret ridiculing Kathy Hodgins. She and her husband would see to that.

—
42

"THE BUCK STOPS WITH ME."

The weekend before Herb Stephen was scheduled to testify at the AJI he and his wife were spotted on an Air Canada flight home from Toronto. The flight attendant who recognized them asked Faye Stephen what they had been doing down east.

"We had to get away," she said.

Herb "Suitcase" Stephen got away a lot in 1989. He was absent from Winnipeg and his office, at various conferences, and other functions, a total of seventy-seven days.

On November 8, 1989, the day the Berlin Wall fell, Winnipeg's chief of police took the witness stand. There was a poppy pinned to his tunic and his arms were folded across his chest, a defensive, even defiant pose in keeping with much of his testimony over the next two days.

Perry Schulman had drawn the job of conducting the examination-in-chief. He quickly zeroed in on Exhibit 87, the press release the chief wrote and delivered on March 10, thirty-six hours after Harper died. Schulman quoted from the conclusion. "The Police Department Firearms Board of Enquiry convened and reviewed the details of this incident. They reached the conclusion that the death was precipitated by the assault on the officer by Harper and the subsequent struggle for his service revolver which accidentally discharged. They found no negligence on the part of the officer and I have concurred with their findings."

Then Schulman put a question to Herb Stephen: Was the press release intended to suggest that a fairly thorough investigation had already been carried out?

"This press release was developed based on the information that I had learned from these reports. Everything appeared to be consistent with what I have said in there. The markings on Constable Cross's clothes, the powder burns, the blood on the boot and the foot. All these appeared consistent with the story that Constable Cross had given."

Schulman pointed out that the canvass wasn't complete when Stephen issued his findings, nor had the revolver been fingerprinted.

"There was more work to be done, yes," Stephen replied.

"But wouldn't you acknowledge that, on March 10th, in releasing Exhibit 87 and the board's findings and your concurrence, that you were leading the public to believe that a pretty thorough investigation had already been done?"

"The conclusions I drew on that date, on the 10th, were eventually borne out by the inquest," Stephen replied. He went on to explain that the media might have accused him of stonewalling had he delayed issuing a statement until the investigation was complete. Then he added, "The word has come out that I exonerated him [Cross]. I take exception with that word because I never used that word."

"But didn't you create the impression by the content of Exhibit 87 that you had exonerated Constable Cross?"

"That was not the intention. I said that I found no negligence on the part of the officers."

Schulman next focussed on Spryszak's cursory canvass of the neighbourhood on the morning of the shooting. "In a case like this, where a citizen has been shot and there is one witness there alive, a police officer, and the event takes place in a residential area with a number of homes nearby, is it fair to say that it was important for the police department to do a canvass?"

"Yes, and it was my understanding that the canvass of the immediate area had been done."

Then Schulman referred the chief to Gordon Sinclair's column from March 12, 1988, "Circling the paddywagons," describing the interview with Herb Stephen in which the journalist had told the chief that there were people in the neighbourhood police still hadn't interviewed.

"Did the meeting take place at 2:30?"

"That would be fairly accurate. In my office on the fifth floor, where I was wearing my 'whiter than white shirt,' which I don't know what that means."

Sitting in a front-row gallery seat, Gordon Sinclair smiled. Apparently the chief thought it was a reference to racism, which Sinclair hadn't intended. At least not consciously.

Schulman quoted from the column: "'I began by asking if the police investigation into the Harper shooting was handled the same way as any other homicide investigation. He said it had been.' Is that accurate?"

"Yes, sir."

Judging by Dowson's report to Stephen, in which he recommended new procedures, Harper's death had not been treated like a homicide, but Schulman didn't pick up on that. He just kept reading excerpts from the column.

"'Stephen went on to repeat what he had told a news conference Thursday, that medical reports and physical evidence that police had gathered at the scene would back up the officer's story.' Did you say that?"

"Not all of that."

"What did you say?"

"I said the first part of it, and then I said that the physical evidence that we had gathered at the scene would be tendered at the inquest."

"You deny saying it would back up the officer's story?"

"That's correct, sir."

Schulman didn't know about a CBC radio interview with Herb Stephen broadcast two days after the shooting and the day after the chief's news release blamed Harper for his own death. If Schulman had, he might have challenged the chief.

"Our investigation goes forward now to the chief medical examiner," Stephen had told the CBC interviewer. "It's mandatory in the case of a police officer involved in a shooting that there be an inquest, so that will be held. And, there will be evidence brought forward there which will certainly, I'm positive, substantiate our findings."

Schulman continued, instead, to read from Sinclair's column: " 'But what about Harper's eyeglasses? After Ident had finished at the scene, newspaper reporters had discovered Harper's broken, blood-splattered glasses 2 ½ meters from where he had fallen.' Did he say that to you?"

"Yes, sir."

"Well, he wrote: 'I wondered if that affected his confidence in the job Ident did at the scene.' Did he wonder that out loud?"

"Yes, he put it in the form of a question."

" 'Not really,' he said, 'I think they did a thorough job.' Did you say that?"

"I'm not sure about the word 'thorough,' but I agreed that I still had confidence in them."

Schulman moved on. " 'I asked again if he was confident the investigation had been complete.' Did he ask you that?"

"Yes."

" 'Listen,' the chief replied, 'we did a thorough job on it.' Did you say that?"

"Not those words and I wouldn't have confirmed that the investigation was complete because I had already assured the media when I talked to them that the investigation was not complete."

Schulman wanted to clarify the chief's answer. "Are you saying that he has inaccurately recorded what you said on this point?"

"Yes, yes."

Schulman read the next paragraph, which Stephen agreed with. "That's when I told him about the three neighbours who hadn't been interviewed by police."

"But I'm sure that I didn't look 'momentarily startled,'" Stephen said. He explained why. "At the time I was talking to Mr. Sinclair I was under the impression that the canvass was still ongoing on the 9th and 10th."

As he sat in the gallery taking notes, Gordon Sinclair was shaking his head.

Earlier, when Schulman asked if it was important that a canvass be done, Stephen said, "Yes, and it was my understanding that the canvass of the immediate area had been done." And, in fact, Hrycyk had assured him there were no witnesses in his special report on the morning Harper was shot.

Schulman was at the end of the column.

"'So the investigation continues?' 'Oh,' he said, 'there's always little pieces to clean up on it, certainly.'"

"I disagree with that comment," the chief said before Schulman could ask. "That's not the way I would talk, about 'little pieces' to clean up on it."

Schulman asked the chief what he did say.

"That the investigation is continuing, or words to that effect."

Gordon Sinclair hadn't been aware that his column was going to be an exhibit and he was even more surprised at the chief's denying parts of what he had said during the interview.

Harvey Pollock swivelled in his chair, looked at Sinclair, and silently mouthed a question. "Have you got your notebook?"

Sinclair shrugged and shook his head. Then, he thought, it might still be on his paper-strewn desk, in a pile of other notebooks. At the lunch break, the columnist went back to his office and found the notebook. He was rereading the quotes, confirming in his own mind that they were accurate, when the phone rang. It was Phil Fontaine, the Grand Chief of the Manitoba Assembly of Chiefs. He had some information for Sinclair. About Dowson.

The following morning Hersh Wolch got his chance to cross-examine the chief. Stephen seemed to have some respect for Wolch, judging by the fact that before testifying, the chief introduced his wife to the defence lawyer.

"So it was your view that the job had been thorough when you spoke to Mr. Sinclair?" Wolch asked.

"Other than the fact that the glasses hadn't been found. I wasn't aware of that at the time."

Wolch directed Stephen to that part of the column in which he was quoted as saying that medical reports and physical evidence would back up the officer's story.

"I said some parts of that."

"Well, perhaps you can tell us what you said?"

"I see really nothing wrong with it. The medical reports and the physical evidence the police had gathered at the scene would back up the officer's story."

"Well, yesterday you said you didn't say that."

"Well, if I said that yesterday, I am in error. I don't recall saying that yesterday."

Wolch moved on, referring to the quote in which the chief said his department had done a "thorough investigation."

"Now is that also something that you didn't say to him?"

"I think they did a thorough job, other than missing those glasses."

"Well, yesterday, you said that those were not accurate quotations. The first one you weren't certain, the second one was not accurate."

"I made a comment to him about it being a thorough job. Now which one of those he wants to choose . . . but at one point I said they did a thorough job."

"Well, the difficulty I have, sir, is that you left a clear impression with me yesterday that Mr. Sinclair was either dishonest, incompetent, or possibly clairvoyant. But, in any event, all of us can make mistakes, and if your view today is that he is none of those and did his job properly, then I will move on."

"I have no comment to make about Mr. Sinclair at all," Stephen said coldly.

"Well, where is he inaccurate? You pick the spot. I mean, I have quoted where you said he was inaccurate yesterday and now you have told us no, he wasn't inaccurate."

"Yesterday I said that the investigation was continuing. I never made the comment 'little pieces to clean up on it.'"

Wolch suggested the quote was close to what he was thinking at the time.

"Absolutely not."

"Well, what were you thinking then?"

"I was thinking that the investigation was continuing."

"Into what?"

"They had a lot of canvassing to do."

"And what else?"

"Forensic reports to come back."

"I have real difficulty that if you felt there was lots to be done, such as canvassing and forensic, why you were publicly offering a personal opinion that there isn't even negligence on the part of the officer."

"Because that was what I felt based on what I had learned and, as I testified yesterday, in hindsight that may not happen again."

Wolch returned to the accuracy of the column and suggested to the chief that the only area he disagreed with now was the "little pieces" quote.

"I also don't agree with his comment – although he may have thought that – but that I looked momentarily startled. I doubt that very much."

The chief had one more complaint. Stephen said Gordon Sinclair was inaccurate in writing that Harper's broken glasses were blood-splattered when Darryl Sterdan found them. The glasses, he suggested, had blood on them because they had been dipped in a nearby pool of blood by a *Free Press* photographer.

If the chief had done his homework he would have known Darryl Sterdan had found only pin-sized blood spots on the lenses.

Harvey Pollock started his examination of Stephen by referring to something the chief had mentioned the day before.

"Yesterday you seemed to make a distinction between racial and ethnic jokes. Remember?"

"Yes."

"What is the difference?"

"An ethnic joke is one of these ones that can be used – and I've heard these things – where you talk about a Newfoundlander . . . Or if it's a Scotch person, you talk about a Scot."

"I don't see the difference. What's the difference between a racial and ethnic joke?"

"Well, I don't see anything wrong with the jokes that I'm talking about."

"No, I know. But I am just asking you, can you tell us the difference between an ethnic and a racial joke? Is there a difference?"

"No," Stephen said. "Possibly not. I can't describe the difference between them."

"Would you not agree with me that through the vehicle of humour, a person can show prejudice?"

"Oh, it's entirely possible, yes."

Pollock carried on in the same vein. Had Herb Stephen ever heard police officers refer to Aboriginals in a derogatory way?

"Not recently, but I suppose at some time in my career I must have heard it."

"How did you respond?"

"Just disregarded it."

"You didn't rebuke them?"

"No, I'm talking a way back in my career. No, I didn't."

"It doesn't make any difference how long ago it was. I just want to know what you did about it."

"I did nothing."

Eventually, Pollock turned to the night of the shooting. He reminded the chief about the discrepancies between the description Cross had of Pruden and what Harper actually looked like: the fact that Harper was nearly thirty-seven, not twenty-two as broadcast; that he was wearing a black jacket, but not leather as Cross claimed Allan had said; also that Harper was walking towards the scene, not running away. What were the reasonable and probable grounds that permitted Cross to grab Harper?

"In my opinion, and this will be up to a court to decide, if I had been there, knowing all those circumstances, I would have felt I had reasonable grounds and I would have arrested the man," Stephen said.

"So any person walking down the street wearing a black jacket, being Native, was a suspect. Is that what you are saying?"

"Well, there were other things to it. The man was uncooperative, and wouldn't answer any questions."

"He didn't have to answer any questions."

"That's right, but that still drew attention to him." Herb Stephen continued to stick to his opinion that there were grounds to arrest Harper.

"So, given the circumstances," Pollock said, "you are saying that at that particular point in time it was Harper that assaulted Cross and not Cross that assaulted Harper?"

"That is how I see it, yes."

"You want to stand by that answer?"

"Yes, sir."

As it turned out, the chief didn't stand by his answer for long.

When Pollock had finished, Al Hamilton started paging through his notes, looking for questions he had jotted down during the cross-examination. The commissioner reminded the chief that, according to Cross's own testimony, he had no intention of arresting Harper when he stopped him.

"And I think others – other of your officers – suggested there might have been an assault caused by Constable Cross on the person of Mr. Harper."

"I would agree," Stephen said. "If he wasn't planning on arresting him that would be an assault."

Hamilton then referred to the Firearms Review Board report that

Stephen had read the morning after the shooting. It described how Cross had grabbed Harper first.

"I'm just wondering, in view of all that, if it wasn't precipitous, both for the board to say, and for you to concur, that there was no negligence on the part of Constable Cross. In retrospect, do you think the evidence – all the evidence that was available – really supported that conclusion? Or do you think it was still up in the air?"

Stephen crossed his arms tight, again.

"I felt it did that at that time. But, as I said, in hindsight, it's something that I would wait longer on in future."

Hamilton had another concern. "One of the things that I've felt is that it was that initial apparent clearing that caused so much of the trouble and so much of the concern."

"Yes," Stephen said.

"Not only among the Aboriginal community but among some others as well. It just seemed a very precipitous sort of thing to do to say everything was fine. Would you agree with that?"

"I agree," Stephen said. "Although, as I reiterate, we did say the investigation was going on and there would be the inquest that ultimately would have all the results."

Hamilton was finished.

There was one remaining piece of business for the day. Murray Sinclair wanted Dowson's suicide note tendered as an exhibit.

The mention of Dowson reminded Gordon Sinclair of an earlier exchange between Hersh Wolch and Herb Stephen. Wolch had suggested that Dowson's report to Stephen outlining the mistakes in the investigation didn't read as if it were written by the man in charge of the Harper investigation. And the chief had allowed that there was a chain of command.

"Ultimately, I am the man in charge," Herb Stephen said. "The buck stops with me."

Minutes later, though, Wolch had asked again if the chief still believed Dowson was in charge of the Harper investigation.

"He was in charge of the investigation, yes."

When the chief finished, Gordon Sinclair waited for him to make his way through the gallery. After what Hersh Wolch had done to Stephen's attack on Sinclair's credibility, he was feeling vindicated and slightly smug.

"Shall we walk out together?" he asked the chief.

Stephen scowled and kept walking towards the open door and the glare of the TV cameras waiting for him in the hall.

Meanwhile, the tip Phil Fontaine gave Gordon Sinclair had given the columnist something else to pursue. "Dowson had a Native girl-friend," the grand chief had disclosed.

43

"SHE'S NOT INVITED TO THIS PARTY."

The walk-up apartment where Eunice Woodhouse lived was directly across the street from the Elmwood Cemetery and the family plot where three generations of Sinclairs, including Gordon Sinclair's parents, were buried. Sinclair wasn't sure what he expected Dowson's alleged Native girlfriend to look like, but whatever he was anticipating, it wasn't the woman who opened the door when he knocked. She was big. Tall and plump, but dressed primly in a pink cardigan, a frilly white blouse, and a skirt.

It was a short drive from her apartment across Redwood Bridge to Main Street, the last place she had seen Dowson just days before he died.

Eunice had an aversion to Main Street, but it wasn't because of that. "I hate the people on Main Street," she said, "because everyone looks at Main Street and they think it's the whole Native population. Society doesn't see us. They only see the bad. Ken often said there were more whites on Main Street than Natives, but that's the way people saw it . . ."

Gordon Sinclair and Eunice Woodhouse settled on going to

Kelekis, a landmark north-end restaurant. On the way to the restaurant, Eunice mentioned that the police had had her under surveillance for a time after the suicide. At least, she thought, she had been followed after she contacted one of Dowson's police pals, the guy he'd told her to call if something happened to him.

"The way he thought he would die was somebody he convicted would come back and get revenge on him for putting him away."

Eunice met Dowson because of someone they both put away for murder. She was seventeen, he was thirty-three.

It was the spring of 1978 and Eunice was working at a Tempo gas station and coin car wash on Logan Avenue. The police were doing a canvass of the area where a woman had died in a house fire. Her husband, who was later convicted, had knocked her unconscious in their second-floor bedroom, torched the bed, and then coolly rounded up their young children and taken them to McDonalds. Firefighters, searching for the source of the blaze, found a plastic container of gas under the bed. Eunice had sold the husband the gas.

Dowson was one of the detectives on the case. He walked into the filling station and asked if she sold gas there.

"Yeah," Eunice said cheekily, "that's what we do here."

And that's how it started. Eunice picked out the husband from three or four mug shots and, later, she even found the bill for the gas.

Dowson took her name, address, and phone number and promised to be in touch. Just as he was about to leave, he turned back to her.

"Why don't I do you a favour? I'll send someone younger."

"Yeah, sure," she said.

Not long after, Dowson returned to the gas station.

"Hey," Eunice smiled. "What happened to the young guy?"

Dowson looked flustered for a moment.

"Do I seem that old to you?"

Across the table at Kelekis, Eunice's round face lit up.

"He dropped by a couple of times after that for cigarettes. I sold cigarettes and gas. Why would I think anything of it?"

Then in October he called to make sure she'd received her sub-poena and ask if she wanted a ride to court. Eunice said she could get there herself. After she'd testified, Dowson showed up and arranged for another officer to drive her back to work in a red Corvette con-vertible she assumed was Dowson's.

Eunice had turned eighteen a month earlier. She had been a lonely little girl, an outsider on the Fairford reserve, where she grew up, and in the city. She was naive. She didn't get it. Even after Dowson kept popping in at the school where she worked. Even after he helped find her an apartment, just a five-minute drive from his home, when Eunice casually mentioned that she and a girlfriend were looking for a place.

Late one night, in the spring of 1979, Dowson called her and asked, "When I get off work, do you want me to come over for coffee?" That's how the late-night visits started. Eunice's place became a safe house for the stressed cop.

"He'd sit for a while and he'd leave again. He'd pace for a while. Then he'd say 'I have to go.' I think of how many nights I got out of bed to get him. I was so afraid he would get into a car accident in his condition. Or he'd kill someone in a car accident if it wasn't himself he was killing because he'd had so much to drink."

That first night he came over, it was two or three in the morning by the time Dowson and another detective showed up. Eunice and her girlfriend had already gone to bed, but they got up. Dowson and his police pal had brought vodka and rum and they started playing cards. But Eunice didn't know the game they were playing, or the one that the other cop was playing with her roommate. Dowson's buddy wound up dancing her roommate all the way from the living room into the bedroom. Nothing happened that night between Eunice and Dowson, or for many nights. Eunice kept him at a distance.

Sinclair wondered how long it was before they slept together. "I would say four years," she said. He rarely talked about his wife. "He used to always say, 'She's not invited to this party.'" Eunice laughed when she remembered that. Actually, it wasn't all that funny.

"I used to say, 'What are you doing? Why can't you just straighten out what's at home so you can get along with your life?'"

"No," he'd say. "I don't want to go home. Everyone is sleeping. I'm lonely. I have nobody to talk with. I'll go when I'm ready."

By 1986, Dowson's drinking was getting worse and he wasn't coming over as often. One night he was so drunk when he arrived in the middle of the night that he started banging on the wrong apartment door, yelling for her to get up. Another night, she and a girlfriend stopped by a Chinese restaurant for a take-out order and she saw him and another cop with two women. Eunice could tell it wasn't business, at least not the official kind.

Eunice and her girlfriend grabbed their take-out order and took off. Dowson followed out the door after them.

"Aren't you going to ask me what I'm doing here?" he pleaded.

"No. It's quite obvious what you're doing here."

"By the time I got home, he was on the phone. He came over and he wanted to talk about it. But I didn't want to and he was getting annoyed. He said, 'Like slap me. Don't just sit there and not say anything. Please promise me you'll never leave. Where else am I going to go?' I'd never seen him as upset as he was. Because I think from that day on he realized I wasn't a little girl any more.

"And that's what came to mind when I met him at Arby's." He had called and suggested they meet for lunch. Eunice thought he was getting ready to say goodbye. She was right, but for the wrong reason. Eunice thought Dowson was going to tell her he was seeing another woman.

"I was starting to drift farther away from him. He had gone through one period where there were other women, and I knew there was something wrong."

When they finished eating, Dowson asked her if she wanted a ride to her mother's. She said no, she could walk. As she looked back, he was still standing by his car. Eunice walked back to him.

"What is it?" she asked. "Do you want to call it quits?"

"He said, 'No. What makes you say that?'" She asked if he'd met another woman.

"Why would you think there was another woman?" he said. "Go see your mother."

Eunice began to leave again, and when she glanced back he was still standing there. Watching her walk away.

Eunice finished another cigarette and her coffee mug was empty.

"Ken had a theory about things," Eunice said. " 'Give me a hug and I'll go back to work. It won't feel so bad, knowing you care.' "

"Did you love him?" Sinclair asked.

"Did I care for him?" she responded, altering the question to make it more comfortable. "Yes. He's probably the best friend I ever had. Because he saw me. Does that make any sense? When he looked at me, he didn't see my father, who was white, or my mother, who was Native. He saw me."

The days and weeks after Dowson's death were especially hard for Eunice because she was alone. His police pals, the ones she was supposed to go to for support, didn't want to acknowledge her. She first met Dowson's best friend, Rex Keatinge, at a time when police thought she was going to testify at the Aboriginal Justice Inquiry.

"He said, 'In all the years I knew Kenny I never heard of you.' And I said, 'I've never heard of you, either.' "

Keatinge tried to dissuade her from contacting the AJI.

"He said, 'If you testify it's going to hurt the kids.' "

"How embarrassing can it get?" Eunice said. "He shot himself in the basement."

Afterward, Eunice realized what Keatinge and the other cops were really concerned about.

"If they had admitted the fact I existed, they'd be admitting the fact there were problems with Kenny, instead of painting him with the golden brush. Instead of this wonderful man with the wonder life that didn't exist."

Eunice never did testify.

"I don't have proof that I had a relationship with him, because I destroyed everything."

44

"Where are the glasses?"

Herb Stephen was followed on the stand by the last major witness at
the Harper hearings, Crown Attorney Bill Morton. Randy McNicol
examined Morton in his typically methodical, stern-voiced style,
establishing at the outset that the Crown attorney's role was to put
before the court any and all evidence.

"Did you, in that regard, view yourself as being in an essentially
independent role?"

McNicol clarified that he meant independent of the Harper family
and the Winnipeg Police Department.

"Yes, I did," Morton answered as he sat with his hands folded on
the table before him. In his twenty-four years as Crown attorney,
Morton went on to concede, he had never conducted an inquest in
which a police officer's conduct was at issue.

"Did that, sir, in view of the Crown's ongoing relationship with the
police . . . provide you with any special problems or considerations in
terms of your role as Crown counsel?"

"I see no problem, Mr. McNicol," Morton said, his hands still folded.
"I felt it was specifically very important that I remain independent."

Morton said the Winnipeg police investigation hadn't concluded
when the inquest started, and he was still getting reports.

"I also wanted to make abundantly sure that counsel for the
Harper family obtained every and all bits of relevant evidence . . . well
in advance so they would be in a position to cross-examine any and
all witnesses."

McNicol wondered if Morton had been concerned that the city
police were doing the bulk of the investigating while the inquest
looked at the conduct of the department in general and one of its
officers in particular.

Morton said it had caused him concern, but he had others in the
attorney general's department looking over the police reports, and

RCMP Sergeant Wes Border had been seconded to him to do any additional investigation.

Morton unfolded his hands when McNicol asked about Dowson's and Keatinge's involvement with the inquest.

The Crown attorney said he viewed them as the senior investigators on the Harper investigation whose responsibilities included doing "whatever they felt necessary to provide police evidence for purposes of the inquiry as it was required by the inquiry."

"Did you ask either Dowson or Keatinge to carry out any investigation for you for the purposes of the fatality inquiry?"

"No."

McNicol then referred Morton to Dowson's report to Herb Stephen in which he listed the mistakes in the Harper case and suggested policy changes to officer-related shootings.

"In particular, Mr. Morton, I direct your attention to the opening paragraph wherein Inspector Dowson reports to the chief, 'On 88 04 05, the writer and Staff Sergeant R. Keatinge were seconded to the Special Prosecutions Branch of the Attorney General's Department at the request of Senior Crown W.W. Morton, QC, to assist in the J.J. Harper Fatality Inquiry.' "

"Is that statement factual?"

"No sir, that statement is not correct."

"Were either of those individuals seconded to you at your request or otherwise?"

"Definitely not."

McNicol went on to confirm that Morton was in charge of the calling of witnesses and the production of documents.

"Were you at all selective in terms of the materials that you provided to Mr. Pollock? By that I mean did you disclose to him some things and not disclose others?"

"The only thing I did not disclose to Mr. Pollock was a certain videotape that had been taken by the city of Winnipeg Police Department of a re-enactment of the incident."

Morton contended that he had withheld it, and instructed

Detective Sergeant Harry Williams not to mention it when he testified, because he thought the video re-enactment was unfair to Harper. It had been rehearsed four times and the detective who played Harper's role wasn't intoxicated.

McNicol reminded Morton that Judge Enns had recalled Cross on the last day of the inquest to demonstrate the struggle.

"Did you think at that point you ought to disclose the existence of the videotape and offer to make it available to the court?"

"No," Morton said, "I considered it what I would call tainted evidence, and I decided that I would not make any reference to it."

But the videotape wasn't the only evidence that Pollock and the inquest hadn't received from Morton. There was also the first police statement made on the day of the shooting by the driver of the medi-van, Jeff Bedosky. In it Bedosky said he saw an officer carrying a gun or a portable radio. The only report Pollock received was the second police statement, dated six days later, in which Bedosky said it was a portable radio.

Morton said he thought he'd sent both reports to Pollock. McNicol was curious to know why Morton hadn't asked Bedosky about the first statement when he took the stand. The officer was Randy Hampton, the same cop four other witnesses said they saw with his gun out. Because, Morton replied, before Bedosky took the stand he'd asked him, "Did you ever say to anyone you didn't know whether it was a radio or a gun?" and Bedosky had said no.

McNicol wanted to underscore what Morton had just said.

"Do I understand you to say then that, prior to Bedosky being sworn as a witness, you interviewed him and specifically asked him, 'Did you ever say to anyone that you didn't know whether it was a radio or a gun?'"

"Mr. McNicol, I am positive I did and his answer was definitely no."

"I am almost done, Mr. Morton," McNicol said.

But Hersh Wolch had more questions about the Bedosky matter. Wolch read to Morton from the inquest transcript where Pollock,

246 GORDON SINCLAIR JR.

working in the dark because he didn't have Bedosky's first police statement, asked him if the object he saw could have been a gun.

"Mr. Pollock says, 'And you're not able to say here today, now,
under oath positively, that it was a radio. It could have been something
else?' And you indicate, 'Well Your Honour, I really don't know –,'
which appears to be the beginning of an objection to the effect, 'How
would the witness know?'"

Morton carries on, Wolch said, and seems to suggest that Pollock's
question was unfair.

Morton agreed with Wolch. He felt Pollock's questioning was
adversarial and not proper at an inquest.

Wolch wanted to delve deeper into Morton's thinking. He suggested to Morton that he would have assumed Pollock had Bedosky's
first statement.

"Yes."

"And I take it, it somewhat surprised you that he wasn't putting it
to the witness. Or did you think he was going to put it to the witness
and didn't feel he should?"

"No, I don't agree with – I can't say either one of those things."

Morton said his throat was getting sore. He excused himself and
took a sip of water.

Then Wolch turned to the issue of the Crown's conflict at the
inquest, given that the senior Crown for the city of Winnipeg, Bruce
Miller, had concurred with the police report the day after the shooting and decided criminal charges should not be laid against Cross.

"I would think that would put you in an awkward position in that
the credibility of the inquiry is then put in issue," Wolch said.

"It didn't help." But Morton said he ignored it. "I was conducting
a fatality inquiry and I can tell you that if I found evidence was coming
forward from the subsequent reports that indicated that there might
very well be criminal misconduct, I would have consulted my superiors about further action."

"Mr. Morton," Wolch said sympathetically, "let me assure you your
integrity is beyond reproach. I am interested mainly in perception."

"What?" Morton asked.

"The perception that the public would have, not those who know you . . . A fellow who works directly with you, Mr. Miller, has already passed judgment and the police chief has passed judgment, that it puts you in a very awkward position in terms of perception."

"No, well, I can't tell you how the public perceives things, I can't act that way. I act only in the best way I can."

"Of course," Hersh Wolch said.

It was clear from follow-up questions by Murray Sinclair and Al Hamilton that both were deeply troubled by Morton's testimony. Hamilton seemed to sum up their concerns in this exchange.

"I think you have said in this case that there wasn't any wrongdoing here, this was a . . . tragic accident. I would like to ask you when you came to that conclusion?"

"That it was a tragic accident?" Morton asked.

"Yes."

There was a long pause. Morton clasped his hands together again before he answered. "I suppose, basically, at the end of the inquiry."

"I would be concerned," Hamilton said with a smile, "if you had come to that conclusion before the inquiry."

During his questioning of Morton, Randy McNicol had asked about the report in which the Crown attorney had recounted praising the testimony of the police officers during a visit with Herb Stephen and his deputies soon after the inquest ended.

During that exchange Morton referred to the still-puzzling issue of why the police had missed Harper's shattered eyeglasses.

"I, quite frankly, felt that I didn't quite see the criticism in not finding the glasses. I still am baffled as to how those glasses and those pieces got to be in one place in such a convenient way."

"Sorry," Murray Sinclair interjected. "Are you suggesting somebody placed them?"

"I don't know, Your Honour."

In late November the Aboriginal Justice Inquiry hearings ended. Then early on the morning of Friday, December 1, Gordon Sinclair dropped by Martin Pollock's office. The young lawyer had something to show him. Martin had had police photos of the sidewalk shooting scene blown up to poster size, and he rolled one out on his desk.

"Where are the glasses?" Martin asked.

On the jagged fringe of the blown-up photo – which had been cropped out on the Identification photos – Sinclair saw a black, hook-shaped blurry object sticking out of the snow just inside the park.

"Right here?" Sinclair said.

It was one of the detached arms. The glasses hadn't been uncovered later in the day by melting snow, as Herb Stephen had suggested when reporter Darryl Sterdan found them. At least one of the arms had been visible when the police were at the scene, as the photo clearly showed.

But looking at the enlarged image of Harper's blood on the sidewalk left Sinclair believing something else crucial had been over-looked. Twenty months, and two public inquiries later, there was still no evidence on where Harper was shot, fell, and was found in relation to the blood and to Cross's account of what happened. There were three pools of blood, a small one on the boulevard, and two signifi-cantly larger amounts four to five feet away from each other on both edges of the sidewalk. There was also a trickle of blood trailing from the park for perhaps ten feet.

On Tuesday, December 5, 1989, Sinclair went to see Herb Stephen's executive assistant, Joe Gallagher. The columnist wanted to know if the police had a shooting scene diagram.

"There are some people who think you're obsessed with this case," Gallagher said.

Sinclair was caught off guard by the comment. Later he wondered if Gallagher would have said that to one of his detectives who was working overtime to solve a homicide.

Gallagher checked. There was no scene diagram.

Sinclair wanted answers to the questions he'd raised. Gallagher said he felt obliged to look into it, but that didn't mean the police would share the answers with Sinclair.

"We don't answer to Gordon Sinclair," Gallagher said icily.

Sinclair wasn't through. He contacted Dr. William Mulligan, a specialist in accident scene reconstruction, who was also the surgeon called out to the hospital when Harper was shot. When he saw the police photo showing two large pools of blood Mulligan concluded that Harper had "spent some time" on the ground in both locations. That meant Harper had moved, or was moved, four or five feet from where he fell.

Sinclair called Randy McNicol with the information. McNicol said he would pass it along to the commissioners.

A few days later they spoke again. "I have instructions to make further inquiries with respect to the issue of the bloodstains," McNicol said.

An RCMP blood-splatter expert was being consulted.

PART IV

THE TOUCH

Freedom of the press is guaranteed only to those who own one.
— A.J. Liebling

$$\overline{}$$

45

"No, Mr. Speaker."

The late winter of 1990 brought some good news and some bad news for Harvey Pollock. In February the Manitoba Police Commission overruled Herb Stephen's old detective partner, Law Enforcement Review Agency Commissioner Des DePourcq. The LERA hearing into Cross's conduct would proceed. And on March 1, Pollock finally filed suit in Court of Queen's Bench on behalf of Lois Harper, her three children, J.J.'s parents, and his 15 surviving siblings. The statement of claim sought compensation for damages and costs, and it named Robert Andrew Cross, Herb Stephen, and the city of Winnipeg.

But later the same day, Justice Minister Jim McCrae announced that no charges would be laid against Constable Bill Isaac for rewriting his notebook because there was "no wilful intent to do anything wrong."

McCrae had sent the case to another provincial justice department for a decision because of what Ticketgate had taught the government about perceived conflict of interest between the Manitoba Crown and other officers of the court, in this case a cop.

Pollock said he was surprised by the decision. He thought there was a *prima facie* case for obstruction of justice.

Then, on the second anniversary of Harper's death, the *Sun* reported that Pollock had received a letter of reprimand from the Law Society of Manitoba for remarks "inappropriate and capable of bringing the profession into disrepute." The letter related to the comment Pollock had made to reporters after Hodgins's testimony. "We were given Valium with Constable Cross's testimony," Pollock had said. "I don't know whether we're getting 222s or 292s with Constable Hodgins."

254 GORDON SINCLAIR JR.

The *Sun* didn't mention where it had obtained a copy of Pollock's letter of reprimand from the Law Society. "Life hell since shooting cop's husband charges," the *Sun* reported. The article said Hodgins had been "subjected to brutal, never-ending scrutiny" since the Harper shooting.

Gordon Sinclair received some bad news of his own about the same time. The RCMP forensic lab in Ottawa had concluded Cross's testimony about how the shooting happened was "entirely consistent" with the blood pattern analysis. "In my opinion," wrote the chief scientist of the blood pattern analysis section, "Cross would have been laying [sic] with his head facing south and his feet north at the time of the shot. Reportedly he was on his back with Harper over top of him. Cross states that he [Harper] took one or two steps back. This is the probable time that the blood fell onto the ground creating the pool on the north side of the sidewalk. Reportedly he then fell to the ground and was holding his chest. Shortly thereafter he was rolled over by police. This would cause the second pool of blood seen on the south side of the sidewalk."

The scientist theorized that the trickling trail of blood in the park could have been made by Rick Poneira, who said he went into the park to wash his hands in the snow after treating Harper. But any scientific analysis is only as accurate as the facts it gathers. The report didn't mention the location of the car keys Danny Smyth had picked up six feet east of Harper's body. Nor did it include the location where Darryl Sterdan had discovered the dead man's eyeglasses. The police could have argued that they didn't have any precise knowledge of where the glasses were. But they had the evidence on the photograph Pollock and Sinclair had seen. Sinclair was sceptical of the RCMP's conclusion, and wrote a column saying so.

It seemed the inquiry commissioners weren't impressed with the RCMP report either. Perry Schulman told Sinclair the AJI would not reopen to hear testimony about the report.

"It's not evidence," Schulman said.

Sinclair got more bad news on the same day that Pollock's reprimand hit the *Sun*. His biggest pal and protector at the *Free Press*, managing editor Murray Burt, was fired by publisher Art Wood, who had been brought in to supervise the newspaper's move to morning delivery and relocation to a new plant. Burt was dismissed just before Wood retired. Sinclair felt badly for Burt, who had been the target of anonymous poison pen letters addressed to the publisher, but his sympathy for his colleague soon turned into concern for his own position. Wood named Burt's assistant, Dave Lee, as the new managing editor. Lee cut Sinclair's column from five days to four and moved it from the entertainment page to the city section. Henceforth Sinclair would report to city editor Brian Cole, a Lee loyalist.

Lee and Sinclair had started their newspaper careers together as copy boys. But Sinclair had long felt that Lee did not like him. In 1987, Sinclair, in a dispute over one of his stories that had appeared under another reporter's byline, had stormed into Lee's office and cleared the desk with one swipe of his long arm. Sinclair had been suspended for two days.

Sinclair wondered how much longer it would be before the column was taken away altogether. At the time he didn't know that losing his job wasn't the only thing he had to worry about.

On June 12, about 9 a.m., two Winnipeg police officers knocked on the apartment door of dancer Cyril Assiniboine. He wasn't home, but Assiniboine had guests, Rick and Debra Coyne. Their two preschool children answered the door, and the cops walked in. They didn't have a search warrant, but they knew what they were looking for: eagle feathers. Bald and golden eagles were protected species and people in possession of their feathers were supposed to have a permit, although the wildlife branch normally didn't make a fuss about Natives possessing them as religious emblems. The police had been at the apartment on a different matter the day before when they saw the feathers hanging on the living room wall. Rick Coyne was in the bedroom when the police returned.

"He just walked right by me and started taking the things down from the wall," Coyne told a reporter later. "I told him he couldn't take them. I was going to take them back and he pushed me."

The timing of the eagle feather seizure was interesting in more ways than one. On March 21 Herb Stephen had issued a policy that was supposed to send a message to the force that racism wouldn't be tolerated. Stephen had assumed the presidency of the Canadian Association of Chiefs of Police, and in that capacity he had also written to the membership and to other chiefs urging them to support the International Day for the Elimination of Racial Discrimination. Stephen's declaration was announced a month after Nelson Mandela was released from prison to coincide with another historic South African occasion, the thirtieth anniversary of the Sharpeville Massacre. At the press conference, Stephen announced, "I have today issued the following police notice to the members of my department.

"Members of the Winnipeg Police Department shall at all times refrain from remarks or actions which may be interpreted in a way that is detrimental to citizens, themselves, the Winnipeg Police Department, or the City of Winnipeg. Every member of the Department shall avoid any exhibition or display of racial or sexual harassment, prejudice, discrimination, or bigotry . . .

"Any violation of this policy by a member of the Department will result in disciplinary action."

When he had finished reading, Stephen added that there was no problem with racial discrimination on his force and he challenged anyone to demonstrate where members of his department had been racist.

"If they've got something specific, something more than sweeping generalizations, they should file a complaint with me or the Law Enforcement Review Agency. But I haven't received any complaints and as far as I know neither has LERA."

When a reporter reminded Stephen that his department had been criticized during the Aboriginal Justice Inquiry for being racist, the chief was dismissive.

"They choose to look at it as though we're treating them that way as a racist matter rather than facing up to the fact they broke the law in the country."

The next day, Harold Rampersad, the coordinator of the city's race relations committee, reported that Stephen had had to deal with complaints about racist remarks made by his officers twice in the last year.

Ironically, on the same day that the police confiscated the eagle feathers, the whole country received a lesson in their significance when MLA Elijah Harper, holding one, uttered the "No, Mr. Speaker" that killed the Meech Lake Accord. Elijah Harper's no gave his people a sense of control and power. An anonymous teenager, quoted in the *Free Press*, summed up that feeling in one sentence. "They are not going to push Native people around anymore."

A month after Harper raised his feather in the Manitoba Legislature, Mohawk Indians at Oka, Quebec, raised barricades and rifles on their reserve. Gordon Sinclair found the story on the wire. "Nine extra holes for the local golf course sparked a bloody battle yesterday between Mohawk Indians and Quebec police in which a 31-year-old police officer was shot and killed."

Seventy-eight days later the Canadian Army marched into Oka and ended the stand-off.

The LERA hearing into whether Cross used excessive force the night Harper died was now drawing to a close, and in preparation his lawyer, Al McGregor, requested an update on Cross's mental health from Linda Loewen. She reported that Cross had been off work for nine months following the incident with his neighbour Sheila Elliot. By early April 1990, he still feared going out in public, but Loewen felt his anxiety had abated enough for him to take on a sheltered, part-time office job with the police force. Within three weeks of returning, however, despite the support of his fellow officers, Cross's violent nightmares grew worse, and he and Diane were having trouble coping with the three children. He wanted them placed back in foster care. She didn't. It was his family problems that were causing him the most difficulty and were the most difficult to remedy, the doctor wrote. Her letter concluded: "With regard to Mr. Cross's attendance at the Law Enforcement Review Agency . . . Mr. Cross is not acutely suicidal, nor has he been for quite some period. I do not think that his appearing would precipitate a catastrophe, but it certainly would have an impact on his mood."

Loewen's opinion didn't serve Al McGregor and Marty Minuk's effort to block the LERA hearings, so they filed a motion with the Court of Queen's Bench that questioned the province's right to hold the hearings. In any event, by law, Cross couldn't be compelled to testify at LERA. But he would have to testify during the examination for discovery on the Harper family's civil suit against the city. And it would be there, a year later, that Martin Pollock would ask Bob Cross if he knew who his next-door neighbours were at the time J.J. Harper was shot.

"No," Cross would swear under oath.

—

46

"Were you ever followed?"

Martin Pollock was preparing a witness list for the LERA hearing when, by chance, he learned about Cross's neighbours, Sheila and Mike Elliot, from Robert Doyle, a colleague at Pollock & Company. One of Doyle's clients had told him that the Elliots were getting divorced. On Tuesday, June 26, a week before the third judicial inquiry into the Harper shooting was scheduled to begin, Martin arrived at lawyer Ron Laxer's office to interview Sheila Elliot. When he got back to his office Martin began dictating from his notes: "Background Information re: Mrs. Elliot's Relationship with Constable Cross," he began.

The dictation covered the period from the first time Sheila Elliot had seen Cross drinking beer and building his deck to a detailed account of the previous summer when Mike had caught her having sex with Cross. She left her husband that day and filed a restraining order with the courts, accusing him of threatening to kill her. Two months later, around the time Ken Dowson killed himself, she attempted suicide, and was hospitalized. Martin took it all down, including a graphic detail about the liaison that he marked "NOT TO BRING OUT AT HEARING . . ."

Martin was more interested in what Sheila had to say about Cross's other behaviour, as his notes would show.

Drinking Episodes
Mrs. Elliot never saw Cross drink to the point where he was stumbling, but his words were slurred and his actions were those of an impaired individual, totally intoxicated, his eyes were bloodshot. Mrs. Elliot saw Cross drink constantly and extensively . . .

She could never really figure when he would go out on his shifts, but she was sure that when Cross went out on his shifts there would definitely be alcohol in his system. This was before and after the shooting. After the shooting Cross's drinking did increase immensely. Very early in their relationship, in 1987, Bob told Mrs. Elliot that he had several different types of drugs in his house, such as heroin, coke, acid, as well as grass and an assortment of guns. She never saw any of the drugs or the guns . . .

Cross's Machismo
Bob's image of himself is sexy, desired. He never spoke of any extra-marital affairs and he always said that he loved Diane . . . Mrs. Elliot was suspicious Cross and Hodgins had something going between the two of them . . .

Racist Comments
Sheila Elliot thought Bob was a racist. She formed this opinion on the basis of numerous comments made by Cross. She recalls Cross telling her about a dog, Tanner, Mrs. Cross's dog. Cross made it

clear that the dog didn't like Natives or any minorities. Cross told Mrs. Elliot, "Tanner don't like Indians."...

The Shooting of J.J. Harper
Several nights when they were drinking Bob Cross would describe the scene to Mrs. Elliot. There were several versions of the incident. The versions Mrs. Elliot got were that the actual approaching of Mr. Harper and showing her how he swung him around were not the way he says ... Cross told Mrs. Elliot that he was forced to re-enact the incident on videotape ... Mrs. Elliot doesn't get the picture of Cross showing respect and saying, "Excuse me sir, could I please see some ID."... One day, in the driveway Bob showed her the way that he was trained to stand. What concerned Cross most was how Harper got him to the ground ... The impression that Mrs. Elliot got sometimes was that the gun was already out of the holster and that Harper did not take the gun from the holster and at other times Cross led her to believe that Harper was fighting with the latch and trying to pull the gun out. Harper sometimes has the handle. Cross sometimes has the handle. Cross describes the struggle but describes it differently every time ... Mrs. Elliot's opinion is that it really bothered Bob that "an Indian had put him on his ass." This is really the purpose of the demonstration ... for Bob to figure out how he got knocked down ...

Martin's entire dictation went on for eighteen pages. It concluded with these two sentences: "As well, Mrs. Elliot said that Bob felt a great deal for Kathy Hodgins. Sheila did not think that Cross was suicidal."

A couple of months later, the Pollocks hired private investigator Milt Brown to interview Mike Elliot. His recollection of Cross coincided closely with his estranged wife's. Mike went into more detail about the night he caught Sheila with Cross. And it was apparent he didn't believe Cross's version of how Harper was shot, either. Brown's notes, quoting Mike Elliot, started with the night Harper died.

He said the Indian was getting the best of him. I took it they were fighting. He used the term, 'It was either me or him.' It was either him or the Indian. He did not say how the gun got out. I didn't want to pressure him. If I would have asked him I'm sure he would have told me. I have that gut feeling that it wasn't the way it was said it happened.

Later in the report, Mike Elliot elaborated:

I told Cross I didn't believe him as to how Harper got shot. I said, "He just walked up and pulled it out of your case?" Then I said, "Bullshit." He did not reply . . . Cross told me when Harper was dying on the ground after the shooting, he was pulling on his (Cross's) pant leg. Cross said, "He was a fucking tough Indian." . . .

Cross's father-in-law was an optician and made Cross a pair of breakaway glasses He calls them his "Indian glasses." He said when fighting or wrestling with Indians the glasses would fall apart and not break. He was very prejudiced. He said the man was an Indian and good enough reason to stop him. He hated Indians . . . He made no bones about hating Indians . . .

I remember fishing with him at Shoal Lake after the shooting. He referred to an Indian burial ground there and said Judge Sinclair should be put there. He even remarked about wanting to run up and cut Judge Sinclair's ponytail . . . He drank pretty good before the Harper shooting. After the shooting he drank more. He would get drunk in a stupor. He wanted sympathy. He said, "Of all the goddamn Indians, I had to shoot a chief." He said this when he was drunk . . . At one time my partner Val Steinman and Walter Thompson were over with Cross. Cross was stupefied. He was talking about rewards for him, police vans in front watching 24 hours a day. He went to work hungover. I more or less carried him home at 3:30 to 4 a.m.. He went to work a couple of hours later.

The morning after Brown filed his report, the private investigator wrote an addendum to his notes. Something he had purposely left out. Mike Elliot had mentioned that Cross used to talk about his marital sex life in great detail. Brown, who was a Jehovah's Witness, had been repelled by the example Elliot had related. But Martin Pollock wanted it included. Reluctantly, Brown obliged.

Late on the same day Martin met with Sheila Elliot, Gordon Sinclair called him. He had been interviewing Ken Dowson's academy instructor, retired superintendent Dennis Scott-Herridge, about his new job. He was in charge of a government program designed to help visible minorities qualify for the Winnipeg police department, and he was frustrated. Back in 1971 he had given Dowson a break when he had only a grade 10 education. Now, nearly twenty years later, he felt the police department was finding ways of failing his students. In the course of the interview, Sinclair chanced upon one of those students, a Native woman who had driven by the shooting scene on Logan Avenue while the police were still treating Harper. At the time she had been afraid to come forward with what she saw, and by this time her account didn't add anything to what was already known. But Sinclair had phoned to tell Martin about her anyway. Martin listened. Then he asked Sinclair something that startled him.

"Were you ever followed?"

Sinclair knew he meant followed by the police.

"Why?" he asked.

"Just expect they would," Martin said.

It was only much later, when he saw Martin's dictated notes, that Sinclair understood why Martin had asked. The section was headed:

Police Shenanigans
Cross told Mrs. Elliot . . . the police were waiting for Gordon Sinclair to come out of a cocktail lounge or a bar and the police were waiting to nail him. Cross told her that the police were following Sinclair. He was very proud of the fact the police were following Sinclair. No names were given, but Mrs. Elliot got the

impression they were Cross's buddies. Cross let Mrs. Elliot know that whole shift was very close and that they would cover for one another . . . Cross hated Sinclair with a passion, because Sinclair was literally tearing him apart in the newspaper . . .

Before they hung up that day Martin told Sinclair that the LERA hearing might not start the following week. Two days later, Marty Minuk filed an appeal in the Court of Queen's Bench. Citing the Charter of Rights and Freedoms, it claimed a third inquiry into Cross's conduct constituted "cruel and unusual" punishment. The police association lawyer also argued that LERA was invalid because the province lacked the authority to create it.

The court reserved judgment. It was fall before the Manitoba court dismissed Cross's appeal. Then Minuk appealed that decision to the Supreme Court of Canada, and it was the following year (1991) before Martin knew whether he could subpoena his surprise witnesses and reintroduce Cross to the neighbours he swore he didn't know.

Early in July there was a verdict in another high-profile case. A jury convicted Christopher Glenn Grywinski of murdering taxi driver Gurnam Singh Dhaliwal. Ten days later, Grywinski closed his case the way Dowson had closed his. Guards found him hanging in his cell at the Public Safety Building.

Soon afterwards the police announced that an internal review had determined there had been nothing wrong with Dowson's lead investigation, which had led to Bunn and Ross being charged for the murder.

The announcement reminded Gordon Sinclair that it had been ten months since Ken Dowson killed himself, and nine months since the inquest that was supposed to explain the suicide, but no one had yet really explained the man. Not the doctor who had medicated him, not the best friend who had found his body, not his wife who had buried him. The closest anyone had come was the writer of a letter to the editor of the *Free Press*, which said that Dowson's pattern of behaviour suggested he was the adult child of an alcoholic. Sinclair wanted to follow this up, but he doubted that anyone in the Dowson family would speak to him. Except maybe Dowson's kid sister.

47

"ON ONE CONDITION."

Gordon Sinclair heard about Nancy Arsenault the way that Martin Pollock had heard about Sheila Elliot. A lawyer had mentioned to him that Ken Dowson had a sister who was in the middle of getting a divorce.

On a perfect summer Friday, six days after Grywinski hanged himself, Sinclair phoned the only N. Arsenault listed in the telephone book. At first the woman who answered was angry, even distraught, when Sinclair explained who he was and what he wanted.

"I don't want to upset you," he finally told her. "If I'm going to upset you, I'll just forget it."

Sinclair was ready to hang up, when suddenly her mood swung.

"On one condition," she said calmly.

"What's that?" Sinclair asked.

"You pick up twelve beer."

"What kind?" he said.

The cab dropped him at an apartment at the top of Ken Dowson's street. As he was lugging the beer to the front door he heard a woman calling his name.

Sinclair looked behind him. There was no doubt she was Ken Dowson's sister. She had the same facial features, but she was slimmer.

Once inside her small apartment, Nancy sat down on the sofa and then, in a wandering way, as she rolled her own Player's Mild and drank her beer, she recounted the family history.

Nancy and Kenny were born in Winnipeg, to English immigrant parents, but when she was in grade 4 and Kenny was in grade 5 the family moved to Dauphin, a farm service community northwest of Winnipeg.

"It was a bad childhood," is all Nancy said.

Then, in the mid-1950s, their mother went into a sanitarium and they never saw her again.

Nancy was twelve, Ken thirteen when she died.

After their father remarried, the two children were shipped off to junior high in Winnipeg, where they each lived with a different, much older sister. Ken joined the army when he was sixteen, leaving Nancy behind.

"I was so homesick for my family. My father came to Winnipeg and I cried and cried and cried when he left. But the stepmother hated Ken and me."

Sinclair asked if their father drank much.

"He drank. I'll be honest with you."

"Was he an alcoholic?"

"I would say yes, he was."

Once Ken had told her about a childhood incident that Nancy was too young to remember. Ken might have been four and Nancy two and they got up Christmas morning to find there were no gifts. Their parents had got drunk the night before.

What Nancy remembered was how, after her mother died, her father would go out drinking and forget where he'd parked his car and she and Ken would have to go looking for it.

"When he drank heavy one of us had to stay home because he was terrible with his cigarettes."

Then, abruptly, the way her mood had swung when they were talking on the phone, Nancy changed topics.

"But I still don't understand why Ken shot himself."

The last time she'd seen him was about three weeks before he died. She ran into him at a drugstore, which was what their relationship had been reduced to: chance encounters. She was under the impression his relationship with Jill had deteriorated too, and that they were having problems in their marriage.

Ken seemed fine the day she saw him at the drugstore. Then he shot himself without saying goodbye.

"I've got all the articles on him. I still can't take them out and read them. I just don't think it's fair what he did."

Nancy said she'd been "out of it." She couldn't even go to the funeral. "I lost a whole week of my life between drinking and Valium."

Her brother had been taking tranquillizers secretly for years and drank heavily, too.

"I suffer chronic depression," Nancy continued. "My pills are right here." She picked up two containers of her antidepressant medication, amitriptyline and perphenazine. "And I think Ken did, too, to be honest.

"It's not a physical illness, it's a mental illness. Anyway, I think Ken had the same problem. His job, the pressure he was under, his marriage. I know depression is hereditary.

"I don't eat. I can't sleep. I cry. I don't want to talk to anybody. I can't live without my pills. If I didn't have the pills I would die. It's what they call the silent illness. The psychiatrist told me it's a chemical imbalance in the brain."

"Did your brother have the same problem?"

"I think he did. All I know is Ken had to be very depressed to shoot himself. That's all I know."

Nancy was sobbing. "People tell me my brother killed himself to cover up for Cross and he just couldn't handle it, so he killed himself because he was a perfectionist. He only had five more years and then he would be retired . . .

"You know what? I wish I knew the truth. All I know is my brother was a perfectionist and on the day of the inquiry he couldn't take it and he shot himself. That's all I know."

Years later, after he retired as medical examiner, Dr. Peter Markesteyn told Sinclair that shortly after the suicide he showed Dowson's "I'll be the sacrifice" note to a psychiatrist.

"He said he thought the note was an indication of mental illness," Markesteyn said. "In psychiatric terms, he said, for a man to assume that responsibility solely on his own shoulders, that's not reality. He's not the only one responsible."

Not long after the interview Sinclair called Eunice Woodhouse and told her about Nancy. Two months later, on the first anniversary of Dowson's death, Sinclair and Eunice drove to Dowson's grave. It was raining and nearly dark when they arrived. From the entrance they could see two figures at the grave, a tall man standing, and what looked like a woman sitting in a lawn chair. From that distance Eunice couldn't tell for sure but the man looked like Rex Keatinge. She figured the woman must be Jill.

The man drove off first, then the woman. Sinclair followed her car for a while, trying to get close enough for a look at the driver, but it was too dark and she was too far ahead. Then he and Eunice drove downtown. On the Legislature lawn a teepee was pitched in front of the statue of Queen Victoria. Behind Her Stone-Faced Majesty a ring of Aboriginal people was standing in the rain, talking about the significance of the circle in Indian spirituality. They were demonstrating their support for the Mohawks at Oka.

It was a long, hot Indian summer across Canada. At the end of it, as the national chiefs gathered in Winnipeg for a conference, Manitoba Grand Chief Phil Fontaine issued a warning to the country that there could be more Okas to come.

Sixty-five per cent of the Native population was under twenty-five, unemployment was epidemic, and the suicide rate among Aboriginals was six times the national average.

"If non-Aboriginal governments refuse to change, the message for our young people will be that governments only act when there is a threat of violence," Fontaine said. "We are tired of waiting for justice."

What few people knew, and what the police wouldn't even acknowledge for another three years, was that young Aboriginals in

Winnipeg were already acting out their frustrations, making a political statement without their even knowing it.

In March 1988, at the time of Harper's death, disfranchised, bored, and often neglected Native teenagers formed the city's first street gang. They called themselves the Indian Posse.

Many of them had started out by stealing bikes, then graduated to the kind of joy-riding car thefts that Pruden and Allan had been up to the night Harper died. Break and enters followed, and then armed robbery.

The nature of Aboriginal crime, which AJI Commissioner Murray Sinclair had identified as being largely petty and driven by alcohol abuse, was changing.

By the late 1990s, the inner city streets of Winnipeg were divided into turfs marked by the graffiti of rival gangs, and a Native boy named "Beeper" Spence, mistaken for a rival gang member, was murdered in a drive-by shooting. The incident reminded Sinclair of something he'd read on the *New York Times* letters page: "Why do young black men kill other young black men? Because they're shooting into a mirror."

Sinclair had known one of the founders of the Indian Posse when the kid was growing up. Ray Armstrong was still a child in the early 1980s when his white father, an ex-con named Bob Armstrong, became a friend of Sinclair and a Runyonesque character in his column. Big Bad Bald Bob, he called him. Bob's weakness, or specialty, was forging cheques. Ray tried living with his father for a while. He even worked bagging groceries in St. James. When Ray reached his early teens, his dad was dead of natural causes and the boy was back with his Aboriginal mother Nancy, an alcoholic living in the inner city. Sinclair used to say hi to Ray when he saw him riding a bike around downtown with other kids. Later, he'd see him hanging out in downtown shopping malls. By that time Ray was on his way to becoming the leader of the Indian Posse. Out of the chaos of his childhood, Ray Armstrong had found structure, order, validation, and purpose in the brotherhood

of the gang. Much the way Ken Dowson had found a sense of family
in the police force that he didn't have growing up.

That's why Dowson had gone out of his way to help Ellen Gordon's
young Native client, Sinclair thought. He was looking into a mirror.
And he was trying to save himself.

48

"You don't know who this is."

Around the time the national chiefs were meeting in August 1990,
John Campbell abruptly resigned as president of the Winnipeg Police
Association. The union executive had voted to suspend him, although
they wouldn't say why. Campbell had been an outspoken critic of
Herb Stephen and what he saw as the old boys' club that ran the
police department and used the buddy system to promote like-
minded cops. The buddy system, he discovered, extended into the
police association's executive, which had voted to suspend him.
Campbell took it hard.

The following month, Campbell and Linda Loewen, Cross's psychiatrist, were married. What had happened to him with the police
association was still troubling him, though, and Loewen had been pre-
scribing medication to help him through it. Just a couple of weeks
later Campbell was drinking Scotch. The next thing he knew he was
being arrested for impaired driving, although he didn't really remember much of that because the mix of booze and pills had left him in a
disoriented fog.

Three days later, on October 9, Martin Pollock's wife, Randee, called
Gordon Sinclair's house and told Athina that Martin needed someone
to talk to. The two men had become friends during the previous year.
While Sinclair and Deputy Chief Johnston would occasionally eat

breakfast together, Martin and Sinclair went for late-night walks. Randee was watching a bris scene on "Thirtysomething" when Sinclair arrived. Just the week before she had given birth to their first child, a boy they named Ethan. The Sinclairs had been at Ethan's bris a few days earlier.

On his way to the Pollocks' house Sinclair recalled what Martin had told him the last time they were out for a walk. "You're being followed," Martin had warned him. "Cross hates you."

Sinclair had already suspected the police were watching him. Marty Minuk had casually mentioned something when he'd bumped into him at an Italian Street Festival that summer that suggested the police had been looking for something on him. "They know a lot about you," Minuk had said with a smile. "You should be honoured."

Then, in the spring, Sinclair, his brother David, and a visiting boyhood friend had gone for a beer at a strip bar. The three of them sat near the railing that separated the customers from the floor show. A couple of unfriendly-looking young guys with short haircuts were sitting at the table behind them. One of them got up and headed for the telephone soon after Sinclair arrived. Sinclair had already had a couple of draught, and the stripper was rolling on a throw rug, when he turned to the two short haircuts and made a crude joke. They didn't laugh. When he looked back again a few minutes later, the two humourless guys had disappeared and two older men in suits had taken their places. Sinclair didn't think anything of it until one day, months later, his brother mentioned he had seen one of the older guys from the bar stopped for a traffic light. The guy was driving an unmarked police car.

The cold, clear autumn sky was shimmering with Northern Lights as Sinclair pulled into the Pollocks' driveway. He paused to look up as he got out of his Honda. The dancing lights looked like restless spirits to Sinclair. It was as if the heavens were alive with the dead.

As they walked around the hushed residential streets of his neighbourhood, Martin didn't pay much attention to the spectacular light show. He seemed bothered about something, although he didn't say what. Maybe it was a hangover from what happened to his friend John Campbell, Sinclair thought. Clearly Martin was concerned about the police.

"They could plant something on you," Martin cautioned Sinclair. But, that night, it wasn't Gordon Sinclair who needed the warning.

At 7:40 a.m. the next day, Bruce Owen's home phone rang. The former *Sun* and CBC reporter had been working at the *Free Press* for only a few months. Owen stumbled out of bed naked and scrambled down the stairs to the antique cradle phone that was still ringing. His shift didn't start until noon; who the hell was phoning that early?

"Hello," he said groggily.

"You don't know who this is," a voice said.

Owen knew who it was, of course. And by the time the brief conversation was over, he knew what it was about, too.

Harvey Pollock arrived for work around 9:00 that morning, ahead of his son, Martin, who wouldn't be in till later. He was on the phone when his secretary buzzed him on the intercom. There was someone to see him. The someone turned out to be two detectives. He recognized one of them.

"Kushneryk, isn't it?" Pollock asked as he motioned them to follow him down the hall to his inner office.

Harvey Pollock remembered Ron Kushneryk from a recent case. He was tall and gangly, with a clump of hair that dangled over his forehead like frayed rope. Pollock didn't recognize Kushneryk's new partner, the round-faced, beefy Don Feener. Pollock closed the door to his office. Moments later he flung it open again and began shouting for his law partner, Bob Doyle.

Kushneryk and Feener had come to arrest Harvey Pollock.

"Sexual assault," Kushneryk said.

By the time Doyle arrived, Pollock had flicked on his Dictaphone and slid the microphone forward on his desk. Kushneryk continued talking as if he were addressing the tape.

"Just giving him his rights. Told him it is my duty to inform you that you have the right to retain and instruct counsel without delay. I asked him if he understood. He didn't answer. If you can't afford it, you have the right to legal advice without charge from Legal Aid duty counsel. Do you understand that, Mr. Pollock?"

"Keep on talking. This is just absolute nonsense."

"Who's laid a complaint?" Doyle asked.

"I'll get to that. Anything you do say may be taken down in writing and may be used as evidence, do you understand that?"

"That's insane," Pollock said.

"We have – some allegations were made by a lady we personally reinterviewed yesterday because the charges are very serious. She made the complaint, I believe it was last week."

The alleged offence had happened a week earlier right in the office where they were sitting.

"At night or in the daytime?" Pollock asked.

"Afternoon."

Doyle asked who the woman was. Kushneryk spelled her first and last name. Harvey remembered her. Her name was Florence, and she'd had an appointment about a personal injuries automobile insurance claim. She was Native, and she had been drinking, and . . .

"Now," Doyle said, assuming the role of Pollock's lawyer, "what is the nature of the sexual offence?"

Kushneryk answered. "She says she was assaulted. He allegedly rubbed her buttocks several times."

"Rubbed her buttocks?" Pollock said in disbelief.

"Calls it her bum."

"Her bum?"

"Several times. She says three times."

"Several times?" Pollock repeated.

"Three times," Kushneryk said. "She was asked to take her coat off. He was going to examine her. She came around the side of his desk when this allegedly happened."

"And that's it?" Pollock said. "Have you discussed this with a Crown attorney?"

Kushneryk ignored the question. "As a result he is being arrested and is going to be taken into the Public Safety Building. Processed. Released."

"We can go down and meet you there," Doyle said. "Can't we?"

"No," Kushneryk said. "He has to come with us. He's under arrest."

"He is in custody," Feener said.

"Is there absolutely any need for this?" Doyle pleaded.

"That's the rules," Kushneryk insisted, "and I'm not breaking the rules."

"Can you not take him into custody at the PSB?"

"No," Feener said.

"He can't be treated anyone else." Kushneryk was stumbling over his words. "Like anybody" he said, trying to correct himself, "any different than anybody else. It would look worse if it happened that way. Him and . . ."

"This is absolutely insane," Pollock said.

"We are not saying you have done this," Kushneryk told him. "We are saying there is an allegation."

"I hope you notice," Doyle said, "that at this point there has been absolute denial of the offence. I hope you are taking note of the immediate response."

"This is absolutely insane," Pollock repeated.

"It's noted," Feener said.

Pollock asked if he could say something about the "alcoholic lady" who'd complained. Then he said, "Do you know what you are doing to my reputation if the newspapers were to get an inkling of the fact that a policeman came down to my office and suggested for a moment that I had – that I had sexually – that I had sexually assaulted somebody? Do you know what that would do to my reputation?"

The two detectives didn't reply.

Bruce Owen had been ducking anxiously in and out of the building's lobby waiting for Harvey Pollock to appear. He had *Free Press* photographer Glenn Olsen with him. Owen and Olsen had driven from the paper to Pollock's office building and parked their marked *Free Press* car in the lot a few stalls away from the front doors. They had seen the unmarked police car arrive and park directly in front of the entrance.

Owen ducked into the building again. This time he heard whistling. It was the distinctive warble of Harvey Pollock, the former world champion whistler. Feener came through the door first, followed by Pollock, with Doyle and Kushneryk trailing. As soon as Pollock saw Owen and Olsen he knew what had happened.

"This is a set-up," he said.

Wearing trench coats, Pollock and Doyle walked together as Kushneryk headed for the driver's door and Feener went around to the passenger side. Olsen got into position to get a good picture, while Owen asked Pollock for a comment on the arrest.

"It's nonsense, absolute nonsense," Pollock said. "It's the police at their best."

Ten minutes later Pollock was at the Public Safety Building, being escorted to the second-floor detective office. Feener asked Pollock if he had any questions.

"Can you stop the *Free Press* from printing that picture?"

Feener told him it was out of his control.

Gordon Sinclair was in the newsroom when he heard that Pollock had been arrested. He tried to reach him at work, but Pollock was still being processed at the police station. City editor Brian Cole was sitting at his desk, in front of the police radio, when Sinclair walked up and asked how Owen had found out.

"It was a regular contact," Cole said, adding that it didn't necessarily mean it was a cop. "It could be someone in the court system."

Herb Stephen was away again, this time on business in Oklahoma City, and knew nothing about the Pollock arrest until he returned, two days later. Sinclair called his friend Acting Chief Paul Johnston and asked him if he knew that a *Free Press* reporter and photographer were waiting downstairs when Pollock was arrested. Johnston seemed taken aback. He said he didn't know that the media had been present.

It took more than an hour to print, photograph, and process Harvey Pollock at the Public Safety Building. He phoned his wife, Sylvia, as soon as he could, so she wouldn't learn of his arrest on the radio, then he called a press conference for 2 p.m. in his office. Beryl, his secretary, was typing up his one-page statement, and the TV cameras were being set up, when Sinclair arrived. Martin was by his father's side. Bruce Owen was there, too. Pollock seemed surprisingly composed, even relaxed. "You don't have to be afraid of the truth," he said with a smile.

As they all waited for the news conference to begin, Pollock shared something his father had told him: "If you don't have a name, you don't have anything. And it's easy to have a name besmirched." Then he began to read the statement: "I have asked you to come here this afternoon so that I can tell you, and the public, that the allegation made against me by a woman client that I sexually assaulted her in my office during office hours by touching her buttocks, is false." His voice was quivering. He went on to mention that a reporter and photographer had been waiting outside his office when he was arrested and that, obviously, they had been tipped off.

When Pollock finished his statement, Bruce Owen asked him if he thought this was police payback? Harvey Pollock just smiled at the reporter.

Sinclair walked back to his office, sat down at his terminal, and began typing the headline of the next day's column: "SOMETHING'S ROTTEN IN . . . *The arrest of Harvey Pollock raises disturbing questions.*"

The column detailed events as Sinclair knew them then. Pollock's accuser had gone to the Law Society of Manitoba with her complaint on the day that Sinclair and Athina had attended the bris for Harvey's eight-day-old grandson. He reported that Owen had been alerted to the arrest by a "contact." The column ended with something else that had happened at Pollock's office: "Just before the news conference started, as Pollock was thinking out loud about not being afraid of the truth and how one's name and reputation is everything, Martin asked Owen a question.

"'Were they laughing downtown at the police station?'

"'Yes,' Owen said."

The next day, a story in the paper quoted Acting Crime Superintendent Randy Bell's denial that Pollock's arrest had anything to do with the lawyer's involvement with the Aboriginal Justice Inquiry. Bell was a former partner of Ken Dowson and had been one of the pallbearers at his funeral. Bell had been consulting on the Pollock case with all the senior officers in the crime division: Johnston, Crime Superintendent Dennis Toyne, and Inspector Ron Dawson.

It was Bell who disclosed that the police had consulted Crown Attorney Rob Finlayson about the wording of the charge against Pollock, but not about whether it should be laid. "We felt we had reasonable and probable grounds against the man based on the complaint of the woman," Bell said.

Sinclair's headline for his column that day was "THE STATE OF THE POLICE."

The column quoted University of Manitoba law professor Jack London, a friend of Harvey Pollock, saying that the police handling of the case was "vindictive." Hersh Wolch used another expression, he said it "smacked of malice." By that time it had been learned that the police hadn't sought a warrant to arrest Pollock, and they hadn't interviewed his staff until after he was arrested. Sinclair questioned the legality of proceeding without a warrant, and the propriety of arresting first and asking questions later. The column concluded: "There are lots of other questions about this case, for which there are no answers. The police are supposed to protect us, but who protects us from them? Where is our justice minister and why isn't he investigating this? And who's next?"

The day after Pollock's arrest, Ron Kushneryk visited Bruce Miller, the Justice Department's head of public prosecutions for Winnipeg. Miller was the Crown attorney Herb Stephen had named on the day after the Harper shooting as having agreed that no charges should be laid against Cross.

Miller had the police reports on the Pollock case, and he also had a surprise. The police had learned about Florence's complaint only by chance. In the early hours of October 6, 1990, two constables went to an apartment in downtown Winnipeg, in response to a woman's complaint that her son was damaging a screen door. When the man and woman police team arrived, the fifty-three-year-old Native woman launched into a rambling narrative about her teenage son's wayward ways. She couldn't control him anymore. The male officer taking her statement had a Polish accent, and every so often he asked a question for clarification. The female officer was just listening, until the woman abruptly changed the subject.

"You wouldn't believe what my lawyer Harvey Pollock did," she said.

At the mention of Harvey Pollock, the female officer straightened up and leaned forward.

"We'd believe you," Kathy Hodgins said.

49

"THEY MIGHT BE THE FIRST TO LAUGH. THEY WON'T BE THE LAST."

A couple of weeks after Pollock's arrest, Sinclair dropped by Martin's place after supper to keep him company. Randee was out with Sylvia, Martin's mother, at a Hadassa Wizo fundraiser. One-month-old Ethan was asleep in a baby seat on the living room rug.

"He reminds me so much of my brother," Martin said, staring down at his baby boy.

Nathan and Martin used to share a room when they were boys. Martin would stay awake until his brother fell asleep because he was afraid Nathan would suffocate. "His face would always be buried into his pillow and I'd go over and depress the pillow. I'd never fall asleep until he fell asleep."

"It was like shutting off a light. That's how he died."

Martin was at Dalhousie University studying law. His mother had been visiting him in Halifax earlier in the week Nathan died. At three one morning, Martin was sitting at a drafting table, working on a school paper. His mother was sleeping in the bed next to him, the white sheet pulled up to her neck. The harshness of Martin's fluorescent desk light had turned her face to the bloodless shade of the sheet. "I looked at her and the first thing I thought of was death."

Nathan was killed four days later.

"Nathan," Martin said, "had a dream that he died and he wanted to see who came to his funeral. He had the dream that night I looked at my mother and saw death."

Sinclair thought that was odd, but a bit like revisionist history. Then Martin told him about coming home that summer and driving out to the cemetery where Nathan was buried. He pulled up outside the gate, and stopped. Then he looked down at the car radio.

"I said, Nate, if there was a song I could play right now it would be 'Funeral for a Friend.'"

"Did you say it out loud?" Sinclair asked.

"Yeah. And I turned on the radio and I pressed the middle FM button and, I swear to God, on came the very beginning of Elton John's 'Funeral for a Friend.'"

Martin paused and leaned forward on the couch. "You never get over it. You get through it. But you never get over it."

Martin lived with his brother's death every day, and the arrest of his father was making it even harder.

"My dad is the quintessential professional. To think he would throw away his career over that. He has treated people with respect.

Dignity. There's something in him that wants to help people. His life has been law. Law and his family."

Then he got to what was really bothering him. "This is such a violation. If someone wanted to hurt my father, our family, they succeeded. But what they don't know is we've been through it. You're ready for the next time, and if people think it's going to destroy us, they're messing with the wrong people.

"They were laughing down at the police station. They might be the first to laugh. They won't be the last."

It was 10:39 when Randee and Sylvia arrived home.

"You'll never guess who won the chocolate-chip cookie contest."

They gave up.

"Herb Stephen's wife."

Martin started laughing. They all started laughing.

50

"ALL IN THREE-AND-A-HALF SECONDS."

Late on the night of November 15, 1990, Winnipeg's new commissioner of parks, culture, and protection got home from his first day at work. Loren Reynolds had taken over from Robert Lunney, who had moved to Ontario to be chief of the Peel Regional Police. Reynolds was short, balding, and quiet-spoken, nothing like the stereotype of what he had been, a military pilot who had just retired as the commander of Canadian Forces Base Winnipeg. As he walked in the door of his large home in the Crescentwood district, Reynolds's wife was waiting for him.

"I hope all your days won't be like this," she said.

The next morning the police issued a press release. A forty-two-year-old man was in intensive care after being shot in the head by the police just after midnight. The police had been dispatched to the New West Hotel on Main Street in response to a complaint about a man making threats. When they went to his room, the release said, they were confronted by a man holding a handgun. He was ordered to drop the weapon "a number of times," the statement continued. He refused, pointed the gun directly at the police, and one of the officers fired.

The release saved the worst for last. "It has been determined that the weapon the male was holding was in fact an imitation plastic hand gun."

The release left out something even worse. The man was Métis.

When Gordon Sinclair learned about the shooting it sounded to him like Harper all over again. The toy gun made it also sound like a bizarre, one-sided game of Cowboys and Indians. It didn't make sense. Anyone who pointed a toy gun at an armed police officer either had to be very high on drugs or extremely low on intelligence. Anything was possible, of course. Even the unlikely coincidence that "Suitcase" Stephen would be out of town yet again for a major occurrence. He was.

Paul Johnston was the acting police chief. Sinclair had always believed that the Harper investigation would have been conducted differently if Johnston had been in charge on March 9, 1988. Now he was going to get a chance to see how Johnston would handle the first shooting since Ken Dowson rewrote the officer-related shooting policy. Johnston had a tough one by the sounds of it. A toy gun?

At the news conference, Johnston elaborated on the release. Two constables had been dispatched to the hotel after a Manitoba Telephones System operator called the police about a man threatening violence. The officers had gone to a room on the second floor where the suspect lived. They identified themselves, the door opened, and the man in the room went for a handgun. The police retreated down the hall and repeatedly told the man to drop the gun. Johnston said the man then emerged from the room, pointing the gun.

"Constable Malcolm Dawson crouched down," Johnston reported, "his feet separated, and pointed the weapon, at which time he was shot."

Judge Murray Sinclair.
(Jeff De Booy, *Winnipeg Free Press*)

Judge Al Hamilton.
(Courtesy Al Hamilton)

Perry Schulman (left) and Randy
McNicol, co-counsels for the
Aboriginal Justice Inquiry.
(Courtesy Randy McNicol)

Robert Cross testifying at the
Aboriginal Justice Inquiry.
(*Winnipeg Free Press*)

Kathryn Hodgins testifying at
the Aboriginal Justice Inquiry.
(Dave Johnson, *Winnipeg Free Press*)

Left to right: Police Association lawyer Al McGregor, Marty Minuk, Butch
Nepon, and Constable Glen Spryszak while trying to oppose the Inquiry's
demand to see police notebooks. (Michael Raine, *Winnipeg Free Press*)

Sergeant Harry Williams.
(Courtesy Winnipeg Police Service)

Constable Bill Isaac.
(Courtesy Winnipeg Police Service)

Constable Danny Smyth.
(Courtesy Winnipeg Police Service)

Hersh Wolch (left) and Ken Dowson. (Bruce Rapinchuk, *Winnipeg Sun*)

Police Chief Herb Stephen and Gordon Sinclair at a fundraiser for Crime Stoppers. (Kevin Frayer photo)

Grant "Butch" Eakin in 1998
(Wayne Glowacki,
Winnipeg Free Press)

Dale Cummings's apt cartoon.
(*Winnipeg Free Press*)

Eunice Woodhouse, Ken
Dowson's alleged girlfriend.
(Gordon Sinclair photo)

At Ken Dowson's funeral, his
widow, Jill, clutches his hat while
being steadied by Inspector Rex
Keatinge. To her left and behind
her are her sons Mark and Kirk.
(Joe Bryksa, *Winnipeg Sun*)

The arrest of Harvey Pollock
1. Harvey Pollock is flanked by
reporter Bruce Owen (left) and
Detective Don Feener. (Glenn Olsen,
Winnipeg Free Press)

2. Pollock and his colleague Robert
Doyle with detectives Ron
Kushneryk (far left) and Don
Feener (far right). (Glenn Olsen,
Winnipeg Free Press)

Police–shooting victim Dan De La Ronde. (*Winnipeg Free Press*)

The toy gun on the distinctively patterned carpet. (Winnipeg Police Service)

Billyjo De La Ronde indicating where the bullet entered his brother's head. (Glenn Olsen, *Winnipeg Free Press*)

Dale Henry in 1991.
(*Winnipeg Free Press*)

J.J. Harper's half brother, Harry Wood, at the LERA hearings.
(Gordon Sinclair photo)

Deputy Chief Joe Gallagher testifying about "cowboy cops" at the LERA hearings.
(Gordon Sinclair photo)

Diane Eastwood (left) finally meets J.J.'s daughter Lori (centre) and widow, Lois (right), at the scene of the shooting during the tenth anniversary commemoration. (Ken Gigliotti, *Winnipeg Free Press*)

Gordon Sinclair and wife Athina Panopoulos accepting Manitoba Human Rights Award with daughter Erin and son Ian in 1989. (*Winnipeg Free Press*)

The bullet hit the man in his forehead, but it did not kill him.

To make their point about how real the fake gun looked, the police released a colour photograph of the large, black plastic handgun. The toy was lying on some blue broadloom that had a swirling fingerprint pattern.

The shooting victim was identified the next day. Dan De La Ronde was the brother of Billyjo De La Ronde. Billyjo was a ruggedly hand-some guy who favoured buckskin jackets and cowboy boots and drove a four-wheel-drive truck. He was also the executive director of the Manitoba Métis Federation.

Sinclair spent the next few days investigating the shooting, check-ing out the second floor of the jaundiced-coloured hotel where it hap-pened, knocking on doors looking for witnesses. Four days after the shooting he found one. The hotel owner. Tony Panchhi was East Indian and only twenty-five. Panchhi had escorted the two police officers to De La Ronde's room on the night of the shooting and he agreed to do the same for Sinclair. Panchhi remembered it beginning much the way the police press release described it. He had led the two constables up to the second floor. Room 109 was at the far end, near the fire escape. The two cops took positions on either side of the door. They could hear music coming from inside. Panchhi knocked. There was no response.

"Excuse me, sir," one of the cops said. "We just want to talk to you."

Still no response. Panchhi used his pass key to open the door, but it was chained from the inside and so it opened only five or six inches. Panchhi could see De La Ronde sitting in a chair.

"The cops are here to talk to you," Panchhi said.

"Fuck off," De La Ronde said.

Panchhi watched as De La Ronde got up and started rummaging through his bureau drawers. Then De La Ronde turned and Panchhi yelled. "He's got a gun."

The police pulled their revolvers as De La Ronde moved towards the door. It closed, and Panchhi and the two cops bolted down the hall. Police took cover ten metres away, at a corner in the hall. Panchhi kept going straight and took cover behind the stairway door. He opened the door a crack and peeked out. He couldn't see anyone. Then, way down the dimly lit hall, under the hundred-watt bulb recessed in the ceiling in front of Room 109, Panchhi saw De La Ronde poke his head out. Just his head.

"Where is he?" one of the cops yelled to Panchhi.

Panchhi told them he could see the guy's head. Like a turtle, De La Ronde pulled his head back into the room. Panchhi screamed for De La Ronde to throw his gun out in the hall and surrender. There was no answer. Panchhi yelled down the hall to the cops. "I'll go call the back-up for you and you guys hold him."

There were twenty-one steps from the second floor to the first-floor landing where the payphone was. Panchhi told Sinclair he was just reaching for the phone when he heard the shot. He dialed 911 and ran back upstairs to see De La Ronde sprawled across the hallway. The two officers were standing on either side of him, their weapons holstered. Panchhi didn't remember seeing the toy gun in the hall.

Sinclair looked at the carpet in the hallway. It didn't match the colour or texture of the broadloom in the police photograph showing where the toy gun had been found. He asked Panchhi to open De La Ronde's room, and there was the blue broadloom, complete with the swirling fingerprint design. How could De La Ronde have been in the hallway "crouched with his feet separated" pointing the fake weapon, the way Paul Johnston described the shooting, when the police had photographed the toy gun where they found it, in his room? There was more. The hotel room door was spring-loaded. If De La Ronde had been in the hallway, "crouched and his feet separated," the door would have closed behind him. So how did the toy gun end up inside his room?

Panchhi re-enacted his movements for Sinclair, running down the twenty-one stairs to the landing so Sinclair could time how long it took to reach the phone and hear the shot. It took three-and-a-half seconds.

In the column the next day, Sinclair reported what Panchhi had described and likened the three-and-a-half seconds to a blink of an eye. Then he posed a question: "Do you think a man who had been drinking most of the day could step out of the room, assume a crouched position, point the toy gun and be shot in the head at 10 paces? All in three-and-a-half seconds?"

On the morning the column appeared, and two days after Billyjo De La Ronde and the Manitoba Métis Federation had demanded that the RCMP investigate the shooting, Herb Stephen was back in town and had issued a statement.

> I reject any suggestion that an outside police agency be asked to investigate this incident. I have full confidence in the thorough and professional investigation being conducted by the members of my department, and they will complete this investigation.
>
> I am well aware that some persons have a perception that we should not investigate incidents involving our members. I reject this and assure the citizens of Winnipeg that we are conducting a thorough and impartial investigation.
>
> After giving serious consideration to the concerns that were expressed recently, I made the following decision in an effort to alleviate these concerns.
>
> I have today written to the assistant commissioner of the Royal Canadian Mounted Police in Manitoba and requested that he give consideration to having his members review our completed investigative file on this incident.

Stephen went on to say his department had nothing to hide and that he was tired of having to defend his officers' actions in public. What he didn't say was that Justice Minister Jim McCrae had pressed him into allowing the Mounties to check the facts.

That night, after Sinclair finished a column lecturing the police on what they hadn't learned from the Harper shooting, he decided to go back to the New West Hotel. He asked Panchhi to come back upstairs to the hall where De La Ronde was shot and to answer a couple of follow-up questions. Had the police dropped by to see Panchhi that day? They hadn't. Sinclair was surprised, as he had said in his column, that De La Ronde had been shot so quickly after Panchhi left to call 911.

Next question: Had he seen anything in the hall other than the body? Like the toy gun?

Panchhi said he hadn't been looking for a gun, so he couldn't say. Then, as they stood where De La Ronde's body had fallen, Panchhi said something that shocked Sinclair. He said he had been wrong about the three and a half seconds and that he hadn't heard the shot until after he called 911. Maybe ten or fifteen seconds after he ran downstairs. Maybe even longer.

"I know I told you that," Panchhi said. "But I thought more about it . . . I didn't think it was going to be such a big thing."

Sinclair went straight back to the paper and rewrote the column for the next day to include the correction.

It's 9:42 p.m. Friday night now, and I sit here wondering what happened, why his story changed. How can someone make a mistake that big?

Is he stupid?

Or is he scared?

—
51

"WE ARE VERY WORRIED OVER HERE."

A week before Christmas, Constable Kathryn Hodgins was standing outside courtroom 408. It was the first day of Harvey Pollock's trial. Inside the starkly modern, compact courtroom a couple of dozen spectators had taken every available seat, among them Constable Glen Spryszak.

Gordon Sinclair spotted other familiar faces: Hersh Wolch and his partner, Sheldon Pinx, lawyer Hymie Weinstein, city councillor Al Golden, and Provincial Judge Harold Gyles, who had lost his position as chief judge as a result of the fallout over Ticketgate.

The presence of all these people was also noted by a person Sinclair didn't recognize, Winnipeg Police Inspector Ron Dawson. Crime Superintendent Dennis Toyne had sent Dawson to monitor the trial, which was being conducted by one of the few women on the Provincial Court bench. Linda Giesbrecht had been appointed to the bench in March, 1988, at the same time as Murray Sinclair.

Harvey Pollock was seated in a swivel chair, beside his lawyer, the dapper D'Arcy McCaffrey, a brilliant barrister who was known more for civil litigation than for criminal work.

Across the room sat the Crown attorney who was prosecuting the charge. Matthew Britton was slight and youthful looking. Pollock didn't know Britton. No one in the room really did. In an effort to distance themselves from any charge of conflict in the Pollock prosecution, Justice officials in Winnipeg had searched for someone who didn't know Pollock and who wasn't a part of the city's incestuous court scene. They had found Britton in Brandon.

Britton's youthful appearance, and the fact that he had been with the Attorney General's Department for only two years, gave the police the impression that he was inexperienced. In fact, Britton had been a lawyer for eight years, six of them with the Brandon firm of Hirschfield & Hunt. In all, he had been involved in more than a thousand criminal cases. So Britton knew as soon as he received the memo from his boss Michael Watson that this was a trial no one in the Crown's office wanted to prosecute.

To Matthew from Mike
Subject: Harvey Pollock.
Unless you have some personal difficulty with it, you have drawn the short straw in the prosecution of the above noted Lawyer on sexual assault charges.

Britton's first reaction was that he was being punished for something. He knew the media scrutiny would be intense, and he also knew that if he won, he would still lose. If he won the case, he would be seen by some as being party to a malicious prosecution. And if he lost, he would be criticized for blowing it.

Before he met the complainant, he had gone over the file with Ron Kushneryk, one of the officers who had arrested Pollock, and his immediate supervisor, Randy Bell. "She'll like you, she'll like you," Kushneryk had assured Britton over the phone the first time they spoke about Florence. Britton met with the complainant, Florence, twice at the Public Safety Building prior to the trial, both times in Kushneryk's presence. Florence struck Britton as a nice person, straightforward and honest, but unsophisticated, with a tendency to give lengthy answers unrelated to his questions. On both occasions she had demonstrated Pollock's touch by reaching back and rubbing the small of her back. Then her hand would move down between the cheeks of her buttocks to the bottom then back up.

Britton felt this was consistent with the statements she had made to the police. But he also felt it was a weak case because, given that Pollock had been checking for an injury at the time, it didn't seem that sexual gratification had been intended. Plus there was no physical or eyewitness corroboration. The central issue in the case, Britton decided, was Florence's credibility.

When she took the witness stand, she was dressed in the same clothes she had been wearing on the October 3 lunch hour that she went to see Pollock: a brown corduroy blazer, white blouse, and baggy blue jeans. Judge Giesbrecht ruled that her name couldn't be made public because she was the alleged victim of a sexual assault, but certain background information could. She was fifty-three, divorced, the mother of five, and a former taxi driver in Dauphin. She was also Métis.

Britton took her through the history of the personal injuries claim, which dated back to a January 20, 1989, traffic accident. She explained that the day before the alleged sexual assault, Pollock had told her over the phone that he had some good news for her on her insurance claim and he wanted to see her. Florence assumed that meant he had a cheque. The next morning, she'd set out for Pollock's office with her seventy-three-year-old friend and neighbour, Charlie Lucier. Her appointment was for 11:30. On the way she and Charlie stopped at the Downtowner Motor Hotel to celebrate with a drink.

"Why did you go there?" Britton asked.

"I felt happy," she said. "It was a beautiful day and I felt happy and I wanted to stop so I can pay all the money I owed people." Britton asked how many drinks she had. One or two beers, she wasn't sure.

It was 12:10 before Pollock was ready to see her. She took a seat in his office and waited for the good news she had been expecting. Instead, "He started lecturing me about liquor and everything like that. 'I could smell booze on you,' he said." Pollock told her she should go to Alcoholics Anonymous and wondered how she could afford to buy booze on her welfare income. "I didn't say nothing. I just listened to him lecturing me... Then I got mad, and I says, 'Look, I didn't come here for a lecture. I come here for my Autopac settlement.' That's all the truth. I'm not telling no lie."

Pollock had been silent for a while, then he'd asked her to take her jacket off so he could examine her injuries. Florence had walked around the desk to Pollock, who was still seated, and stopped beside him, within arm's reach. She had pointed to her various injuries. "First my ankle, then my knee, and I came up towards the back part where my spine was injured, eh? Or my bum. Whatever you want to call it."

Britton asked what happened next. "The only thing he done was check my spine here – like he touched me a couple of times. Then he said, 'There's a bone sticking out there.' I said, 'Well, naturally.' That's when I got mad. After I turned around and I says, 'Hey, you're not a doctor.'"

Pollock had the doctor's report on her injuries on his desk. He had been "fingering" it while he was lecturing her. After she told him off, Pollock started the tape recorder and dictated a letter to her doctor, describing her as having an alcohol problem and being depressed. She had left the office crying.

The most vital part of her testimony was precisely where Pollock had touched her. Britton asked her to demonstrate.

"Right here, like this," she said, moving her hand up and down near the base of her spine.

McCaffrey started to describe the area for the transcript. "I think she's describing an area from her waist downwards and her –"

"He didn't go far down," Florence said.

"He didn't go down far?" McCaffrey repeated in a surprised tone.

"No, no. Not far down." Her hand wasn't going down between her cheeks the way she had demonstrated to Britton during the two pre-trial interviews.

Judge Giesbrecht tried to describe what she had witnessed. "My observation of the witness appeared to be from the waist down, perhaps four to six inches down from the waist. . . . Down her spine. Would that be a fair description of what the witness –?"

Florence clarified that Pollock's hand had stopped at the base of her spine, where she said the injured bone was sticking out.

"How many times did he touch you like that?" Britton asked.

"I think – I think a couple of times and the third time, that's when he said, 'There's a bone sticking out there.'"

"Then you said you got mad," Britton said. "What did you say?"

"I did get mad after that because I told him, I said, 'You've got no business touching me like that,' I said, 'and lecturing me.' And I said, 'You're not a doctor. You got all the reports on your desk.'"

When it was his turn to cross-examine the witness, McCaffrey walked over to her and leaned close. "Have you had something to drink before you came here today?" At first Florence denied that she had, but then admitted she had had one drink.

Then McCaffrey turned to the point at which Pollock asked her to take her jacket off.

"You said you hesitated at first?"

"Well, I sort of wondered. Am I supposed to be like this, 'cause I always watch Perry Mason on TV and I never seen Perry Mason tell anybody to take part of their clothing off."

"Just so I have it. You then kind of ran your hand up and down your back."

"Yeah," she agreed.

McCaffrey was trying to stress that if Pollock had touched her, he touched her only in the place on her lower back where she said it hurt.

"That's the only place he rubbed me, too," she said. And the touch had been gentle, she agreed.

It was clear that Florence had been upset about the way Pollock treated her. She had called Jeff Oliphant, her former lawyer in Dauphin, but Oliphant had been appointed to the bench. He passed her to another Dauphin lawyer, John Menzies, who passed her to the Manitoba Human Rights Commission, which passed her to the Law Society of Manitoba. Two days after the incident, she went to the Law Society's offices to deliver a letter of complaint.

The letter was filed as an exhibit at the trial. McCaffrey asked Florence to put on her eyeglasses and read it.

To Whom it may Concern

Today I went to the Lawyer, Harvey Pollock of Winnipeg M.B.. He started saying that I smelled from Booz and he called me an Alcoholic, Then he asked me to take my jacket off. I didn't know if I should, (It made me think for a few minutes before I did and I showed him my arm & wrist & my knee, ankle, also my spine. And that's where he touched me is my bum, where my spine is broken.

To my self I don't think he's doctor that he has to examine me he has no right.

Another thing he told me your drinking and I said so if I did its none of your bussiness and he said your only getting 376.0 per months where do you get money to drink. So I told him its none of your business that I come here for Auto Pack.

I said my friends buy drinks for me then he tell me, tell your friends not to buy you any drinks & I said I don't have a car if I want to drink its none of your bussiness. (I hate him)

Yours truly
P.S. He doesn't have to touch me.

McCaffrey took her through the letter, paragraph by paragraph trying to get her to admit she was more upset about the lecture on drinking than she was about the touch.

"No, it's not the drinking part," she insisted. "It's true that's all that happened. It's a minor detail really, in a way. But he didn't have to touch me. He's not a doctor."

McCaffrey started to say something else, but she interrupted him. "You're a lawyer. Do you ever touch any of your clients to tell them to take off their jacket or any part of their clothing?"

It was a good question. McCaffrey ignored it.

"What really upset you, I am suggesting –"

"No," she said. "Don't bring that up again."

When the trial adjourned for the noon break, McCaffrey suggested to Britton that he abandon the prosecution and try for a mediated settlement between Pollock and the woman. Britton listened, had lunch with Ron Kushneryk, then went up to discuss the morning with senior Crown attorney Bruce Miller. It hadn't gone well, he told Miller, but the two of them decided it wouldn't be appropriate to discuss mediation with Florence while she was still being cross-examined.

When the afternoon session started, McCaffrey moved to the subject of how the police had heard about the incident. It had been inadvertent. She had called the police in the middle of the night because her sixteen-year-old son had broken a screen in the apartment.

"And a couple of police officers in uniform came out?"

"Umm-humm."

"And there was a lady officer?"

"Yes."

"Would you remember her?"

"I just know her by her first name. I told them to write names on that card – the incident card. Kathy, and I forget the guy's name."

McCaffrey asked for Kathy Hodgins to be brought into the court-room.

Of all the hundreds of cops in Winnipeg, Kathryn Hodgins and her new partner, Jacek Kapka, had been the ones dispatched in response to the distraught woman's call. According to Hodgins's report on the encounter, it wasn't until the complainant digressed from her problems with her son to her problems with her car accident injuries that Harvey Pollock's name came up.

"You wouldn't believe what my lawyer Harvey Pollock did to me," is the way Hodgins remembered how it started.

In a report written by Hodgins and co-signed by Kapka, she described what the complainant demonstrated. "Florence said he then had her turn around and he rubbed her between her cheeks, between her tailbone-anus area. She leaned to one side on her chair and showed Hodgins where."

After Florence identified Hodgins, who then left the courtroom, McCaffrey went back to something Florence had told Britton in her testimony earlier that day: "You said that you spoke to the city police and you talked to a lady, who I take it was Kathy –"

"I just wanted to get a little advice from everybody what I was sup-posed to do."

"She said – and here's the words I took down that you gave this morning – 'You should report this.'"

McCaffrey was still cross-examining Florence when Bruce Miller walked into the courtroom, passed Britton a note, and left. Court recessed shortly afterward. When the trial reconvened twenty-five minutes later, Britton said he had no other questions of the witness and asked Judge Giesbrecht to adjourn until the next morning at 10 a.m. "I would like to have an opportunity to reflect on the Crown's position after hearing the complainant's case," Britton said.

But Britton had already made up his mind, and he decided to tell Ron Kushneryk. They met at the end of the day, along with Inspector Ron Dawson, who had been monitoring the trial. Britton had never seen Dawson before, but he told both of them that Florence's testimony didn't back up the charge of sexual assault or even common assault.

Both cops were upset. Kushneryk said dropping the charge would make the police look bad in the papers. He wanted Hodgins to have a chance to testify or she would look bad, too. Britton offered to put his reasons for staying the charge in writing and to take personal responsibility, but that didn't mean anything to the two detectives.

"There will be women's groups down here that will be upset," Dawson said.

Kushneryk insisted on testifying. He wanted to describe how Pollock had denied the charge when he was arrested but then called the complainant's doctor and, in the course of talking to him, admitted touching her while he was checking out her back problem.

Britton didn't see how that proved their case of sexual assault. "This is shit, Matthew," Kushneryk kept saying. "This is shit."

Britton later met with Bruce Miller and his boss, Stu Whitley, the man Pollock still blamed for "blowing" the case against the drunk driver who killed Nathan. They were in agreement that the sexual assault charge wouldn't fly, but Whitley didn't think the whole case should be tossed out.

"He touched her," Whitley said, "that's a common assault."

Britton didn't think so, but Whitley was an assistant deputy minister, the head of prosecutions, so Britton deferred to his judgment and agreed to proceed with the charge of common assault.

Meanwhile, Ron Dawson was in Paul Johnston's office in the Public Safety Building, briefing him on what had happened at the trial. Dawson said Britton was out of his depth, and that McCaffrey looked as if he was fencing with an unarmed man. The way Dawson saw it, Britton was confused and intimidated and he had just given up. He was going to drop the case.

Johnston was alarmed, and hurried off to tell Herb Stephen what had happened. They decided to call Graeme Garson, the deputy minister of justice. "Graeme," Johnston said when he reached Garson on the phone, "we are very worried over here." They were worried that Britton was about to roll over and play dead on the Pollock case. Garson inferred that the policemen thought that the Crown had deliberately assigned a junior man to lose the case against Pollock and embarrass the police. He promised to look into it.

Britton was still in Whitley's office meeting with the province's two most senior Crown attorneys when the phone rang. It was Garson, and he wanted to see the three of them – Whitley, Miller, and Britton – in his office. It was just across Broadway in the Legislative Building. After Britton finished briefing Garson on Florence's testimony, the deputy minister asked him to wait outside. He wanted to speak privately with Whitley and Miller.

52

"It's over."

Matthew Britton slept fitfully that night. He finally got up shortly after 7 a.m. and began composing a memo to Bruce Miller. Britton had decided that, in good conscience, he couldn't proceed with the common assault charge, either. At the end of the memo, he wrote: "If my recommendation is not accepted, I regretfully request permission to withdraw from the case and ask that a different Crown be assigned."

The second day of the Harvey Pollock trial was late starting. It was 10:15 by the time Judge Giesbrecht entered the courtroom and Matthew Britton stood up.

Reading from a statement, Britton said the Crown would not proceed with the sexual assault charge against Pollock because the complainant's evidence did not support it. As for the lesser charge of common assault, again the Crown did not believe it had enough evidence to prosecute. "The facts in the case, as have been presented in court, disclose that the defendant-lawyer touched his client lightly on the tailbone while presumably examining her injuries." And so he was entering a stay of proceedings.

When Britton finished, Pollock's lawyer D'Arcy McCaffrey congratulated him, then used a metaphor to describe the police investigation. "I think that the lid on the sewer, if I can put it that way, was removed and we got a whiff of the gas yesterday afternoon. . . . It appears there was an enormous amount of energy and taxpayers' money and time devoted to the prosecution of Mr. Pollock . . . It's been an ordeal for Mr. Pollock."

Five minutes after the second day of Harvey Pollock's trial began, Judge Giesbrecht entered the stay of proceedings and adjourned the court.

Across the room, Sinclair watched Ron Kushneryk throw up his arms in disgust. He had never met Kushneryk, at least they had never been introduced, but he followed him onto the street, looking for a comment.

"Sorry, Gord," Kushneryk said, waving him away.

Outside the Law Courts building a knot of reporters and cameramen surrounded Harvey Pollock, as Martin stood by his side. Pollock had already told one reporter that he was considering a civil suit. "It was all brought on – obviously instigated – by the police department, by the vindictiveness of a certain police officer. The police were looking for me. They were waiting for me." He added that he felt sorry for Florence. "The police used her."

Pollock had finally publicly answered Bruce Owen's question about payback. Later that day, Owen asked for a private meeting with the Pollocks and told them he hadn't been acting out of malice when he showed up outside Pollock's office on the morning of the arrest. But, in front of the courthouse on the morning the case collapsed, Pollock had something else to say, this time about Herb Stephen. "He should have resigned a long time ago. It should cost him his job. As a boy I grew up and was told to respect the police . . . What do we tell our kids today?"

Sinclair walked with Pollock and Martin the two blocks to their office. Pollock was whistling again. There was a vase with three yellow roses from the staff waiting for him when he walked in. Once in his office, Pollock told Sinclair that at the Public Safety Building that morning, Kushneryk had asked him if he had a gun. Kushneryk had said, "You know," and pointed a finger to his own temple.

Harvey wanted to play the tape of his arrest for Sinclair to hear. But, first, he had to call Sylvia.

"It's over," he told his wife.

Later that day, Mayor Bill Norrie rejected Pollock's call for Stephen's resignation and asked Police Commissioner Loren Reynolds to put together a report on what had happened. The next day, Paul Johnston was acting police chief again when he issued a news release saying the department was ready and willing to assist Reynolds with his report. The release concluded with what had become the unofficial department motto during the last two years: "I have every confidence that our officers acted in a professional manner."

Paul Johnston was wrong. At least one of them hadn't. But Harvey Pollock was wrong, too. It wasn't over.

PART V

‒‒‒⦵‒‒‒

THE VERDICT

Ishi, the last known Stone Age survivor in North America, stumbled into the modern world at dawn, August 29, 1911. It happened in a remote slaughterhouse in the hills of northern California. The butchers, awakened by the barking of dogs, got up to investigate, then excitedly telephoned the sheriff that they had found an almost naked wild man crouching in their corral. Sheriff J. B. Webber and his deputies presently arrived with guns drawn, but the wild man made no move to resist capture. He was an Indian, Sheriff Webber saw, emaciated, starving and obviously at the limit of exhaustion and fear. Though his black eyes were wary and guarded now, he quietly allowed himself to be handcuffed. The sheriff then motioned him into a wagon, drove two miles to Oroville and, not knowing what else to do with him, locked him in the Butte County jail.

        – Theodora Kroeber, *Ishi in Two Worlds*

53

"There are some things I'll take to the grave with me."

Herb Stephen had hoped that 1991 would be better for the police than 1990 had been. But that wish exploded on his desk two weeks into the new year. On the day before Stealth bombers began dropping bombs on Baghdad at the start of the Gulf War, former armed forces pilot Loren Reynolds fired a paper missile that scored a direct hit on the fifth floor of the Public Safety Building.

Reynolds, the new police commissioner, had been forced to work quickly over the Christmas holidays on his report about the arrest of Harvey Pollock. Other than interviewing senior Crown attorneys Stu Whitley and Bruce Miller, he had relied on written reports from the police officers involved. On January 7, Reynolds's five-page report, marked "confidential," landed on the desk of Mayor Bill Norrie.

Reynolds outlined the chronology of events, including, on October 9, a late afternoon meeting where Ron Kushneryk briefed Dennis Toyne, Randy Bell, and Ron Dawson. It was decided then that a sexual assault charge should be laid against Pollock, but only after consulting the Crown the next morning. Reynolds got to the guts of the matter on the third page.

The charge of sexual assault against any member of our society is a serious matter and should not be done hastily, without considerable evidence and reasonable justification. There is serious doubt in this writer's mind that this case was handled with due care for Mr. Pollock. . . . The Police Department's first contact with the complainant [Florence] indicates that she was having serious behavioral problems, as she was reported to have "broken down.". . . . Yet in spite of this and some definite indications of alcohol problems, a thorough background check was not conducted prior to the arrest, and her statement was taken by the Police Department to be accurate and sincere.

The manner in which Mr. Pollock was arrested is worthy of close examination. . . . The presence of the *Free Press* reporter gives cause to wonder if in fact the arrest was meant to get Mr. Pollock in an embarrassing position. It is clear that only someone at a relatively high level in the Police Department had sufficient knowledge to "tip off" Mr. B. Owen of the *Free Press*.

There are two revelations that surface in this investigation that cause me particular concern. First, there is a serious distrust of crown attorneys by members of the Crime Division, and as publicly stated by Mr. S. Whitley, the necessary level of cooperation between our department and the crown attorneys is non existent. . . . The open criticism by senior police officers of the crown attorney's handling of this case is also cause for concern . . .

Second, there seems to be an unreasonable degree of paranoia, dislike, distrust or all three factors when the subject of criminal lawyers, certain media or certain public figures arise. . . .

There are no reasonable grounds to prove that the Police Department persuaded or coached the complainant to pursue the laying of the charges of sexual assault against Mr. Pollock. However, there is sufficient circumstantial evidence which would indicate that certain members of the department exercised an abuse of authority in this case. . . .

RECOMMENDATIONS. The Crime Division needs to be restructured immediately. The head of this division, the Acting Chief during the Pollock matter, is clearly responsible for the state of affairs and the police actions in the Pollock case. Deputy Chief Johnston should be relieved of his duties immediately and be retired from the force. He will be 60 years old in September, 1991. Superintendent Toyne should be removed from his position in the Crime Division

and transferred to another division. Likewise Inspectors Bell and Dawson should be removed from their current positions and reassigned to positions outside the Crime Division. . . .
Loren H. Reynolds

It was overcast and an unseasonably warm minus eight Celsius on the afternoon of January 15, 1991, when Herb Stephen led his deputy chief across the street to Loren Reynolds's office at City Hall, where Paul Johnston was told his career with the Winnipeg Police department was over. In the next day's newspaper, there was no suggestion from Johnston that his resignation had been forced. "It's time to go," Johnston told a reporter. "Time to relax. Time to do other things."

Herb Stephen denied there was any connection between Johnston's sudden departure and the handling of the Pollock case. "Absolutely not," the chief said. Reynolds was more candid. "If I said this had no connection with the Pollock case, I would be dishonest. Our obligation is to let the gentleman go as honorably as we can. Thirty-seven years of excellent service can't be overlooked. He served the city a long time."

Four days after Johnston left, Dennis Toyne, Randy Bell, and Ron Dawson were transferred out of the Crime Division. The Reynolds report was still a confidential document when Stephen issued a news release explaining the decision: "The reason for the transfers of Supt. Toyne, Insp. Bell and Insp. Dawson was not disciplinary in nature and not related to the Winnipeg Police Department investigation of allegations against Harvey Pollock."

In fact, Stephen had called in the three officers one by one and told them they were being transferred because the Pollock investigation hadn't been thorough enough. But the officers all grieved their transfers, saying they were without just cause. In early April, the *Sun* reported that Stephen had reached a secret deal with Toyne, Bell, and Dawson. In exchange for five weeks of extra vacation, and in Dawson's case, reinstatement in the Crime Division, they would drop their grievances. The chief also issued a public apology to the three men, saying the Pollock investigation was "conducted in a professional manner" and "did not tarnish the image of the Winnipeg Police Department."

Less than an hour after Stephen had made his apology, *Free Press* reporter Paul Wiecek confronted the chief as he was storming out of the Public Safety Building. He was taking off on annual leave and refused to comment further on his statement. When Wiecek asked where he was going, Stephen grew even more agitated. "Away from Winnipeg," he snapped.

Meanwhile, it was as if the mayor hadn't even read the report he had ordered from Reynolds. In public at least, Bill Norrie insisted that the police had done nothing wrong in the Pollock investigation. He pointed the finger of blame instead at the Justice Department for appointing a "junior" Crown to handle the case.

On April 13, a sunny, springlike day, Gordon Sinclair met Paul Johnston at the Polo Park Pancake House for one of their Saturday morning breakfasts. Johnston had called Sinclair at home the week before to arrange the get-together. While the two men sipped their coffees and waited for their orders to come, the former deputy chief talked about being glad to be away from the political quagmire that the police department had turned into in recent years. The boys had already held a retirement party for him.

Sinclair genuinely liked Johnston and even wanted his approval, the way sons do. Sometimes, Sinclair thought, Johnston even seemed to treat him like a son. "Gordy," he once said gently after one of his columns on the police, "I'm disappointed in you."

On this day, though, Johnston's disappointment was with others. He spoke angrily about Reynolds, the man who had forced him to resign: "He couldn't investigate an elephant in a telephone booth." Johnston was upset with Stephen, too. Sinclair got the sense that he felt Stephen should have stood up for him, that he had been let down if not betrayed. Sinclair hoped Johnston was angry enough that he would share some fifth-floor secrets. He wasn't. And when they were saying their goodbyes, Sinclair recalled something Johnston had said when he'd called earlier. "There are some things," he'd said bitterly, "I'll take to the grave with me."

After the case against his client, Harvey Pollock, was dismissed, D'Arcy McCaffrey had written a letter to Mayor Bill Norrie and the rest of city council saying that unless he received an apology and an offer of an out-of-court settlement by April 19, a suit would be filed. The grounds would be malicious prosecution, false imprisonment, malicious arrest, abuse of process, negligence, and defamation. On April 17, city council voted 21–8 to ask the province for an independent inquiry into how the police and the Crown handled the Pollock case. Norrie believed a public inquiry was needed to clear the air and protect the integrity of the police department and the Justice Department.

Whether there would be an inquiry was up to Justice Minister Jim McCrae, whose senior Crown attorneys were being blamed by the police for bowing to pressure. Why, Sinclair wondered, would McCrae risk being damaged politically if an inquiry found his department to be at fault? Unless, of course, his staff felt they had nothing to hide, that the police had been to blame. Coincidentally, on the same day city council called for the inquiry, Senior Crown Attorney Rob Finlayson wrote a memo to Stu Whitley, the assistant deputy minister of justice and head of public prosecutions, detailing how the police had initially notified the Crown about the Pollock case. The memo suggested why Justice would want a public airing of the Pollock case.

Finlayson had been asked what charge would be appropriate for a hypothetical scenario in which a lawyer touches a woman "up the crack of her ass" two or three times. Finlayson had told Bell and Dawson the charge would be sexual assault. Only then was he informed that Pollock was being arrested, at his office, to ensure the police had the "right" Pollock.

The day after Stu Whitley received Finlayson's memo, Justice Minister Jim McCrae met for more than an hour with Norrie. On April 19, the deadline for Harvey Pollock's demand for an apology, McCrae announced there would be an independent inquiry into the circumstances surrounding the arrest of Harvey Pollock, QC. Mayor Bill Norrie later called Pollock to say he was sorry about what had happened, but Pollock never did receive an apology from the city. And, in exchange for his legal expenses being paid, he eventually dropped the suit.

A few days earlier, Sinclair had gone to Martin Pollock's for dinner. Harvey Pollock was there. At one point in the evening, Pollock said he feared for his life. He had a house alarm, but there was a problem. It was connected to the police station.

54

"PLANE TICKETS."

In early March, Ellen Gordon was in Los Angeles, visiting a girlfriend, Nancy Schwartz. Ellen was driving a rented car she'd borrowed for a couple of days. The two of them were speeding along Sepulvada, when a motorcycle cop signalled them to stop. Ellen pulled over and the cop asked for her driver's licence and registration. Ellen knew she was in trouble. She couldn't find the car registration and she was an uninsured driver. The cop asked her to wait while he dealt with another driver whose car he had already pulled over.

Ellen looked in her rearview mirror. She could see the other driver. He was black. When the cop finished writing him a ticket he returned to Ellen.

"I'm not going to give you a ticket," he told her. "Just don't speed any more."

Ellen smiled and thanked the cop. She couldn't believe her luck. Then something occurred to her. She turned to Nancy. "They got the ticket because they were black."

The next morning Ellen turned on the TV, to see footage of a pack of police mercilessly beating a black man, Rodney King.

Back in Winnipeg the Rodney King videotape was all over the TV news, too. The same day, CBC radio ran a news item on the Aboriginal Justice Inquiry. It was expected to report by the summer.

Two weeks later, another videotape was being talked about at the examination for discovery on the Harper family's civil suit against Cross, Stephen, and the city. On March 19, Harvey Pollock had visited the Court of Queen's Bench exhibits room and signed out twenty-four exhibits from the Harper inquest and three from the Aboriginal Justice Inquiry. One of those three was the videotaped re-enactment of the shooting, featuring Cross and Detective Cal Osborne.

The examination for discovery required the lawyers from both sides to declare their evidence. This time the Pollocks met with Al McGregor and Martin Minuk on home turf: the book-lined boardroom in the Pollocks' office. Cross's lawyer offered the new evidence that Cross now acknowledged that the fight had swung off the sidewalk and into the park. That had been suggested in the police photos by a trickling trail of blood that led into the park. But the Pollocks had something more important to prove. It was their contention that Cross already had his gun out before he stopped Harper, and that some of the other constables at the scene denied they had their guns out to fit Cross's contention that he never pulled his. Acting Sergeant Glen Spryszak had noticed that the barrel of Cross's gun had a whitish stain on it that looked like salt.

"Okay," McGregor asked Harvey, "do you know at what point in time the gun was first out?"

"Yes, when he was chasing Allan in the back alley."

"Cross was carrying a gun at that point?" McGregor asked incredulously.

"Yes," Pollock replied. "Allan said, and there was physical evidence, that the gun was dirty."

"So," McGregor said, "the physical evidence that the gun was dirty you relate back to –"

"Cross falling on his knee, and his hand going down on the ground, and the gun was in that hand."

"You don't relate that to the struggle with Mr. Harper?"

"No, not at all, because Cross himself said that it never touched the ground."

Cross's testimony went on for three days, over the next three weeks. At one point, Martin Pollock asked Cross if he knew the names of his next-door neighbours. Cross said he didn't. About a month later, during another instalment of the examination for discovery, this time between Martin Pollock and the city's lawyer, Doug Abra, Martin reminded Abra of Cross's sworn testimony that he didn't know his neighbours' names. On the contrary, Martin said, Cross had a close relationship with his next-door neighbours Mike and Sheila Elliot. Mike had gone fishing with Cross following the Harper shooting, and Cross had told him certain things, including the admission that he'd drawn his gun.

"Now with respect to Mrs. Elliot: Constable Cross had demonstrated the shooting to Mrs. Elliot on a number of occasions."

Then Martin tried to give Abra the boot while he was down. "Constable Cross had more than just a passing interest in Mrs. Elliot. I am satisfied that if you read from . . ."

"Well don't," his father interjected.

There were more questions for Cross about whether any complaints about him had been brought to the Law Enforcement Review Agency. Cross answered that there had been several complaints, all naming the officers involved, but that none of them named him as the "aggressor."

"So the record that the police chief would have of you would be a clean record then?" Martin asked.

"Mr. Pollock," Abra said. "I don't think he could answer that. The chief will be here one day, and you will be able to ask the chief about what the record is. Who knows what the chief has in his files."

"Plane tickets," Martin Pollock said.

Cross still faced the long-delayed Law Enforcement Review Agency hearing into his conduct. About the time of the examination for discovery, another report arrived at McGregor's office from Cross's psychiatrist, Dr. Linda Loewen. It would be Loewen's last report on Cross. After Loewen's marriage to police association president John Campbell, Cross switched psychiatrists.

In her report, Loewen said that while Cross could testify at LERA, it would be best if he didn't, given his fragile emotional state. Family problems were causing him the most anxiety and depression, those and the media attention.

The psychiatric report reminded Martin of an exchange about the re-enactment videotape.

"Is there some reason why you didn't view the videotape after the final shooting of the videotape?" Martin asked.

"It's not something pleasant to look at," Cross said.

"Were you not concerned about the accuracy of the portrayal?"

"To watch someone die is not enjoyable. It's not something that I am interested in," Cross said. Then he began to lose it. "You have made my life hell for three years. I want to forget everything."

<hr>

55

"WHAT WAS THE GUN DOING INSIDE?"

In the midst of Cross's testimony on the civil suit, the De La Ronde case bobbed back to the surface like a bloated corpse. The RCMP submitted their review of the shooting to Justice Minister Jim McCrae.

Dan De La Ronde had survived the shooting and, despite Sinclair's embarrassing experience with the owner of the New West Hotel, he had continued to investigate. All he really had to work with was a suspicion and the colour photo of the toy gun. He'd been unable to get answers to the questions he had raised, namely, if De La Ronde was shot as he emerged from his room, how did he end up sprawled diagonally across the hall? And, how, with De La Ronde in the hall and his door on a spring return, did his toy gun end up in the hotel room? De La Ronde couldn't have been using his hand to keep it open because the police said he was holding the fake gun with both hands. Even if he had propped the door open with his left foot, it still didn't explain how the gun ended up in the room and he ended up in the hall.

The other question nagging at Sinclair was where in the room did the gun land? He decided to take the photo to the hotel and try to find the patch of carpet that matched the photo. He asked Dan De La Ronde's brother, Billyjo, to go with him, and the two of them spent half an hour on their hands and knees trying to find a match. Dizzy from the swirls of blue, they finally gave up.

On the day after the RCMP report landed on his desk, Herb Stephen held an afternoon news conference to discuss the Mounties' findings. Coincidentally, Sinclair had an appointment with Dale Henry, the commanding officer of the RCMP in Manitoba that morning. He wanted to talk to Henry about the De La Ronde case. Henry had a reputation for being exceedingly bright, ethical, progressive, understanding of Natives and Native issues, and egotistical. But on the morning Sinclair met Henry for the first time, the Mountie wanted Sinclair to talk about himself as if he had come in for a job interview.

Finally, they got down to the subject of De La Ronde. It was apparent Henry wasn't going to tell Sinclair what was in the report, so Sinclair told him what he knew and the questions that were bothering him. Henry told Sinclair he was on the right track, and went on to suggest that Winnipeg police investigators had done a good job of gathering evidence on the shooting, but their critical analysis of the facts was wanting.

Later, Henry indicated that he didn't respect the leadership of the city force, particularly the chief's. He recalled Stephen's body language while testifying at the Aboriginal Justice Inquiry: the defiant, arms-crossed posture. Herb Stephen should resign, he said.

That afternoon, in the *Free Press* newsroom, city editor Brian Cole came storming over to Sinclair's desk.

"What are you working on?" he demanded.

Sinclair told him, and Cole promptly ordered him not to go to Stephen's news conference. Sinclair responded that he was going anyway, which infuriated Cole. He warned Sinclair that there had better not be anything in his column that duplicated the news story. And then he gave another order: "No mention of Herb Stephen."

The news conference was held in the fifth-floor boardroom of the Public Safety Building. Herb Stephen sat at one end of the long table. Sinclair took a seat at the other end. As usual, Stephen started by reading a statement. "On March 21st I received a report from the RCMP and I have reviewed it with my executive.

"The RCMP report raises a number of questions which require clarification. Answers to these questions will be obtained and provided to the Firearms Review Board and to the Crown attorney who is presently reviewing the file. I will also provide the answers to the RCMP for their comment if they so desire."

There were six questions, most of them about the door and the gun. The Mounties hadn't been able to figure out from the hundred-page Winnipeg police report whether the door shut after De La Ronde was shot or something kept it from closing. There were two other basic questions. Stephen read them to reporters:

"Four: Was De La Ronde in possession of the plastic handgun at the moment the shot was fired?

"Five: What was the exact position of the plastic handgun in suite 109?"

Stephen said he was puzzled by the RCMP's list of questions. "These are things that were covered," he said, "although they may not be in the actual report." Sinclair was puzzled, too.

When Stephen was asked why the Mounties were asking if De La Ronde was holding the gun when he was shot, the chief replied, "I have no idea why." He had to have known why, but it was apparent that he wasn't going to explain the context of the RCMP questions and that most reporters didn't understand what they meant.

Finally, Sinclair put the question to the chief. If De La Ronde had been standing in the hall, how had the toy gun ended up in his room behind a closed door? Stephen said he didn't know.

There was no mention of Herb Stephen in Sinclair's next column. Instead, he wrote about going back to the New West Hotel with Billyjo and Dan De La Ronde. Dan still had the bullet in his brain and was using a cane because he was partially paralyzed. His memory came and went like a weak radio signal. Billyjo wanted to take him back to the scene to see if he could remember what happened before he was shot.

"Do you remember telling me how you poked your head into the hall, how you couldn't see anything? And then you heard a shot and felt your head exploding. Do you remember that story?"

"No," Dan said.

The bullet had damaged his memory. But as they stood in the room where the gun had been found, it was obvious it hadn't damaged his cognitive abilities.

"If I was standing out there," he said pointing to the hall, "what I don't understand is what was the gun doing inside."

Two months later, Herb Stephen hastily called another news conference, this time to announce triumphantly that the Winnipeg police had proven once again they could investigate themselves; the RCMP and the Crown had finally agreed with their report clearing Constable Malcolm Dawson of any wrongdoing in the shooting of Dan De La Ronde. Stephen held up the photo of the toy gun.

"He was in a threatening position in the hallway with that weapon in his hand. He was pointing it at them. Now if you had that pointing at you, would you know it was a toy weapon?"

But, as was becoming the pattern, the chief neglected to tell the whole story. Later, Deputy Justice Minister Graeme Garson told reporters that De La Ronde might not have had the toy gun in his hand when he was shot. And, most certainly, De La Ronde had not – as the police had initially reported – stood in the hotel hallway, "crouched down, his feet separated, and pointed the weapon at which time he was shot."

"The officers saw a man put the upper part of his body outside the hotel room and some use of his hand," Garson said. "But whether or not the weapon was actually there, I don't know if anyone will be able to determine that."

Ultimately, the Crown had decided there was not enough evidence to charge either De La Ronde or Malcolm Dawson. The RCMP report did make one thing clear to Gordon Sinclair: the original lack of critical analysis about the door and the placement of the toy gun demonstrated that the Winnipeg police department's attitude hadn't changed.

The next day, at a press conference in the Manitoba Métis Federation's office, Billyjo De La Ronde used a metaphor to express his dissatisfaction: "The wound has to be cleaned out before the healing will begin."

56

"I WOULDN'T SAY ANYTHING LIKE THAT."

Diane Eastwood remembered it this way: It was June 15, 1991, the day after the newspaper announced that the Supreme Court had refused to hear Cross's appeal on LERA. She was in bed when she heard Andrew screaming for her. Diane ran downstairs. Cross had one hand over Andrew's mouth and the other pinching his nose. He had been drinking.

"You shut up," he told Andrew. "Your mommy doesn't love you."

"You fucking asshole," Diane screamed. "You get the hell out of here."

A year later Cross swore an affidavit denying that he ever told the children that their mother didn't love them or that he had ever been

312 GORDON SINCLAIR JR.

mentally or physically abusive. He claimed it was his wife who had been verbally abusive, swearing at them, calling them "fucking idiots." What he didn't dispute was leaving the house, and spending the night at a motel, where he signed the register and gave his address as Englewood, Colorado. His sister Judy lived there.

Just a week before the inquiry into Pollock's arrest was set to begin, Police Commissioner Loren Reynolds arrived for work at City Hall to discover that his office had been burgled. Reynolds didn't bother reporting it to police. When Gordon Sinclair eventually heard about the break-in, he was reminded of a newspaper clipping defence lawyer Hymie Weinstein brought back from Los Angeles for him. The American Civil Liberties Association had placed an ad in the *Los Angeles Times* at the time of the Rodney King beating. The ad posed a question: "Who do you call when the gang wears blue uniforms?"

Nine days later, on June 24, 1991, the day the Meech Lake accord officially died, and the news wire reported that Quebec police were trying to undermine efforts at a negotiated settlement to the Oka stand-off, a big-bellied, silver-haired man with the look and demeanour of a country doctor opened the inquiry into the arrest of Harvey Pollock by sitting down in the same high-backed chair from which Judge Enns had presided over the Harper inquest. Ted Hughes was a former Saskatchewan judge who became deputy attorney general of British Columbia, where he had drafted that province's conflict-of-interest guidelines. Five years later, as the province's conflict-of-interest commissioner, Hughes ruled that Premier Bill Vander Zalm had violated those guidelines. Within hours the premier had resigned.

"Well, good afternoon, ladies and gentlemen," Ted Hughes said. "I think we are ready to get under way with the inquiry."

During the next two weeks the details of how Pollock came to be charged with sexual assault would be covered. Much of it had already been made public at Pollock's trial. But there was new ground, too. The Reynolds report was made public for the first time, including the police commissioner's findings that the police had acted with undue haste in arresting Pollock. In Reynolds's opinion, there had been a vendetta.

The inquiry heard that Ken Dowson's former partner Randy Bell and Ron Dawson had sought a Crown opinion on what charges to press on the morning of the arrest at least twenty minutes after Owen had been tipped to the arrest. There was also the manner in which Crown Attorney Rob Finlayson had been consulted. Pollock's name hadn't been mentioned until after Finlayson had agreed the action the police described constituted sexual assault.

The police claimed they withheld Pollock's identity from Finlayson because they feared the Crown wouldn't recommend charges if the Crown knew whom they were going to arrest. They didn't trust the Crown for historic reasons dating back to Ticketgate. In Paul Johnston's firm view, the police distrust of the Crown centred on one person: the tall, professorial assistant deputy justice minister and head Crown, Stu Whitley.

When Whitley took the stand in his own defence, he was just as adamant about the conduct of the police, and their questionable ethics. He related an instance in which the police wanted assault charges laid against striking grocery workers. Whitley had seen video-tape of the picket-line incident, and knew that the police commonly laid assault charges against citizens they knew were going to press assault charges against them. He told the inquiry how Johnston had reacted when Whitley refused to lay charges against strikers. "Stu, you don't back the boys." Johnston denied saying that.

Among the exhibits before the inquiry was Hodgins's initial report from October 6, 1990. In it, Hodgins wrote that after the complainant, Florence, told the two officers that she hadn't liked Pollock's touching her, she mentioned she had complained to the Law Society.

She was asked if she made a report to police or intended to make one. Florence was told that when she made a report to the Law

Society ... that they'd handle everything. So she didn't know if she could make a police report.

Florence was told if she wanted to complain she could speak to the Detectives at the Public Safety Building. Florence asked if the officers could write down where to go, who to speak with and she was given a piece of paper with that information ... [On the piece of paper, Hodgins had jotted down a phone number and address, and had written "Sexual Assault Complaint against Harvey Pollock." Sexual assault was Hodgins's term for what had happened, not Florence's.]

The attending officers decided it was prudent not to take the complaint ourselves due to previous dealings between Mr. Pollock and Cst. Hodgins.

On 90 10 06... the writer received a call from Florence. She stated that she had called the number and the persons on the paper that was left for her. The officer that answered the call told her to wait until she hears from the Law Society and finds out what they are doing before making a police report. She then asked the writer if this means she can't make the report as she wanted to.

The writer stated that I'd speak with my Sgt., let him make the decision and I'd call her back. The writer spoke with Sgt. Vokey and he stated that a call should be entered and a report taken by another crew.

When Sergeant Bruce Vokey took the stand, commission counsel John Scurfield referred him to a memo that picked up the sequence at the point Hodgins's report left off. After Hodgins approached him about Florence, Vokey had written, "Constable Hodgins stated that she had encouraged the woman to provide further details of the assault with full intentions of taking an assault report, but that when the woman identified her assailant as Harvey Pollock, Constable Hodgins felt that she was in a conflict situation due to the Harper matter."

Hodgins's own report suggested that wasn't quite the way it happened. Hodgins knew it was Pollock all along.

Scurfield read the rest of the memo: "Constable Hodgins then advised that she had advised the woman that a criminal offence had occurred when Pollock touched her, and that if she wanted the police to investigate she would have to contact the Crime Division, and provided her with the phone number."

When Hodgins took the witness stand, she picked up the story of what happened when Florence called the Crime Division and spoke with a detective.

"She was told by the officer that it is a long weekend," Hodgins testified. "To maybe call the Law Society on the Tuesday and ask them what is going to be happening, and then, you know, call the police department back."

That was when Florence called Hodgins.

"She then asked me if this means that the police department isn't going to take a complaint from her, if the police department isn't going to help her now, either. I told her to hang on and I would have to speak with my sergeant. She still seemed adamant she wanted to make a complaint.

"I called her back and told her a car would be dispatched to speak with her. I will not be attending."

"At any time," asked commission counsel John Scurfield, "when you were talking to her, either the first night or during the course of these telephone conversations, did you put any pressure on her to get her to make a complaint?"

"None whatsoever," Hodgins said. "It was totally her decision."

That notion was disputed later by Florence's young lawyer, Chuck Blanaru. But, in the meantime, when Ron Kushneryk's counsel, Al MacInnes, cross-examined Florence, he referred to the note Hodgins had left with her that first night, where Hodgins had referred to a "Sexual Assault Complaint" against Harvey Pollock, and left the Crime Division phone number.

"Do you see that?" MacInnes asked, referring Florence to Hodgins's handwriting on the note.

"I never wrote no statement," Florence said. "I didn't say nothing about sexual assault."

"No, I didn't say you did," MacInnes said. "I'm saying –"

"Because I told you," she interrupted, "sexual assault . . . to me is rape. I wouldn't say anything like that."

The focus of Hughes's attention eventually became the crucial question of who had leaked news of the arrest to Bruce Owen. Pollock's counsel, D'Arcy McCaffrey, had cross-examined Paul Johnston on the call.

"Was it your view that the leak came out of the station?"

"Quite probably."

"Yes?"

"I am sorry to say that, but quite probably."

"And you would agree with me that that would be a vindictive and malicious thing to do?"

"Reprehensible, sir."

One by one, commission counsel John Scurfield asked the cops involved – Paul Johnston, Dennis Toyne, Randy Bell, Ron Dawson, Don Feener, and Ron Kushneryk – the same two questions.

"Did you phone Bruce Owen?"

All six gave the same answer: "No."

"Do you give Bruce Owen permission to expose you if you were?"

"Yes," they all said.

Of the six prime suspects, Sinclair knew only Johnston personally, but he was getting to know Ron Kushneryk better. He seemed to be at the inquiry every day, wearing the same blue blazer, with a tiny gold lapel cross. Then it dawned on the columnist where he'd seen Kushneryk before. He was the guy who had sat down behind Sinclair at the strip bar. The cop his brother saw the next day in an unmarked police car. Sinclair asked Kushneryk about it. He said he'd never been to that bar.

$$\overline{57}$$

"It is just unthinkable."

Harvey Pollock took the witness stand on day two of the inquiry. Scurfield began by establishing that Pollock had been president of Citizens Against Impaired Driving for three years, and that, since his son had been killed he abhorred heavy drinking and would not represent anyone on charges of impaired driving.

Scurfield then turned to Pollock's attitude towards the police as a result of J.J. Harper's death.

"Would it be fair to say, Mr. Pollock, that during the course of the inquest and the inquiry you were a rather vocal critic of the actions of Constable Cross and the Winnipeg Police Department generally?"

"I was. So much so that I believed that there was a cover-up in respect to the death of Mr. Harper and I am still of that mind."

"And did you make any public announcements in the media of that sort?"

"I did. I was often approached by the media for comment and inadvisably or advisably I made them because of the way I felt about what was happening. And my position was noted by the media as being one who was critical of the police department and the investigation of the shooting of Mr. Harper . . ."

Scurfield moved on to Hodgins's involvement with Pollock during the Harper case.

"Did you personally criticize the quality of her evidence?"

"I did."

Pollock explained that he had cross-examined her twice; once at the inquest and then at the AJI, and that her testimony had been inconsistent. He admitted he'd been critical of her.

"Did you in fact make a comment which was published in the press to the effect: 'I don't know whether we are getting 222s or 292s with Constable Hodgins. Every witness suffers from stress, but to blame that. It will be up to the commission to decide if she is a credible witness'?"

"I said that, and that comes from the fact that Constable Cross had been on tranquillizers and we had been cautioned by the commissioners in dealing with his testimony and so, therefore, knowing that Constable Cross was in that state I made an offhand statement which in retrospect was inadvisable. But again I was emotional and I spoke what I felt. That's what I said."

Having put the case in context, Scurfield moved to Florence's visit to Pollock's office. Pollock said that he had spoken to her the day before about some good news on her claim. He had managed to get the Manitoba Public Insurance Commission to agree to a settlement for $6,000, but she needed to sign some papers. When she arrived the next day, he could smell alcohol on her and he'd told her so.

"Would you have used the word alcohol?" Scurfield asked. "She indicated to us yesterday that you may have used the word booze."

"It is possible that I may have used the word booze."

"Was there any discussion about Alcoholics Anonymous?"

"Oh, yes. I got into that as we sat down and we started talking."

Pollock said Florence was hyper and began complaining about how she was feeling.

"She complained about her right arm, her shoulder, her – I think it was her wrist, her elbow, her knee. She talked about her back. She said – she used the word broken spine or something and she took out some pills, some pill boxes out of her purse and she showed me what she was taking, I guess to reaffirm her condition and her complaints."

"Did you have any concerns about her consumption of drugs?"

"I did. I guess maybe in retrospect I shouldn't have concerned myself with it, but I was concerned about it. I am concerned about all my clients."

That, Pollock testified, was why he said what he did.

"I told her that I thought she had an alcohol problem and had she thought about AA. At which point in time she got angry. She said, 'I didn't come here for a lecture.' And I continued on to, I guess, press the point. And then finally I said to her, 'Would you like to take off your jacket and come around my desk and show me, point to me on your body, where it is that you are complaining?'"

Scurfield wanted to know about Pollock's decision to examine Florence's injuries.

"It wasn't that I wanted to examine her injuries, I wanted her to tell me about her injuries. And I asked her to take off her jacket and come around my desk and point to where the problem is. I had the medical reports in my file. I had acquainted myself with them at the time. And some of the things that she was saying to me didn't seem to bear out what the medical reports had indicated."

Scurfield asked if there was any reference in the medical files to a broken spine.

"None."

"Why did you ask her to come around the desk to examine her?"

"Well, I wanted her to point out to me where her problems were. I just wanted to get an idea exactly where it is that she continues to complain so that I can be knowledgeable in dealing with the matter, talking to the adjuster."

Pollock said Florence showed him all the places where she hurt. The wrist, elbow, shoulder, knee, and her lower back.

Pollock said she had been wearing high-waisted blue jeans and her shirt was tucked in. He had remained seated. "I extended my hand – my right hand – and I put it up against the back of her lower part of her spine." Pollock was demonstrating. His thumb was pointing down. Thumb up would have been a more comfortable motion. But having his thumb down would have kept his hand away from the intimate part of his client's body.

"That's what I did," Pollock insisted. "And I let it rest there for, you know, I didn't just touch it and pull away. I thought I was going to find or feel a bump, like a ridge or something that would indicate that here we have got a vertebra that had been chipped or broken and it is extending beyond the normal surface. And that's what I was expecting to find. I found nothing. My hand came away. It was there only momentarily."

"She also indicated with her hand, if I may," Scurfield said, "that you had reached around behind her and with the fingers pointed downwards, I believe, towards the legs, that you rubbed up and down in what she either called the bum area, or the spine area, or the tailbone area. Now, is that the motion that you used in order to examine her for her injuries?"

Pollock said no and suggested it would have been an unnatural movement because his hand would have been upside down and his elbow in the air.

"Besides, I wouldn't do that. I had no interest in this lady. I wasn't interested in her sexually in any way. I am not interested in other women. I love my wife. I have wonderful children. I think I enjoy reasonable respect in this community. I am not about to jeopardize or compromise my position. It is just unthinkable. I wouldn't do it."

The encounter between Pollock and Florence ended that day with her signing a contingency agreement on the insurance claim, witnessed by her friend Charlie Lucier, and then leaving.

"Did you notice if she was crying?" Scurfield asked.

"She was not crying."

Pollock went on to talk about his belief that the police were getting even with him for his involvement in the Harper case and with Dowson's suicide.

"What was your basis for making that allegation, sir?"

"Well, first of all, the police were sort of hung out to dry in Harper, so far as I was concerned. Their investigation, what they did, how they did it, was incompetent and, from my point of view, was a cover-up. Then there was the Aboriginal Justice Inquiry, and again that came out. Inspector Dowson was to testify. He killed himself the morning that he was supposed to testify."

Pollock continued, saying that he'd read a police statement in the newspaper, blaming people involved in the AJI for Dowson's death. He'd felt that the police were after him, that they wanted to get even with him.

"Was anything ever said to you, in a direct fashion, which led you to believe that there was some vindictive act taking place?" Scurfield asked.

"Not in specific words," Pollock answered. "Just by conduct, action, and people."

Gordon Sinclair waited for Pollock to mention what he had told him about Ron Kushneryk's behaviour when they got to the police station the morning he was arrested. Asking Pollock if he was armed. Then putting a finger to his own temple and pantomiming a trigger pull. But Harvey Pollock said nothing.

—
58

"I HAVE GOT TO SEE YOU."

Bruce Owen was about to make national headlines in the same court-room where he'd covered the Harper inquest more than three years earlier. Owen was facing the same dilemma *Saturday Night* writer Don Gillmor had struggled with at the Aboriginal Justice Inquiry. Reveal his source on the Harvey Pollock tip, or face a jail sentence for contempt.

John Scurfield took him through the sequence of events that started with the phone ringing at Owen's house at 7:40 a.m. on October 10, 1990.

"What happened when you answered the phone?"

"I answered the phone and a voice said, 'You don't know who this is.'"

"Did you in fact know who it was from listening to the voice?"

"I recognized the voice."

"What did that voice then tell you, sir?"

"I cannot remember word for word. But the gist of it was, 'They are going to arrest Harvey Pollock sometime this morning.' I said,

'What for?' Like my first impression was, Oh, boy. And the voice said, 'Sexual assault.'"

Scurfield wondered about the use of the word "they." "Could the voice have equally said, 'We are going to arrest Harvey Pollock this morning?'"

"No, it struck me as kind of weird when he said they."

"Did his voice belong to a police officer, sir?"

"Yes."

Owen had driven to the *Free Press*, where he spoke to Brian Cole, the city editor, about what he'd been told. "Did he ask how you knew that?"

"Not at that time."

"Has he subsequently asked how you knew that?"

"Yeah."

"Did you tell him?"

"Yeah."

Owen said he met up with photographer Glenn Olsen and the two of them drove the three blocks to Pollock's office building. It was half an hour to forty-five minutes before the police arrived. Owen said he was outside the building, hiding behind a pillar.

"Did you recognize the police officers who arrived?"

"I didn't see them. All I saw was a car."

While he and Olsen waited for the police to return with Pollock, Owen checked the elevators to see if one was on the way down from Pollock's sixteenth-floor office.

"The last time I ducked in I heard Mr. Pollock whistling. He has a distinctive whistle. I said, 'Well, here he comes.'"

Owen said he asked Pollock if he had anything to say about his arrest.

"Immediately he responded: 'This is the Winnipeg Police Department at their best.' Or, 'It's nonsense. It's absolute nonsense.'"

"Did you ask the police officers who were attending Mr. Pollock to comment on why it was that the police had tipped off the media that this arrest was about to take place?"

"No."

"No?" Scurfield echoed.

Owen shook his head. "From past experience at either crime scenes or arrests or whatever, the police don't talk to reporters at those scenes. From what I knew, it was pointless asking them anything. They wouldn't give me the time of day."

Asked when he next spoke to his source, Owen said he didn't talk to him again until after the Hughes Inquiry was called.

"That source said: 'I screwed up. I'm sorry. I screwed you. I screwed me.'" Those weren't the exact words, Owen acknowledged. Scurfield asked him to try to remember the exact words as best he could. "The source said: 'I'm sorry that this ever happened, that I have called you.' The source asked about my position at the paper, whether or not I was the subject of persecution by my supervisors, fellow reporters."

"What did you respond?"

"Nope."

"Did they say anything about the forthcoming inquiry?"

"Yes."

"What was it that the source said?"

"The source asked that I keep my word as to a prior, I guess you could say long-standing agreement of confidentiality."

Owen's source was worried about his career and how what he did reflected on the police department.

Scurfield had interviewed Owen prior to his appearance, so the commission counsel knew where he was going with the next question, even if the young reporter didn't at first.

"Did the source indicate that they had any significant, deep-seated, personal concerns?"

"Yes."

"What did the source tell you?"

"They were afraid of losing their job."

"Yes, and what else, sir? How would that impact on them?"

"During our conversation, the source talked about Ken Dowson and about the decision Ken Dowson made before he was about to testify at the AJI, and I know he didn't come out and say it, he said Dowson had made a decision that was admirable, and he – I know you are going to ask me, but, well, did he say he was going to kill himself? No, he didn't say that. He – he –" Owen was choking up. "The impression I was left with, was that that was an alternative to this whole thing."

After a five-minute break, Scurfield waded into the legally uncharted area of journalistic privilege.

"You are aware, Mr. Owen, that Sergeant Kushneryk, Sergeant Feener, Inspector Bell, Inspector Dawson, Superintendent Toyne, and former Deputy Chief Johnston have all sworn under oath that they did not give you this information."

Owen knew that. He also knew each of them had given him permission to disclose his identity if he were Owen's source.

"You are further aware that each of them has, under oath, relieved you from any form of journalistic privilege that you may claim, sir?"

"I am aware of that, whatever that means."

"I take it you are further aware, sir, that as a result of this incident, there is a shadow hanging over the career of each of these individuals which only you can clear up, sir?"

"I have made an ethical decision and one I am going to stand behind, where I am not going to reveal my source to you at this inquiry."

One by one, Scurfield named the six officers who may have tipped Owen, asking the reporter if this was the one. Six times Owen refused to answer the question, on the grounds that his relationship with his source was privileged.

When he had finished, before Owen's *Free Press* lawyer, Jonathan Kroft, took over, Scurfield told Hughes he wanted him to compel Owen to answer, "and I would be asking that you use such powers as you have under the Evidence Act if necessary to commit Mr. Owen to jail."

Next, Owen's lawyer asked the reporter to explain the principle of journalistic privilege.

"It's a principle that exists, whether in law or not, but it exists that a reporter, if he's going to be worth his or her salt, has to maintain that integrity.... If I chose to burn my source, it would be the end of my career. I want to go back to work after all this is over. I want to be able to call people up and get information. I want to be able to do stories. Who is going to trust me with confidential information? Nobody. What are my peers going to think? Nothing. How does it reflect on other reporters if I burn my source? How does it reflect on their work at the *Winnipeg Free Press*, or anywhere else in the city? I'm not prepared to jeopardize that. I may be in contempt of [court] here, but I'm not going to be in contempt of myself and what I believe in."

"Thank you," Kroft said.

Scurfield had some re-direct questions about whether the story would have broken anyway. Owen agreed that it would – it was an incredible story. Then Scurfield asked him, "Did it ever cross your mind that the source was concerned that possibly Mr. Pollock would not be charged, and he wanted to make darn sure that the media at least picked up the fact that he had been arrested and, therefore, for malicious reasons, embarrass him?"

Owen didn't know.

Scurfield continued to focus on the nature of the tip. "In fact," he said, "the tip that you were getting, to your certain knowledge, was at best gossipy and at worst malicious?"

That was an interesting question, coming from Scurfield, whose sister was a gossip columnist for Owen's former employer, the *Winnipeg Sun*. But Owen answered the question straightforwardly.

"I don't know."

A few moments later, Scurfield asked Owen if he had ever considered that he shouldn't have extended confidentiality to his source.

"No," Owen said.

"Do you believe that reporters should be allowed to extend confidentiality to malicious sources?"

"Well, malicious, you prove that. I have no knowledge of that."

Indeed, in an interview years later with Gordon Sinclair, Owen said he knew what it was about as soon as he got the phone tip about

Pollock's impending arrest: "*Payback*. This was a great story. The shit was going to hit the fan. And I wanted to be there for it."

Scurfield had finished, but Hughes wanted to make sure he understood Owen's view.

"Even if you were able to identify maliciousness in the motive, the assurance of confidentiality should still be given?"

"Yup," Owen said. "Yes, sir."

Next, Ron Kushneryk's lawyer, Al MacInnes, asked Owen a number of questions, including why Owen had revealed his source to city editor Brian Cole.

"Did you not consider that to be a breach of confidentiality to your source?"

"No, Brian Cole demanded it from me."

"You were prepared to breach the confidentiality agreement that you had with your source when your superior asked for the information?" MacInnes asked.

"Yes."

"But you are not prepared to come clean with this commission and do the same here?"

"Exactly."

When Sergeant Feener's lawyer, Randy McNicol, questioned Owen, he tried to get the reporter to narrow down the list of police suspects.

"Did you recognize the identity of both the officers accompanying Mr. Pollock?" McNicol asked.

"I only recognized one," Owen said.

"Prior to October 10, 1990, had you met and made the acquaintance of Sergeant Don Feener, my client?"

"No, sir, I don't believe so."

"You didn't recognize him outside Mr. Pollock's building the morning of October 10, 1990, did you?"

"No, sir."

The shadow hanging over the career of one of the officers had been lifted. And then there were five.

Bruce Owen had come to the inquiry with his toothbrush packed, but he wouldn't be going to jail that day. Hughes put over a decision on whether to find Owen in contempt until the following week, when he would hear evidence and argument on journalistic privilege. Then Hughes read from a statement, deploring the cloud hanging over the Winnipeg Police Department and asking for Owen's source to come forward. It was an emotional speech. Afterwards, as Sinclair left the courtroom, he saw Ron Kushneryk standing in the hall. Sinclair noticed his eyes. They were welling with tears.

The next morning Al McGregor met in his office with Bruce Owen and his lawyer, Jonathan Kroft. He had a letter he wanted Owen to pass to his police source. McGregor gave him the letter, a list of police home phone numbers, and told Owen to go into another room and pick out the one that belonged to his source.

That evening Owen called his source from home.

"What are you doing?" a panicky voice answered. "Why are you phoning me?"

"I have got to see you," Owen said.

The cop suggested they meet in Woodhaven Park just off Portage Avenue in the police district known as Sleepy Hollow. A mounted T-33 jet marked the spot.

It was after dark when Owen arrived. It was a hot night and he was wearing shorts. As he got out of his black Plymouth, up ahead, partially illuminated by the street lighting, he could see a dark figure nervously smoking a cigarette. The two of them headed into the park together, where the mystery cop had a question for Owen.

"What's this crap about suicide?"

328 GORDON SINCLAIR JR.

"I CAN'T KEEP IT FROM YOU."

D'Arcy McCaffrey, Pollock's dapper lawyer, called Sinclair on Saturday morning. He wanted the columnist to come over to his Wellington Crescent apartment, but he didn't say why. Sinclair assumed he had something to tell him. He assumed incorrectly.

"Who do you think called Owen?" McCaffrey asked when Sinclair arrived.

They ran down the candidates. They knew it wasn't Feener. Owen didn't know him. Toyne? Nah. Sinclair wasn't sure about Kushneryk. Bell seemed a more likely candidate, given that he'd been Dowson's partner and pallbearer. Sinclair suspected it might be Paul Johnston. Then again, he said, it could be all of the above.

It was standing room only in the inquiry room on July 17. Word had leaked out. Ron Kushneryk, the cop who had arrested Pollock, was standing in the witness box.

"Sergeant Kushneryk," Scurfield said, "I am advised you have something that you would like to tell the commissioner this morning."

"Mr. Commissioner, I am the person who phoned Bruce Owen, the reporter, the morning of the arrest. I would like the opportunity to explain why, if I might."

"Yes, certainly," Hughes said.

"So I could apologize," Kushneryk said, sounding as if he were having trouble controlling his emotions. Scurfield slowly took him through the morning Pollock was arrested, beginning with the call he said he made from his office in the Crime Division. Kushneryk claimed no one else knew he was making the call. He had met Owen years earlier when the young reporter was covering the courts, and thought him an honest person and a fair-minded reporter. But, he swore, he could not recall ever giving Owen a tip before.

"So why did you decide to call him with respect to Harvey Pollock?"

"That was a very, very foolish thing to do. I realize this. I don't even – I've put this through my mind. I have lived with this for ten months. I looked at this like a little favour for Bruce."

Kushneryk wanted to talk about his meeting with Owen after the reporter had refused to name him.

"We met at a location in St. James. It was night, about 10 o'clock. And I told Bruce, 'I apologize, I am sorry, Bruce. I have hurt you. Look what I have done to you.' And he said, 'Ron, don't apologize. You have done nothing wrong. You know, you are carrying all of this on your back. You didn't hurt anybody.' ...

"I said, 'But it was still – I hurt you. I have made you go through this. I put you on the spot. And there is a chance that you can go to jail.' And he says, 'Ron, I will go to jail.' He says, 'I am quite set. I am going to go to jail.' He says, 'I am never going to tell your name.' And he says, 'Neither is my editor.'

"And then I said . . . 'What is all of this bunk about me being your constant source for three years? What is all that?' And he kind of laughed, and this is the part, I don't want to get Bruce in trouble. But I don't think he will. I hope he won't. I hope nobody hurts him over this, but it is the truth, this is what happened. He says, 'Ron, I had to convince the commission that I had a source, or else I couldn't protect you . . . so I made up this scenario that you were my source and it kind of gave the groundwork for my defence.'"

Before his client came forward, Kushneryk's lawyer, Al MacInnes, had negotiated a deal with the Justice Department. Kushneryk wouldn't be prosecuted for perjury. According to police regulations, Kushneryk should have been fired for leaking news of Pollock's imminent arrest and for lying under oath. Instead, he was fined and demoted from sergeant to first-class constable. Later, it was reported that an intermediary for Kushneryk had struck a deal with the city administration, including Police Commissioner Loren Reynolds, before he'd agreed to identify himself.

At 6 p.m. the TV set at the back of the newsroom was tuned to the supper-hour news on CKY TV, and Bruce Owen was watching. When the segment came on about Kushneryk accusing Owen of exaggerating their professional relationship, Owen just shook his head.

"Well," he said, "tomorrow it'll be forgotten."

Years later, in a conversation with Sinclair, the young reporter who had once been so eager for the Pollock story now felt angry about the telephone tip.

"People accused me of being a tool of the police department. Whether I was a tool of the department, I don't know."

If he felt used, Bruce Owen wasn't the only one.

A week later, Florence's lawyer, Chuck Blanaru, read his closing argument to Judge Hughes. In part, he said it was Kathy Hodgins, not Florence, who formed the opinion that a sexual assault had taken place. Blanaru said Hodgins based that opinion on what Florence showed her, but "the police conclusion that sexual assault occurred was reached without even enquiring from Florence as to whether she considered Mr. Pollock's actions to be in any way sexually motivated... In essence, what became the focal point for the police investigation and subsequently the crucial factor for the Crown, was the specific location of the touching. Lost in this process was what I have suggested to be Florence's state of mind and her essential complaint – the verbal and physical unprofessional conduct of her lawyer."

Blanaru called Pollock's conduct "demeaning." Florence's feelings were hurt, but he reminded Hughes that Pollock touched her only in the area where she said she was injured, and that it was clear that Florence never considered Pollock's poking and prodding to be sexually motivated.

"Lastly," said Blanaru, "I feel it worthy to mention that Florence was not informed by the police in advance that Mr. Pollock would be arrested and charged with sexual assault. Florence was not consulted on the nature of the charge and had to find out by reading the newspaper the next day. Similarly, when the criminal proceedings were stayed, Florence was not informed of the reason why in advance. Nor was she consulted in any way. Given these matters, I would submit that either the system of justice in this province is insensitive or, in this case, Florence was viewed as a non-entity."

Hughes was clearly impressed with the young lawyer's summation. He asked for a copy.

The Hughes Inquiry had concluded by the August long weekend when the *Free Press* moved from downtown to a sprawling new plant in a north-end industrial complex. The new brick building was surrounded by walls and fences and gates; Fortress *Free Press*. Booze flowed in the old newsroom on the last night. Mayor Bill Norrie even dropped by to say goodbye to the old building. As Gordon Sinclair packed his belongings into cardboard boxes, he wondered what his dad would say if he were alive, and what fate awaited him at the new building. Would he die on the job, as his father had?

On August 22, Sinclair arrived at work and went straight up to city editor Brian Cole.

"What's new?" he asked.

"Nothing much," Cole said.

Sinclair smiled and turned to walk away.

"I can't keep it from you," Cole said, grinning.

But Sinclair already knew. Herb Stephen had submitted a letter of resignation to Norrie. The chief would retire in six months.

Your Worship:

On January 30th, 1992 I will complete 36 years of service with the Winnipeg Police Department, and will have served as Chief of Police for almost eight years.

I respectfully wish to advise you that I will retire as Chief of Police and from the Winnipeg Police Department on February 7th.

This five-months notice of my retirement will serve several purposes. This should provide adequate time for the City to seek out and appoint my successor for the position of Chief of Police.

Secondly, it will provide me with an opportunity to review the reports of the Aboriginal Justice Inquiry and the Hughes Inquiry, and perhaps implement some of the recommendations which have not yet been addressed . . .

On the day the story broke, Stephen was holed up in his office at the PSB, refusing comment. Reporters who came hoping to question him were escorted out of the building for what the police termed security reasons. The next day, a CBC reporter who had spoken with Robert Lunney told Gordon Sinclair that a month before he resigned as police commissioner, Lunney had asked the mayor for Stephen's resignation, and some city councillors had also called for Stephen to quit, but Norrie wouldn't go for it. There could be only one reason for Stephen deciding to leave at this point, Sinclair assumed. He'd been told what was in the AJI report.

60

"THE VISIBLE EXPRESSION OF AN ATTITUDE."

The Manitoba Aboriginal Justice Inquiry was released on August 29, 1991, eighty years to the day that Ishi, the last Stone Age Native North American, had been jailed because a sheriff didn't know what else to do with him. Al Hamilton and Murray Sinclair's three years of work had been summarized in two volumes and 1,100 pages. Their overall findings on the state of Aboriginal justice were summed up in two paragraphs on the first page of Volume I.

The justice system has failed Manitoba's Aboriginal people on a massive scale. It has been insensitive and inaccessible, and has arrested and imprisoned Aboriginal people in grossly disproportionate numbers . . . It is not merely that the justice system has failed Aboriginal people; justice also has been denied to them. For more than a century the rights of Aboriginal people have been ignored and eroded. The result of this denial has been injustice of the most profound kind. Poverty and powerlessness have been the Canadian legacy to a people who once governed their own affairs in full self-sufficiency.

The commissioners' key recommendation was a separate justice system for Aboriginal people, one that gave them power over their own police, courts, and parole system.

The second volume of the report included their findings on the shooting of J.J. Harper.

Al Hamilton and Murray Sinclair's conclusions on the Harper case contrasted starkly with Judge John Joseph Enns's report. The commissioners concluded that the inquest had been conducted with a police bias. Where Enns had believed all of the police witnesses and none of the Native witnesses, Hamilton and Sinclair more often found the contrary to be true.

The commissioners blamed Robert Cross for the Native leader's death, and Herb Stephen for the constable's hasty and premature exoneration, which had effectively foreclosed further meaningful investigation.

It was Cross, they said, through his racially motivated, unnecessary approach and illegal grabbing of Harper, "who set in motion the chain of events which resulted in Harper's death."

"Harper did not push Cross down," they wrote, "Cross pulled Harper."

The authors also found that racism had been openly displayed that night, that some police officers at the shooting scene had collaborated to protect Cross. The commissioners said that an "official version" appeared to have been developed to shield him and hence the police department, which those involved saw as one and the same.

As evidence of collaboration they pointed to what happened after Kathryn Hodgins broadcast Melvin Pruden's description: "Cross said that he had been told by Allan that the suspect was wearing a black leather jacket and Hodgins transmitted a description to that effect, but did not refer to the jacket's being leather. Cross said he approached Harper because he was wearing what appeared to be a black leather jacket."

Butch Eakin and his partner Rick Poneira adopted "black leather" in their notes, even though Poneira had radioed that the second suspect he was chasing across the park was wearing a grey jacket.

Clearly they did not obtain that description from the radio transmissions or from their own observations. We believe that the officers inserted the reference to "black leather jacket" in their notes to support Cross' story. That is the only reasonable conclusion to draw.

We accept Allan's evidence that he did not give Cross and Hodgins specific information on Pruden's clothing. This suggests that Cross and Hodgins got a much better look at Allan and Pruden than they acknowledged, and that their radio description was indeed based on their own observations rather than on their questioning of Allan. It also suggests something else: in both their note taking and their testimony at the inquest and at this Inquiry, several officers were less than truthful.

The commissioners couldn't say exactly how the shooting happened, but they suspected that Cross had his gun out when he approached Harper because they had already concluded that at least two other officers – Randy Hampton and Kathryn Hodgins – had theirs out. What they could say with certainty was that Cross had acknowledged having his finger on the trigger and having pulled it.

"We also know that Cross had hold of the revolver during the entire scuffle. It would be reasonable to conclude that if Harper did have any control over the revolver at such a close range he would not have allowed it to be pointed at him, let alone be fired. We conclude that Harper never had any significant degree of control over Cross's revolver." Investigators, they said, hadn't paid sufficient attention to Cross's words about the incident to constables Danny Smyth and Doug Hooper: "He went for my gun, and I shot him."

The commissioners referred to Hodgins again when they said that they believed she had called Allan a "blue-eyed fucking Indian." "We found Hodgins to be forgetful and in some instances clearly wrong in her evidence," the two judges wrote. "Her comment to Allan was racist."

If the commissioners thought they knew who advised Cross to say it was an accident – a point on which they accepted Allan's testimony – they didn't say. But the report went on to heap blame for the shoddy initial stages of the investigation on Duty Inspector Eric Hrycyk and Acting Sergeant Glen Spryszak. Hrycyk, they suggested, acted irresponsibly when he told Herb Stephen that "all officers acted in a professional and competent manner," when he knew Spryszak, for one, hadn't.

As for Spryszak, the commissioners said while he made numerous errors in judgment, some of the fault must lie with others for having placed him in a position of responsibility for which he wasn't properly trained.

The importance of the commissioners' criticism of the inquest was buried in the volume of material that the press had to sort through and report on the next day. But it was nevertheless a stinging indictment. Hamilton and Sinclair said they couldn't understand why Enns had taken such a narrow interpretation of the Fatalities Inquiry Act and limited the cross-examination, although they were careful to point out that Enns had a reputation as an impartial judge.

They weren't as charitable when it came to Bill Morton.

"Crown attorneys are supposed to be fair-minded, even-handed and concerned only to see that justice is done and is seen to be done," the commissioners wrote. Then they added: "Those are admirable thoughts indeed . . . The difficulty is in this case they did not match reality."

The commissioners also said the Crown should have handed the inquest over to independent counsel because it was in a perceived conflict as soon as the city's top Crown attorney, Bruce Miller, agreed with the police that no charges were warranted. They also pointed to Ken Dowson's and Rex Keatinge's involvement with Morton as a conflict of interest.

Considering that Dowson was identified by several police witnesses as the officer in charge of the Harper case, and that he had shot himself on the morning he was supposed to testify, the commissioners said surprisingly little about him. In part, they suggested, this was because the Dowson inquest report had yet to be released, although the AJI had used a private investigator to gather information of its own about "the invisible inspector," as Gordon Sinclair called him. In the columnist's view, the commission didn't do enough analysis of Dowson's role in the creation of the "official version." And they should have subpoenaed Keatinge, who knew as much about the investigation as his dead friend had. Gordon Sinclair thought that Dowson's sacrifice, and the emotional aftermath, had caused the inquiry to back off.

Whatever the case, the commissioners didn't believe Dowson had been responsible for the Harper investigation:

It may well be that Inspector Dowson was nominally in charge of the investigation, but lines of supervision and communication appear to have been so ineffective that no one actually took responsibility for determining all the facts of this case.

"Ultimately, I am the man in charge. The buck stops with me." These are the words of the man who has the final responsibility for the Winnipeg Police Department . . . Despite Chief Stephen's apparent willingness to take ultimate responsibility, he did not appear to exercise any supervision over the investigation. It was the Chief's responsibility to see that an independent investigative approach was taken by his staff. He did not assume the responsibility. He did not even recognize there were serious deficiencies in the way the investigation was conducted. It is he who ultimately must be held accountable for the breakdown in standards and supervision which marked this investigation.

Judges Hamilton and Sinclair also said this of Herb Stephen: "His conduct was just the visible expression of an attitude which was prevalent in his department – an attitude which viewed the public image of the police department and the interest of one of its officers as more important than finding out the truth about the death of a citizen."

In conclusion, the commissioners said: "Society requires capable and professional police forces. We sometimes impose upon them responsibilities that are burdensome and expectations that border on the unrealistic. For those reasons, we must understand and accept that on occasion errors will be made and mistakes will happen. We do not demand perfection from our police force.

"At the same time we are entitled to insist that they perform their obligations and duties in a professional manner . . .

"We have every reason to believe that the vast majority of police officers in the Winnipeg Police Department perform their jobs with a sense of professionalism that would stand up well to any scrutiny and which would do any department proud. The City of Winnipeg has enjoyed a long and proud history insofar as its police department is concerned.

"This incident need not be a permanent blemish upon that history. It can provide important opportunities for the City and the department to begin a new era in which the citizens of the City of Winnipeg will receive policing services from an abler and wiser force."

To that end, the Aboriginal Justice Inquiry made thirty-six recommendations involving the police. Some of the recommendations led to others.

The report called for a special investigations unit to look into police shootings and alleged wrongdoing. The probes into police-related shooting deaths should be conducted as homicide investigations, with audio- or videotaping of police statements taken in such cases.

338 GORDON SINCLAIR JR.

Grade 12 should no longer be a criterion for hiring because of the built-in bias towards Aboriginal people, who don't have the same levels of education. Instead, the police should develop other ways of testing a recruit's ability to do the job. The police should no longer identify suspects by race in their broadcasts, the commissioners said, because it tends to reinforce stereotypes and because Native people share no common look, or way of speaking. Instead, suspects should be described more specifically by their colour.

The report also recommended a recruit-screening process be used in an attempt to weed out "bigots or racists" and an employment equity plan instituted with clear targets and target dates. For population ratio reasons, the commissioners said, the target should be 133 officers.

Herb Stephen was away the day the AJI report was released. Against the advice of his new deputy chief, Joe Gallagher, Stephen had decided to attend a week-long meeting of the Canadian Association of Chiefs of Police in London, Ontario. Three city councillors called for his resignation the day the report was released. There was talk of an investigation into criminal conspiracy, but Acting Chief Laurence Klippenstein told reporters it was too early to say whether the AJI report would result in an investigation of Stephen or another criminal probe of Cross's conduct. (Neither ever happened.) On the next day's front page, under the headline "AJI Damns Native Justice," there was a photograph of Herb Stephen taken at a dinner the night before. He was wearing his black-tie dress uniform. Reporters had left messages in Stephen's hotel room. He didn't return them.

It was early evening when Sinclair drove up to the Harper's house on Elgin Avenue. He knocked on the back door, and Lois Harper appeared behind the screen door.

"I don't really want to say anything," she said.

But she stepped out and sat down on the back step and Sinclair asked her the obvious questions.

"How do you feel?"

"Lonely," she said.

He asked about the Aboriginal Justice Inquiry's report.

"It's good they've confirmed everything we've always said."

Lois had read parts of the report at the Island Lake Tribal Council, where she was now working. But she had purposely left it there. "I don't want my kids reading it."

She said her eldest, Vince, now sixteen, wanted to read it. He was starting to understand what it was all about. "He's been having a few problems with racism. I don't like to talk about it."

But she did. She talked about the time Vince went downtown to buy a pair of Reeboks and just missed his bus in front of the St. Regis Hotel. He'd begun running with the shoes, and as he passed two men in business suits he heard one of them say, "Oh, it looks like somebody stole something."

Lois and Sinclair sat on the back step for nearly an hour until Vince opened the back door. He was wearing a ball cap and a Coke T-shirt, and Sinclair could hardly believe what he was seeing.

"You look just like your dad," he said.

Vince just smiled shyly, and walked away.

Sinclair looked at Lois. "You fear for your children, don't you?"

Lois Harper nodded her bowed head and wiped away a tear.

Less than a month after the AJI released its report, something startling happened that lent credence to what Murray Sinclair had said years earlier: that police go after Natives because they're easy targets. The latest example was the police handling of a double murder that dated back to the same summer weekend that Cross was caught next door with his pants down. An eighty-six-year-old woman, Kiyo Shimizu, and her fifty-nine-year-old daughter, Chieko, had been repeatedly knifed during a break-in at their downtown home. Both later died of their wounds. Police, answering a 911 call from one of the victims, had found a twelve-year-old boy inside when they arrived. The boy was Native. In November 1989, the boy, now thirteen, had become the youngest person ever convicted of murder in Manitoba. But six months later, the

Manitoba Court of Appeal unanimously overturned the conviction, saying the facts supported what the boy had initially told police: that his accomplice in the break-in had actually murdered the women.

Less than six months later, police arrested another Native suspect in that case, Bryan Tait, who was twenty. He was a victim of foetal alcohol syndrome, which had left him mentally handicapped since birth. At first Tait had denied any involvement, but when the police told him someone had fingered him, Tait broke down weeping and confessed. The police had provided him with details of the murder when they told him what his accuser had said. But any details they left out – such as how the youths had broken into the house – Tait got wrong. He was charged anyway. Then in late September 1991, after spending eleven months in jail awaiting trail, Bryan Tait was freed. His lawyer had discovered an alibi that was literally iron-bar clad. Tait had been in jail at the time of the murders.

In anticipation of the AJI report's release, the police had already started to make many of the recommended policy changes. But the Manitoba government's general reaction to the findings was not unlike Sheriff Webber's exactly eighty years earlier upon finding the half-naked, starving Ishi. They studied it with curiosity for years, and then put it away because they didn't know what else to do with it.

$$\overline{61}$$

"IF I WAS TOLD, I CAN'T REMEMBER."

Just after noon on Labour Day, nearly two years after Dowson shot himself, Sinclair drove over to the home of his widow. Jill Dowson had given an interview to the *Winnipeg Sun* a few days earlier, so he decided he wouldn't be intruding. But he didn't know who would be home or what to expect. "Keep the damn media away," Dowson had instructed Rex Keatinge in the suicide note.

"You're the last person I want to see," Jill Dowson said when Sinclair introduced himself. But she opened the door, and invited Sinclair into her living room, where they talked for five hours. She talked about her family, how she'd met Ken, their twenty years together, and Ken and Nancy's hard childhood as the kids of alcoholics.

Eventually, Sinclair asked Jill about the night Harper died. She said the phone had rung in the middle of the night, the way it often did. Ken answered it and Jill held her breath wondering what terrible thing had happened in the city.

"I have to go," he said. "Somebody's down."

"Is it a cop?"

"No."

"Oh, shit," Jill said.

It took him about ten minutes to get ready. "And then he was gone."

Jill confirmed that her husband oversaw the investigation, but she said he didn't go to the shooting scene until the following morning.

About a week before he died she talked to him about the Harper case.

"I said, 'Do you blame yourself because you didn't go to the scene? You weren't a street cop.' And he just hung his head. He had no answer."

Martin Pollock had long suspected that Dowson might be the phantom officer, the "old man cop" Allan said he overheard tell Cross to say the shooting was an accident. Sinclair was suspicious, too. At the inquiry Herb Stephen first said Dowson had been at the scene that morning, then the chief said he'd been wrong about that.

But Sinclair decided Dowson wasn't the cop Allan heard. For one thing, Dowson would not have been in uniform, which the kid recalled the cop was wearing. Also, he would have been called out about the same time as Harry Williams, who testified he arrived at the PSB simultaneously with Dowson at 5 a.m.

Now, at the Dowson house, Sinclair listened to Jill talk about the last line of the letter left for Rex Keatinge: "Don't forget to print the gun."

"The gun was being mishandled," Jill said, "and he knew it was being mishandled."

Then she said something her husband had suggested in his note, but the AJI had never determined. "He made the decision not to have it printed."

Jill said Ken had taken a course on fingerprinting and knew how rare it was to get a fingerprint off a revolver. "So he knew there was no point. And he proved it with his own suicide."

Sinclair asked Jill about her outburst at the wake when she saw Faye Stephen come in. Jill avoided the question. Whatever anger she might have had back then towards the chief was gone now. She had told the *Sun* that she blamed both the AJI and the department for her husband's death. The AJI because of what it put cops through, and the department because it didn't allow Dowson to admit he had problems.

"Don't blame Herb Stephen," she told the *Sun*. "Don't hang him out to dry. He's a good man."

In his long note to Keatinge, Dowson said that those who knew him would understand why he had killed himself, but it was evident that Jill still hadn't come to terms with the why of it. "Was there something so awful?" she asked. "What was he afraid of?

"I just think it's very sad Ken never knew how many people really loved him. It was so evident the day of the funeral. I just couldn't believe it myself."

Just then a teenage boy walked into the living room. Fifteen-year-old Mark Dowson was tall, thin, and blond, the way his dad had been when he was a kid. He had his dad's face, too.

"You look like your dad," Sinclair said, the way he'd said it to J.J. Harper's oldest boy. Mark didn't say anything either. He just flashed a big smile.

While he was talking with Jill, Sinclair brought up the existence of Eunice. Jill knew about her, but Rex Keatinge had told her she was just a friend of Ken's.

Sinclair didn't know this when he mentioned Eunice's claim of a more intimate relationship with Jill's husband. The shock of finding out her husband had been seeing another woman sent Jill into a fit that teetered between rage and tears. She didn't want that made public. Sinclair told her Don Gillmor had talked to Eunice, too, and he was writing a second article for *Saturday Night*. Jill was in tears.

By the time Sinclair left, Jill had calmed down and seemed to be all right. But she wasn't.

The next day, Eunice called Sinclair. "You don't know how mad the department is," she said. Rex Keatinge had been talking to her. Eunice was not supposed to have told Sinclair about her relationship with Dowson. Jill had phoned Keatinge after the interview, and he'd stayed with her till two in the morning. "If they would just admit the guy had problems prior to the AJI. It wasn't totally Harper," Eunice said.

Sinclair thought that had been the point of the inquest, to show that Dowson was having problems handling the stress on the job. But the problems Eunice was referring to were related to alcohol and his marriage. Maybe if the city knew the rest of Dowson's story, Eunice said, they would view what he did differently. "Maybe they wouldn't blame the Native community and the AJI for Dowson's death."

Then Eunice turned bitter. "What are they worried about protecting? His image? It's all over the goddamn basement."

Three days later, on the same day Sinclair's column on Jill Dowson appeared, a colleague told the columnist that Mayor Norrie had refused to comment on the AJI report; he hadn't read it, he was too busy painting his cottage. Right away Sinclair started a column suggesting the attitudes of the mayor and the police chief were representative of the city's when city editor Brian Cole walked over and looked at what Sinclair was writing.

"I hope you've got another column," he said, and went on to deliver the message that Sinclair could not write about the AJI anymore.

"Why not?" Sinclair asked.

"If I was told," Cole said, "I can't remember."

That same day, September 5, a city hall committee met to consider the Aboriginal Justice Inquiry's recommendations affecting the city. Police Commissioner Loren Reynolds had already reviewed them, and the day before the meeting he had sent Herb Stephen a letter commending the chief for already anticipating and instituting twenty-two of the thirty-six recommendations.

A week later the CBC "I Team" broke a story alleging that officers on the force were involved in a break-and-enter ring. The allegations were made by Martin Shaver, a petty hood who claimed the police had paid him to recruit rounders off the street to commit burglaries. The police officers would then lie in wait to nab the culprits in the act, taking credit for the busts while letting Shaver escape. The CBC had been tipped to the story by a lawyer who had been contacted by Shaver. The lawyer's name was Harvey Pollock. The same day the CBC ran the Shaver story, Ted Hughes delivered his report to Attorney General Jim McCrae.

—
62

"A SACRIFICE I AM WILLING TO MAKE."

The Hughes report was released on September 18, 1991, Yom Kippur, the Jewish day of atonement. Gordon Sinclair drove to the Legislative Building to get his copy, then settled into a chair in the basement cafeteria and began to flip through the 105 pages.

The police probe of Pollock smacked of payback, Hughes wrote. While Pollock was wrong to have touched the woman, it did not constitute sexual assault, and Crown attorney Matthew Britton was right to stay the charges.

Hughes admonished the police for the "indecent haste" with which they arrested Pollock. He called the police policy on sexual assault arrests "inflexible" and "probably unlawful." Referring to Ron

Kushneryk's tipping Bruce Owen on the arrest, he said: "There is evidence that the attitude displayed, if not the act, was embraced by his immediate superiors . . . I conclude that Kushneryk's action was consistent with the prevailing attitude of his immediate supervisors. Therefore I do not view it as an isolated act." Hughes also criticized the city administration for backing Herb Stephen when he said the transfers of Toyne, Bell, and Dawson weren't related to the Pollock investigation.

He exonerated the Crown, finding the police paranoia about Stu Whitley to be just that. "The allegations with respect to the lack of integrity and absence of trustworthiness made about the Assistant Deputy Attorney General, Criminal Justice, S.J. Whitley, QC, were unfair, unjust and totally without any merit whatsoever."

But the full force of the Hughes report landed on Stephen's chin. Hughes called his leadership "woefully inadequate." As for Pollock's contention that what motivated the police treatment of him was payback for being the Harper family's lawyer, Hughes wrote: "There is no doubt in my mind that Pollock was not liked by these members of the Crime Division. I am equally convinced that this animosity substantially accounts for the special treatment of this complaint, the premature arrest, uncritical investigation, manipulated Crown opinion and emotional, sometimes irrational, commitment to the prosecution.

"While I stop short of finding an overt conspiracy, the influence of payback was at work in a far from subtle fashion and must be condemned."

Sinclair noted that Hughes found no fault with Hodgins's conduct.

He had almost finished reading, when he looked up and saw *Free Press* legislative reporter Don Campbell walking towards him.

"The chief is gone," Campbell said.

Sinclair knew he didn't mean on a trip.

Campbell had seen a press release from Justice Minister Jim McCrae: "As a result of the findings, Stephen has advised the city of Winnipeg that his retirement will be effective immediately . . . Public confidence in the Winnipeg Police Department will only be restored," said McCrae, "if the Winnipeg Police is able to recruit a progressive, decisive and fair-minded leader. I urge Mayor Norrie to expedite the nationwide search for a new chief."

Later the same day, a copy of a letter written by Herb Stephen to Mayor Bill Norrie arrived at the *Free Press*. It was dated twenty-four hours earlier. After saying he was "disappointed and dismayed" that others weren't given the opportunity to participate in the review of the AJI report, Stephen concluded: "If my immediate departure will assist in restoring the credibility of the Winnipeg Police Department then this is a sacrifice I am willing to make for the citizens of Winnipeg and the Department . . ."

Stephen was commencing "pre-retirement leave" immediately, two years less two days from the second anniversary of Ken Dowson's "sacrifice" for the department.

Later it was reported Jim McCrae had told Bill Norrie that the chief had to go and that Stephen, on his way out the door, received a golden handshake from the city.

The story appeared on the *Free Press* front page the next day, beside a photo of his deputies Gallagher and Klippenstein sitting at a table, wearing their funeral faces.

"Today," said McCrae, "we begin the rebuilding of a service vital to the safety of all residents of Winnipeg." Gordon Sinclair considered what had just happened. An Aboriginal man had been shot dead, but it took the arrest of an establishment lawyer to bring down the chief of police. In the end, though, Herbert Bishop Stephen had received a form of Aboriginal justice, banishment – from the police department.

Four months later, at a downtown hotel, Stephen stood in a reception line for more than an hour and a half and greeted the 500 people who turned out for his retirement dinner. Among the well-wishers were high-ranking representatives from the Montreal, Toronto, and Vancouver police departments, and even the FBI.

Bill Norrie was also there, still playing the nice guy and loyal friend. "I guess he took retirement a little earlier than he intended," the mayor told a reporter, "but he retired with honour. You can see that by the turnout."

Stephen and his family were piped into the room, and serenaded through the pork tenderloin dinner by the Winnipeg police band. The icing on the Black Forest cake served as dessert featured the City of Winnipeg crest.

"It's been a difficult three or four years," Stephen said, "not just for me, but for the entire force.

"It was a good job," he added. "If I had to do it over again, I would."

PART VI

THE SENTENCE

Injustice is relatively easy to bear. What stings is justice.

– H.L. Mencken

63

"How can one man ruin so many lives?"

On March 10, 1992, exactly four years after Herb Stephen absolved Robert Cross of any negligence in the shooting of J.J. Harper, the Law Enforcement Review Agency's hearing into the incident finally convened. But Cross wouldn't be appearing. He had taken his youngest son, Stephen, and gone to Denver to visit his sister, Judy. Two months earlier, Dr. Marilyn McKay, Cross's new psychiatrist, wrote a letter to his family physician outlining Cross's psychiatric problems: the "post-traumatic stress disorder" and "episodes of clinical depression requiring antidepressants." The letter was also a window on what Cross had been doing at the Winnipeg Police Department since the Harper shooting.

In the days, weeks and early months after the shooting, it was anticipated this incident would be resolved in the usual fashion for such incidents. However, as the incident became embroiled in controversy and unprecedented complications, the stress took its toll. He became progressively unable to function . . . By October of 1988 he was unable to work.

In March of 1989, in an attempt at rehabilitation, he returned to a special work-placement with the Winnipeg Police Force. He was to work as a "community-based policeman responding to no calls, but driving around the district identifying himself as a policeman to citizens and businesses." He was not able to function in this limited protected role and this approach was abandoned in July of '89. From July of 1989 to March of 1990, he did not work.

In March of 1990, a second attempt was made to have him return to a sheltered position within the Winnipeg Police Force. It was agreed that he would work four hours a day. . . . He was assigned to work on the various tasks relating to the ongoing investigation and litigation arising out of the shooting. Because of significant cognitive difficulty, he had to leave this program in April of 1991. From April 1991 to the present he has not worked in any capacity.

Dr. McKay also wrote this analysis of Cross's situation: "He has become the scapegoat of long-standing Canadian problems, current crisis, provincial and city turmoil, televised enquiries, endless litigation, threat of loss of employment, possible imprisonment and threats of injury from community vigilante groups ..."

McKay's report made no mention of what was happening in Cross's private life, including an incident earlier that month at The Forks. Diane and Bob had gone out for dinner with his parents and his sister Judy, who was visiting from Denver. In the midst of the table chatter, Diane said, Bob began boasting about how much weight he could bench press. Diane said she mocked him, suggesting the amount kept getting heavier and heavier. In a sworn affidavit that alluded to the incident, Cross accused his wife of "calling me vulgar names and trying to goad me into a fight." But they both agreed on what happened next.

He struck her across the head. "Cuffed" was the word he used. "Slapped," Diane said.

The LERA panel was made up of four lawyers and a Brandon police officer, all white. The lone woman, chairperson Martha Chuchman, sat between the four men, in the middle of the folding tables that had been set up for the hearing on the eighth floor of the Woodsworth Building.

Martin Pollock's first witness was Mike Elliot, Cross's neighbour, the guy Cross swore under oath he didn't know.

Martin wanted to establish that Cross and Elliot had been not only next-door neighbours for four years, but were also close friends. He established that Elliot and Cross became friends while landscaping the backyards of their adjacent new homes.

PART VI: THE SENTENCE   353

"We both liked to drink," Elliot said. "He just seemed to absorb more alcohol than me."

"So if you had one beer," Martin said, "how many would he have, for example?"

"He could drink three to my one."

"And what did he like to drink, do you recall?"

"My liquor."

The gallery reacted like a studio laugh track, but Elliot kept a straight face.

Eventually Martin manoeuvred his way to an area he wanted to exploit: Cross's sense of humour. And Elliot related several racist jokes that he'd heard from Cross.

Martin looked down at his notes. "Did he mention anything about Indians on the lake when you were on the fishing trip? What they were doing in the lake?"

"They're ruining the lake."

"Tell us the words that he used."

"Oh, piss in the lake. We get our water supply from there and they're pissing in the lake and shitting in the lake."

"Okay. I understand that Cross's wife had a dog. Do you know the dog's name?"

"Tanner."

"What kind of dog was Tanner?"

"A golden lab. Something like Yeller. A nice dog."

"Did he say anything about Tanner?"

"The dog didn't like Indians that were drunk. His wife worked at the Minaki hospital, or something like that, and [there were] a lot of drunks out there and the dog was very protective of Diane."

Martin asked about another dog, a neighbour's dog at the lake, which Cross claimed to have tied up and shot because a year earlier it had attacked and killed his Cairn terrier.

"He told me that several times," Elliot said.

That gave Martin his segue. From Cross shooting a dog, he asked about Cross shooting Harper.

"What did he say to you?"

"He said, 'I shot the wrong Indian.'"

Cross had told him this a few months after the shooting while they were sitting on his backyard deck.

"Now, about the evening of the shooting. Did he mention anything to you about police officers and their guns?"

"Yes."

"What did he say to you?"

"'Of course we had our guns out.' Not referring that he had his out, but 'we.'"

Had Cross explained why the guns were out?

"Well, yes, the situation they were under. Not knowing the situation they were under. They were in pursuit of somebody."

Martin had got as much as he was going to get from Mike Elliot. It was McGregor's turn. He focussed on the breakdown of the friendship between Elliot and Cross. McGregor wanted Mike to admit he'd once threatened Cross, but all Mike would say was "I was disappointed in him." McGregor was straying into a dangerous area. He stopped there.

Sinclair followed Elliot as he hurried out of the room. He was trying to put his trench coat on and get on the elevator at the same time.

"I'd like to talk to you sometime," Sinclair said.

Five months later, in late August, Sinclair drove across town to the suburb of Island Lakes. It was dark by the time he reached Cross's former house on the bend of a street without curbs or sidewalks.

Mike was surprised to see Sinclair, but he was friendly. Sinclair explained why he had dropped by and suggested they go out somewhere for coffee. Mike agreed. But first he wanted to show him the backyard, particularly the deck where he and Bob had sat drinking so often, before the high, wooden fence went up between the families. Sinclair climbed on a wobbly picnic table to see over the fence to the deck Cross built. After so many years of conjuring up the scene, of hearing about all the personal sadness, paranoia, and pain acted out on those wooden planks, the deck seemed small and empty, like a deserted stage. He could imagine what it had been like four years earlier when Don Gillmor sat in the backyard with Cross, listening sympathetically to his boyhood pal's story, while the twins romped around. He thought about how this typical suburban neighbourhood closeness, this working-bee togetherness and sharing beers afterward, had ended so unhappily.

Sinclair drove Mike to Bellamy's restaurant, across from the St. Vital Shopping Centre. It was close to Clancy's, where Cross and Mike used to hide out at happy hour. Over coffee Mike began to remember that Friday July long weekend. The night when he lost his wife and his friend.

It was July 1, 1989, Canada Day. Diane had left for the lake, so Cross was home alone. Mike was hung over from the night before, so Sheila and Cross had been drinking together, but later that night, as it got darker, Mike had wanted to watch the holiday fireworks with his son, which they could see from their upstairs bedroom. It was late by the time they were over. Time for bed. Mike sent his son downstairs to get his mom, then went around the house shutting off lights. A few minutes later the boy returned.

"Where's mom?" Mike demanded.

"I don't know," the boy said.

Mike asked again. This time the boy said his mom was with Mr. Cross.

"He's hurting her," he said.

Mike went looking. Checking the deck first. Calling Sheila's name, then storming next door. Through a torn curtain Mike could see what his little boy had seen. Cross was on top of Sheila. Straddling her chest. His shorts were down, and he was pumping. Pushing her breasts together with his hands, and pumping between them.

Mike burst through the front door.

"What the hell's going on?" he roared.

Sheila scrambled to her feet. Mike went after her first. It wasn't the first time she had cheated on him. And it wasn't the first time he had hit her. Just as Mike connected he heard Cross gasp, "Oh, my God."

"He knew he was next," Mike said, his eyes clear, his voice firm again. "And he was."

Then Mike was out the door. He wanted out of there. Cross followed him outside, trying to explain. Mike wasn't interested. What he had seen was self-explanatory. All he wanted to do was hit him again.

"But it was the strangest thing," Mike said. "I've been in a lot of fights, but I couldn't get near him."

On the way back to his house, Mike kept talking about Bob and Sheila. It was obvious he missed them both. In spite of everything they'd been through, Mike still loved Sheila. They were almost at the Island Lakes turn-off when Mike asked Sinclair a question: "How could one man ruin so many lives?"

The next witness, a man with thinning light brown hair, had a presence that seemed to command the LERA panel's attention and respect. But then Deputy Chief Joe Gallagher was not only a senior police officer like one of them, he was a lawyer like the rest. After a series of questions about Gallagher's background, Martin Pollock focussed on an area of Cross's training that he wanted the panel to hear about: the use of force.

"If an officer does not have reasonable and probable grounds to believe that somebody is a suspect, what are they taught . . . in terms of detaining people? Are you allowed to detain somebody in that particular situation?"

"No. Unless you have the right to detain that person, to hold him against his will, to arrest him, then you must allow him to proceed."

Gallagher didn't tell the board what Herb Stephen had told the AJI – that Cross grabbed Harper when he wasn't under arrest. But then he wasn't asked. Martin turned to Gallagher's testimony at the examination for discovery in December 1991.

"Do you recall using the term 'cowboy'?"

"Yes, I do, sir."

"What do you mean by the term 'cowboy'?"

"Someone who is prone to drawing his revolver when there doesn't appear to be any basis for doing that," Gallagher said.

Martin referred Gallagher to the incident in September 1988, on the day Diane came home from the hospital, when Cross had chased a speeding car and had put a gun to the head of one of the passengers. Afterwards, Cross had boasted to Sheila Elliot, "I almost shot another one."

Gallagher replied, "I don't think in that situation – as you describe it – I don't think he was acting professionally. I think he was acting in a grossly. . . ."

Martin cut in. "Like a cowboy?"

". . . negligent manner," Gallagher said, finishing his thought. Then he caught what Martin had said.

"Yes," the deputy chief conceded, "I would say it definitely would fall within the definition of 'cowboy.' "

While the LERA hearings were going on in March 1992, two more city cops were in trouble, but the case never reached LERA or even the newspapers. Two Native women claimed to have been beaten up when the patrol partners answered a noise complaint. A neighbour testified she saw one of the officers assaulting them. At the trial, the charges against the women of obstructing a police officer were stayed and when they filed a civil suit, the city settled out of court. There was one condition, though. The women were not to disclose the settlement. The cops were Butch Eakin and Rick Poneira.

By the end of March, the Los Angeles trial of four white police officers charged in the beating of Rodney King was under way in front of a jury with no black members. There was a clip of officer Lawrence Powell's testimony on CNN.

"I was completely in fear of my life," Powell said. "If this guy got back up, he was going to take my gun away from me."

$$\overline{64}$$

"Are you all right, Gordy?"

Less than a week after Mike testified at LERA, Diane walked up the path of cracked concrete blocks and opened her front door. Cross was standing in the living room.

"Are you thinking of leaving me?" he asked.

Oh God, Diane thought. She had been having violent visions of his flipping out when he found out. Now he was confronting her before she had even found a way to tell him she was leaving.

"Why?" she asked, nervously.

"Because I found this."

Cross was holding forms that Diane's lawyer had given her to fill out about the family's monthly expenses. She had buried them at the bottom of a tea wagon, but Bob had found them. That much of the cop within Cross was still there.

Finally, Diane answered. Yes, she was leaving him.

Then, to her surprise, he just sat down on the sofa. There was no scene. Little dialogue. There wasn't much else to say.

"I have to pack a few things," he said.

Bob got up and walked towards the hall that led to their bedroom. But as he passed the kids' bedroom, Stephen wandered out. The dark-haired tyke who had been born less than a month after Harper was shot looked up at his father.

"I love you, daddy."

Cross's dark eyes squinted ever so slightly, as if a shaft of light had flashed in front of them. He bent down and hugged his little boy. Diane could see Bob was trying not to cry, trying to hold himself together. So was she. For an instant, as they were pulling apart, they had been pulled together.

"Oh God," Diane thought, "What am I doing?"

And then he was gone.

He drove across town, past the police station he had left from that night, past the park where Owen and Kushneryk had secretly met, to the Courts of St. James, where his parents lived. He had nowhere else to go. The next day, Cross returned to pick up a few things he had forgotten. Diane's father was there changing the locks.

A month later, on April 24, just as LERA was reconvening to finish its sittings, Diane filed for a divorce. The four years and seven months of their marriage she summed up in an affidavit that read like an indictment.

> During the course of our relationship I found the respondent to be drinking quite heavily. His drinking increased with the recent difficulties he has experienced around the Harper inquiry. Our relationship deteriorated over the years and included incidents of infidelity on his part culminating with an incident with our neighbour in July of 1989. The next day after our neighbour caught the respondent with his wife the respondent went into the hospital suffering from nervous stress. There were numerous incidents of infidelity on the respondent's part over the course of our marriage. On two occasions I contracted pubic pediculosis. Those times being in April of 1986 and July of 1986.

Diane also mentioned the night he'd hit her at The Forks. In his affidavit of response, Cross didn't deny the adultery or giving her pubic lice, including once while she was pregnant. But he did offer an excuse for hitting her: "On one occasion I cuffed the petitioner on the head . . . We were having dinner with my parents and the petitioner was calling me vulgar names and trying to goad me into a fight."

About a week before Diane filed her affidavit, Dr. Marilyn McKay wrote to Al McGregor, updating Cross's emotional state. He was now taking antidepressants, she reported.

> In recent weeks he has been further traumatized by the unilateral decision of his wife to terminate the marriage. During the time I have

known Mr. Cross, the degree of his symptomatology has fluctuated from time to time, but through this time he has remained unable to work. As a result of the anxiety and depression Mr. Cross suffers from disabling cognitive deficits. At times it becomes a struggle just to maintain his self care and carry out small routine activities of daily living. During these periods of time, during an interview, his attention, concentration, memory are markedly impaired. He reports serious cognitive errors in even the routine activities of daily living and has long periods of severe levels of dysfunction . . .

The shooting of J.J. Harper, and the name Robert Cross, have achieved a very high level of public awareness in the city. Consequently, Mr. Cross has a name which is recognized everywhere on a day-to-day basis as he moves about his life in Winnipeg. . . . Mr. Cross is psychologically ill-equipped to deal with this level of recognition and adverse attention.

She concluded with the observation that Cross should leave Winnipeg.

A month later, Robert Cross filed his affidavit, asking for access to the children.

I am prepared to take the children on a regular basis, every Sunday from 11 a.m. until 5 p.m. At the present time, I can not undertake to take the children any more often. I am currently residing with my retired parents. I am sleeping on a couch in their living room. I do not have any overnight accommodation for the children.

In Los Angeles at about the same time the LERA hearing was ending, the verdict was returned on the police officers charged in the beating of Rodney King. Not guilty. By early afternoon L.A. time, the rioting had started. The next day Gordon Sinclair wrote a column referring to the riots and the fact that there was a similarity between the jury that cleared the L.A. cops and the LERA panel that was deciding whether Robert Cross used excessive force. There were no blacks on the L.A. jury and there were no Natives on the LERA panel. But the next morning, when Sinclair picked up the paper, the column wasn't there.

Dave Lee called Sinclair into his office. The philosophy of the paper had changed, Lee told Sinclair, and the column had to change, too. It had to freshen up. Lee didn't elaborate, but Sinclair knew what he meant about the paper changing.

In March, a new publisher had arrived. Maurice Switzer had been publisher of the comparatively tiny *Sudbury Star*, another Thomson newspaper. Switzer was in his late forties, short, dark-haired, seemingly affable on the surface, but volcanic underneath and a man who courted the establishment, joining the board of the Winnipeg Symphony Orchestra and the like. Sinclair learned that Switzer's father was Jewish and his mother Aboriginal. He had a treaty card. This should have given the columnist some comfort, but it didn't. Switzer wanted more soft stories, more advertiser-friendly "good news" in the paper.

Sinclair was more vulnerable than ever. But he wasn't alone. On the same day that Sinclair was warned by Lee, Barry Mullin, the paper's Ombudsman and former city editor, stepped in a bear trap. Mullin had criticized the paper's new direction in a column where he pointed out that the *Free Press* had buried the L.A. riots on a back page in its first 30,000 papers. When he read it after the paper came out, Switzer immediately summoned Mullin and read his own riot act. Henceforth his column of comment on readers' concerns about the paper would be submitted forty-eight hours in advance to Dave Lee. And Mullin would have to apologize for the L.A. riot column. Mullin refused and submitted his resignation.

The story of what amounted to Mullin's forced dismissal made papers all over North America, including the *Chicago Tribune*. Mullin wasn't replaced. At least not by an Ombudsman. Instead, Maurice Switzer began writing a weekly column in the space formerly occupied by Mullin. It was obvious that there was only one opinion that counted in the paper now. The publisher's.

Later that week Gordon Sinclair went to see his childhood friend Susan Thompson at her cowboy store on Main Street. Bill Norrie had decided not to run for mayor again, and Susie Thompson had decided to go after the mayor's chair. She had the backing of a lot of establishment people, but that was okay with Sinclair, who thought Susie would be good for the city. Since they had grown up together and she wasn't well known, he decided to write a background column on her. But after he interviewed her, Sinclair had second thoughts. He didn't know what he could or couldn't write. He decided to postpone the If-You-Knew-Susie-Like-I-Know-Susie column. A week later Susan Thompson phoned Sinclair at the *Free Press*.

"Are you all right, Gordy?" she asked in a concerned voice. It sounded as if Thompson had heard something about Sinclair's precarious position at the paper. In fact, as she would tell him when it was over, some people in powerful political positions were putting pressure on the paper to get rid of him.

By summer Gordon Sinclair was smiling again. He had found a story on the news wire, dated July 29, 1991.

Winnipeg (CP) A retired RCMP officer who is considered sympathetic towards Native concerns has been recommended as the new chief of Winnipeg's police force. Dale Henry, a former assistant commissioner with the RCMP in Winnipeg, was the unanimous choice of city council's executive policy committee today.

"We wanted someone who would be an agent of good change within the department," Mayor Bill Norrie said. "We wanted someone who would restore the morale of the department and the public confidence in the department."

The committee also felt Henry was sympathetic towards Native concerns and was knowledgeable about their situation, Norrie said.

Henry had been living in retirement in Kelowna, B.C., and had been hounded by a head-hunter for five months about assuming the chief's position. But it was a call from Norrie that convinced him to take the job. Norrie sounded desperate.

Sinclair's man was going to be the new chief.

In early fall there was more good news. LERA had come out with its decision. Cross had been found guilty of using excessive force and of abusing his authority. The LERA panel would hear arguments on sentencing later. Sinclair's choice for chief was taking over the police department and his childhood friend, Susan Thompson, was favoured to be the new mayor. Maybe, he thought, this is going to have a happy ending after all.

$$\overline{65}$$

"Don't let the bastards grind you down."

Dale Henry took over as chief in September 1991. A message from the troops was waiting for him that first day. It was on the *Free Press* front page under the Quote of the Day: "A gun will be waiting for him at the range and he'll have to qualify with it."

The speaker was Eric Hrycyk, the inspector who went to the Harper shooting scene nearly five years before. Henry was not amused.

A week later Sinclair was out having dinner with his wife and her family when Henry and a bunch of friends arrived. He told Sinclair he had given his first speech to the graduation class on September 23 and no one had covered it. Sinclair asked him to fax it to him and he'd get it in the paper. Henry also mentioned he took his service revolver to the range. And he shot a perfect score. Sinclair told him he'd take care of that, too.

At 2:18 p.m. on September 28 the speech was transmitted. Two hours later Sinclair was writing the column about Henry's answer to Hrycyk – about what a straight shooter Henry was – and about his vision of the Winnipeg police, when the phone rang.

"Are you taping this?" a male voice asked.

The man on the other end of the line told Sinclair that a group of cops had beaten up a Native man down by Alexander Docks. The cops had been partying after shift. He said a cop friend was bragging about it. Sinclair phoned Henry and asked if he was aware of the incident. The new chief said he wasn't. An hour later he called back to confirm that the story was basically true, that his deputies knew about it, and that their not briefing him had been an oversight. The next day in his column Sinclair wondered how Henry's deputies could have neglected to inform him when he had been brought in specifically to address the department's image and dealings with minorities. Sinclair's column had somehow gone to press without management noticing it. The following morning, city editor Brian Cole told Sinclair that the story should have been on the front page. Encouraged, Sinclair wrote another column quoting Henry's inaugural speech to the department, but the column never ran. Dave Lee killed it.

Early in October, Amnesty International marked the 500th anniversary of Columbus's arrival in the New World with a report on human rights violations throughout the Americas. Under "Canada" the shooting of J.J. Harper was singled out for special attention.

Then, on the morning of Tuesday, October 20, 1992, Gordon Sinclair received a phone call at home. It was the office. "Are you coming in this morning?" Brian Cole asked. "Dave wants to see you."

Cole didn't say what Dave Lee wanted to see him about. He didn't have to. Given the persistent harassment, the sporadic killing of columns, Mullin's forced resignation, and the publisher's ties to the city's establishment, Sinclair knew it was just a matter of time. And this was the time.

Sinclair reached the office shortly after noon and talked for a minute with Lee before Brian Cole joined them.

"Gord says he's expecting bad news," Lee said.

"Well," Sinclair said, "why else would Dave want to see me?"

Lee was smiling, but he wasn't looking Sinclair in the eyes.

"Okay, I think it's time to, ah, there's no question, re-evaluate the column. You know, you've been writing it for a long time. Eleven or twelve years. I know you're not going to agree with me."

"Go ahead," Sinclair said meekly. "No, I'm listening." Sinclair felt beaten already. He was starting to think that they were right. Maybe he had been writing the column too long.

Lee cleared his throat, then referred to the number of columns that had "had to be pulled" in recent weeks.

Then he got to the next reason.

"And, ah, sadly, whether you believe it or not . . . I don't think you have the readership that you once had. And I know that isn't an easy thing for the ego to take."

Lee shuffled some papers on his desk. "Um, I feel fairly strongly about this and, ah, you're going to, I know what you're going to, you're going to try and say there's always been a motive, an agenda. There isn't, believe me. It's pure and simple –" Lee paused. "What are you smiling about?" Lee asked Sinclair. "It's that simple. You don't believe me, do you? Uh?"

Sinclair wasn't going to start accusing Lee of anything at that point. Especially not when he felt he was being baited. Lee seemed to want to get it on the record that Sinclair had been warned repeatedly about his work.

It was Sinclair's turn to bait Lee.

"What happened again and again?"

"Types of columns."

"Like what? What types of columns?"

"You get into areas –"

"Like what?"

"– you were told not to."

"What was I told not to go into?"

"Not to write about letters. Not to – then you ran, what was it? – Dale Henry's inaugural address. Something or other . . ."

They argued for several more minutes. Then Sinclair said: "You're telling me I'm going to lose the column."

"I'm killing the column," Lee said, "Yeah."

Sinclair wanted to know what his options were, but he said he needed to get a drink of water first.

"I'll be right back," he said.

He didn't need a drink of water to think about what he was going to do. He just needed to rewind the tape in the recorder he had slid into his jacket pocket before he went into Lee's office. Like Harvey Pollock when he was arrested, Sinclair had a feeling he would be needing some back-up one day.

That night Sinclair sat his children down on the living room couch and told them what had happened. Erin had just turned fifteen, Ian was twelve. Months of harassment were over. "They," whoever "they" were, had got their dad.

The kids were confused and angry. So was his wife, Athina. Later, when they were alone, she directed the anger at her husband. "What were you going to do?" she asked rhetorically, "write columns for another twenty years and die in the newsroom the way your father did?"

Later Justine Spiller, a friend of Athina's, phoned Lee to protest the cancellation of Sinclair's column. In defence, Lee read a letter from someone who blamed Gordon Sinclair for Ken Dowson's death. Paul Johnston phoned Sinclair after he heard what had happened and sent him a trophy engraved with the Latin words he had lived by while with the civic bureaucracy. "It means, 'Don't let the bastards grind you down,'" Paul Johnston said.

Sinclair took heart from Johnston's kind gesture. He told his lawyer to file a grievance through the newsroom union. He wanted his column back.

66

"It's all on a road map."

On the night before Susan Thompson was sworn in as mayor, and Bill Clinton won the U.S. presidential election, winter lowered a shroud over Winnipeg while the city slept. The fresh snow made the streets more slippery than the night Harper was shot, making Gordon Sinclair late in getting to Robert Cross's penalty hearing. Cross wasn't there though. He'd taken his psychiatrist's advice and moved to Denver to stay with his sister Judy. He would be sentenced for the shooting of Harper in absentia in the same basement room where he had testified before the AJI.

Outside the hearing room, Meno Zacharias, the inspector in charge of training, was waiting to testify about Cross's service record. It was clean. No disciplinary defaults. No regulation breaches. No commendations.

Zacharias was wearing a Remembrance Day poppy on his blue tunic lapel and standing flag-pole straight.

"How's the chief?" Sinclair asked as he hurried by.

"Not bad," Zacharias said, his head swivelling, his stare cold. "Better than you are."

By that time Sinclair had been sentenced himself. He'd been demoted to reporting. Lee had moved Sinclair from his private cubicle to a reporter's desk, where he was to take assignments. He was also expected to work a month on nights each year.

Sinclair didn't say anything. Zacharias had a question. "Was it a management decision?"

"You could join the police force," Zacharias said, his long, thin mouth curling.

Sinclair didn't know it then, but John Campbell later told him the police believed they'd "got him." Campbell said the word was that the new chief Dale Henry had complained about him. Long afterwards, Sinclair asked Henry if this were true. Henry denied it.

368 GORDON SINCLAIR JR.

Kathryn Hodgins was already inside the hearing room. She looked different all dressed up, with her hair long, sitting beside a baby carriage and her recently promoted sergeant husband.

Martin Pollock, wearing a new suit, stood up to make his final argument. Without the sound system that the AJI had used, and facing away from the gallery, Martin was hard to hear. Sinclair leaned closer in his second-row chair.

"The key is this. When Mr. Cross shot Mr. Harper he was not suffering from post-traumatic stress disorder . . . what happens after, I submit, is irrelevant."

Dismissal is harsh, he argued, but employees are dismissed for just cause.

In his turn, McGregor argued that dismissing Cross amounted to economic capital punishment, far too harsh a sentence.

It was well after noon by the time Zacharias finished with Cross's service record, and Martha Chuchman adjourned the hearing until 3:30, the time the board hoped it could report its verdict.

Martin and Sinclair trudged through the slushy snow to Eaton Place, where Athina's parents had a Greek food kiosk. The next day would be Martin's thirty-fourth birthday. In ten days it would be his sister Karyn's birthday, and Nathan would have been dead ten years.

Martin started retelling the story about going to see Nathan's grave and stopping at the cemetery gate, where the car radio eerily answered his prayer and played "Funeral for a Friend."

"My feeling was Nathan was there to meet me at the gate. It really threw me into a different level of thinking. Fatalism. Determination. It was meant to be."

Martin took a bite of a mini doughnut. "I believe it was fate that Harper happened to be walking along Logan at that time," he said. "Some people say they're in the wrong place at the wrong time. The corollary of that is you're in the right place at the right time for reasons unknown to us. We're all on a trip. It's all on a road map. It was meant to be that Harper was shot by Cross. That was how Harper was meant to die. Cross happened to be the poor sucker, for whatever the reason, who was chosen to be the executioner. The question was, why was Cross the guy who was picked?"

Sinclair thought Mike and Sheila Elliot's portrait of their neighbour as a remorseless, vindictive racist had answered that question. That, and Joe Gallagher's definition of a cowboy cop. But Martin was worried about the LERA board and their impending sentencing decision.

"This is when you wish there was Native participation. Someone who is sympathetic to the Native position," he said.

The board was late getting back with its decision. Outside the room, in the hall, Al McGregor was seated in the electric cart Dowson had raced with at the inquest victory party. McGregor looked despondent.

"I'd bet every penny I have that they dismiss him," he said.

It was after 4 p.m. by the time the board members finally filed in and took their places. Martha Chuchman announced the outcome of the three-to-two decision.

She said the board had considered the submissions of counsel, the service record of Constable Cross, and the recommendation of the Manitoba Police Commission that Cross be dismissed. Then she noted that the Law Enforcement Review Act penalty provisions are strict and rigid, and that the board had no right to deviate from them.

McGregor was right, Sinclair thought. They were going to be forced into dismissing him.

Then Chuchman said: "We have the discretion to order a lesser disposition. It is our opinion, because of the mitigating factors, namely, this was an isolated incident, the respondent's current state of health, previous clear record, and the undue economic hardship that would result, a lesser penalty is justified."

Sinclair couldn't see McGregor's face, but he could see Martin's expression and the reaction of Harry Wood, J.J. Harper's half-brother. They looked as if they had just seen J.J. shot again, this time, right in front of them, in the same room where the AJI had heard evidence that found Cross's actions racially motivated.

Chuchman was still talking. "It is trite to say, but no penalty which we impose will reverse the tragedy which occurred March the 9th 1988. The board's decision is that Constable Robert A. Cross should be reduced in rank to a fourth-class constable which, in effect, would place him back into training. That is the board's decision. Thank you. The proceeding is now concluded."

In the press scrum that followed, a television reporter asked Martin Pollock if he thought the decision was fair.

"The question that has to be asked," Martin said, "is how many people does one have to kill in order to be dismissed?"

After the scrum had scattered, as he made his way out of the room, Martin let his feelings out in one loud outburst. "The AJI has taught us nothing."

PART VII

──✺──

THE SUMMING UP

Death cancels everything but truth.
                        – William Hazlitt, *The Spirit of the Age*

$$\overline{67}$$

"She said she loved him."

One day in January 1993, Gordon Sinclair dropped by the Pollocks' office to see Martin. Randee was due with her second child. It was noon when Sinclair arrived and everyone was out for lunch except for a young articling student.

"I guess you heard," he said.

Sinclair thought he was talking about Randee giving birth.

"They've settled the Harper case."

Finally it was over, at least all the court cases.

A few minutes later, Pollock and Martin came through the door. When Pollock saw Sinclair he grinned and held out his hand. "This says we were right."

Pollock mentioned Pruden had been in the office that morning. He was twenty-four now, and he had stopped drinking, Pollock reported, and felt guilty about what had happened that night.

The amount of the settlement wasn't disclosed, so Sinclair tried calling Lois to find out. When he couldn't reach her, he called her sister Bonnie Ross, who had moved from her apartment on Kennedy to a house a few doors down from Lois on Elgin. Bonnie was the only one of Lois's six sisters who lived in Winnipeg. She didn't know what Lois had received. Sinclair asked how Lois was doing.

"She can't let go. She still has his picture up all over the house. She still celebrates his birthday."

Then he asked about the kids.

"They seem to have adjusted."

Sinclair wondered why Lois hadn't.

"Probably because things weren't the best when he died and she's trying to make it the way it should have been."

Eventually Sinclair heard what the settlement with the city had been. It was $450,000. But after the Pollocks' costs and contingency fee, Lois Harper would receive close to $300,000. She had already received $180,000 from an employee insurance policy.

The following month, on an overcast late winter day, five years after the shooting, Gordon Sinclair and his son, Ian, pulled up outside the home of Robert Cross's estranged wife. She was expecting them. Sinclair had called Diane Eastwood earlier in the week, the same day Brian Mulroney had announced he was resigning as prime minister. She had just come in from grocery shopping when she heard the phone ring. It was difficult to know who was more surprised when she answered it, Sinclair thought afterward, she that he had phoned or he that she hadn't hung up. Sinclair had never been able to speak to Cross; his requests for interviews through his lawyers and family had always gone unanswered. He told Diane he wanted to put a human face on her husband.

"I don't think he is very human," she replied. "Or his parents."

Diane was upset because neither Cross nor his parents had seen the three children in months. Sinclair had taken Ian along to babysit while he talked with Diane. Sinclair drove her to Bellamy's, the same neighbourhood restaurant where he had interviewed Mike Elliot. As they turned north onto St. Anne's Road, he asked her if what Cross had told Elliot was true, that they had named their youngest son Stephen after the police chief. She laughed. "You have to take everything he says with a grain of salt."

They spent a couple of hours together over coffee. She remembered the day the shooting happened, how Cross's face was twitching and his hands were shaking when he came to the hospital to tell her he'd shot someone. "It was either him or me," he said. She talked about her sorrow at watching her once-robust husband shrivel and hide himself away at home. She recalled how relieved she'd been when she saw the news on TV that LERA would let Cross keep his pay cheque. And then she mentioned something that had happened one night in the fall of 1988, just after she had arrived home from her stay in the psych ward. It was 3 a.m. Cross was downstairs and she was upstairs in bed when the phone rang. Diane picked up the extension phone by her bed, turning the mouthpiece upside down. "Someone was on it."

It was Kathy Hodgins.

"I started to listen. I don't know why. Maybe because I thought there was something going on."

Sheila Elliot also thought there had been something going on between Cross and Hodgins by the way he talked, but she had no proof.

As Diane listened to the obvious closeness between the former police partners, she began to blame herself for not being more supportive. "He had no one to talk to. He had an outlet with Kathy."

Sinclair asked Diane what she had heard on the phone.

"She said she loved him. He didn't say he loved her. He just went along with what she said. But he didn't commit himself to anything. 'Yeah,' he would say. As if he was elsewhere.

"I almost said, 'What the hell's going on here?' I don't know why I didn't." Then she remembered why. "Because I didn't want to rock the boat. I was very fragile emotionally, and there was no way I thought I could look after three children all by myself. And then I kept hoping things would get better."

Diane said she never did tell her husband or Kathy what she'd heard, but sometimes, after she went to bed and left them together in the family room, she would sneak downstairs and try to catch them embracing. She never did.

Sinclair asked her about the day the phone rang a year after that and Cross learned about Dowson's suicide.

"He was very shaken."

That's when she thought he might do the same thing.

When Sinclair asked what Cross had told her, what he'd said about Dowson, Diane thought for a moment.

"I don't remember," she finally answered. "That whole time for me was a blur."

376 GORDON SINCLAIR JR.

"He never discussed hardly anything with me," she said later. "I guess he discussed it with Kathy."

Diane's emotions seemed to be in a tug-of-war. Every so often her anger towards Cross over what he had done to her and the children would yank her feelings one way, then a memory of how it once was would tug her emotions the other way. Then the anger would return; her bitterness at what had happened to him, and them, because of the process.

"I still get very resentful. Just about the whole thing. I didn't do anything wrong. I'm just trying to build a better life for my children and me . . .

"I always wondered, what if it had been Rob who was dead? Probably it wouldn't have been a big deal. Just like the officer at Oka."

Sinclair wondered if Cross had ever shown any remorse about Harper's death. Several seconds passed before she answered. Sinclair looked down at his notebook, and scribbled her answer: "I don't think so."

Then he told her about Lois Harper. As he watched Diane's face, Sinclair could almost hear her thoughts.

"Would you like to see her?" he asked

"I was going to ask you," Diane said.

"What would you do?"

Diane paused for a second.

"Probably hug her."

"What would you say to her?"

"That I'm sorry."

They drove back to her house. Diane had promised to find a wedding photo for Sinclair. The kids were waiting at the door. Sinclair picked up Stephen, the boy born a month after Harper died, and followed Diane upstairs to the living room where their marriage had ended a year before. Stephen made him stop at the dining room table. He pointed down at something he had drawn. As Sinclair held Robert Cross's son in his arms, the little boy asked him, "Are you my daddy?"

Later, when Sinclair went to Cross's parents' home trying to get an interview with Cross, he saw a mirror image of himself. Ten years earlier Sinclair's first wife had told him he was no longer welcome in the family home. But he felt that, like Cross, he deserved what he got. He, too, had cheated on his wife. He had asked for and was granted joint custody, access to his then five-year-old daughter and two-year-old son. But he remembered the sense of loss and isolation, a feeling of being exiled in a one-bedroom apartment where the children slept in his bed when they came over and he took the living room couch.

68

"Do you ever talk to Harper?"

In the fall of 1993, on the night Jean Chrétien and his Liberals swept to power, Gordon Sinclair got some surprising news when he called home from Portage la Prairie where he was covering the election.

His wife, Athina, told him that the *Free Press* had backed down on the eve of an arbitration hearing after the journalist's lawyer, Robert Tapper, disclosed the existence of the tape recording that showed the way the demotion had been handled.

Sinclair was getting his column back. A week later, Dave Lee received a severance package, and was gone. Less than six months later, Maurice Switzer was replaced by Rudy Redekop as publisher of the *Free Press*.

About the same time, the daddy the Cross children wanted so desperately married in Las Vegas. His third wife was Nora Jane Horigan, a thirty-nine-year-old Denver divorcee and mother of three children under ten. They had met in the spring of 1993, at Jimmy's Grill, a Denver reggae bar. Soon afterwards, Cross had moved out of his sister's basement and into a rental townhouse with Nora Jane, where he spent the afternoons by the swimming pool, charming some strippers who lived in the same complex.

"It's kind of like he's taken the opportunity to become a child again," Nora Jane's brother, Dan, told Sinclair over the phone. He had called the *Free Press* one day looking for information on Cross. When his sister met the Canadian, Nora Jane's brother, Dan Horigan said, Cross confided that he was in hiding because he was a former undercover cop. The way Dan understood the story, Cross said he had been wounded in some shoot-out. There was supposed to be a $100,000 contract on his life. Cross had told them that the Indians wanted him dead and he was sleeping with a suitcase by his bed.

Cross's relationship with Nora Jane had been one never-ending party since they met. Except, maybe, for a somewhat sobering incident three months earlier. On July 13, 1993, Cross had been driving his Corvette in the 7500 block of Yosemite, near his sister's home, when Patrolman Terry Reibeling pulled him over on a traffic violation. Cross was subsequently charged with driving under the influence and cited for not obeying a traffic signal and having no proof of insurance. On October 28, when he didn't show for a pretrial hearing, a warrant was issued for the arrest of Robert Andrew Cross.

A year later, in the fall of 1994, the CBC managed to get Cross to do his first media interview since his backyard chat with Don Gillmor. A team of three had flown to Denver to videotape it.

Cross was topical again because of a play about the shooting called *InQuest* being staged in Winnipeg. Coincidentally, on the evening the CBC piece aired, Gordon Sinclair had arranged an interview with Cross's first wife, Charlene, who had remained deep in the background throughout the Harper case.

Charlene lived just west of the city. Sasha answered the door. Robert Cross's first child was almost ten and had his dark hair and looks. She smiled sweetly, shook Sinclair's hand, and ran off down the hall for a bedtime bath.

Charlene was petite and pretty with a gentle, shy quality. She introduced her new husband, George, an affable, bearded guy who sat across the kitchen table as she poured tea. She said she was concerned about offending Cross and his family by saying something she shouldn't. His dad was "just the nicest guy," and Judy, his sister, was "just super." Cross was extremely close to his mother, too. They talked nightly on the phone, she remembered.

"He loved to talk," she said, "just like his mom."

"About what?" Sinclair asked.

"Mostly about the future. And dreams. What he was going to have. What he was going to do."

Then, without prompting, she started talking about the other Cross. The person he became when he'd had too much to drink.

"When he was drinking he was sort of a mean drunk." But not all the time, she said.

Sinclair wanted to know what she meant by "mean."

It was verbal mostly, she said. "He would get very insulting. I knew when to stay away. I used to get very upset about the drinking."

Sinclair asked if Cross had ever been violent when he drank.

"Just the one time," Charlene said. "He ripped the counter top off in the kitchen."

She didn't know what had prompted that. Drinking just seemed to turn him into a completely different person. "He was just a very unattractive personality. Very down on everything and everybody. It was evident even when we were dating, but it was more under control."

"But he never harmed you physically?" Sinclair asked. Charlene looked at George as if asking his permission. Then she said there had been a couple of incidents. Once he had put her in a wrestling-style arm lock and told her to shut up and just let him drink. Another time he'd thrown her in a snowbank.

"The day after," she said, "he was sincere about how he wanted to reform."

When he joined the police department, what kind of cop had she thought he would be, Sinclair wondered.

"I have to admit I was apprehensive."

Charlene recalled an officer coming by their house to do a screening interview the second time he applied.

"I can still see her sitting across the table. She said, 'Do you think he would ever get violent?' And I said, no. I remember in my mind feeling guilty."

But Charlene was just looking forward to him having steady work. Besides, she decided, he was only violent when he drank and he wouldn't be drinking when he was working.

Sinclair asked about Cross's attitude towards Natives.

"He did make a remark that when you were in the line of work and you saw the type of Natives you did, you couldn't help but come to a certain frame of mind. Because of the exposure to the Natives that are always getting into trouble, having too much to drink and going to jail, you couldn't help but form some sort of negative opinion."

Late in the interview Charlene referred to something else that happened at the lake when they were married. She was out jogging on a gravel road near the cottage with their dog Duffy when a bigger dog attacked and killed their little Cairn terrier.

Sinclair thought there was something familiar about the story. Then he remembered. Mike Elliot had mentioned it. Cross had said he'd tied up and shot the other dog.

Sinclair asked Charlene what Cross had done.

"He grabbed his gun and said, 'I'm going to get that dog.'"

"Did he?"

"No."

Charlene said she insisted Cross drive her to the vet. A moment later, Charlene smiled. "He probably claimed he shot the dog."

Sinclair was surprised, and asked her how she knew that.

"That's the kind of thing he would fabricate," she said.

The face on Winnipeg TV screens that night was puffy and lined. Robert Cross's Wyatt Earp moustache had turned from black to grey, like Pruden's jacket. It had been six years since the Harper shooting, but he looked as if he had aged twenty. Cross told the CBC crew he would meet them at a hotel. He was still in hiding and he still had a packed suitcase open at the end of his bed so he could make a quick escape if the Indians showed up looking to kill him. But there was no one after Robert Cross, except maybe the Denver cops who, a year later, still had a warrant out for his arrest on a drunk driving charge. None of that was mentioned in the television piece. Nor was his marriage to Nora Jane, which was on the rocks, like the rum and Diet Coke Cross binged on. He'd already had a couple before he met the TV crew at 10 a.m. The interview lasted several hours, primarily because Cross kept wanting to stop in mid-answer and start over again. What the CBC ended up showing was a series of quick clips that captured the essence of the man, or what was left of him.

"I don't understand why the wife of the poor deceased gets half a million and I sort of get shafted. Why does she get rewarded for that? I mean, the guy took my gun away and she gets money because of that. And I'm exiled?"

Cross said he wanted a $250,000 settlement from the city and he would walk away from the police pay cheque.

He called the AJI a joke.

He seemed to be down on everything and everybody again, the way Charlene remembered him when he drank.

At the end of the interview, CBC arts reporter Robert Enright asked what he later described as a throw-away question.

"Do you ever talk to Harper?"

"He talks to me in my dreams," Cross answered. "I have to put up with that. That's enough. The occurrences keep going over."

Then Robert Cross said, "I think the one reason I don't suicide is I'm scared of having to meet him again. I don't know how he feels, but I don't want to see him again."

$$\overline{69}$$

"I'm the only one who knows."

Soon after Dale Henry took over as police chief in the fall of 1992, he ran into Rex Keatinge in the Public Safety Building's basement garage. Keatinge was still bitter about Dowson's death, as was evident from his opening remark: "You probably know I don't like white shirts."

Henry didn't know that. Keatinge quickly added that he didn't include him and offered some advice: "Watch your back. This is a treacherous place to work." Then Keatinge walked off.

Over the next three-and-a-half years, Henry felt that his deputies, such as Joe Gallagher, supported him, but he also came to understand what Keatinge meant. "Sometimes I felt I was just a bystander watching the treachery go on, with the other cops at each other."

Dale Henry had inherited a police department with a severe image problem, both publicly and within its own ranks. He had taken over a rudderless ship and a demoralized crew, some of whom were openly mutinous and resistant to change.

Later, working from his diary notes, Henry summarized what he'd found when he arrived: "Internally there existed a large body of dispirited personnel, generally low morale, lost pride, and a poor sense of responsibility and accountability. A feeling of turmoil was evident. It was driven by a lingering bunker mentality due primarily to strained relations with the Justice Department, most of the practising criminal defence lawyers, City Hall, the public at large, and the embarrassingly high number of police under investigation for allegations of both on- and off-duty wrongdoing."

Henry's note to himself went on, "Perhaps most problematic was a deeply rooted, malignant culture of cover-up, deceit, and concealment." Henry felt that it was only a relatively small number of cops who were to blame, but they were a constant source of animosity towards him and others who wanted to make changes. He also thought the heart of the police department was good and wanted change.

Henry was able to accomplish much of what he was hired to do. He reached out to the Aboriginal community and his own members by including them in decision making. He established a structure for community policing, which would take the department back to its beat-cop days and allow its members to reconnect on a street level with the people of Winnipeg. He also went after the elitist, incestuous detective division, cleaning it out by transferring some cops to other divisions and bringing in new, young members. Among the casualties were the storied homicide team of Dave Shipman and Ron Morin, who were split up and transferred out of the division. He also made some important, symbolic changes that were incorporated in a new badge and a new motto on the side of the cruisers. The department became the Winnipeg Police Service, which was supposed to send a message about its true mission to both the membership and the public. The motto became "Community Commitment."

By the time he left in March 1996, Henry thought the police culture was finally changing, in part because of the new recruits, most of whom were Aboriginal, from other visible minorities, and women.

His successor, David Cassels, had been the deputy chief in Edmonton, whom Henry had consulted about the change to community-based policing. As much as Henry had hopes that the police service had changed significantly, Cassels ran into the same problems that had greeted Henry.

In February 1998, Cross was back in Winnipeg for his father's funeral. The obituary didn't run until after the funeral was over, so nobody knew Cross was back in town.

Then, in March, shortly before the tenth anniversary of the shooting, Gordon Sinclair received an invitation from Jonathan Flett, who had assumed J.J. Harper's position as executive director of the Island Lake Tribal Council. They were having a commemorative ceremony and prayers at the shooting site on Logan Avenue. It would be a small gathering of family and friends. Lois and the children would be there.

Sinclair decided to take Diane in hopes of fulfilling her wish to meet and speak with Lois. They had a lot in common, including what the shooting had done to them and their families. Both were forty-three, both had three children.

"I didn't sleep last night," Diane said when Sinclair picked her up at her home.

It was a cool, overcast day. About forty people were already gathered on the sidewalk when they arrived. Sinclair asked Lois's sister Sherry Meade if Lois would speak to Diane. It was fine if Diane wanted to participate, Sherry said after she checked. But Lois didn't think she could talk to Diane.

Lois kept her distance, even when they were standing in the snow-covered park, in the healing circle, separated only by Lois's pretty seventeen-year-old daughter Lori.

The Lord's Prayer was recited. Jonathan Flett spoke of forgiveness and moving on. And then, as people took turns moving around the circle greeting each other, something happened that surprised Diane. Lois stopped in front of her, put out her arms, and hugged her.

But said nothing.

When the group learned who she was, everyone embraced Diane. Then the service was over. As Diane walked away from the place on the sidewalk where J.J. Harper died, Lois reached out and touched her shoulder to stop her.

It was the very opposite of what happened between their husbands ten years earlier.

Lois hugged Diane again and apologized for not being able to say more. They were smiling and their eyes were welling.

Then Diane said what she had wanted to say for five years. "I'm sorry."

On the drive home, Diane said more.

"She had to realize it wasn't my fault. We were both innocent bystanders. We were both victims."

On March 9, 1998, the shooting of J.J. Harper dominated the front page of the *Free Press*. Phil Fontaine was quoted as saying it was a turning point for Aboriginal people. "It brought the community together. It exposed our issues in a way that wasn't imagined.

"There's a much higher degree of sensitivity about Aboriginal people. We have I don't know how many Aboriginal police officers."

Ten years after the shooting there were ninety-eight Aboriginal officers. There had been only nine when Harper was shot. The AJI's recommended target had been 133.

Dale Henry, the man who oversaw the changes brought about by the AJI as both the head of the RCMP in Manitoba and as Winnipeg's chief of police, called it a watershed event.

"It took the policing community in Manitoba and shook it up and forced it to recognize that Aboriginals were not treated equally or fairly. And that improvements had to be made." But Judge Murray Sinclair wasn't satisfied. "I think their recruitment needs to be strengthened. I still think they need to root out racists in the police force, which they haven't done . . . I still think we have a problem in the police department in terms of their relationship with Aboriginal people generally."

The administration of justice had changed little in Murray Sinclair's view, and the root causes of Aboriginal crime – poverty, unemployment, hopelessness, and systemic racism – remained unchanged. More Aboriginals were being charged, not fewer, and the crimes were more serious.

"I think the situation in terms of the criminal justice system and Aboriginal youth is going to get worse," Murray Sinclair said. And he suggested the need to belong and the search for identity would be channelled from crime to political activism, as it was with the American Indian Movement in the United States.

"I think it's going to be protests and demonstrations and some form of civil disobedience. I think that will become more and more a part of the relationship between frustrated Aboriginal people and the rest of society . . . unless we begin to develop ways of dealing with that frustration."

Six months after Murray Sinclair spoke those words, in September 1998, a group of mostly Aboriginal youths began a five-month arson spree, burning dumpsters, garages, and most seriously, derelict homes in the heart of the north end.

By that time the Harper home was up for sale. In the ten years since the street gangs had emerged, the price of homes in the inner city had fallen by half. That's if they sold at all, which was part of the reason the homes were being abandoned.

Winnipeg, the perennial contender for the title of the country's child poverty capital, had been given a new dubious distinction: arson capital of Canada. Many residents of the area, especially the elderly, feared for their lives.

The police later rounded up sixteen kids, three of them too young to charge and none considered gang members, and charged them with setting at least eighty fires. Kids with nothing to do but look for trouble were responsible. One of them cheekily told the cops the arsons were an urban renewal project, something like the way Indians used to burn the tall grass prairie to generate regrowth. In effect, that's what the bored youngsters had done. Their smoke signals had got the attention of complacent civic leaders. They even reached Ottawa, where Foreign Minister Lloyd Axworthy, the MP for Winnipeg South Centre, helped earmark $2 million from a federal fund to fix up houses in the inner city.

As the smoke was just beginning to billow, Police Chief David Cassels had had enough. Before he could leave he was reminded why he had resigned with two years remaining on his contract. The service was hit with a series of rotating strikes, as officers phoned in feigning the flu, "the Blue Flu," as the papers called it. Whole shifts booked off in support of an officer who had been suspended without pay after being charged with severely beating a young South African–born man after answering a noisy party complaint. The officer's name was Butch Eakin.

To Cassels, the Blue Flu was indicative of everything that was still wrong with the Winnipeg police force. Despite Henry's and Cassels's reforms a culture persisted, which Cassels saw as destructive. "The people of Winnipeg will never get a real efficient, committed, dedicated service as long as that culture exists," Cassels told Gordon Sinclair the day before he left the city.

Cassels was succeeded by Jack Ewatski, the first non-Anglo Saxon chief in the city's history; another sign of change. Ewatski was a north-end boy raised in the Ukrainian tradition, who had risen through the ranks and had a reputation as a no-nonsense disciplinarian. Before he left, Cassels had turned over to Ewatski the task of determining Eakin's fate, and it was the then deputy chief's decision to suspend Eakin without pay. His decision was overruled by an arbitrator, and Eakin was reinstated and assigned to desk duties until his criminal case was resolved.

While the fires were still burning, and shortly after Cassels left, in the late fall of 1998, Cross quietly moved back to Manitoba and bought a rambling bungalow in Sandy Hook, a Lake Winnipeg cottage community seventy-five kilometres north of the city. The house, at Number 4 First Avenue, was a few hundred metres from the lake, and two doors away from the local post office.

He and a woman friend, thirty-eight-year-old Linda Fisher, took possession on November 1, after driving north from Colorado. Cross still had a drinking problem, but evidently so did Fisher. Soon after they arrived she was pulled over by the Mounties and charged with impaired driving.

That didn't stop them from driving to Hecla Island Resort two months later, where, on New Year's Eve, Cross and Linda were married.

For someone who had left Winnipeg ostensibly because he couldn't go to the grocery store without being recognized, Cross had been surprisingly open about his background with the people of Sandy Hook.

At the liquor store, where he bought vodka, the owner said Cross would flash his police badge when he opened his wallet to pay. At the curling rink, where he drank, Cross was overheard telling people, "I shot a guy."

Few people knew Cross had returned to Manitoba. Gordon Sinclair didn't know when he dropped by to have lunch with Al McGregor and Marty Minuk in February 1999. Afterwards in his office, McGregor did share something with Sinclair, who had casually asked him what he thought had happened on Logan that night eleven years earlier.

"I'm not going there," McGregor said.

Sinclair laughed.

"But I'll tell you one thing," McGregor added. "I'm the only one who knows."

Sinclair took that to mean that McGregor was the only one Robert Cross had told what really happened the night he shot Harper.

But then on March 12, 1999, a man called Sinclair at work and left a message. Bob Gill was a former Winnipeg police officer who had lost his job in 1990 because of a drinking problem. Gill had been suspended just before Ken Dowson's funeral, and when he showed up, one cop told him he wasn't welcome. Gill left in tears. He had been a police classmate of Dowson's. He had also been one of the officers who had taken Gordon Sinclair's mother to the hospital when she was committed. On the phone he said he didn't have long to live and he had something he wanted to get off his chest.

"Bring a tape recorder," he instructed.

Gill was staying at the Sherbrook Inn, the place Harper was afraid to go the night he died because he might get shot. He was a big, bearded guy, a little shorter than Sinclair, about six foot two, and a little younger, about forty-nine. What Gill wanted to get off his chest – and what Sinclair would speak to him about again when he was sober – was that after the Harper shooting he used to run into Cross occasionally at a liquor store in Windsor Park and they'd sit in his car and drink together.

"We were both pissed as a cricket."

And he said that one day Cross told him the real story of the shooting. "What happened was Bob Cross walked up to him with a gun out. He reacted. They had a struggle. He got shot. They all lied. We all lie for each other. I've lied for my brother officer."

Sinclair didn't know if Gill was lying now, but why would he? Gill became more specific. He said Cross had been holding the gun down by his leg, hidden.

Gill had decided to tell what he knew after he was diagnosed with liver disease. "So I figured I'd tell you," he said to Sinclair, "and cleanse my conscience." He said he felt sorry for Cross. "Bob's destroyed. Bob could never get better."

Bob Cross had rarely felt worse than he did twelve days later, on March 24, 1999. NATO was beginning its air war on Yugoslavia, and Cross had been restless all evening. He wasn't hungry, and by the time Linda went to bed about 1 a.m. he'd had only one drink.

Then, about 3:30 a.m., Cross stumbled into their room and collapsed on the bed, waking Linda. He told her he had fallen in the bathroom and struck his forehead on the sink. Cross raised himself and sat up on the edge of the bed. He was sweating profusely and his breathing was laboured. Linda stayed up with him for the next two hours, until he slid off the bed and onto the floor. He seemed to be sleeping, so Linda covered him with a blanket. It was about 6:30 a.m. when she noticed he didn't seem to be breathing. Linda phoned the woman next door, the community's post mistress, who rushed over. They couldn't find a pulse. At 6:45 a.m. Linda called an ambulance.

Winnipeg's new police chief, Jack Ewatski, called Gordon Sinclair shortly after 11 a.m. and left a message to call him. Minutes later, Sinclair returned it.

"Bob Cross is dead," Ewatski said.

"Oh, no," Sinclair said.

Ewatski said he didn't know much more. Later Sinclair learned from the RCMP that an hour after Linda called the ambulance, and twenty minutes after arriving at Gimli Hospital, Robert Andrew Cross had been pronounced dead.

Cross had died in the place where Harper talked with him. In his sleep. He was one month shy of forty-five.

Sinclair thanked Ewatski for the call. Fifteen minutes later the *Free Press* columnist phoned the Island Lake Tribal Council and told Lois Harper that Cross was dead.

There was a momentary silence. Then Lois said, "Well, that's good news for me. I'm not sure it's good for his family, but . . . he killed my husband and he got away with it."

By noon Cross's death had been reported on the radio. Almost three hours later a colleague at Victoria General Hospital told Diane that the father of her three children was dead, just as Cross had taken her aside in the same hospital hall eleven years earlier to tell her that he had shot a man.

When Diane heard how Lois had reacted, she said: "Maybe she'll find closure with this.

"Poor guy," she said of her former husband. "He didn't have a very good life after that."

Around suppertime Diane sat her three children down to tell them that now they would never again see the father they hadn't seen or heard from in seven years.

"They thought he was still in Denver," Diane told Gordon Sinclair when he phoned that evening. "They wanted to fly down for the funeral."

Later, when he learned more about the circumstances of Cross's death, Sinclair called Diane back. He passed on the details RCMP Sergeant Steve Saunders had given him, including why Linda Cross hadn't phoned an ambulance when Cross first stumbled into their bedroom. Saunders said two months earlier, when Cross had been in distress, she had called an ambulance and he had refused to go with them. Just as he had refused to keep doctor's appointments.

"What does that tell you?" Saunders had asked.

Sinclair asked Diane the same question.

"It was like a slow suicide," she said.

The official cause of death was "acute alcoholism."

Gordon Sinclair wrote a column the next day. In his view, Cross had died because he had never forgiven himself. He suggested there was a lesson for everyone in that.

The service was held at a chapel on Main Street. There was a police honour guard and his brother-in-law, Judy's husband, gave the eulogy.

It was a relatively small gathering, with less than a hundred people. Chief Jack Ewatski was there, but the new chief didn't notice Herb Stephen in attendance. Neither did Al McGregor, who was there on his scooter without Marty Minuk, who had a prior commitment. Kathy and Ron Hodgins were among the mourners, so was Rick Poneira, but his old partner Butch Eakin wasn't. He was vacationing with his family at Disneyworld. Eakin, Cross's bodyguard at Stephen's birth, missed his buddy's funeral. But there was no body to guard this time. Cross had been cremated.

Diane and the children weren't invited. But at the last minute, the police association intervened, and they were allowed to come to the chapel when everyone but the honour guard had left. The flowers were still there, too, and a large photo of Robert Cross.

By coincidence, Diane had planned Stephen's eleventh birthday party for the same day. Stephen had asked for a limousine ride around the city, and Diane had booked it without knowing that she and the children would be taking another limousine that same day – to Cross's memorial service.

The Island Lake Tribal Council issued a press release after Cross died. It said they were saddened by his death and offered condolences to the Cross family. The statement continued: "The Aboriginal Justice Inquiry came about as a result of the past events involving the lives of J.J. Harper, Robert Cross, Helen Betty Osborne and others.

"The recommendations of the AJI, when implemented, will be an honorable legacy to all who are part of these tragic events.

"The chiefs feel that we are all still victims of the justice system due to the fact the Manitoba government has not recognized or endorsed the AJI report and its recommendations."

There was one more line. It suggested Cross had nothing to fear in meeting Harper again.

"We the people of Island Lake commit the soul and spirit of Robert Cross to our Creator and with that we know that he will rest in peace."

That reminded Gordon Sinclair of something Mike Elliot had said about the Harper shooting: "It was just two guys who didn't understand each other. And the guy with the gun won."

Nearly six months after Cross died, Gordon Sinclair met with Sheila Elliot, who added credibility to Bob Gill's story. She said Cross had told her his gun was out when he approached Harper. She also confirmed the central testimony of Allan, although she had never heard it. Cross had admitted to her that someone told him to say it was an accident. She told Sinclair that she hadn't revealed this key information at the Law Enforcement Review Agency hearing because she had been frightened and no one asked those two questions directly.

Sheila told him something else. On the day Sinclair's first column appeared, a few days after J.J. Harper was shot, Cross showed it to her. He said he found the headline, "Circling the paddywagons," amusing. Then Cross joked about his house being encircled by paddywagons. "Like Cowboys and Indians," he said.

EPILOGUE

By the mid 1990s, the Winnipeg Police Service, as it was now known, had replaced the .38 Smith & Wesson Police Special revolver with the Glock 40-calibre semi-automatic pistol. But that was not the weapon Gordon Sinclair noticed Danny Smyth carrying when he ran into him in early 1999. The one cop who seemed to have done the right thing at the Harper shooting was standing in the hall of the law courts. He was dressed in battle fatigues and a flak jacket, with a MP5 semi-automatic machine-gun over his shoulder.

Three Manitoba Warriors, who had been convicted on a vicious gang-related murder, were appealing their verdicts, and the city police and RCMP Emergency Response units had been given the job of securing the courthouse. By that time the Warriors had graduated to pimping and drug dealing, and were believed to have connections to bike gangs.

Catching up on old times in the hall, Sinclair asked Smyth about the changes in the police service since the Harper shooting. Smyth said the list was lengthy, and that whenever he paged through the procedure manual he saw the night Harper was shot reflected over and over.

By the time Dale Henry arrived in late 1992, the city had addressed, if not complied with, all of the AJI's recommendations aimed at its police. Under Dale Henry's leadership, every officer had to take a Native Awareness course and the police academy had expanded its cross-cultural program. Police even had a Cultural Relations Unit. But there was still no independent Special Investigations Unit.

Moreover, the recruitment of Aboriginal officers had slowed to a trickle after Henry's departure. The number of Aboriginal officers jumped from twenty-two at the end of 1991 to eighty-eight when

Henry left at the beginning of 1996. Under Cassels, police had recruited another ten by the fall of 1998, but by midway through 1999 they had added just one more, making the total ninety-nine, well short of the 133 called for eight years earlier by the AJI report.

Dowson's death also had a profound impact on the police service. It took Judge Charles Rubin more than two years to deliver his report. Job stress had caused Ken Dowson to take his own life, Rubin concluded. That was the surface reason, but it didn't speak to the combination of factors that usually underlie suicide. Rubin knew nothing of Dowson's background growing up, how Ken and Nancy were left to fix things when their father drank and forgot where he left his car or was careless with a burning cigarette. And how, in Gordon Sinclair's view, the police force had become the family Dowson as a child had never had.

Sinclair was reminded of all that one day when he was talking with Dowson's old recruit classmate Bob Gill. Gill mentioned that because Dowson was so well-respected as an investigator, the department called on him to "fix" tough cases.

The cases didn't come any tougher than the Harper shooting. And Sinclair believed that when Dowson tried to fix it and couldn't, the childhood memories of trying to save his father kicked in. That would account for what a psychiatrist saw as his exaggerated sense of responsibility during and after the investigation that led to the suicide. That, his chronic depression and alcoholism, and the fear that not only would he be humiliated on the witness stand, but ultimately he would be rejected by his police family, the way he and Nancy had been rejected when their father remarried and they were sent to live with their older sisters.

Nor did Judge Rubin know anything of Dowson's domestic problems as an adult when he released his inquest report. By that time, police had already responded to the suicide by hiring a full-time psychologist, creating the position of "wellness officer," and beefing up their post-traumatic peer counselling team, moves initiated by Herb Stephen before he left office.

To that point, compared with the Manitoba government's response to the AJI report, the city police were a model of progress. Then, on the tenth anniversary of Harper's death, the government took what Al Hamilton called a good first step, even though, he said, it didn't come close to meeting any of the major recommendations. Justice Minister Vic Towes and MP Lloyd Axworthy announced a $1.5 million pilot project aimed at keeping Natives convicted of non-violent crimes out of prison. The "restorative justice" project was centred on the traditional Aboriginal sentencing circle concept, where a repentant wrongdoer meets and is judged by the victim and the community. A second joint provincial-federal project was aimed at helping First Nations create their own police services.

Gauging the impact of Harper's death on the community is more difficult. But in the 1996 census Statistics Canada discovered something curious. Winnipeg's Aboriginal population had swollen by 60 per cent in five years, making it the largest Aboriginal city in the country. But the addition of 17,000 Aboriginals since 1991 couldn't be explained solely on migration and birth rate. The theory was that more people were now willing to declare that they were Aboriginal. Native leaders credited the new-found pride in being Indian and Métis to the aftermath of Indian resistance at Oka and defiance over Meech Lake. But it had been what Murray Sinclair referred to as "the process" of the Aboriginal Justice Inquiry, from 1988 through 1991, that had set the historic stage for the actions of Elijah Harper and the Mohawks.

And it had been the timing of John Joseph Harper's death, the day the provincial election was called, that caused the AJI to be created.

Gradually, the city and the province is waking up to the reality that the future must include First Nations people. In a move symbolic of that recognition, millions of dollars are being spent to turn the Main Street strip of seedy hotels into a spiritual centre for Aboriginal people in Winnipeg.

But some things never change. The Alexander Docks case against the after-shift cops who allegedly beat up a Native man fizzled at trial, as did the charges against the cops allegedly involved in a break-and-enter ring. And in 1999, the Crown admitted it had a chronic problem trying to convict cops charged with criminal offences.

In spite of nearly a decade of enlightened leadership, and the hundred of pages the police service has stuffed into its procedures binder, police continue to make the same kinds of mistakes that led to J.J. Harper's death.

Early on New Year's Day 1999, while Bob Cross was celebrating his fourth marriage, police patrolling a north end neighbourhood stopped a Native teenager as he was running along the street. They wanted to know why he was running. Sixteen-year-old James Zebrasky was on his way home from a party, and he told them he was running because it was cold. The temperature was minus thirty-six Celsius with the wind chill. Police were suspicious. They said they were looking for a burglar.

In a newspaper interview a few weeks later, Zebrasky described what happened next. He said he was thrown against the cruiser, punched in the jaw, handcuffed, and placed in the back seat. Police then drove around berating him about being stupid and threatening to take him to the drunk tank, Zebrasky said. "I told them I didn't drink, smoke, or do drugs, and I told them to do a breath analysis on me."

As it turned out, the cops had picked on the wrong Native teenager. Two months earlier, Zebrasky had been honoured with a provincial Aboriginal Achievement Award for his volunteer work at his high school and in his community. He was literally a poster boy for the United Way, and his dream was to be a police officer.

"I respected the police," Zebrasky said, "but am now having second thoughts. I just don't know."

For ten years, First Nations across Manitoba have commemorated J.J. Harper's death with a Martin Luther King–like day of remembrance, highlighted by a hockey tournament. But on the tenth anniversary, the framed photograph of Harper that hung in the offices of the Island Lake Tribal Council was taken down. Now there is talk among Island Lake leaders that the memorial day should end.

There is a feeling, said J.J. Harper's successor, Jonathan Flett, that it's time to move on.

For the people who were part of this story, a decade has changed some more than others:

Jim Walding, the MLA who toppled the government on the night Harper died, bought a bed and breakfast in Victoria soon afterwards. In 1995 he sold it and returned to Winnipeg, still maintaining he did the right thing on the night of March 8, 1988. Gary Filmon's Progressive Conservative government was re-elected for a third time in 1995, although an inquiry was later called into a vote-rigging scheme. It transpired that Tory election organizers had financed independent Aboriginal candidates in traditional NDP ridings in an effort to divide the predominantly Aboriginal electorate's loyalties and split the vote. In 1993, Elijah Harper was elected as a Liberal MP, but was defeated in the next general election. He was appointed an Indian Claims commissioner in 1999. Former Manitoba Premier Howard Pawley moved to Windsor, Ontario, where he is president of the university faculty club. Former Attorney General Vic Schroeder had to rekindle his law practice when he was defeated at the polls in 1988.

Melvin Pruden and Allan both have lengthy criminal records. According to police, Allan is a gang member. There are court orders prohibiting both of them from owning firearms.

Ellen Gordon moved to Vancouver, where she practises criminal law. She still has a weakness for handsome, compassionate cops. When she's in Winnipeg she always calls on Danny Smyth, her new favourite cop. Smyth works as a crime analyst in Vice. His partner on the night Harper was shot, Doug Hooper, has retired. Rick Poneira and Butch Eakin have been split up. Poneira works in the crime division. After working in the gang unit for several years under Ron Hodgins, who's still there, Eakin is doing desk duty while his charge of assault causing bodily harm is before the courts. Kathryn Hodgins, who was criticized for her racist comment to Allan, is an investigator in the youth division. Randy Hampton is a plainclothes vice officer, and the right-eous Bill Isaac is in Identification. Eric Hrycyk retired two months after Cross died, and joined the Winnipeg Hospital Authority as its director of emergency preparedness. Big Glen Spryszak is walking the beat. Bob Parker has been promoted to Staff Sergeant.

Darryl Sterdan, the *Sun* reporter who found Harper's broken glasses, now works on the newspaper's features desk. Linda Morisette works for Air Canada's personnel department. Randy Houston, who fathered her two children before they broke up, worked in Eaton's grocery department until the store's demise. His pal Larry Yaworek still lives in Pine Falls, where he works for a paper company. Dr. Peter Markesteyn retired in the summer of 1998 and the following year was selected to be part of the Canadian team that went to Kosovo to investigate alleged atrocities.

Judge John Enns has retired, as has Bill Morton. RCMP Sergeant Wes Border died of cancer, and Rex Keatinge works for the provincial sheriff's department. Keatinge travels regularly into northern reserves, and has become deeply concerned about the plight of Aboriginal women and children, something the AJI report also commented on.

Jill Dowson still does the books at Munroe Pharmacy.

Eunice Woodhouse is a nurse on a northern Manitoba reserve. Kathy Bushie works for the Southeast Tribal Council.

Garry Bunn and Gordon Ross made headlines twice on the same day in the fall of 1993. First, they were denied compensation for the year they spent in jail waiting to be acquitted of the murder of the taxi-driver. And second, Bunn was acquitted of murder for a second time. He had viciously stabbed a companion at a hair-spray drinking party, and the Crown attorney argued Bunn had used excessive force when he wrestled the knife from the man and stabbed him twice in the chest and back.

"Others might have said he was the author of his own misfortune," Hersh Wolch said, sounding like Robert Cross talking about J.J. Harper.

"I'll probably beat this on self-defence," Bunn told police. "There was only him and me fighting, so the judge will only hear one side."

Bunn was acquitted. Said the judge: "How do you determine in that split second what's reasonable and what isn't?"

Hersh Wolch now splits his practice between Calgary and Winnipeg. In the spring of 1999 he settled a $10-million compensation suit for David Milgaard, the largest settlement for wrongful imprisonment in Canadian history. Little more than a week later, the fifty-nine-year-old Wolch suffered a massive heart attack and was clinically dead for several minutes before he was resuscitated at Foothills Hospital.

Randy McNicol and Doug Abra continue to practise law. McNicol represented the Manitoba Progressive Conservative Party at the inquiry into vote rigging. Marty Minuk moonlighted as a chef for a time, but still maintains his law practice and runs marathons. Al McGregor is still wheeling around the law courts, although the firm Simkin and Gallagher is no more and he and Minuk no longer represent the Winnipeg Police Association. Bill Olson, the lawyer appointed to represent Cross at the AJI, handles most of the Association's business now, although Hymie Weinstein (the man who gave Gordon Sinclair the *Los Angeles Times* advertisement with the catchy question, "Who do you call when the gang wears blue?") is representing Butch Eakin at his trial. Perry Schulman and Al MacInnes have been appointed judges, as has Bruce Miller. Don Gillmor continues to be a contributing editor at *Saturday Night* and has a major book project in the works.

Al Hamilton has retired from the bench and is writing a book on Aboriginal issues. In September 1998, Murray Sinclair finished hearings at the longest inquest in Canadian history, the two-and-half year probe of baby deaths at Winnipeg's Children's Hospital.

Billyjo De La Ronde went on to become president of the Manitoba Metis Association for a time. His brother continues to suffer from a short-term memory deficit. Malcolm Dawson, the officer who shot him, served a stint as a polygraph officer. He is now in the traffic division.

Ted Hughes is conducting yet another inquiry, this time into the RCMP's conduct at the APEC conference in Vancouver. His counsel at the inquiry into Pollock's arrest, John Scurfield, was elected president of the Liberal Party of Manitoba.

Of the police involved in the Hughes Inquiry, Dennis Toyne, Randy Bell, and Ron Dawson are all retired. And, after being demoted to First Class Constable and losing a month's pay, Ron Kushneryk was reinstated as a sergeant two years after he perjured himself at the Hughes Inquiry. Kushneryk is now a street supervisor in a suburban division.

Bruce Owen is an assistant city editor at the *Free Press* and was one of a team of *Free Press* reporters who won a National Newspaper Award for their coverage of the 1997 Red River flood.

Paul Johnston lives happily in retirement, and lunches regularly with retired Crown counsel Jack Montgomery.

D'Arcy McCaffrey, who represented Harvey Pollock, died of a stroke while vacationing in Florida in January 1998. He was sixty-one.

Rob Finlayson, the Crown whom police asked for an opinion on what charges to lay against Pollock without naming the lawyer, is assistant deputy attorney general, Stu Whitley's old job. Whitley is deputy attorney general in Yukon, where he also writes novels.

Bill Norrie continues his community work as chairman of the United Way. Ironically, in the summer of 1997, an Indian band in northwestern Ontario laid claim to the island in Lake of the Woods where Norrie has a cottage. And tragically, Bill and Helen Norrie lost one of their sons in the fall of 1992. Duncan Norrie, a university classmate of Martin Pollock, perished in a plane crash in the Himalayas. The city named a street in memory of the former mayor's son. Susan Thompson, having kept a keen and watchful eye on the police service's rebirth, and having guided the city through the Flood of the Century in 1997, decided not to seek a third term. She was succeeded by the country's first openly gay mayor, Glen Murray, and in the summer of 1999 was appointed Canada's consul general in Minneapolis.

Joe Gallagher joined the Law Society of Manitoba as legal counsel. John Campbell and Linda Loewen live in Kelowna, where Dale Henry returned to retirement. Henry's successor as chief, David Cassels, is back in Edmonton. Herb Stephen is a partner in a Winnipeg security training company. The Winnipeg Police Service named its bomb disposal robot "Herbie" in his honour. He still enjoys travelling.

Martin and Randee Pollock have three sons, and he continues to be successful in representing clients who have suffered at the hands of police officers. Harvey Pollock has grown a goatee, still practises law, and has taken up whistling again.

J.J. Harper's friend Victor Harper still resides in Island Lake, as does Harry Wood, who unfortunately has lost his sight.

Diane Eastwood became engaged the week after Robert Cross died. Her fiancé is a farmer, and the children have decided to change their last name to his. Lois Harper has also moved out of the city, to a rural bedroom community. She is in a relationship and the children are reported to be doing well.

Dave Lee does the occasional contract work for *Free Press* special sections. Brian Cole moved to Mesa, Arizona, in the summer of 1999, where he is metro editor of the *Tribune*. And Maurice Switzer works as communications director for the Assembly of First Nations in Ottawa, where Phil Fontaine is grand chief.

Gordon Sinclair continues to write columns for the Winnipeg *Free Press* and to enjoy the occasional restaurant meal with Paul Johnston.

Acknowledgments

After writing this story on and off for more than a decade, it's difficult to remember everyone whose support contributed to this book. But I'm going to start by thanking my long-suffering agent and friend, David Wolinsky, and my publisher, Doug Gibson. I would not have finished without their patience, guidance, and their belief in this project.

It was Doug's idea that I include myself in the story as a third-person character, a device I resisted at first, but a kind of out-of-body experience I grew more comfortable with over time.

The list of others to be thanked is long:

A Canada Council grant allowed me to take time off in the early 1990s, when much of the first draft was completed. But to get the grant, I required the letter-writing support of Sandra Birdsell, Lesley Hughes, and in particular my long-time friend and former coach, Maurice Hogue, who knew the ropes for grant writing and delivered the application to me wrapped in a nice, neat package. Many others shared their time and, in some cases, especially the women, their painful personal memories. Among them were Lois Harper, Diane Eastwood, Jill Dowson, Charlene Junkin, Kathy Bushie, Eunice Woodhouse, Nancy Arsenault, and Sheila Elliot, which is a pseudonym, as is her husband's name. "Florence" is also a pseudonym.

The insights and cooperation of my police pals and acquaintances, Paul Johnston, John Campbell, Dale Henry, Joe Gallagher, and latterly Jack Ewatski and Bob Gill, were invaluable. So were Ellen Gordon's insider stories and Sylvia Schulman's loan of her video collection from the AJI. Cec Rosner of the CBC also helped out with videos, and Tim Killeen kindly went to court and got the prohibition lifted on Dowson's suicide note to Hersh Wolch. Vic Schroeder was especially helpful, as were Murray Sinclair, Al Hamilton, Perry Shulman, Randy McNicol, Phil Fontaine, RCMP media-liaison sergeant Steve Saunders, Wyman Sangster, Brian Savage, Bob Urbanoski, Ken Cameron, and Dr. Peter Markesteyn.

Victor Harper brought J.J. Harper to life for me, as did Dave Tomasson. The people of Island Lake also generously shared their community and a trip by boat to J.J. Harper's burial site. I also was touched and honoured by Jonathan Flett's invitation to the tenth anniversary service.

I am particularly grateful to those who stood by me during my year of banishment from the column; among them: my lawyer Robert Tapper, Trevor and Caroline Kennerd, Vivian and Bob Prince, David and Isabel Wolinsky, Catherine Morrisseau Sinclair, George Katsabanis, Archie Cham and Marion Golfman, Justine Spiller, Paul Johnston, Costas Nicolaou, Leo Dufault and Daryl Kuhl, Hymie and Shaaron Weinstein, my wife's parents George and Anna Panopoulos and brother Tim Panopoulos, my friend Jamie Macleod, and countless other Manitobans who wrote in support of me to the *Free Press* and whose letters were never published. I received many other letters of support during the period I was writing columns on the Harper investigation, but the one I hold dearest was a card signed by a woman whose signature I can't make out. Inside she simply wrote, "Thank you for writing about J.J. Harper on Logan Ave." I keep it on my desk, along with the trophy Paul Johnston gave me.

I owe a general acknowledgement to my colleagues at the *Free Press*, reporter Heidi Graham, librarian Lynn Crothers, Rosalind McIntyre, photo editor Jon Thordarson, Joe Bryksa, Morley Walker, Margo Goodhand, and particularly *Free Press* editor Nicholas Hirst for generously permitting the paper's photos to be used in this book. Also thanks to *Winnipeg Sun* publisher Gordon Norrie for permission to use their photographs. The staff at Manitoba Archives were also of assistance.

Harvey and Martin Pollock were enormously helpful, both professionally and personally. Their wives, Sylvia and Randee, were also gracious and supportive. There have been many others who have offered general support over the last decade: my brother David Sinclair; my uncle, Clayton and aunt Marcelle Sinclair; the man who hired me at the *Free Press*, Murray Burt; Walter Schoenhausen; Morley and Charlene Shatsky, who put up with my endless book-talk; and Robert Doyle, whose encouragement to finish the book was always in the back of my mind. The editing assistance of Marion Lepkin, my father's trusted colleague at the *Free Press*, was invaluable. Marv Terhoch's help was also appreciated.

But there is one person who deserves special praise, my editor, Dinah Forbes. She faced the formidable assignment of helping me turn the original 700-page-plus manuscript into a book. It was like an overgrown yard – at times a jungle – that needed slashing back to find the path again. Dinah was wonderfully patient, professional, and kind in the way she used her pencil to whack the weeds.

Finally, an acknowledgement to my late parents, Dorothy and Gordon, whose influence and spirit guided me throughout this story. And a special thank you to my wife, Athina Panopoulos, and my now grown children, Erin and Ian. They sacrificed and endured much because of my obsession. Athina also offered sound editorial advice when she read over the work in progress, although doing so was difficult for her because of the painful memories it evoked. But thankfully, unlike three other families, when it was over, Athina had her husband, and Erin and Ian their father.